The English Urban Landscape

The English Urban Landscape

EDITED BY *Philip Waller*

Oxford New York
OXFORD UNIVERSITY PRESS

OXFORD
UNIVERSITY PRESS

Great Clarendon Street, Oxford OX2 6DP

Oxford University Press is a department of the University of Oxford.
It furthers the University's objective of excellence in research, scholarship,
and education by publishing worldwide in

Oxford New York

Athens Auckland Bangkok Bogotá Buenos Aires Calcutta
Cape Town Chennai Dar es Salaam Delhi Florence Hong Kong Istanbul
Karachi Kuala Lumpur Madrid Melbourne Mexico City Mumbai
Nairobi Paris São Paulo Singapore Taipei Tokyo Toronto Warsaw

with associated companies in Berlin Ibadan

Oxford is a registered trade mark of Oxford University Press
in the UK and in certain other countries

Published in the United States
by Oxford University Press Inc., New York

First published 2000

British Library Cataloguing in Publication Data

Data available

Library of Congress Cataloging in Publication Data

Data available

ISBN 0-19-860117-4

10 9 8 7 6 5 4 3 2 1

Printed in Great Britain by
T.J. International Ltd
Padstow, Cornwall

Contents

List of Cameos

Acknowledgements

Authors' acknowledgements these days can be a trial for their readers, presenting them with an unwanted mystery tour of the writers' psyche and inventory of their professional and domestic life. The editor of a symposium is potentially the most dangerous creature of all, having it in his power to inflict on readers the corybantic celebrations and confessions of an entire team of contributors, like the excesses of Oscar night. Common honesty and courtesy dictate that authors should acknowledge intellectual debts and other help; but they should also strive to be decorous about this. Some individual acknowledgements, explicit and implicit, may be found in the bibliographies and section on further reading at the end of the book; but here, with one exception, a collective reticence will rule and readers must assume that those contributors who are seized with an urge to hug and kiss their Uncle Tom Cobbleigh in gratitude for his *aperçus*, without which their chapters would have fallen marginally short of perfection, will be doing so in the privacy of their own homes. The exception is the editor's thanks for the secretarial support he has received from Clare Bass, Julie Gerhardi, and Judith Kirby at Merton College, Oxford; and he hopes that that particular expression will not cause the many more people—family, friends, colleagues, and others—who have assisted in the book to feel unregarded.

Philip Waller

Information on Contributors

JOHN ARMSTRONG is Professor of Business History at Thames Valley University, London. He is interested in all aspects of transport history and especially the British coastal trade. He edits *The Journal of Transport History* and is Series Editor of 'Studies in Transport History' published by Ashgate Press. His most recent book was *Coastal and Short Sea Shipping* (Aldershot: Scolar, 1996).

PETER BORSAY is a Senior Lecturer in the History Department at the University of Wales, Lampeter. He is a committee member of the Pre-modern Towns Group and an associate editor of *Urban History*. His publications include *The English Urban Renaissance: Culture and Society in the Provincial Town, 1660–1770* (Oxford University Press, 1989), and, as editor, *The Eighteenth-Century Town: A Reader in English Urban History, 1688–1820* (Longman, 1990). He has recently completed essays on spa and seaside towns, and the culture of improvement, for the forthcoming *Cambridge Urban History of Britain* and *The Oxford History of the British Isles: The Eighteenth Century*, and is currently preparing a monograph for Oxford University Press on the Image of Georgian Bath 1700–1900.

JOHN DAVIS is Fellow and Praelector in Modern History and Politics at The Queen's College, Oxford. His study of municipal reform in nineteenth-century London, *Reforming London: The London Government Problem, 1855–1900*, was published by Oxford University Press in 1988, and he has contributed the chapter on central–local government relations, 1840–1950, to the forthcoming *Cambridge Urban History of Britain*, ed. M. J. Daunton.

MARGUERITE DUPREE is the editor of *Lancashire and Whitehall: The Diary of Sir Raymond Streat 1931–1957*, 2 vols. (Manchester University Press, 1987) and the author of *Family Structure in the Staffordshire Potteries, 1840–1880* (Oxford: Clarendon Press, 1995) and articles on the social history of medicine in Britain in the nineteenth and twentieth centuries. She is a Senior Lecturer and core staff member of the Wellcome Unit for the History of Medicine at the University of Glasgow and a Fellow of Wolfson College, Cambridge.

DAVID A. HINTON is Reader at the Department of Archaeology, University of Southampton. Books include *Archaeology, Economy and Society* (London: Routledge repr. 1998) and *The Gold, Silver and Other Non-Ferrous Alloy Objects from Hamwic* (Stroud: Alan Sutton Publishing, 1996). He was Editor of *Medieval Archaeology*, 1979–89.

DEREK KEENE is Director of the Centre for Metropolitan History at the Institute of Historical Research, University of London. His *Survey of Medieval Winchester* (Oxford, Clarendon Press, 1985) reconstructed the physical, social, and economic environment of a medieval city, and he has applied similar techniques to the study of London. He has published widely on the history and archaeology of English towns between the early Middle Ages and the nineteenth century, and is contributing chapters to the forthcoming *Cambridge Urban History of Britain* and a chapter on towns and trade in eleventh- and twelfth-century Europe to the *Cambridge Medieval History*. He is a member of international and national committees and commissions on urban history and the historic environment.

R. J. MORRIS is Professor of Economic and Social History at Edinburgh University. He has written extensively on class, urban history, and voluntary associations, notably *Class, Sect and Party: The Making of the British Middle Class, Leeds 1820–1850*, (Manchester University Press, 1990).

STANA NENADIC is Senior Lecturer in Social History at the University of Edinburgh. She has written on various aspects of art, literature, and society, most recently 'The Enlightenment of Scotland and the Popular Passion for Portraits', *British Journal for Eighteenth-Century Studies*, 21/2 (1998) and was Editor of the *Urban History* 1995 special edition titled *Art and the City*.

ANDRZEJ OLECHNOWICZ is Lecturer in Modern British History, University of Durham. He is the author of *Working-Class Housing in England between the Wars: The Becontree Estate* (Oxford, 1997).

RICHARD RODGER is Senior Lecturer in Economic History at Leicester University and, since 1987, has been Editor of *Urban History*. He has written and edited several books on the economic, social, and business history of cities, including *Scottish Housing in the Twentieth Century* (Leicester University Press, 1989), *The Victorian City: A Reader in Urban History* (London: Longman, 1993) (with R. J. Morris), *European Urban History: Prospect and Retrospect* (Leicester University Press, 1993), and *Housing in Urban Britain 1780–1914* (Cambridge University Press, 1995).

DAVID SHOTTER is Senior Lecturer in Roman History in the Department of History at Lancaster University. He has published in the fields of the history of the early Roman principate, Roman numismatics, and Roman Britain. Most recent published works include a *Commentary on Suetonius' Lives of Galba, Otho and Vitellius* (Warminster: Aris and Phillips, 1993), *The Roman Frontier in Britain* (Preston: Carnegie Publishing, 1996), *Roman Britain* (London: Routledge, 1998), and an assessment of the evidence of Roman coins in north-west England in *British Numismatic Journal*, 63 (1993).

GEOFFREY TYACK is Director of Stanford University Programme in Oxford, and Fellow of Kellogg College, Oxford. He is the author of *Sir James Pennethorne and the Making of Victorian London* (Cambridge University Press, 1992) and *Oxford: An Architectural Guide* (Oxford University Press, 1998).

PHILIP WALLER is a Fellow and Tutor in Modern History at Merton College, Oxford. He is author of *Democracy and Sectarianism: A Political and Social History of Liverpool, 1868–1939* (Liverpool University Press, 1981), and of *Town, City and Nation: England 1850–1914* (Oxford University Press, 1983); and editor of *Politics and Social Change in Modern Britain* (Hassocks: Harvester Press, 1987), and (with Neville Williams and John Rowett) of *Chronology of the 20th Century* (Oxford: Helicon, 1995 and 1996).

JOHN K. WALTON is Professor of Social History at the University of Central Lancashire, Preston. He works on the comparative history of seaside resorts, especially in England and Spain, and on regional identities, especially in north-west England and the Basque country. His books include *The Blackpool Landlady: A Social History* (Manchester, 1978), *The English Seaside Resort: A Social History 1750–1914* (Leicester, 1983), *Lancashire: A Social History 1558–1939* (Manchester, 1987), *The National Trust Guide to late Georgian and Victorian Britain* (London, 1989), *Fish and Chips and the British Working Class 1870–1940* (Leicester, 1992); and *Blackpool* (Edinburgh, 1998).

MICHAEL WINSTANLEY is Senior Lecturer in History at the University of Lancaster. He has a particular interest in the social history of small businesses in retailing and agriculture, especially in north-west England. His publications on shops include *The Shopkeeper's World, 1830–1914* (Manchester University Press, 1983), *A Traditional Grocer: T. D. Smith's of Lancaster, 1858–1981* (Centre for North West Regional Studies, University of Lancaster, 1991) and 'Concentration and Competition in the Retail Sector, *c.*1800–1990', in M. W. Kirby and M. B. Rose (eds.), *Business Enterprise in Modern Britain* (London: Routledge, 1994).

Introduction

The English Urban Landscape: Yesterday, Today, and Tomorrow

Philip Waller

This history of the English urban landscape from the earliest settlements to modern times focuses upon the social structures and the changing politics and economies which shaped it. Continuity of development is important to record—some of our existing street plans, as in the City of London, follow medieval lines—but it is first necessary to register the critical distinction between a country that contained towns and a country that was an urbanized nation. Although the difference between urban and rural environments was marked by the Roman period, the crucial point in English history arrived after 1800–50 when urbanization became the cardinal presence in most people's lives. This book endeavours to do justice to these considerations by establishing the principal characteristics of the English urban landscape from Roman times to the nineteenth century in four chapters which are organized around broad periods, before moving to detailed explorations of features which chiefly obtain in the modern age. In addition, a series of cameos highlights certain processes or places as a means of illustrating the representative or the particular.

The urban landscape is not composed of only functional or solid entities. Its history cannot be depopulated. Part of the story consists of personal experiences, transient sounds and smells as well as sights. Historians of the urban landscape must also include those creative impulses which find expression in literature, music, and art. These have contributed much to our perceptions of urban form and character. The townscape is an ideological as well as built environment, carrying iconographic and mythological significance. It is a disputed terrain, fought over from political, economic, and social causes and for metaphysical reasons. Landscape imagery can articulate ethical messages; for example, in *The Private Papers of Henry Ryecroft* (1903), George Gissing execrated industrial conurbations as centres of corruption and apostrophized England's small towns and villages, in harmony with their surroundings, as the ideal environment in which character was formed. Ironically, businessmen whose materialism Gissing deplored exploit this mood as an advertising trope. Cosy, small town images sell countless products, from table mats to Christmas cards. The townscape does not suffer an entirely negative image: the city of Bath is among UNESCO's designated

World Heritage sites. Now, however, conservationism aims to preserve not only the beautiful so much as the historically significant. In 1998, English Heritage awarded Grade II* protected status to notable examples of council housing from what many deplore as the State Stalinist era, the 1950s and 1960s, such as the 'streets in the sky' zigzag blocks of Park Hill Estate, Sheffield, to the incredulity of tenants who think them more worthy of demolition. But clean, modernist urban settings do exercise a powerful hold over imaginations; and the ideal is located in the urban as well as rural landscape. It is no philological accident that 'town' constitutes the stem of 'civilization'.

At the end of the twentieth century England's urban areas accounted for 90 per cent of the population (60 per cent in places with over 100,000 people), 91 per cent of economic output, and 89 per cent of employment; and nearly 60 per cent of UK public expenditure was spent there. Here it is apposite not only to review past trends but also to try to glimpse what patterns might develop. Towns are made and remade for distinct purposes, in response to public and private needs that find expression in particular buildings or spatial organization. These requirements involve defence, political and judicial administration, commerce and industry, transport and communication, religion and recreation; and each will receive consideration in this book for the influence it has exerted on the urban landscape. Needs of defence once were symbolized by castles and walls. These are gone or survive as scenic monuments; yet, the need to protect urban populations has not vanished but taken new forms. Throughout history, accidentally sparked fires probably destroyed more urban areas than did warfare. The towns' capacity for recovery is epitomized by the name of one of the oldest insurance companies, the Phoenix. Outside aggressors have also marked the urban landscape, and air raids during the twentieth century's wars increased the towns' vulnerability. This is represented both in redevelopments of blitzed neighbourhoods and in individual structures, from myriad war memorials to Anderson shelters now serving a pacific role as garden sheds. The threat of aerial bombing has been superseded by terrorism. A strategy of urban disruption was initiated by Fenians in the 1880s. It was repeated by the IRA in the inter-war years and extensively pursued in the past quarter-century. Among the largest explosions was that at the Arndale Centre, Manchester in 1996, but the most ambitious was the attempt in that same year to detonate bombs simultaneously at six electricity sub-stations which supply power to London and the south-east. The IRA is not the only group to employ terrorism: animal rights activists have used incendiary devices against laboratories and shops. We cannot reckon that no new terrorist organizations will arise in future or that they will abstain from using chemical and germ warfare or computer hacking and viruses in preference to bombs and guns. Accordingly, the freedom to enter particular buildings and districts will be increasingly hedged by restrictions and inspection.

Our streets are already cluttered with advisory and imperative features. It was the Automobile Association in 1906 which installed the first road warning and town nameplate signs. Now there are not just countless information and directional notices, but speed cameras, 'sleeping policemen', pedestrian crossings, traffic lights, roundabouts, and islands; and roads are war-painted with coloured lines and symbols. Street lighting was originally introduced to combat crime as well as for commercial and public convenience; but the urban landscape of the future will be characterized by an almost perpetual illumination which practically defies the natural order of day and night. Six million street and motorway lights, the floodlighting of churches and other historic and public buildings, of stadiums, parks, bridges, offices, pubs, and stores, and the spread of security and decorative spotlighting on homes and in gardens, all conspire to make England the third most light-polluted region in Europe, following after the more densely populated Netherlands and Belgium. According to John Mason of the British Astronomical Society, 'children of the next millennium are being condemned to never seeing the stars'.

The urban landscape of the future will contain more surveillance systems, to deter internal forces of disorder as well as external enemies. In the past, citizens sought protection against crime not only by securing their premises with dogs (now sporting studded collars and called Tyson) and with gates, shutters, bars, and locks, but also by policing and by concerted action against districts which they knew (or assumed) to harbour criminals. Such action took the form of zonal segregation and clearance: hence the advent of residential squares and suburban estates and, correspondingly, the demolition of 'rookeries' and relocation of their populations, some few to prisons but the majority to other neighbourhoods which might better convert them into productive citizens or, failing that, better regulate their sociopathic proclivities.

Public policy thus influences the appearance of the urban landscape. The Victorians, using a metaphor inadmissible today, framed the issue as a question, Is it the sty which makes the pig, or the pig which makes the sty? That sidestepped crucial issues of income and wealth distribution, but the twin strategies that flowed from this debate still obtain: the aims of improving both personal character and physical environment. Education and temperance reform, the provision of employment and amusement, these remain the foundations of a constructive approach to reforming character, bounded always by a judicial system which penalizes infractions. Currently, the policing policy gaining favour is 'zero-tolerance'. This involves prosecuting all petty offences from street begging to graffiti-daubing in the belief that if a culture of contempt for the law flourishes, then miscreants will progress to serious crime and the social order will deteriorate. This follows the 'broken window' theory in buildings, according to which, unless minor repairs are undertaken, entire structures will collapse. Libertarians worry about this and about the electronic tagging of potential reoffenders; but most people welcome these moves to avoid whole areas being condemned to vandalism, prostitution, drug-dealing, car thefts, burglaries, and muggings.

The town landscape of the future will see the extension of neighbourhood watch systems, the greater employment of porters, private guards, and security patrols in and around buildings and estates, the use of CCTV to monitor visitors, entryphones and swipecards to control access, pull-alarm and remote-control blippers to alert against intruders, and all manner of automatically operated steel doors and window shutters. In 1999, the number of CCTV cameras in use in Britain exceeded 1 million, the highest in proportion to population of any country in the world; and in London and many towns, a person could reckon to be caught on film over 500 times a week, on the road, in stations, in offices and at work, in shops, restaurants and other places of entertainment, and outside and even inside many private residences. Yet there is also an awareness of the importance of not making townspeople feel as if they live in a fortress: hence the emphasis on security with style. Thorn and holly hedges, ponds and water courses, may curb crime and give pleasure. The popularity (to horticulturists, the scourge) of the fast-growing evergreen Leylandii stands as a symbol of this. There are an estimated 55 million in Britain, planted mostly by suburban gardeners. Housing design likewise gives prominence to these needs. Security is a major selling point of luxury apartments; and it is integral to new corporate housing schemes, such as the Waltham Forest Estate in East London.

Town landscapes will continue to be shaped by structural change in the economy. The most important, taking place over centuries, was the shift from an agrarian to a commercial and industrial economy which caused a majority of England's people to inhabit towns by 1851 and some 80 per cent by 1914. What followed was a deepening and diversification of this trend, with a switch from an economy based on primary extractive processes, heavy industries, and staple trades manufacture (coal, iron and steel, shipbuilding and textiles) to one in which retail and services sectors dominate. The surviving manufacture is generally lighter and less labour-intensive, utilizing scientifically devised production methods (automation and computerization) and energy (electricity, gas, and petrochemicals). There remain sizeable industries with a poor record of atmospheric pollution and landscape despoliation. Among the most noxious are the ICI chemical plant at Runcorn and Associated Octel's plant at nearby Ellesmere Port; but England's towns are generally now cleaner and controls stricter. Only the older generation can recall the coal-smoke menace of innumerable steam engines, factories, and domestic hearths which polluted the urban air for a century and more, right up to the 1960s. Then, if not proud of the blackened buildings and soot-laden atmosphere, people were more alarmed when chimneys were clear, because that meant work was scarce.

Urban air quality now is threatened more by motor vehicles than by industrial production. Accordingly, experiments with alternative fuels are being tried. In Coventry, local council, electricity board, and postal staff drive vehicles powered by electrically charged batteries whose radius is limited to 50 miles; and buses and lorries using liquefied gas or electricity operate in Oxford, Bournemouth, and five London boroughs. The car culture saps vitality in other ways too: the average distance walked by individuals has fallen 20 per cent since the 1970s, with a consequent decline in physical and psychological well-being and rise in obesity, heart disease, and osteoporosis.

The economic move away from basic manufacture to services is most dramatically epitomized by activity in the City of London where, over the past century, a quarter of the buildings have been replaced every 30 years. Here a forest of skyscrapers has sprung up and, had not widespread opposition caused the Trafalgar House company to withdraw the plans it unveiled in 1996, all would have been miniaturized by the London Millennium tower. Designed by Sir Norman Foster, with 92 storeys to be built on the Baltic Exchange site that suffered IRA-bomb damage in 1990, this building was planned to scale 1,265 feet, making it twice as high as the NatWest tower and the tallest in Europe. Critics decry such landmark intrusions as aggressive architecture, which reflects confrontational power systems and rejects public concerns about a fragile environment. Others regard it as ineluctable if London is to maintain its position as Europe's finance capital; moreover, a skyline of skyscrapers, conveying strength and line, is not without aesthetic appeal and their presence can shelter the intimacy of old-fashioned quarters below. Indirectly, too, skyscrapers force public authorities to consider transport policy in city centres: Foster's plan included only 100 car-parking spaces for the 8,000 users of his building.

These developments in the City appear remote from most people's lives, yet they are mimicked on smaller scale in the provincial cities. More broadly, the urban landscape is being reshaped by the changing ecology of work, as more businesses adopt flexible labour patterns, eroding old job boundaries and contracting out for particular services or parts of the production process. The proportion of individuals who in whole or in part work from their homes is now the highest in Europe: three in ten men and four in ten women. Increasing car dependency is connected to job mobility. In 1950, a quarter of all journeys were by bicycle; in 1999 the figure was only one per cent. The number of private motor vehicles in Britain first passed 1 million around 1930, rising to 6 million in 1960 and 19.7 million in 1990. There are now about 25 million, more than in China, India, and sub-Saharan Africa. Fewer women than men hold driving licences—12 million out of 29 million drivers—but more women are obtaining them.

New Thames riverside housing in London, with distant views of the Millennium Dome supplying added lustre. (Computer-generated image.)

The anticipated pattern of population growth, around which controversy revolves concerning housing demand and supply and other infrastructural provision at the start of the twenty-first century. Population statistics by Government Office Regions, 1996–2021.

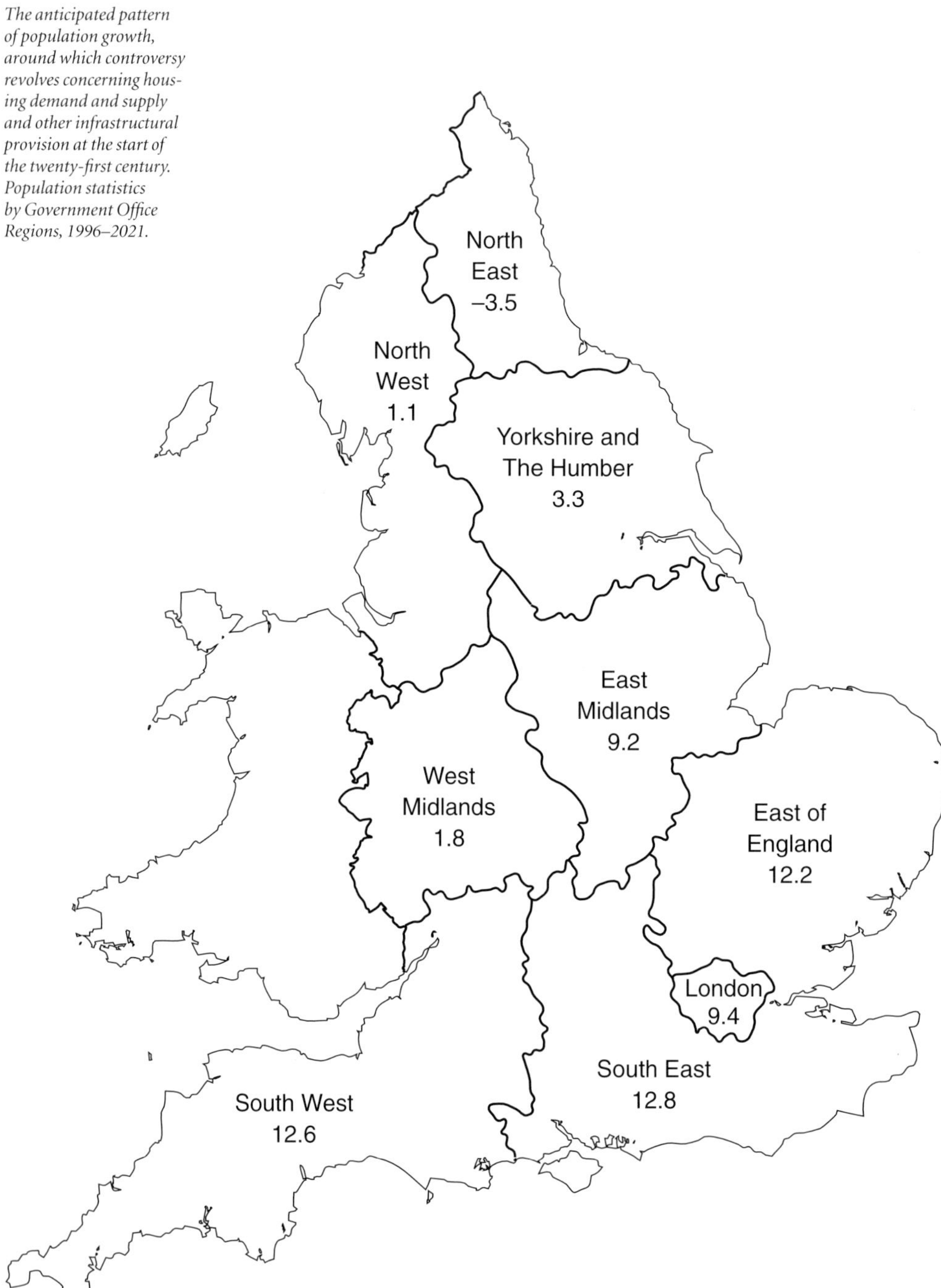

About 69 per cent of households own a vehicle; of these nearly 22 per cent have two. In surveys of reasons for car use, people emphasize their need to get to work at a place or time which public transport does not readily serve. Men travel annually on average one-third more miles than do women, but women make more journeys as they contrive to combine work schedules with domestic chores of shopping and transporting children to and from school. Moreover, car dependency is not confined to working parents and mothers. Many retired and elderly people are similarly placed, and about 15 per cent of adults suffers a disability that makes access to public transport problematic or impossible.

Demographic trends compound these changing work habits. It is not population increases alone, rather its composition and distribution that affect the urban landscape. England's estimated population of 49.1 million in 1996 is expected to grow slowly, to 52.5 million in 2021 (an increase of 6.9 per cent over 25 years), because more women are deferring childbirth until they have established careers or are ceasing to raise families. Nearly one in four women are now childless, compared with one in ten in the early 1960s. Women born in the mid-1930s produced an average family of 2.45 children; those born in the late 1960s, about 1.85 children. This decline is expected to persist, as is the trend towards short-term cohabitation. Over one-third of children are born outside wedlock; moreover, England has the highest divorce rate in Europe, four in ten marriages dissolving. Some 27 per cent of households contain a single person and, though 35 per cent contain children, only 24 per cent comprise a couple with children. The proportion of one-parent families has risen from 12 per cent in 1980 to 27 per cent now. There is a tax burden associated with this, and an unaccountable cost in social dysfunction; but the equation is incomplete without reckoning that people are both living longer and working shorter lives. A boy born in 1998 has a life expectancy of 74, a girl that of 80. By 2034, there will be 15 per cent fewer children and 50 per cent more pensioners. The term 'pensioner' has altered in quantity and meaning during the century. In 1909–10, at the introduction of the state pension, about 5 per cent of the population was aged over 65; nowadays, that group comprises 15 per cent. Of equal significance, over 60 per cent of male workers and 41 per cent of female workers stop work before the official retirement ages (65 for men, 60 for women in 1999). Again, there are financial calculations to weigh. In 1946, social security spending was 3 per cent of national income, in 1996 over 13 per cent. At present the proportion of workers to pensioner is almost 3 : 1, and over the next half century it may approach 2 : 1.

Budgetary implications can be set aside here, although serious consequences arise for the urban infrastructure if the principal tax-base, the working population, is shrinking. Of direct relevance to the urban landscape is the forecast that another 3.8 million households will be formed by 2021, an increase of 19 per cent, with over one-third involving people living alone. Notwithstanding a preference for the two-storey independent dwelling, it is evident that more people will inhabit apartments—young singles, childless couples, and so-called 'empty-nesters'. McCarthy and Stone, the leading builders of retirement-apartment complexes, admit buyers at any age over 50, consistent with the trend towards early retirement and child-free life. Some include swimming pools and other fitness facilities as many retired people enjoy prolonged health as well as wealth. By contrast, one in five who reaches age 65 requires supervised accommodation. Apartment-life is also spreading as a fashion for inner-city living revives. The most well-publicized examples are in London's former docklands, in apartment conversions of disused warehouses. Such developments are replicated in most provincial cities, to discourage, even reverse, urban sprawl. Seen not long ago as wildernesses of dereliction and especially unsafe at night when commuters quit their offices for the suburbs, city centres are reviving as new restaurants, delicatessens, and grocery shops cater for residents who cycle or walk to work and to theatres, cinemas, and galleries in a simulacrum of New York's 'metro-life-style'.

Selling capital chic, in which the best of the past and future are conveniently and sumptuously provided in the present.

Opposite: *Launching a dream of the modern metro life-style: this warehouse-conversion evokes images of pre-war luxury streamlined for the global jet age and commerce with the European Union.*

GATEWAY TO EUROPE
ICE WHARF
LONDON–PARIS–LILLE–BRUXELLES
MANCHESTER–NEWCASTLE–EDINBURGH
BATTLEBRIDGE BASIN
REGENTS CANAL
NEW KING'S CROSS
94 APARTMENTS AND PENTHOUSES

This trend is noteworthy; nevertheless, it would be wrong to minimize the exodus from cities and the lure that the small-town and rural idyll holds. Pollsters in the early 1990s reported that two-thirds of Londoners would like to leave. Since 1980, London's population has fallen by 628,000, close to the 648,000 aggregate loss experienced by the six other chief metropolitan areas. Currently, about 300 people evacuate the big cities daily. Once gone, they rarely move back. Larger migrations are involved than these figures suggest: between 1981 and 1994, 9.2 million people settled in the metropolitan areas but 10.5 million left. Most do not move far, but such migrations cumulatively produce in once rural areas what the Civic Trust dubs 'suburban super-crescents'. The largest arcs around London from Peterborough in the north, through Amersham and Newbury to the west, and so on round into the south-east. This appears much as H. G. Wells predicted in 1901, that by 2001 Londoners would live anywhere south of Nottingham and east of Exeter in connected urban regions. We can analyse the phenomenon more precisely. Certain quarters of London, boasting a 'village feel' in the heart of the city, appeal to young professionals: Kensington, Holland Park and Ladbroke Grove, West Hampstead, Islington, Kensal Rise, Marylebone, Bloomsbury, Clerkenwell, Shoreditch, Spitalfields, and Bermondsey. Doubtless other neighbourhoods will emerge but, overall, they do not compensate for the quitters, and the space which they abandon when they flee to the suburbs and countryside is often filled by ethnic minorities. Greater London receives one-third of all new immigrants; moreover, over 60 per cent of ethnic minorities, old and new immigrants, inhabit council estates or run-down areas, compared with fewer than 20 per cent of whites. The danger is that migrations are deranging the social balance as big cities become polarized, left to the very rich who inhabit price-ringed compounds and to the very poor who are without amenities. Moreover, the smart and affluent young are not so taken by inner-city chic when they start families. The second-home syndrome is well known to estate agents who monitor rising house prices for weekend retreats within 2½ hours' drive from cities which, in London's case, takes people into East Anglia, Nottinghamshire, Worcestershire, Somerset, and Dorset, as well as to the south-east coast. Such is the rural pull that an inverse movement has emerged whereby second-home-owners establish their main residence in the country and a pied-à-terre in town. This trend is strengthened by school league tables: housing in catchment areas for high-performing schools sells at a premium, and most such schools are not in inner cities. Further, it is mistaken to think that single invariably means small. Many single people who are divorced or widowed, have children or grandchildren. Apartment-living cannot satisfy their desire to domicile or entertain offspring, and surplus bedrooms are utilized as office-studies. The demand for out-of-city homes is strongest among the over-55s, fed up with traffic and fearful of crime. This 'grey-wave' is conspicuous in several regions, notably in the softer climate of the south-west. Somerset's pensioners comprise 103,000 in a population of 470,000. In 1996, the Taunton MP David Nicholson speculated that restrictions might have to be imposed on elderly people wanting to move into such areas, a notion immediately denounced as 'a bit silly' by his 82-year-old mother who had retired to North Wales in the 1970s. Nicholson himself left London for Devon in the 1980s.

The Nicholson family tiff illustrates that the fiercest controversy concerns not the type and quantity of homes to be built, rather, where these will be situated. On this decision hangs the future character of the English urban landscape. The

Blair government envisages 60 per cent of new homes being placed in existing urban areas, mostly on previously developed or derelict land; but the Council for the Protection of Rural England (est. 1926) complains that England already loses 27,000 acres annually to urban development (mainly on town edges) and that, if this rate continues, 20 per cent of the country will be built over by 2050. Currently, 87.5 per cent of England and Wales is countryside. The CPRE wants the schedule of new homes built on urban land raised to 70–75 per cent, arguing that 500,000 derelict acres wait to be used and 1.3 million buildings (including 735,000 houses of which 108,000 are publicly owned) stand empty. However, some unused urban land is unusable, being too contaminated by a previous industrial presence to allow home construction; some more is parkland, playing fields, or green space too precious to forfeit; and the distribution of derelict land does not tally with where homes are needed. Seven city authorities state that they expect to run out of land between 2006 and 2011. This imbalance is especially acute in London and the south-east. There is pious agreement about the need to avoid the errors of the 1950s and 1960s when too many people were packed into poorly constructed tower blocks or housing estates, as politicians urgently strived to reduce council-house waiting lists. It is equally agreed that too many houses were demolished, of the Victorian terrace type which required only refurbishment to renew their usefulness. The Greater London Council acknowledged in 1970 that 67,000 houses which it had bulldozed should have been renovated.

It may be that the government's projections will not be borne out. There has been a down-scaling already since November 1996 when the Environment Minister, John Gummer, announced that 4.4 million new homes would be needed by 2016. This caused the architect Richard (Lord) Rogers to pronounce, 'It is imperative to put as much as possible in existing cities and towns. The critical thing is, that if they can take 60 per cent of the new housing needed, that should be the *first* 60 per cent.' Rogers subsequently headed an Urban Task Force, which reported in June 1999. This reckoned that, if present policies continue unchanged, the target of 60 per cent cannot be met. By 2021, only some 55 per cent of a projected 3.8 million extra households will be planted on recycled urban land. The Task Force considered other models by which the proportion might fall as low as 47.4 per cent; but mostly its attention was directed towards advising how the target might be realized, even raised to 62.2 per cent, and comprehensive urban regeneration achieved and sustained. Its report, containing over 100 recommendations, was designed as a primer to an intended Government Urban Policy White Paper—the first for over two decades—and a complementary Rural White Paper. Planning is crucial, but planning in the past (where it has existed at all) has been more reactive than proactive, too partial and too slow, and too confused by overlapping organizations. The history of public provision of environmental services, transport, and housing is shot through with underinvestment, incompetent management, and inadequate maintenance. To advocate wider vision, strengthened authority, streamlined procedure, and better practice is uplifting; but reality has a habit of pulling things down. To suppose market forces can be ignored or easily controlled is naïve. Moreover, to make plans work, political consent—even more elusive, political consensus—is required. The State can devise strategic plans and building regulations; it cannot dictate where every brick is laid. Council-house spending now is one-third what it was when Mrs Thatcher formed her first ministry in 1979. Government reforms—concerning tenant

Designated in 1968, Telford was part of the second wave of New Town formation and now contains 125,000 people. It boasts a forward-looking philosophy together with firm foundations associated with the achievements of Thomas Telford (1757–1834), the Industrial Revolution engineer of roads, canals, and bridges.

rights, the abolition of mortgage tax relief and of VAT on building conversions and renovations, and the corresponding imposition of VAT on new housing or special taxes to deter developments of greenfield sites—will not cancel the public's partiality for individual homes in 'leafy areas'. Homeowners will not be bossed about indefinitely. They constitute a political force. In 1945, 26 per cent, and in 1979, 52 per cent, of all homes were owner-occupied; by 1983, this had risen to 63 per cent and, though the rate of increase has since slowed, it now stands at 68 per cent. This investment expresses the Lockean notion of 'self-ownership', a drive for personal independence and fulfilment. Most homeowners' tastes are traditional rather than modernist. They welcome energy-efficient installations but generally do not want to inhabit a 'machine for living' according to the precepts of Le Corbusier, still less some gleaming sepulchre whose rationally aligned and voided rooms are designed for photographing rather than comfort. Above all, they pursue value for money. They understand that, if they leave the principal cities and suburbs, they can buy more property for the same sum and extend their lives in a healthier environment.

One can reckon on resistance being raised by residents of small towns and country people who do not want to be submerged in a tide of new housing. This is the 'NIMBY' ('Not in my back yard') phenomenon, so called after a Secretary of State for the Environment, Nicholas Ridley, who in the late 1980s bullied local authorities into granting planning permission for housing estates at the edge of many country towns while objecting to development in his own neighbourhood. Most architects and planners believe that dormitory suburbs cannot be grafted onto villages and small towns without injuring their character and multiplying traffic and social problems; why not, therefore, generate a crop of well-designed, self-sustaining new communities? This prospect horrifies others in turn. The requirement of 3.8 million additional households translates into 24 new Milton Keyneses and, if built at current average densities for new developments, would cover a land area larger than Greater London.

Recent town creation by the State has been clustered into two periods, the late 1940s and the 1960s. Most new towns stand out not as realized utopias so much as creatures of their time. No one now wants to replicate the housing standard of Skelmersdale. Almost all have passed through a phase of being judged (more by outsiders than insiders) 'soulless' places. Image problems persist: Paul Hills's debut film *Boston Kickout* (1996) depicted Stevenage as a wasteland where no-hope, drug- and drink-addicted youths rampage. Stevenage was hit in the early 1990s by British Aerospace redundancies and by Kodak and Bowater plant closures; but its unemployment rate stayed below average and its attractions were not nullified. The new towns' aggregate achievement has been impressive. Altogether, they house over 2 million people and do business with 50,000 companies providing over 1 million jobs. Of these companies, 1,200 are foreign-owned. Telford has attracted 140 companies from eighteen countries, including the most Japanese and Taiwanese firms of any town in Britain. New towns have been innovators in styles of urban living now so diffused that they are almost taken for granted: pedestrianized streets, shopping malls, multiplex cinemas, and artificial ski slopes first appeared in one or another new town, as did the first science park, solar-heated home, and system of domestic refuse recycling. New towns have been exemplars in low-density housing, built on reclaimed land as well as on greenfield sites. The standard has been a maximum of twelve houses per acre, each overlooking open ground. Twenty per cent of Milton Keynes is public space, including woods and lakes; but the 1999 Urban Task Force recommended increasing densities for most new urban developments to fourteen or sixteen dwellings per acre, in order to economize on land and encourage a clustering of public amenities which would reduce car use.

In the past, government commitment to new towns was fitful. The Labour ministries which promoted them failed to convince the wider Labour movement that they would not damage the older industrial cities by siphoning off skilled workers and fresh investment; and to Conservative ministries, new towns were suspect as experiments in State Socialism. Future governments can be expected to regard them more positively, as blueprints for urban development partnerships combining Whitehall ministries, local authorities, schools of design, and business corporations. This does not mean that a multitude of new towns will result, although particular sites lend themselves to this, such as surplus military bases. The partnership model is broadly applicable for the regeneration of existing towns and dilapidated industrial regions.

One new scheme is the Bluewater mega-shopping centre near Dartford, opened in March 1999 and conceived as the hub of a future north-west Kent city. It was designed by an American architect and developed by a consortium involving large retail companies, the Prudential Insurance Company, and an Australian property and financial services corporation. Its anticipated 30 million 'shopping visits' per annum were planned to include shoppers from mainland Europe, using the Channel Tunnel. Retail developments such as this are contentious. Some see them as a trigger to revive urban regions, others as spelling the death of the traditional city. The rise of suburban shopping malls has been correlated with devitalized inner cities in America. In 1986, Britain contained 432 'superstores' (shops with over 25,000 square feet of floor space); 1,034 by 1996. Almost all households now do some weekly shopping in supermarkets. Of equal importance is their location: Sainsbury's, for instance, has added 206 new stores since 1986, 10 per cent in town centres, 23 per cent in suburbs, and 67 per cent on outside sites. There are several issues to weigh, particularly increased reliance on cars for shopping; yet city centres may have better prospects of revival if more delivery and shoppers' vehicles are redirected to outside sites. Perhaps, too, the volume of consumer demand, unmatched in history and still growing, will sustain *both* inner-city *and* out-of-town retail centres. The advent of electronic shopping could alter this. Already, at the time of writing, 42 per cent of households possess a computer, of which 30 per cent are online. Electronic shopping appeals to the time-conscious professional. However, convenience is only one fraction of the 'shopping experience' which involves convivial and experimental sensations; moreover, there is disturbing evidence about 'food deserts' emerging in the poorest city areas and in the countryside, where the closure of corner and village shops and inadequate public transport leave people without cars struggling to shop for nutritionally vital fresh foods.

The leading chain of chemists, Boots, with over 1,200 shops, retains more high-street positions than any other retailer; and it has formed an alliance with Marks & Spencer, Sears, Sainsbury's, W. H. Smith's, the Prudential Insurance Company, the National Westminster Bank, and several other firms, linked to university and local authority planning departments, to sponsor town centre management schemes and public and private sector partnerships in 170 places. Town centres, with an average 3.6 parking spaces per 1,000 square feet, cannot match out-of-town shopping centres which average 7.4 spaces. The more towns restrict parking, the more congestion as drivers search for spaces. There are ways round this problem. Tesco's runs 100 free buses for shoppers to its supermarkets; and more local authorities might imitate the park-and-ride facilities introduced at Oxford and York or the tramway system revived in Manchester. Town centres have not lost the war; indeed, there is evidence of victories won. Pedestrianization of town centres is widespread. This increases their attractiveness during shopping hours, although fears must be countered that such zones become no-go areas at night. Town centre revivalism involves a multitude of attentions: more elegant shop façades and smarter public buildings, conscientious street cleansing and floral decoration, well-sited benches, stylish lighting and surveillance systems, and so forth. Such a delicate balance requires constant correction; but town centres are advantaged over out-of-town or suburban malls because their appeal is not exclusively based on shopping. Town centres historically are focuses for the arts and entertainments; and these, joined to tourism, are forces for inner-city regeneration. Vying with Bradford, Bristol, Liverpool, and Manchester to be the next British city designated European Capital of Culture, Newcastle conceived plans to convert the disused Baltic Flour Mill into an arts centre alongside concert halls and a new Tyne footbridge, estimating that it would attract 345,000 visitors a year, create 350 jobs and generate £5 million for the local economy.

Recreation has long been an important function of towns. Its physical symbols in the past were fairs and inns. Now there are dance and bingo halls, theatres and cinemas, parks and sports facilities. A puritan ethos once held this in check. In the nineteenth century, the temperance movement favoured 'rational recreation' to enhance civil society. Only recently have many pubs discarded their image as dingy dens for a predominantly male clientele, in which no respectable woman or family was found. The spending power of the 'teenager' and the 'twenties' has also abetted cultural change, evident first in the rise of Mecca dance halls and gramophone music in the interwar, now in the vogue for 'clubbing'. One hundred and fifty thousand young people are attracted each weekend into Manchester, the clubland capital of the north. Certain towns such as spas and holiday resorts specialize in leisure provision. Historians have analysed the factors involved: changing demographic and work patterns, commercial organization, and cultural philosophies. The impact on the urban landscape is not always lasting: descendants of medieval fairs which survive, such as the Nottingham Goose Fair or St Giles' Fair at Oxford, are transient, yet for a few days bring festivity to city streets. The recently invented Notting Hill Carnival stands in this tradition, as a celebration for people of West Indian origin. More characteristic of the modern age are the fixed sites and purpose-built edifices for recreational participation and spectatorship. The soccer stadiums opened in 1997 at Bolton, Derby, Stoke, and Sunderland are new urban temples, planned as 'leisure villages', providing not just a football pitch and 25,000-plus seats but gymnasiums, rackets courts, athletic tracks, and conference, exhibition, banqueting, and shopping facilities. The pitches have under-soil heating to ensure playability throughout winter; they can also be floored over for pop concerts and other events. Philathleticism in the past was associated with particular social classes, a particular educational curriculum, and for particular public purposes, often of a militaristic and imperial kind.

Nowadays, in a calorie-conscious age, philathleticism is more of a generalized health and aesthetic cult of the body, imbued with physiological and narcissistic philosophy. Music systems, and mirrored walls for preening, are as essential to fitness clubs as exercise bicycles and power-lifting machinery. Offices as well as apartment complexes and ordinary homes include these. Exhibitionism is also a public trait: there is a strong tradition of political and commercial displays such as the Great Exhibition at Hyde Park in 1851, the Empire Trade Exhibition at Wembley in 1924, the Festival of Britain Exhibition on the Thames' South Bank in 1951, and the Millennium Exhibition at Greenwich in 2000. The Olympia Hall at Earl's Court in London and the National Exhibition Centre in Birmingham are other servants of this demand. Advertising sustains it. Posters promoting products, events, and propaganda are ubiquitous in the urban landscape, appearing on special hoardings, on ordinary house ends, on shops, street-stands, and mobiles such as cabs, buses, and even pedestrians. As E. H. Gombrich noted, this marks a development in the history of art, which previously was 'harnessed to the service of power or of religion': now it predominantly sells goods. At their most vivacious, advertisements constitute a poor man's art gallery, brightening as well as defacing the urban setting.

Investment in leisure is a major industry. Over 80 'multiplex' or (the jargon screams hyperbole) 'megaplex' leisure centres exist, providing on one site cinemas, video-game and 'virtual-reality' arcades, artificial ski slopes, indoor hang-gliding, bowling halls, fitness clubs, bars, nightclubs, restaurants, and hotels. There are also some 30 leisure parks, providing funfair rides and/or animal safari experiences. The old-style park, established in the Victorian period, needs to adapt to compete. This is difficult since competitive tendering was forced on local authorities in the late 1980s, whereupon most slashed their parks budgets and replaced permanent staff with mobile contractors. Nonetheless, 8 million people visit public parks and gardens daily. There are ambitious schemes to revitalize some of the largest, such as the 90-acre Mile End Park created in 1947 as a lung for half-a-million East End residents. Holiday resorts likewise need to refurbish to sustain their competitiveness. It is not now so certain that the English do like to be beside the English seaside, although Butlin's camps at Bognor Regis, Minehead, and Skegness attract 2 million visitors annually and operate at 85–90 per cent capacity. Competition is not just in the volume and variety of excitements but also in environmental quality. Most resort authorities publish data regarding hours of sunshine but, with fears rife concerning skin cancer, attention is now directed to cleanliness; and a priority is to improve coastal sewerage systems. Environmental health is a quest pursued on macro- and micro-scale, from the global warming campaign involving statesmen and scientists to the canine faeces vigilantism involving park and beach attendants. Actually, the number of dog-owners in towns is falling (and cat-owners rising) because working couples and single persons cannot manage a dog. So-called 'cyber pets'—electronic toy animals—are being marketed instead. Tourism, however, is big business: in 1996, Britain attracted 25 million overseas visitors who spent an estimated £12.67 billion. More Britons, 43 million, went abroad, but many take more than one annual holiday. The Bank Holidays, instituted from 1871 and constituting a long weekend, are stretched into several days. Every August Bank Holiday about 5 million people leave home, 1.75 million for the airports and the rest for the roads. Their destination is no longer invariably the seaside, although Blackpool's Pleasure

Beach, with 7.3 million visitors, led the country's list of free attractions in 1995, ahead of the British Museum (5.7 million) and National Gallery (4.5 million) in second and third place. The most popular venues which charged for admission were the Alton Towers theme park in Staffordshire and Madame Tussaud's waxworks in London (2.7 million), followed by the Tower of London (2.5 million). Towns with historic associations attract as many visitors as the most vibrant resort. Stratford-upon-Avon is the mecca for Shakespearians; and Oxford's colleges draw 4 million visitors annually, the equivalent of 30 visitors per resident. It is also a sign of the soap-opera times that in 1995 Granada's TV studios, where *Coronation Street* is made, overtook Stonehenge, with 750,000 visitors.

The torrent of urban tourists generates difficulties as well as revenue. Slow-moving, open-topped buses, equipped with loudspeakers, anger locals in historic towns. Noise is now among the most generally felt nuisances, with amplified music blaring from pubs, clubs, shops, and passing vehicles. A special irritation is caused by mobile phones in public places. Traffic noise is most grievous. It affects the countryside as well as towns. Resurfacing roads with noise-reducing materials is a palliative. The cure lies in traffic reduction; yet road traffic, which has increased by almost two-thirds since 1980, is forecast to grow by another third over the next 20 years. Protest is favoured by nomadic 'eco-warriors' whose tactic of encamping on sites scheduled for road-building was initiated in 1992 to block an extension of the M3 motorway across Twyford Down. Civil disobedience also appeals to people wanting *more* roads. In 1997, the mayor of Tetbury organized residents to process continuously over the pedestrian crossing on the main road along which 400–600 lorries thunder each day, thus to publicize their need for a bypass. Politicians chant a mantra about an 'integrated transport policy'. This sounds wholesome but signifies little. All transport systems in all periods of history have been integrated because at some point one mode of transit connects to another, the pedestrian to the horse and cart and boat, or the cycle and car to the train and airplane. In the horse age, 25 miles was a reasonable day's journey; now the limit is set by frustration, not vehicle capacity. An 'integrated transport policy' is a euphemism for forcing people to surrender their cars, by steep rises in fuel prices, vehicle duties, and parking charges, by introducing road tolls, more bus and cycle lanes, park-and-ride schemes, and by closing areas to traffic. The snag lies in the complementary package, the investment required to cheapen, improve, and extend public transport so that the choice people make about travel is not automatically their own car. Fiscal incentives are required, such as allowing companies to buy rail and bus season tickets for their employees as a tax-free benefit while phasing out company-financed motoring. Persuasion plays a greater part than compulsion in a democratic society, but it is unlikely that public transport can so expand as to satisfy needs and expectations. No planning can bring homes, schools, shops, and workplaces into desired proximity for most people most of the time. Neither motorist nor non-motorist—13 million people belong to households without a car—has flourished in recent years. Commuting time is an average 40 per cent higher than 20 years ago and, since 1986, there has been a 29 per cent *reduction* in bus passengers in spite of a 25 per cent rise in bus mileage. Bus fares have soared 22 per cent over inflation, and public subsidy has been cut by more than 50 per cent. The 1999 Urban Task Force recommended dedicating at least 65 per cent of transport public expenditure over the next decade on schemes that favour public transport users, cyclists, and pedestrians. Currently there are no votes to be won by compelling people to stand in the rain at bus stops for unpunctual buses which do not take them where they want to go. People are sceptical of the ability of the State—in practice, partisan politicians and far-from-omniscient civil servants—to get things right. Why trust an organization that, having nationalized the railways in 1948, then commissioned the Beeching Report in 1963 which recommended the closure of over a quarter of all passenger railway lines and 2,100 stations? The

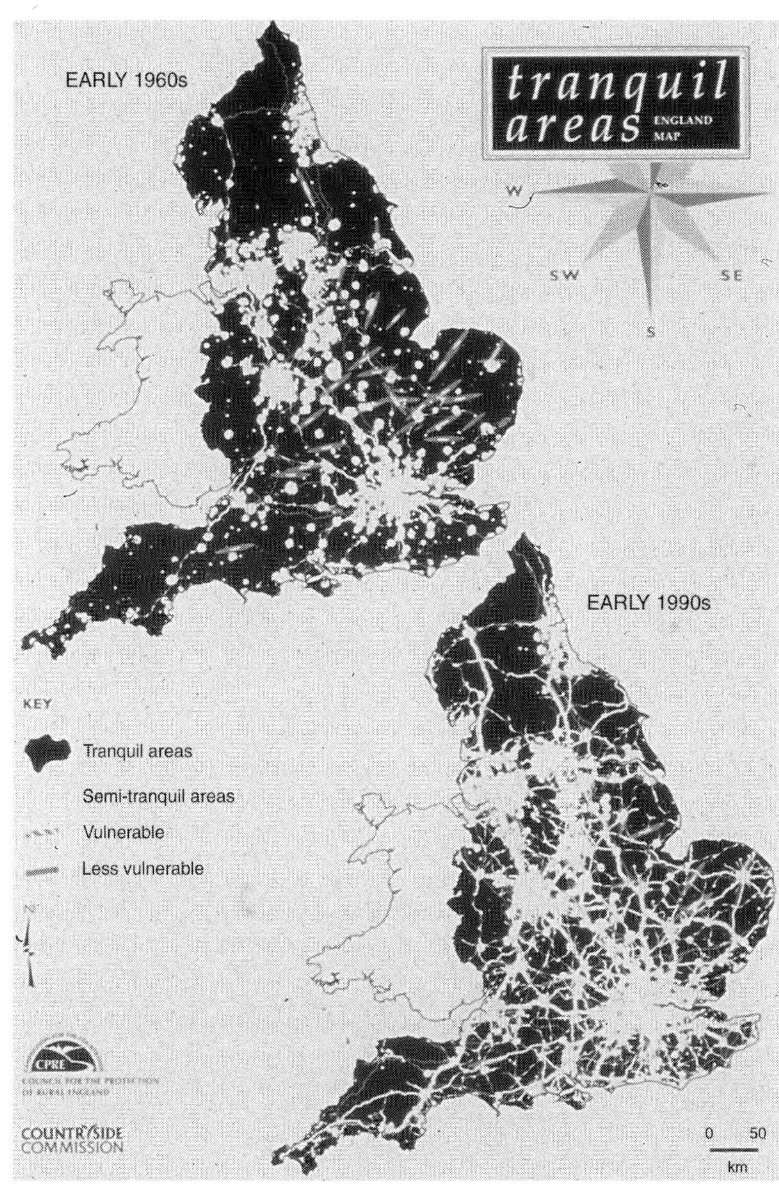

The shrinking state of peace or three decades of din diffusion, according to the Council for the Protection of Rural England whose criteria involve various degrees of proximity to busy roads, railways, and airports, towns, power stations, and sites of industrial activity and open-cast mining.

State-run system was not renowned for rail and bus timetable 'integration'—or for responsiveness to passenger complaints. England's towns will suffer congestion so long as public transport cannot match the private car for versatility, convenience, comfort, cleanliness, dignity, safety, and cheapness. Politics involves the distribution of finite resources: subsidized fares spell higher taxes, unless revenue allocation is changed. Currently, only £7 billion of £28 billion raised from motorists is invested in transport. Such spending amounts to a mere bagatelle compared with the costs of the Trident missile system or Eurofighter. Every form of travel—whether buying a car or travelling by bus and rail—costs more in Britain than in most European countries and America.

The urban landscape is shaped by changing economic and social structures, refracted through political systems. Religious practices too have stamped the town with characteristic features, from the earliest pagan formularies through the centuries of Christian worship. The churches' physical dominance, lording it over most ordinary habitations, has largely disappeared. The suffocation of St Paul's Cathedral, which lost its supremacy in London's skyline in the 1950s, remains the most pathetic symbol of this. In future, churches will be proportionately fewer and less significant; they will also diversify more, as the country's population that derives from immigrant origins and adheres to non-Christian faiths grows in wealth and influence in particular areas and erects buildings whose religious architecture owes little to Western European tradition. Britain now has 1.2 million Muslims and 600,000 Sikhs; there are also more Scientologists (500,000) than Hindus or Jews (300,000 each). Social surveys suggest that about two-thirds of people profess belief in a God of some kind; yet only 11 per cent attend a weekly service and over a half never, or hardly ever, attend. Possibly, some receive religious ministration through services broadcast on television and radio, but probably most reserve their communion to private thoughts. The record of falling church attendances stretches back into the nineteenth century; nevertheless, the argument that urbanization and/or industrialization created an environment antipathetic to religious worship is not convincing. The nineteenth century was a great age of church building and sectarian animation, when ecclesiastical agencies wielded considerable influence in public affairs, over the educational system and through social administration. This has not expired; indeed, when four of the country's five top-performing primary schools in 1997 were Anglican, with an emphasis on Christian moral education, it is plain that the Church communion remains attractive on calculative as well as confessional grounds. However, for all the evidence of a diffused Christianity persisting outside of regular churchgoing, it is equally plain that churches no longer command automatic respect. Symptomatic is the number whose windows require protection by grilles and whose doors are kept locked to prevent the theft of sacred ornaments, charity boxes and anything portable. At St Martin-in-the-Fields, off Trafalgar Square in London, every pew bears the warning: 'PLEASE. In your own interests DO NOT leave handbags or any valuables unattended in the pews.' This notice is plastic and screwed to the benches, otherwise it also would be vandalized. Needless to say, it was not designed by James Gibbs when his masterpiece was completed in 1726. Most historians would accept, however, that, while periods of outright hostility have been rare, superstitious beliefs and practices have always coexisted alongside orthodox Christianity. The current fascination with the paranormal and resort to amateur psychics, fortune-tellers, faith-healers, and nature gurus as well as to professional counsellors and psychiatrists, are fashionable representations of age-old phenomena. The conviction remains widespread that there are many things beyond scientific explanation. Half the population believes in the existence of aliens or intelligent life on another planet. Ours is an age of alternative, even do-it-yourself, faiths; accordingly, institutional religion commands a smaller place in the urban landscape. Without a structured system, religious emotion expresses itself in spontaneous acts of reverence such as the laying of flowers and lighting of candles at roadside shrines or at the scene of an accident. Committals of the deceased are an everyday part of the urban scene, but it is their cumulative impact that matters most for urban form. Cemeteries cover over 16,000 acres—a necropolis almost the size of Nottingham—and a serious problem of land use will be averted only by cremation. This began in 1885, but no more than 240 bodies were cremated in 1898, and it was not until 1960 that over half the dead were so disposed of. Currently, cremation results in an annual saving of 200 acres; but burial is preferred by 30 per cent of people, and many local authorities are close to exhausting their available space. Annual deaths now amount to 640,000 people, equal to the obliteration of Bristol and Hull combined; by 2050, that is expected to rise to 829,000. The mausoleum tradition, expressed in the sepulchral pomp of the Victorians' Brompton, Highgate, and Kensal Green cemeteries, must surrender to utilitarian dictates.

How should we summarize what the future urban landscape may look like? Writing his *History of England* in 1848, Macaulay trumpeted the superiority of mid-Victorian England over its predecessors; yet, as an apostle of progress, Macaulay predicted that

> We too shall, in our turn, be outstripped; it may well be, in the twentieth century, that the peasant of Dorsetshire will think himself miserably paid with twenty shillings a week; that the carpenter of Greenwich may receive ten shillings a day; that labouring men may be as little used to dine without meat as they now are to eat rye bread; that sanitary, police and medical discoveries may have added several years to the average length of human life; that numerous comforts and luxuries which are now unknown or confined to a few may be within the reach of every diligent and thrifty working-man.

Nowadays, science visionaries prophesy that, by 2020, people will be inhabiting 'smart' homes stocked with intelligent robots, not just entertainment features but common objects such as chairs and utensils which respond to our presence and serve our whims. Advances in bioengineering will be such as to add years, even decades, to life expectancy, with incalculable consequences for all existing social and economic systems, housing patterns, and urban structures. Thirty years ago, men landed on the moon; thirty years hence, according to one of those first astronauts, Buzz Aldrin, there will be tourist shuttles to the moon. In contrast, other scientists espouse doomsday eschatologies about environmental despoliation, global warming, and meteor collisions. In a fast-moving and uncertain technological world, historians will be wise not to try to read the tea leaves. It is more pertinent to note how relatively recently the idea of progress took hold and how limited its operation has been. Though long fermenting in Judaeo-Christian theology, progress was essentially an Enlightenment creation of the late eighteenth century. Two centuries on, viewed from parts of Africa, progress seems so much a Western myth; even in that Western world, to cite only the Holocaust and Communist mass murder, it would appear that material progress has not been accompanied by moral progress. As for mass culture and civic virtue, despairing cries resound: at worst a neo-barbaric regression, at best a diffusion of vulgarity and banality. It was this quality-of-life test that W. G. Hoskins applied at the conclusion of *The Making of the English Landscape* (1955) when he lambasted contemporary planners for their zeal in concreting over the 'cultural humus of sixty generations or more' to produce an 'England of the arterial by-pass, treeless and stinking of diesel oil'. There is no need to chorus this, rather to appreciate that the character of the urban landscape is among the most significant questions to occupy us. Over half the world now lives in towns and cities. England, as the first urban nation, has more experience of town life than any other country and should heed its lessons in order to get things right. Recently, instead of occupying the vanguard, England has appeared to flag. In general quality of urban life, the Urban Task Force reckoned in 1999, England has fallen far behind the experience of Germany, the Netherlands, and Scandinavia; and the Task Force chairman, Lord Rogers, specifically cited 'the quality of our urban design and strategic planning' as being 'probably 20 years behind places like Amsterdam and Barcelona'. Concerted effort is required to realize the Task Force's ambition of a sustainable urban renaissance such that, by 2021, 'at least five major English cities will be in the European "top 50" on any reasonable set of measures of quality of life [and] none will be in the bottom third'. The good city is the well-managed city, and the urban landscape is the visible record of this.

1 The Roman Contribution

David Shotter

Whether we regard the period of the Roman occupation as marking the beginning of the urbanization of England depends largely upon our chosen definition of that word. Undoubtedly the Romans were the first to build in England structures which a modern generation would recognize *visually* as urban, although some at least of the centres of the pre-Roman Iron Age provided for functions which we would reasonably associate with town life.

The Roman View of Towns and Empire

Traditionally, the Roman entertained a nostalgic regard for the countryside, believing it to be the source of such vital national characteristics as honesty, simplicity, integrity, and a capacity for hard work. In practice, most aristocratic Romans, while they continued to derive much of their wealth from agriculture, found the countryside tedious and peopled by men who knew little or nothing of city life and who, therefore, lacked the quality of *urbanitas*—a mixture of grace, wit, and sophistication with regard to cultural and political matters. Such Romans needed the city and its facilities to lead a fulfilling life.

Furthermore, towns were seen as closely related to the emergence of oligarchic forms of government, both nationally and locally, in which the few who were privileged by wealth governed and, as patrons, provided for the essential interests of the less fortunate. Accordingly, in the Empire the Romans looked to identify and cooperate with men who entertained attitudes similar to their own. In the case of England, the hierarchical nature of the tribal society made this objective relatively straightforward.

The Roman attitude to the provinces of the Empire and their administration changed greatly from the time of Julius Caesar and Augustus in the second half of the first century BC. First, the process of imperial growth acquired a philosophy—

that of providing a buffer of Romanized territory between Rome and Italy on the one hand and the real enemies of civilization on the margins, just as walls provided the civilization of town life with a protection from 'untamed nature' beyond. Second, it was apparent that the resources to administer the Empire were not limitless; economically and politically, it was not feasible to sustain an army of the size that would be required to keep subject-populations under control. Thus, it was essential to devise methods to encourage Rome's subjects to *want* to be part of the Empire.

The Augustan poet Virgil summed up these objectives as to 'war down the proud, and offer the olive-branch to those who submit'; Tacitus, in his *Life of Agricola*, shows Agricola, during his governorship (AD 77–83), following such a policy in his dealings with the Brigantes of northern England. The detail of Agricola's encouragement of the British reads much like a programme of urbanization. The same was noted by the historian Dio Cassius in describing the Germans in the Augustan period: that they 'were adapting themselves to Roman ways, were becoming accustomed to hold markets, and were meeting in peaceful assemblages ... and were becoming different without knowing it'. There is in such passages an implicit emphasis on wealth-creation, and in largely urban environments.

It is important to register the significance which was attached to leaving as much money as possible in the pockets of provincials: the Emperor Tiberius (AD 14–37) enunciated the policy that 'sheep should be sheared, not flayed', whilst Nero (AD 54–68) attempted to reform the tax-system in order to encourage commerce, and thus wealth-generation. Most provincial governors, like Agricola in Britain, set out to check abuses in tax collection. At the heart of such moves lay the conviction that, through wealth-generation, provincial communities would more easily become Romanized; the wealthy would then be in a position to take on administrative responsibilities and financial burdens, such as those associated with town management and upkeep. It was, in truth, a long way from that scathing judgement passed upon Romanization by Calgacus, the chief of the Caledonians, when he spoke before the battle of Mons Graupius in AD 83: 'they create a desolation and call it peace.'

Types of Town in Roman England

Urban centres in the Roman world conformed to a hierarchy which depended upon the ownership or acquisition of some or all of the privileges of Roman citizenship, although technically such distinctions disappeared as a result of the universal grant of citizenship (*constitutio Antoniniana*) made by the Emperor Caracalla in AD 212. In Roman England, the inhabitants of two types of town—*coloniae* and *municipia*—enjoyed some form of Roman citizenship, whilst those of two further types—*civitas* centres and *vici*—did not.

At the top of the hierarchy were *coloniae*; these were purpose-built and intended in the first instance for legionary veterans, though in time the military character of such towns was ameliorated by a variety of local liaisons, social and economic. One of the English examples—York—represented a later grant of status to an already-existing community, but the original three—Colchester, Lincoln, and Gloucester—followed a Roman tradition which derived from the fourth century BC, whereby Roman citizens were given an opportunity to settle in newly won territory. They received grants of land both inside and outside the town itself, ran their own local affairs with constitutions modelled upon that of republican Rome, formed a military reserve, and assumed some responsibility for promoting Romanization in the areas in which they were set up.

The original three *coloniae* in Britain were developed on and adjacent to the sites of legionary fortresses and the urban settlements which had grown outside them. Although little is known in detail of the actual establishment of *coloniae* at Lincoln (AD 92) and Gloucester (AD 97), Tacitus records that the foundation of Colchester in AD 49 caused a good deal of local resentment; land and money were expropriated, and local people treated in a high-handed fashion, especially in connection with the construction, as a prestige project within the town, of the temple of the Imperial Cult, which was regarded as a 'symbol of an alien domination'. These factors served to make Colchester a principal target for Boudicca's rebels in AD 60.

Although the *coloniae* were integrated into the province's administrative system, they probably, because of their status and because of the hereditary nature

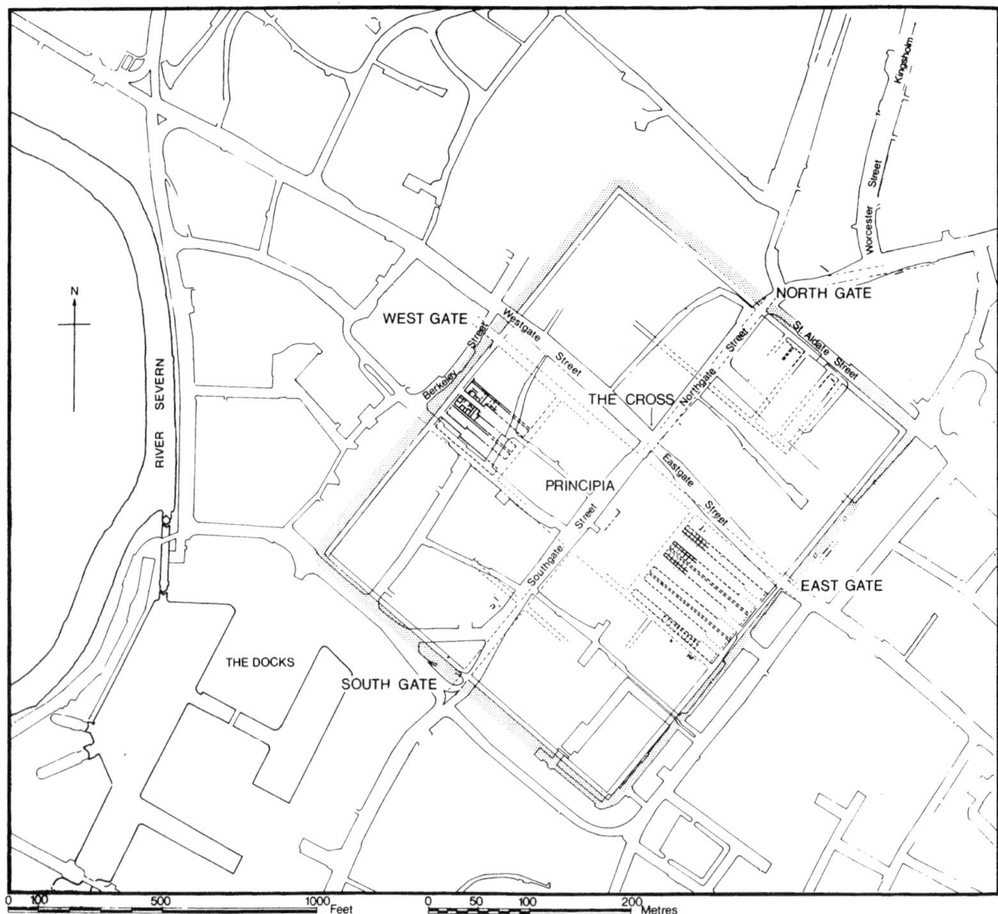

Plan of the colonia *at Gloucester: this shows well the 'military' style of planning appropriate to a settlement of veteran legionaries. The* forum *occupied a dominating central space, as the* principia *(headquarters) would have done in a fortress. (Plan after Henry Hurst and John Wacher.)*

of much of their office-holding, retained an air of exclusiveness in relation to other urban settlements. It is known that in Gaul (France) the *colonia* of Lugdunum (Lyons) maintained a superior attitude to its native neighbour Vienna (Vienne); in England, the social and economic vibrancy of Cirencester was probably encouraged by the exclusiveness of its neighbour, the *colonia* at Gloucester. Such exclusiveness should not, however, be equated with a lack of physical development; after all, these towns were intended as exemplars and as a means of impressing on the native population a conception of the physical might and sophistication of Rome. Roman architecture had a definite political edge.

Like the *colonia*, the *municipium* had a long history in the urban and social development of the Empire. The status represented a grant of citizenship privileges to an existing community, although this did not necessarily involve retention of the pre-Roman site. In England, it appears that Verulamium (St Albans), which took over from older Catuvellaunian centres, enjoyed this status, presumably in recognition of the tribe's earlier rank. Again, an amount of local autonomy was involved and, in practice, a *municipium* was much like a *colonia*; as with Colchester, Verulamium attracted the hostility of Boudicca's rebels. The determination of other *municipia* in England is difficult because of the lack of epigraphic evidence, although strong cases have been made out for both London and Leicester. Confusion may arise where *municipia* 'doubled' as *civitas* centres.

The *civitas* centres were the chief towns of the non-citizen subject-population. Their role in the administration of the province was of crucial importance, for England was divided into tribal administrative units known as *civitates*, which were largely, though not totally, based on the pre-Roman tribes. Strictly, these

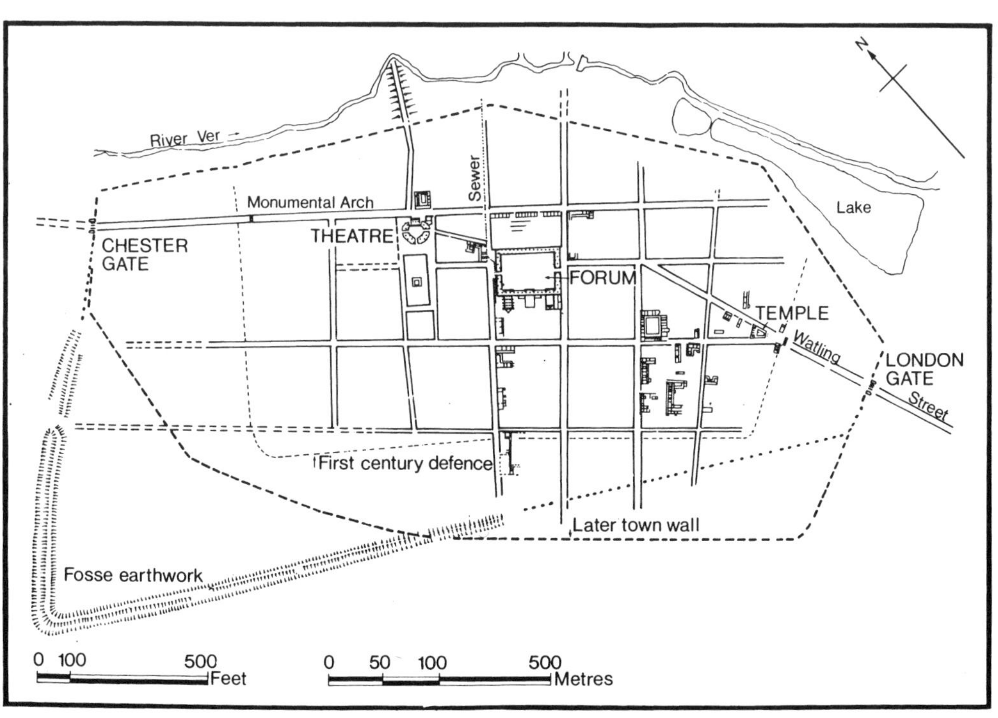

Plan of the municipium *at Verulamium (St Albans). Note that although the street-system shows signs of regularity, the perimeter defences/walls do not, presumably because they were built to enclose an area regarded at the time as 'worth defending'. (Plan after S.S. Frere and John Wacher.)*

Aerial photograph of Vindolanda (Northumbria), showing the fourth-century fort (in foreground) and the extramural settlement beyond (to the west). The early frontier-road (the Stanegate) can be seen running from the bottom-right to the top-middle of the photograph.

towns were not independent urban entities, but existed as conveniently placed administrative centres for their *civitates*; similarly, those men who exercised a degree of local administrative power within them were officers of their *civitates*, not solely of their towns. In appearance, the *civitas* centres differed relatively little from the *coloniae* and *municipia*, equipped as they were with a planned layout and a range of public buildings.

Alongside these larger and more prestigious towns was a considerable group of usually smaller towns, which had developed not as a result of administrative decisions, but for economic and/or social reasons. These towns—commonly called *vici*—might be found at road intersections, where their principal stimulus was probably the need for market facilities, or adjacent to forts where servicing the needs of troops was a mutually beneficial enterprise for soldiers and civilians.

Whilst such towns occasionally had some kind of local administration—as is indicated by inscriptions from such sites as Old Carlisle (Cumbria), Vindolanda (Northumbria), and Carriden (at the eastern end of the Antonine Wall)—it was not on a level comparable with that found at larger towns. Also, within this group should be included towns, such as Bath and Buxton, which, though architecturally more impressive than the normal *vicus*, had come into being simply as a result of their having unique facilities—in these cases, the healing waters which made them places of pilgrimage. In another case, that of Stonea (in Cambridgeshire), evidence suggests that this was a Hadrianic foundation—perhaps a personal initiative of the emperor—to celebrate the prosperity which was expected to flow from drainage work in the Fens. Significantly, this town had no obvious role to distinguish it from its near neighbours, and within a century of its foundation it was evidently a failure, with its principal buildings in decay.

The Origins and Development of Towns in Roman England

This bronze head is probably that of the emperor, Claudius. It was found in the river Alde in Suffolk, where it is believed to have been thrown by Boudicca's rebels as an offering to a local god after it had been wrenched from the body or base at the Temple at Colchester.

Whilst it is not appropriate to regard the inhabitants of England in the late Iron Age as entirely unused to an urbanized lifestyle or their leaders ignorant of the responsibilities involved, previous experience was very different from what the Romans introduced. The question thus arises as to how far a direct Roman initiative was involved, and what form(s) it took. We have noted that, according to Tacitus, Agricola offered encouragement. This has been taken to indicate that, through him, the Roman government was pursuing an urbanization drive; the basilica inscription from St Albans, which names Agricola, appears to offer confirmation of this. Further, we have noted the apparent involvement of Hadrian in the foundation of Stonea, and there is little doubt that Claudius was directly involved in the foundation of the *colonia* at Colchester, as was Nerva in the *colonia* at Gloucester. It is also possible that the policy revision which followed the rebellion of Boudicca provided for town-building initiatives.

We can assume that the *coloniae* came about not only as a result of government decisions but also, because provision for military veterans was a government responsibility, with the help of funds made available centrally from the Military Treasury (*aerarium militare*), which was itself supplied from tax-receipts. It is far less likely that finance was made available in the form of grants for the building of other kinds of town—except perhaps in a limited and specific way. The Roman attitude in general was that those who accepted the privilege of local power also accepted financial obligations, which will have included such responsibilities as providing and maintaining buildings and services, and making good shortfalls in the tax-expectations for their *civitates*. In the later imperial period, with its increases in bureaucracy and taxation, such an obligation came to be seen as a weighty burden, which fewer were able to sustain.

It is possible that in some circumstances and on certain occasions an emperor might step in with tax-incentives to help 'beleaguered' town builders. It is thought that, when Wroxeter was demilitarized as a legionary fortress (probably around AD 86), the civilian settlement that had developed outside the fortress was designated as the administrative centre of the *civitas* of the Cornovii. Yet, we learn from an inscription that it was not until the late 120s that the *forum*—the public square which was normally the first building to be erected—was dedicated. It is possible that Hadrian, on his visit to England in AD 121–2, noticed the length of time which it was taking to develop the *civitas* centre, and took measures to help it along. It is likely that in England, as elsewhere, local leaders were carried away with plans that were impracticable and over-costly, as Pliny noted in his province of Bithynia. Alternatively, *civitas* leaders might borrow on the money market to finance their projects; we hear of the consternation that was caused in England when Nero's chief adviser, the philosopher Seneca, who had lent money to the developing *civitates*, decided to call in his loans.

Aerial photograph of the site of Caistor-by-Norwich (Venta Icenorum; civitas *centre of the* Iceni*), showing the division of the urban area into approximately regular blocks (*insulae*) created by the intersecting street-system.*

Tangible help was clearly available in the building process itself; a comparison between legionary and urban buildings leaves little doubt that legionary architects and manpower were available for building and infrastructural projects. The Romano-British *forum*, as a building design, was virtually identical to the fortress headquarters (*principia*), and the similarity in bathhouses is as close, with many urban suites conforming to the predominant military linear plan. The legions, too, possessed the necessary skills to survey sites, lay out street systems, and thus create the blocks of space in which public buildings were located; they also had the engineering expertise and manpower to construct theatres and amphitheatres and to provide water supplies and sewers, which were essential features of town services.

Most of the small towns—particularly those outside Roman forts—lacked the element of formal planning; with no obvious town centre they developed in a ribbon pattern along the fort's exit roads, presumably, since they were rarely provided with wall-circuits, tailing off into a rural suburbia. Again, some technical help was probably available for such structures as bathhouses and for the provision of services. Although the plans of the 'strip-houses' (long, narrow houses with their gable ends facing on to the street) which are commonly found in the small towns are simple, their ubiquity might of itself suggest that some organization lay behind their construction.

An obvious distinction between Roman urban centres and most of their pre-Roman equivalents lay in the matter of their siting. The great majority of Romano-British town sites probably began as settlements outside the forts; military considerations thus initially determined their positions, though some of these—proximity to communications and water—involved considerations intrinsic to all urban sites. Although, in general, the Romans set out to use the pre-Roman tribes as *civitas* units for administrative purposes, and whilst it might have been an objective to site *civitas* centres as close as possible to pre-Roman centres, there was no room for sentiment. A hilltop position was of no real relevance to the Roman system, thus some competition for town sites will have resulted, with the chief criterion being the administrative needs of the *civitas*. In the Roman mind, the *civitas* was probably of greater importance than the town which acted as its administrative centre.

The establishment of the major towns came about, therefore, not so much as part of a rolling policy of urbanization, but from a need to put in place administrative units to replace the army as it moved on. This was in all probability equally true of *coloniae*, *municipia*, and *civitas* centres. Thus, when the decision was taken by Vespasian (AD 69–79) to resume the course of northward conquest, the removal of troops from further south to facilitate this left administrative vacuums. This led to the organization of vacated areas into *civitates*—the Dumnonii, the Durotirges, the Dobunni, the Coritani, and the Cornovii, of which the centres were designated respectively to be Exeter, Dorchester, Cirencester, Leicester, and Wroxeter. At around the same time, the long-standing treaty with Cogidubnus of the Atrebates came to an end (presumably with the king's death); out of his territory three *civitates* were formed—the Atrebates, the Regni (or Regnenses), and the Belgae, of which Silchester, Chichester, and Winchester were the designated centres. As an illustration of the lack of sentiment involved in this process, we may cite the abandonment of the old Atrebatic centre at the coastal site of Selsey. In contrast, the other territory left originally under treaty was that of the Iceni; for obvious reasons, the tribe was in no state in the immediate aftermath of Boudicca's rebellion to be organized as a *civitas*. Thus, there was a delay until the end of the first century, when the establishment of Caistor-by-Norwich heralds the introduction of the *civitas*.

The process continued intermittently thereafter; the eastern portion of the Brigantes was organized around Aldborough (as distinct from the pre-Roman centre at Stanwick), perhaps as a result of Hadrian's visit, whilst in the third century the north-western Brigantes were formed into the *civitas* of the Carvetii around Carlisle. This may have been accompanied by recognition of a north-eastern group, the Tectoverdi, who are described on an inscription as possessing a *curia* (assembly). Some earlier *civitates* were split; thus Ilchester became the centre of the 'western Durotriges'.

It is thus hard to see urbanization itself as an organized governmental initiative; rather, the priority was to replace the army's administrative role in specific areas. Towns were the inevitable concomitant of the wish to establish the *civitates* as local wealth-based oligarchies.

In such cases, towns frequently developed on the sites of former military *vici*. Assuming that these had resembled the longer-lived *vici* of the north, although a basis of their prosperity was already established, nonetheless a completely new start was required to provide sites which were well laid out, and equipped with the public buildings that befitted their status and enabled them to do the job required of them. It is evident from the pace at which this took place that local financial resources were a key factor in the development, and in the nature and style of what was produced.

These towns acted as market centres for their *civitates*, facilitating the exchange of goods and produce between country and town. In this sense, town and country were equal partners in an administrative, social and economic enterprise. No effort was made to ensure level development between the *civitates*; that would have required far more central intervention than the imperial government had in mind. Some enjoyed a steady development; some, like Wroxeter (of the Cornovii), had, as we have seen, a rather slow start. Others seem not to have found a real position for themselves. We have already noted the evident lack of a role for Stonea; similarly, the *civitas* centres at Brough-on-Humber (the Parisi) and Chelmsford (the Trinovantes) were unable to make significant social and economic headway against nearby—and more thriving—towns, respectively York and Colchester. Whilst both of these were *coloniae*, a town type which did not always display great vibrancy, York's status represented the relatively late promotion of a thriving extramural settlement, and Colchester continued to be regarded in some senses as the capital of the province.

Other towns emerged as real success stories: a striking example is Cirencester, which merited its role as the capital of one of the four provinces into which England was divided by Diocletian in the late third century. The range of its buildings and their quality provide evidence of the economic success of the leading figures amongst the Dobunni, which seems to have been based on a continuing ability to respond to new challenges and opportunities. Not only did Cirencester merit the building of a market place (*macellum*) to supplement the provisions of the *forum*, but the town also developed a school of mosaic artists who serviced the buildings of the town itself and the expansive villas of the Cotswolds. The strength of Cirencester is demonstrated by its rapid supersession of the pre-

Above: *Altar depicting a personification of* Corinium, *the tutelary deity of Cirencester, which stood in the town* forum.

Above right: *Decorated capital from a 'Jupiter-column', which stood in the* forum *at Cirencester. The capital is of the Corinthian order and, though badly weathered, still shows the relief – a head of Jupiter on the two visible faces.*

Roman sites of Bagendon and Minchinhampton, also by its clear dominance in economic terms of the 'senior' city represented by the *colonia* at Gloucester. The keys to this success derived from the propriety of Cirencester's geographical position, as well as from the wealth that was generated for the *civitas* leaders by sheep-farming, which was of sufficient significance to find mention in an imperial *panegyric* of the fourth century.

In each case, the ability to prosper and the degree of that prosperity depended upon the winning of large and lucrative contracts (particularly with the army) and the provision of goods and services which had a ready market. Key factors in this were obviously the density and wealth of that market, the location of the market town, and, in particular, its relationship with the systems of communication (by road or water).

Similar criteria might be employed in a discussion of smaller towns which occupied lower positions in the hierarchy. Thus, Carlisle thrived because of its

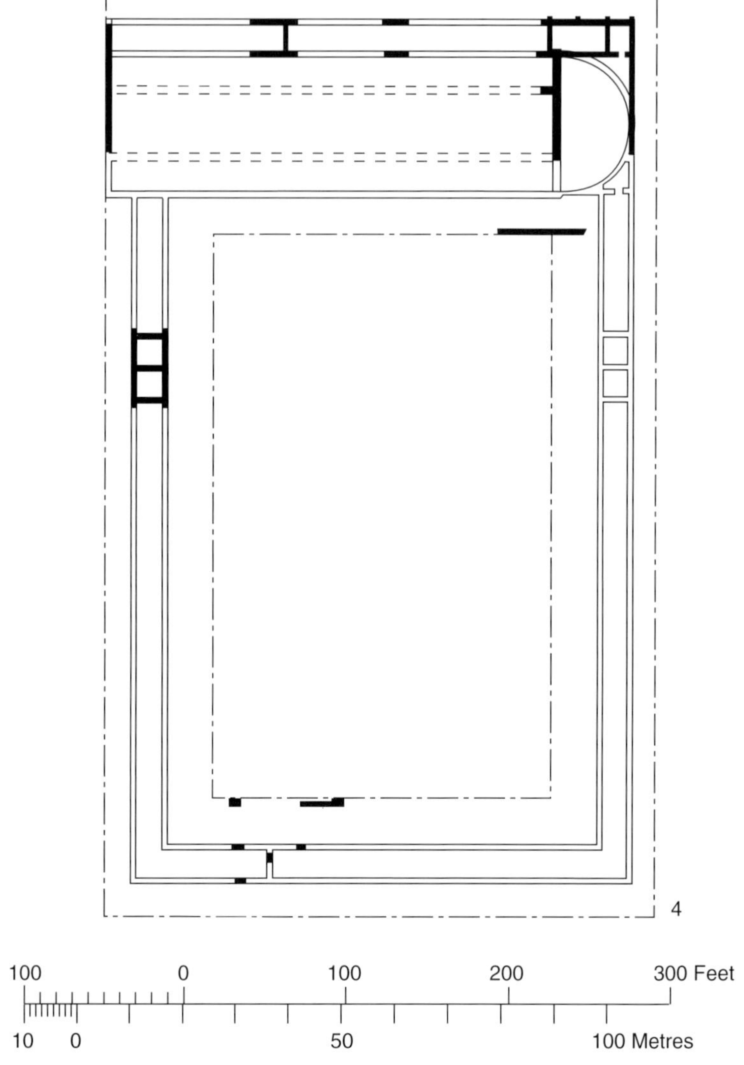

Plan of the forum *at Cirencester, which consists of a large rectangular space for market-stalls, leading into a basilican structure which constituted the 'town hall'. At the rear of this were shops/offices. As with Gloucester (see illustration p. 34), the complete plan closely resembles that of the military headquarters. (Plan after D. Macketh and John Wacher.)*

proximity to its markets which, as for Corbridge at the other end of the frontier, were principally of a military nature, and because of the success and consequent wealth of the Carvetian leaders; these will have been leading factors in determining their promotion. Corbridge, and Catterick too, which also developed into thriving commercial entities, did not emulate Carlisle's promotion, not because they were less successful, but presumably because there was not a ready place for them in the administrative system.

The small towns which remained attached to forts thrived so long as their markets survived which, in the military zone of the north, depended both on the preservation of peace and communications and on the continuing need for and presence of a military force.

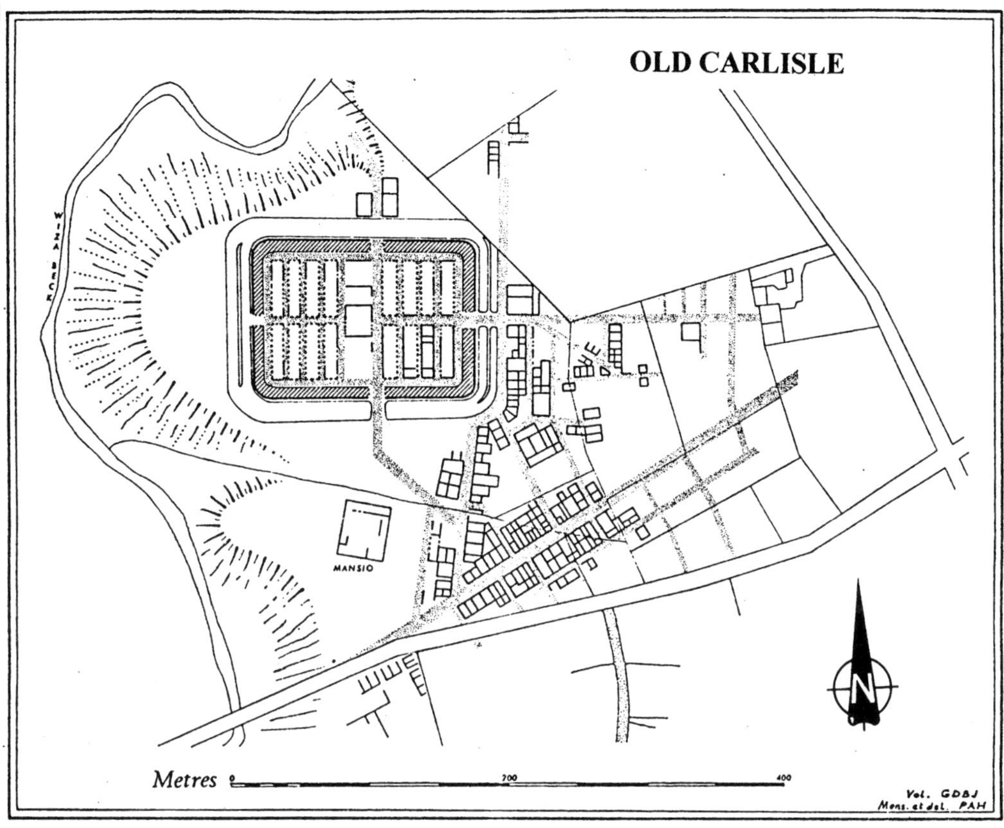

Plan of the fort and extra-mural settlement at Old Carlisle (Cumbria), based upon aerial photographs. Note that, although buildings sprang up around the fort, the chief focus of settlement appears in this case to have been the nearby road from Carlisle to Maryport. (Plan reproduced by permission of Professor Barri Jones and Dr Paul Holder.)

The strength of the *vici* was their ability to service their markets and to occupy a middle position between those markets and agricultural producers further afield. Units of the Roman army required food, manufactured goods, and a range of services; the limited evidence available suggests, as at Manchester, the organization of 'heavy industry' into areas of the *vici* to process locally exploited raw materials and to produce from them marketable goods—utensils, tools, jewellery, pots, building materials, as well as a range of objects of religious application. Agricultural produce required processing—grain for food and drink, and meat which probably came into the *vici* on the hoof for butchering; tanning and weaving were obvious by-products of the food industry.

A good idea of traded items is provided by the writing tablets from Vindolanda; they include grain, eggs, gruel, pepper, beer, socks, boots, bootlaces, cloaks, shirts, blankets, and larger items, such as parts for wagons. The contexts indicate that Vindolanda was involved in commercial activity both locally and at considerable distances. There is no reason to believe evidence from this site to have been different from others of a similar nature. In addition to manufacture and commerce, the *vici* housed the unofficial 'families' of serving soldiers, fast-food outlets, restaurants, bars, gambling establishments, and brothels—not to mention a large and changing range of religious establishments.

There is no evidence of planning in such towns, but rather 'spontaneous growth'; nor is it likely that there was much scope for administrative responsibility, which in these cases resided largely with the military authorities. Few *vici* were apparently walled—principally a matter of status—though one known exception to this was Ribchester (in Lancashire), where a clay bank and ditch were located outside at least part of the extramural settlement. This may be explained by Ribchester's Roman name, Bremetennacum Veteranorum, indicating the presence of a settlement of military veterans within the town, on an organized basis. The populations of the small towns were evidently varied—some veterans, people from the near locality and from other (sometimes relatively remote) parts of England, and from much further afield. South Shields contained a sculptor from Palmyra (in Syria), whilst Maryport had a resident from the eastern territory of Galatia. A fuller collection of inscribed tombstones—the best evidence for personal origins—would probably show even more cosmopolitan populations. These were small to medium-sized towns, bustling with activity—though, in the main, almost totally dependent on the presence of the nearby army unit. For most, standing on their own would have proved impossible, as is indicated in those cases where a decline in local military activity (temporary or permanent) often meant a consequent decline in the *vicus*, too, as many of the traders and other residents followed the units with which they had become associated, and upon which they were dependent.

Success or Failure?

There has long been a tendency in Romano-British studies to create models of occupation on the basis of a relatively small—perhaps, therefore, untypical—body of evidence; all sites of similar type have been seen as conforming to such models, and thus enjoying very similar histories under the influence of the same sets of events. Hadrian's Wall, for example, has been treated as a single unit, without allowing for the local individuality that is now recognized. The discussion of towns has tended to follow similar lines—an urbanization-drive in the first century, followed by a period of prosperity in the second, decline in the third, and then a rebirth in the fourth. The one area in which individuality was allowed its head was in the matter of their ultimate fates.

Whilst conditions throughout the province were relevant to the histories of individual towns, allowance has to be made also for a range of local circumstances, particularly if we rule out the availability of government assistance and accept that towns had to make their own way, and that this depended upon the prosperity of their leaders. If we take the view that these were in the main wealthy landowners, then the fortunes of individual towns can be seen to have been bound up with those of their hinterlands. This should not, however, encourage us to embrace the view that the towns were parasitic upon the countryside; rather, the nature of their relationship was interdependence. We have already seen this clearly over a long period in Cirencester. Bath, too, enjoyed long-term success, though here the stimulus was completely different. A lot depended upon the location of individual towns; few areas were so prosperous as to be able to bear urban competition over an extended period; one town's success in such situations was won at the expense of a neighbour. The only exception to this was in the military zone, where there was a close and unique relationship between individual forts and individual *vici*, and where success depended largely upon local military imperatives.

The criteria for judging success or failure are similarly difficult to establish, particularly since very few Romano-British town sites are available for the extensive excavation necessary to reveal the fortunes of their whole townscape. A state of disrepair in some buildings might point to a number of possible explanations—lack of interest, changes of taste, fluctuations in the material fortunes of those responsible for them, even hostile disruption. None of these necessarily points to a town's complete or temporary failure, unless, of course, such evidence can be shown to have been widespread in an individual site, or even over a number of sites, or perhaps to have affected a town's principal buildings.

It is often suggested that the *civitas* leaders, although initially persuaded to become urban dwellers, found the experience distasteful and migrated back to their country estates; but the generalization involved here strains credibility. The risk attached to making such an assumption is again the small sample of relevant material to hand. Aerial photographs have been used to suggest that some major towns had few domestic buildings; other methods of study, however, have on occasion revealed a different picture, and some buildings may be of such a nature as to be insusceptible to all methods of survey. Houses have been recognized in towns; those at Verulamium show in their early stages a marked similarity with contemporary villas, and over time they underwent development in style, decor, and materials used. Some houses became almost palatial, even in relatively small towns (for example, Carlisle). However, quantifying houses and establishing the proportion of them that were opulent is an extremely hazardous business.

In any case, a town's success or failure would not necessarily be determined by a decision of some *civitas* leaders to spend considerable amounts of time on their country estates. As we have seen, the principal function of most larger towns in

The theatre at the municipium *of Verulamium (St Albans); the revetted earth banks which supported the tiered seating can be seen in the foreground, while the 'dancing-area'* (orchestra) *separated the seating from the stage building, of which a single column – part of the 'scenery' – survives.*

Roman England was to act as administrative centres of their *civitates*. Thus, the existence in towns of vacant space which was put to agricultural or horticultural use does not prove that a town had failed; indeed, we might just as well point to extensions to public buildings and an increasingly opulent domestic provision in Cirencester to draw the opposing conclusion.

In larger and smaller towns alike, it is safer not to overgeneralize, but to relate evidence to particular towns. Yet, it does not appear that in Roman England the surviving evidence supports the contention that the urban experiment had failed; it answered a range of political, social, and economic needs in a province that was becoming increasingly Romanized.

Survival

'Later Roman England' is a term dogged by misconceptions and half-truths which stem in part from the difficulties of interpreting the evidence. Traditionally, the departure of the Romans was viewed as an event, which freed the Britons from four centuries of shackles and enabled them to resume old lifestyles. Such caricatures are not tenable, and whilst it is true that some reuse of hill forts occurred, the reasons for this stemmed from the exigencies of the present, not from memories of past glories.

The temptation to view the end as a clear-cut event must be resisted; as we shall see, the nature of the Roman army in the fourth century—its composition, deployment, and functions—argues strongly against any notion that in its entirety it was ordered to return to Rome, so leaving England to the mercy of events. This is not to say that it remained an effective weapon for peace and security. The idea of an end has also been inextricably tied up with a rescript of the Emperor Honorius, issued in AD 410, which was once taken to indicate the formal termination of the Roman

The bronze figurine of a ploughman, from Piercebridge (Co. Durham), showing the ritualistic turning of the furrow which marked a town's limits.

occupation of England; but if, as is now agreed, this rescript does not refer to Britain at all, the need for new interpretations is ineluctable.

Certainly, from the middle of the third century AD, England had been under pressure from raiders from a variety of quarters. This is an indication both of the insecurity of these raiders and of the perceived prosperity of Roman England. In the main, such raiders were not set upon wanton destruction so much as grabbing something that they found desirable—either by removing it as loot or by settling and participating in it. This is in itself a positive comment upon the assimilation of Roman culture and the enjoyment of its material benefits by the Romanized British.

Whilst there is mixed evidence if we compare individual towns in the fourth century, the general picture that emerges is one of development—particularly in the cases of the smaller towns, such as Corbridge and Catterick. Plainly, however, whilst military requirements might continue to provide good markets in the military zone, continuing development outside it has to be reckoned against a background of times which were for many economically harsher. In the larger towns, the responsibility for physical upkeep must have imposed greater burdens on the upper class, and thus inevitably some economies became necessary. There is little or no evidence of a lack of will on the part of local leaders.

Aerial photograph of the extramural settlement outside the fort at Piercebridge (Co. Durham); the irregularity of the street layout contrasts sharply with the plan of Caistor-by-Norwich (p. 38). The fort area lies off the bottom of the picture, while the settlement is concentrated upon the road leading from the fort's east gate and its intersection with Dere Street.

The amphitheatre outside the walls of the legionary fortress Caerleon (Isca). The arena consisted of an elliptical area surrounded by earth banks which supported the tiered seating.

A portion of the walls of the 'Saxon-shore' fort at Porchester Castle (Hampshire). The bastions supported pieces of heavy artillery. The lower two-thirds of the surviving masonry are of Roman date. This late military architecture was in the fourth century 'transferred' to towns.

One obvious consequence of a deteriorating security situation was the need to offer improved protection to towns in the form of physical defences. It was traditional to mark an urban boundary; as is shown by the figure of the 'Piercebridge Ploughman', this was done by turning a furrow, which in practical terms is probably represented by the earth-and-turf banks with which most larger towns were equipped early on. Gateways should be regarded differently from walls; indeed, many towns probably had gates before the provision of stone walls began—probably late in the second century AD. Gates were prestige symbols, as is shown by a gated personification found at Carlisle; gates impressed upon those entering the might and sophistication of Roman civilization, and the wealth of the town's leaders. They also served a traditional purpose of offering a clear demarcation between Romanized civilization and untamed nature. Although probably few towns in Roman England boasted the imposing gates with double carriageways, often seen on the Continent (as in the Porta Nigra at Trier), nevertheless the construction of gates and walls greatly added to the expenditure of the *civitas* leaders; and the relatively late arrival of walls for Romano-British towns was perhaps due less to a fear of what the inhabitants might do behind their protective curtains than to a realization that a certain level of prosperity had to be attained before their building and upkeep could be afforded. The fact that England contains the remains of few large and luxurious villas may indicate how difficult it was, even for willing subjects, to find the necessary resources.

In the main, the walls of Romano-British towns enclosed generous areas, reflecting the state of a town's physical development; and there is evidence—for example, from Lincoln—that suburbs which developed after walling might be subsequently enclosed within an extended wall circuit. The defensive nature of the walls became more apparent in the fourth century when bastions of many shapes and sizes were added—at least, partially—to the circuits of many towns. These, following the prevailing military architecture of the day, were intended to provide stable bases for the mounting of pieces of artillery. It is not clear how these defences were manned, but it has been suggested that settlers from outside—for example, Saxon federates—undertook the task in return for land within the towns. Some evidence for this may be seen in the introduction in a number of places—for example, Canterbury and Caerwent—of a new style of house, constructed of wattle and daub and with sunken floors, the so-called *grübenhausen*. There must also have been some formation of local militias, as happened in the *vici* of the military zone.

The towns of Roman England thus came to take on the appearance, as their Gallic counterparts had in the late third century AD, of Roman forts. This was particularly evident as the forts themselves emerged in a new, castle-like, form in which ease of access was replaced by strength in defence characterized by high, thick walls equipped with bastions, and with relatively narrow entrance-ways. The Saxon-shore forts of Roman England probably took the Gallic town walls as their model—appropriately enough, since the English sites were having to cope with an invasive pressure similar to that already evident in the Gallic towns. Although the change of style of military architecture in England cannot be precisely dated, *c*. AD 280–300 would not be an unreasonable estimate. The towns' adoption of this military style indicates an increasing blurring, as new threats were faced, of rigid distinctions between soldiers and civilians.

Evidence is lacking of any standardization or coherence of approach in the provision of town walls; not only are different appearances found, but also they

A Romano-Celtic temple at Caerwent (Venta Silurum: the civitas *centre of the Silures). A small square cella, with an apse in which the image of a god would have stood, was surrounded by a low wall which supported the columns of an ambulatory.*

came into being at different times. Naturally, the major towns were provided with walls, but so too were some smaller settlements. This in part perhaps reflects the proliferation under Diocletian's new provincial arrangements of officials who required protected centres, but it also suggests that there were facilities—particularly industrial and agricultural—which were seen to merit protection. The presence in some smaller towns of 'police groups' suggests that they at least were intended to act as centres of refuge for rural populations. Only where such protection was not afforded do we find in some measure an abandonment of Romanized centres in favour of a limited reoccupation of old hill-fort sites.

Although the early part of the fourth century provides strong evidence of a continuing rural prosperity which would have translated into many towns, it is clear that through the middle of the century—*c.* AD 340–70—a marked deterioration occurred in the military situation. The visit to England in the winter of AD 342–3 of the Emperor Constans suggests that by that time the security situation was causing disquiet. The growing harassment of Britain by outside enemies—Picts, Scots, Saxons, Angles, Franks—culminated in AD 367 in the so-called Conspiracy of the Barbarians. Finds of metalwork in towns and town cemeteries suggest that troops—regular or irregular—were at some stage in the fourth century being stationed either in or close to towns. In AD 367, the Emperor Valentinian I sent Count Theodosius (father of the later emperor of the same name) to restore the situation. It was at one time thought that town bastions belonged to this phase of activity; but since Theodosius' restoration work is evident in the

The remains of late Roman walls at Caerwent (Venta Silurum). The bastions on these walls are of polygonal configuration. Such architecture illustrates the way in which towns came to be seen as defended 'strong-points'.

north, the fact that no northern towns have bastions calls this into question. Theodosius may, however, have been responsible for the walling of some northern towns. It is, of course, a sign of the continuing soundness of the towns of Roman England that such large-scale restoration work was regarded as viable.

In the military zone of the north, the effects of the disaster of AD 367 were probably more fundamental; precise dating of the *vici* is not readily available and, in any case, it is not likely that all followed an identical pattern. It has been argued that some may have gained a greater independence of status from their neighbouring forts, but some at least appear to have become run down. The reason is not far to seek; without walls, they were incapable of protecting their inhabitants—a particular weakness if, as seems likely, the prevailing military philosophy was one of defence-in-depth. Under such circumstances, the ability to absorb attack was of crucial significance; thus, some *vici*—for example, Lancaster—appear to have been abandoned in favour of the use of the forts themselves as protection for civilians as well as military personnel. Changes in the design of the interiors of many forts—with the emergence of chalet-blocks replacing rigidly proportioned barracks—argue for living-arrangements which were less formal. Some forts probably assumed the character of fortified villages, with mixed populations providing for their own day-to-day needs and defending themselves. In this way, each village became in large measure self-sufficient, preserving the urban idea but losing the coherence that had been the hallmark of Roman influence.

Roman England was thus embattled, but not giving way; indeed, contrary to the traditional view of disgruntled civilians relying on the defence provided by an ever-dwindling body of Roman troops, the Romanized natives were now faced effectively with the task of defending their own land. Nor does the evidence suggest any lack of will in this, even though differences arose over the most appropriate method. It has been argued that the emergence of the Pelagian heresy, which proposed that 'man was the master of his own salvation', was a religious reflection of contemporary social, political, and military preoccupations; indeed, its existence argues for the presence of men with the courage and independence of mind to maintain the essential qualities of a Romanized lifestyle. There are signs that locally such attitudes achieved considerable hold.

There is now widespread acceptance that, although Roman England did not come formally to a clear end, the inhabitants, after three-and-a-half centuries, thought of themselves as Romanized British, and were anxious to maintain their material culture as best they could. However, the word 'continuity' has to be employed with great caution, and an attempt must be made to take into account individuality of circumstances in different localities, and again to remember that we do not have the evidence of widespread excavation upon which to rely. There is, therefore, a particular danger in seeking to generalize from a few fragmentary examples.

The bath-house at Wroxeter (Viroconium Cornoviorum, the civitas *centre of the Cornovii). The remains of the hypocaust of a heated room can be seen in the foreground, whilst the wall in the background separated the bath-house itself from the exercise area* (palaestra) *beyond. For a plan of this building,* *see opposite.*

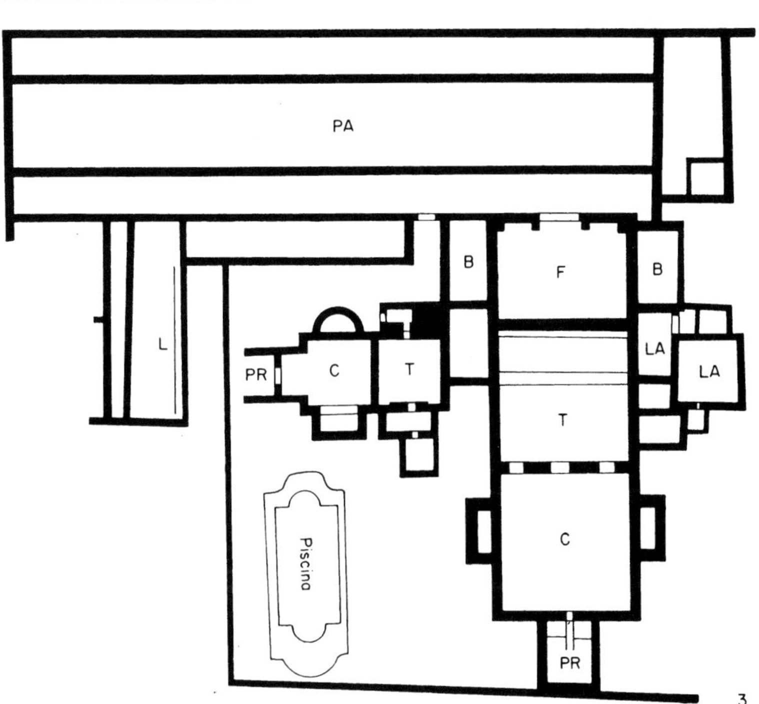

Plan of the bath-house at Wroxeter; the main suite of rooms is the 'linear group' (on the right-hand side). The bath-house was separated by a wall from the exercise area beyond (see also illustration opposite). (Plan after John Wacher.)

The physical state of towns in the late years of the fourth century varied; and despite some indications of at least partial dereliction, it would be unwise to regard such towns as abandoned. We should, in any case, expect that, having regard to the geographical locations of the threats, towns will have survived them in different ways. In general, it is reasonable to suppose that the towns of eastern England were more vulnerable than those of the west.

Towns might remain attractive simply because they had populations and some facilities; certainly, it is not difficult to find examples where facilities of a town's Romano-British period survived and were kept up. In his description of St Cuthbert's visit to Carlisle in the seventh century, Bede talks of surviving town walls and a still-functioning fountain. At St Albans, in one block (*insula*) at least, a large house was being rebuilt in *c.* AD 400 with mosaic floors, and its water supply appears still in operation in the later fifth century. Excavation at Carlisle has shown specifically that a bathhouse continued to benefit from refurbishment in the middle of the fifth century, and that an early 'strip-house' had been repaired in a monumental style at around the same time, possibly surviving as late as the seventh century. Cirencester, too, provides evidence of a functioning *forum* in *c.* AD 450, and excavation at Wroxeter has shown how building work, possibly in the classical style, continued to take place in the *basilica* adjacent to the baths, even though the baths themselves had probably not functioned since the middle of the fourth century.

It is clear, too, that in some cases some form of Romanized administration remained, such as greeted St Germanus in AD 429 when he visited St Albans on a

mission to check Pelagianism. He was taken to the shrine of St Alban by people described as well dressed. Those who wished to combat Pelagianism, it has been argued, were also those who wished Romano-British culture to survive with minimal change; these—the *civitas* leaders—had a vested interest in the maintenance of the status quo. The Pelagians, on the other hand, as befitted the freethinking evident in their religious beliefs, wished to act more dynamically to protect their interests. Essentially, these two groups represented different approaches to the problem of defending the integrity of their identities. That this identity was Romano-British seems clear from the choice by 'sub-Roman' leaders of such titles as *dux* (leader), *sacerdos* (priest), *magistratus* (magistrate)—terms with urban or military origins. St Germanus records encountering a man of tribunician rank at St Albans.

How these leaders accomplished their task of defending those for whom they were responsible is hard to say. Towns may have been used if they were defensively viable—the use of Cirencester's amphitheatre provides an interesting example of this. Alternatively, recourse was had to the reuse of hill forts, many of which saw refortification as places of refuge in the fifth century. The shape of society will have reflected this as a new generation of leaders dominated by their dynamism and control of land; those whom they dominated/protected will have been more or less successful farmers.

In these circumstances, towns would not have flourished in the ways in which they did in the Romano-British period, because many of the reasons for and sources of earlier prosperity had gone. Thus, the sense of community dwindled, as society became a matter of those who dominated by providing protection and those who, with varying levels of wealth, accepted that. As in the Iron Age, kingdoms became again the most viable type of organization. In time, Romano-British or Celtic kingdoms gave way to Saxon kingdoms.

In a situation of increasingly rural, and less industrial and urbanized, preoccupations, three factors in particular saw to the preservation of town sites. First, there was their ability to offer protection, even in their relatively run-down states. Second,—and another link with later Roman England—there was Christianity: by the nature of the custom, many during the Roman period would have been martyred in or close to towns, and their shrines became, therefore, an urban phenomenon. The revival of Christianity brought a renewed importance to such sites, and to those where churches had been deliberately placed to take advantage of surviving Romano-British physical protection. Finally, however, the majority of Romano-British town sites survived because those that came later had the same requirements of their centres as had the Romanized British—adjacent good land, easy communications, defensive capability, water supply, and so on. The particular material-contents of these towns may not have survived in a recognizably Roman form—though often street systems did—but the organizational structures in most cases merged with what came after.

The towns which catered for the specific material needs of Roman England were less resilient, unless and until the raw materials which they used came into use again. Thus, the fate of the small, often industrial, town was more questionable, as were those of the fortified villages which represented the late Roman transformation of Roman forts. These were much more narrowly part of a Romanized way of life; although they may have survived for a while, in the long term they lacked the breadth of appeal of the larger towns which has enabled these to offer a link between the past, the present, and the future.

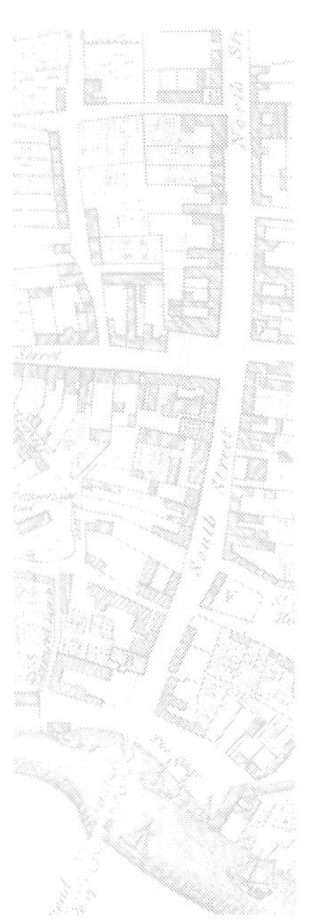

2 Decay and Revival: Early Medieval Urban Landscapes

David A. Hinton

Towns were not needed in fifth- and sixth-century England, as they had been under the rule of the Roman Empire. The tax system that had maintained the government and its armies had partly depended upon a coin-using market network for distributing pottery and many other commodities less archaeologically identifiable; town-based magistrates and other office-holders gained social prestige from an elaborate lifestyle, and had supported an often grandiose civic superstructure. But urban commerce and industrial production were not part of the economic and social needs of chiefs (usually called 'kings' by their contemporaries) who depended upon their subjects for support both in kind—the best of the year's surplus—and through service—land-work or military. Nor did their entertainments and ceremonies demand an urban setting.

Roman towns remained a physical presence, however. Anyone still using Roman roads knew that they led from one walled place to another, just as most navigable waterways eventually took the traveller past a collapsing waterfront. Even if they had no active role to play, walled enclosures were a reminder of a pre-existing world, in which the indigenous Britons knew that they had once participated, and of which the unknown number of immigrants could not but have become aware, even if they did not understand what they saw. The British writer Gildas spoke of the destruction of cities by invaders, but his was a rhetorical work, presenting an image of a society battered by external forces in punishment for its shortcomings. Reality was closer to the image presented in the late tenth-century Old English poem *The Ruin*, which speaks of abandonment and decay; the poet saw the crumbling walls as the work of giants, part of an older world alluded to in the Bible. He knew that they were actually Roman, but he was not presenting historical explanation.

Inside the Ruins

Activity continued within at least some Roman towns well into the fifth century, and perhaps beyond, but it was not an urbanized life. Kings were increasingly likely to rule by travelling around their territories, but a claim to have inherited the authority of the Empire might well be symbolized by holding occasional assemblies at a former centre of power, an old Roman *civitas*. Post-holes outlining the plans of substantial timber-built structures within Wroxeter have been interpreted as a base for whoever controlled the area formerly associated with the Cornovii tribe, but it was not necessarily therefore a permanent residence. The largest structure may have been used to store the tribute brought in for the chief and his leading supporters to consume on one of their regular visits.

At Verulamium (St Albans), grain-driers and a building interpreted as a barn imply quantities of wheat and barley to be turned into flour for bread or malt for ale, but more probably for the enjoyment of visitors than for sale in a market. Similarly, the piped water system that was renovated after the barn went out of use would have been needed if animals were brought in and kept until it was time for them to be slaughtered. The virtual absence of Anglo-Saxon types of burial from the area between London and Verulamium until late in the sixth century suggests that it was a British enclave, with the latter being one of the local leaders' power bases. Whether London was used in the same way is quite unknown; there is no evidence, but would it be identifiable in the redeveloped City? Instead, there is a build-up of 'dark earth' on many sites, some from as early as the third century.

In the few Romano-British towns in which there was any sort of occupation in the 5th and 6th centuries, buildings like these reconstructed at West Stow, Suffolk would have contrasted with the crumbling masonry around them (see also illustration p.58). Timber- or earth-walled buildings with thatched roofs were also the norm in the 7th century and later (see also illustration p.67).

A build-up of soil over Roman floors and streets, often with ruined walls sticking up through it, has been recorded not only in London, but at the majority of properly excavated urban sites. Its composition varies; analyses indicate that some of it results from deliberate dumping so that small plots could be cultivated or fenced off for stock pens; in other cases, a similar effect might have arisen from the decay of earth-floored, daub-walled timber and thatch buildings that are much less identifiable than those that used stone, brick, and tile. If there were many structures using only organic materials, late Roman and subsequent use of towns becomes all the more difficult to recognize. In some, like Winchester, whole areas became quagmires as drainage channels blocked up through lack of maintenance, spreading layers of silt across the Roman streets and floors.

It is even harder to know what happened to smaller towns, whether walled or not, than to *municipia* and *civitates*. A few roadside settlements were later to have small market towns above or adjacent to them, but this is regeneration caused by location, and has nowhere been shown to be from continuous use. A site at a crossroads or at a ford might eventually again become a good place to trade, as an internal commercial network re-emerged. The most complex example is Dorchester-on-Thames; outside its late Roman walls, one interpretation of an early fifth-century male buried with weapons and an elaborate set of belt fittings is that he was a Germanic soldier hired to oversee a toll-payment point, a function maintained for a while by whatever authority ruled the area. Inside the town, 'Anglo-Saxon' pottery suggests Britons and migrants intermixing; there were buildings also, though their dating is obscure, and they may be connected to the seventh-century use of the place as a diocesan centre. Various cemeteries and objects witness the importance of the area, but documentary evidence would put a royal centre at Benson, three miles from Dorchester—perhaps an example of polyfocal settlement.

Dorchester's post-Roman history was partly confused by its position in territory that came to be disputed between Wessex and Mercia. Even worse affected was Silchester, *civitas* of the Atrebates. As elsewhere, usage staggered on into the fifth century, and a stone carved with a name in Irish ogam has been found there; at face value, this suggests that Silchester retained considerable importance, but its authenticity has been questioned. Efforts to protect the *civitas* from the north were made, with the main road to Dorchester cut by Grims Bank. By the time that regular, peaceful communication between the Thames Valley and southern England was restored, Silchester had become isolated, made irrelevant both by new political factors and by changing emphasis towards carriage of goods by water, so that Reading came to replace it as the regional centre. Similarly, Norwich was to replace Venta Icenorum (Caister), although in that case there were no local politics to affect the situation.

In a few Roman towns, sunken-featured buildings were dug into the latest Roman levels; in Canterbury, they are dated by pottery to the mid- or late fifth century, and Colchester has one of the same date. They have floors up to a metre below contemporary ground levels, are crudely rectangular—10 feet by 8 feet would be typical, but there is wide variation—and usually have a post-hole in the centre of each shorter side, implying a gabled roof. Occasionally there are breaks in wall-lines to suggest entrances, and one had a porch with two or three steps down; in some there was evidence that the earth removed from the sunken area was used to create a low wall along its edge. A few might have had suspended floors at ground level, but as so many had had stakes hammered into the bases of the sunken areas, showing that there were internal fittings, and a few had hearths, it seems that in most, if not all, the bottoms of the features provided craftworking and storage space, albeit restricted in area. A single row of clay loomweights implies weaving, though they were not necessarily *in situ* from a collapsed loom, as they could have dropped off a shelf. Another possibility is that some of the huts were used only briefly by occasional visitors, such as itinerant craftworkers. The jeweller who lost a late fifth-century imported gold coin that had been deliberately cut down and still had rouge adhering to it, and who perhaps also lost the cut piece of plain gold found nearby, did not necessarily live permanently in Canterbury.

Canterbury provides better evidence than any other Roman town for a thread of continuous use, although even there a brief hiatus is possible. Its name derives

Artist's reconstruction of the collapse of Roman Canterbury. It shows vividly how uncleared rubble would block streets; as plants and shrubs took root and drainage ditches silted up, the wall foundations would get buried. The outer wall would remain serviceable, however.

from Cantwaraburg, 'the fortress (*burg*) of the people (*ware*) of Kent', which originates from the Cantiaci tribe, and suggests that it was recognized as some sort of centre for the new political unit that replaced Roman administration. Kent can claim to have been the first of these units to be ruled by a migrant dynasty, with origins back to Hengist and Horsa. The sunken-featured buildings can no longer be taken as proof positive of immigrant occupation, as such structures are not found only in the east of the country, but their dates in Canterbury suggest that they belong to the period when British rule there had ceased. The old view that the migrants actively shunned towns is no longer valid.

Canterbury was well placed for assemblies, being on the edge of populous East Kent, and therefore an acceptable place for people from West Kent to come, using the London–Richborough road that passed through Queningate and Ridingate. The fifth-century buildings were found near the old Roman theatre, which might have continued as a focus, as in Italy where some theatres were places 'where discussions were held'. One of the streets leading to it went out of use, but another was respected by the new buildings.

Although Bede was writing in the early eighth century, his description of Canterbury at the end of the sixth as King Aethelberht's *metropolis* may have had reality, in that it was a place to which people came to meet their king, probably at fixed times in the year. Where people assembled, there they also made exchanges, of goods, of marriage arrangements, and of property, in front of witnesses. Such assemblies would have acted as magnets for craftworkers seeking aristocratic patrons, like the jeweller who lost the gold coin. By the early seventh century, gold coins were being struck in England, one of the finest inscribed 'Dorovernia Civitas', to proclaim Canterbury's importance, as well as its old Roman name. By that date, surface-floored buildings were also being constructed inside the walls. It was not a uniformly developing settlement, however; as one area came into use, so another was abandoned.

No other kingdom can be shown to have used a town in quite this way; royal assemblies did not need to take place in such enclosures, even though they might have been perceived as bestowing the prestige of Imperial authority upon English and British kings. Nor was international trade necessarily conducted through towns. The Mediterranean pottery of the fifth and sixth centuries found at western British sites such as Tintagel shows that a landing place where a ship could be safely beached under the protective eye of the local princeling was enough. Facilities for loading and unloading, for repairs, for acquiring fresh supplies and any other services the sailors required, could all be provided at temporary beach-markets. A few of these had the potential to develop into permanent ports, although most were probably replaced because a location satisfactory for short-term use was not solid enough for buildings, and did not offer enough shelter from winter storms and floods.

Towns and Churches

Archaeology supplies one sort of evidence about post-Roman Verulamium, documentary another. During the visit, or visits, made by St Germanus to Britain, in *c.*429–35, he worshipped at the shrine of St Alban, which was perhaps within one of the extramural cemeteries of the Roman town, on the opposite side of the river.

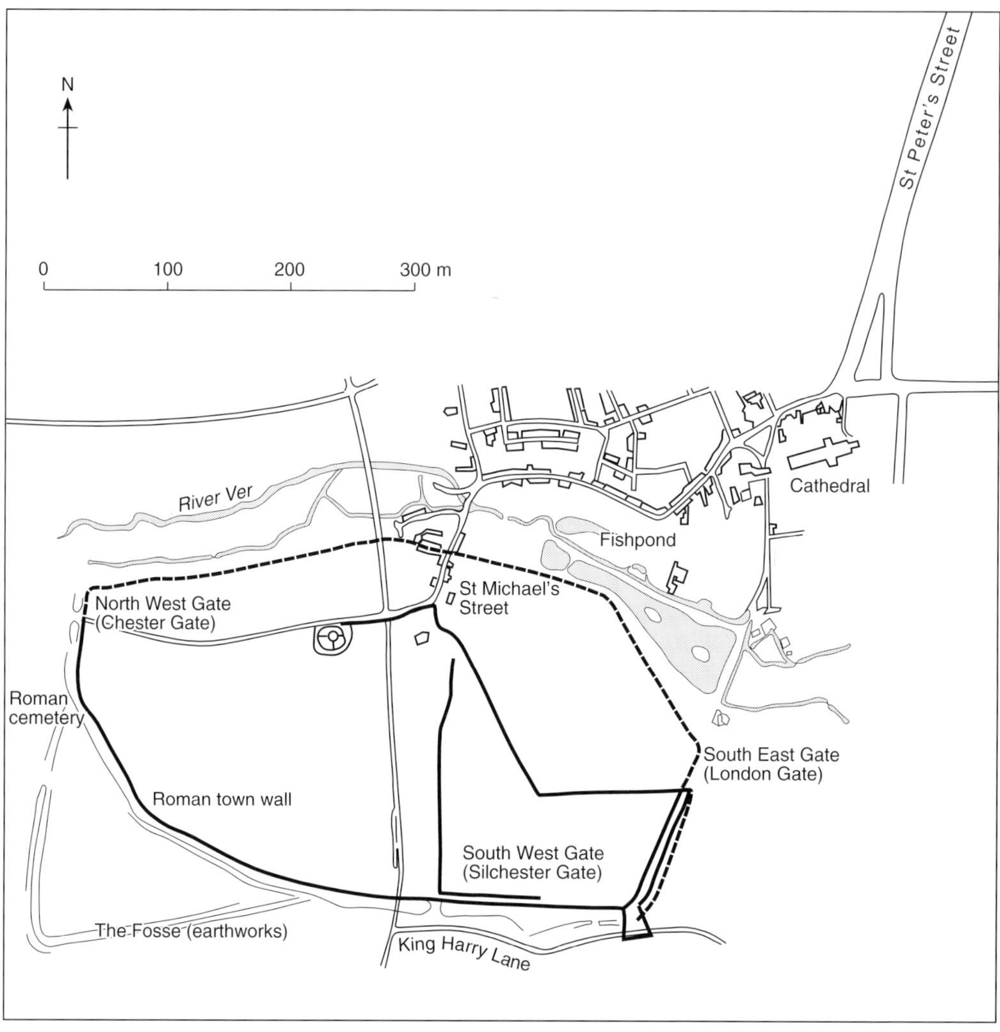

The relationship between Verulamium and St Albans. The cathedral was an abbey throughout the Middle Ages; the development of a market at its gate is clearly shown by the width of St Peter's Street and the very obvious infilling of the triangular market-place at its southern end.

A shrine in such a location could have developed into a cult centre attracting numbers of pilgrims, whose donations would have stimulated the development of a more elaborate structure, leading eventually to the great St Alban's Abbey. Establishment of a market just outside its gate, to supply the church's needs and to provide it with toll income, led to the clustering of the medieval citizenry there too.

As Germanus secured the exiling of some of Pelagianism's practitioners, he must have had the support of a powerful secular authority. The barn and grain-driers appropriate to an estate centre suggest at least a high-status interest, but perhaps already that of an occasionally visiting peripatetic British king coming to a royal residence, rather than remnant Romanized officialdom. In Gaul, many towns survived as diocesan centres. This cannot be shown to have happened in Britain, even in Verulamium where it seems that British control lasted long after 409–11.

Some religious use of a few of the old towns can be proposed. Burials within the demolished basilica in Exeter have radiocarbon dates that put them in the fifth/early sixth centuries; they were aligned to the Roman street pattern, not west–east like a later group probably associated with the abbey that was flourishing by the 680s. But if there had been a British bishopric in the *civitas*, it did not survive (the present bishopric was only transferred from Crediton in the eleventh century). An intramural building claimed, though not proven, to have been a Romano-British Christian church in Silchester's forum was abandoned, and had no direct successor. In Worcester, two graves, one with gold thread from a cap or stole around the head, are dated to the sixth/early seventh centuries, and may be associated with a church that preceded the bishopric there; but Worcester, though perhaps more than a small roadside town, had not been a major Roman centre. No Roman features at all have been found at Hereford, the other western bishopric. The temple at Bath remained in use for a time, and as in Exeter an abbey appeared nearby by the end of the seventh century. A consistent pattern does not clearly emerge from this sort of evidence.

Lincoln presents what is currently a unique case. In the middle of the forum-basilica there, excavations have found a sequence of buildings which current opinion considers late Roman in origin, one with an eastern apse. Burials with dates at least into the fifth century show that even if buildings did not survive, a cemetery was still recognizable or remembered when in the seventh century a stone-lined grave was dug not quite on the centre line of the former nave. In it was a hanging-bowl, a type of object found mostly with well-furnished Anglo-Saxon burials. There was no skeleton, however, and it seems that the occupant had been removed for reburial somewhere else, perhaps at a church underlying the present cathedral which had acquired greater status. A single-roomed stone building enclosed the grave, and this became St Paul-in-the-Bail church. Was it built as a shrine, before the decision to translate the body in the grave?

By 314, Lindum Colonia had a bishop, and the forum-basilica buildings could quite well have included a Romano-British episcopal church. When Lincoln re-emerges in documentary history in the 620s as a place with a *praefectus*, who was visited on a conversion mission by Paulinus, it was part of Lindsey, the only example of an Anglo-Saxon kingdom taking its name from a Roman town. By then, it had had long exposure to Anglo-Saxon culture, and it is unlikely that the British bishopric survived, even if a British political unit had lasted longer than many.

Paulinus also preached at York, where King Edwin chose to be converted; presumably this was at least in part a gesture of recognition of the place's Roman past, but it may also already have been used for periodic assemblies, as has been suggested of Canterbury. The degree of physical survival in York was probably less than once claimed (see cameo), though its outer shell of defensive walls would still have stood in the seventh century. Occasional attention was paid to the circuits of at least some Roman towns; in Winchester, for instance, the archway of the south gate collapsed, but traffic continued to pass through it for a while, until a ditch was dug across the roadway and the gap in the wall was filled, perhaps in the sixth century.

No features have been excavated within Winchester to show how it was used internally in the fifth and sixth century, though some pottery has been found. If the attention paid to the defences shows royal interest, use of the place as a royal centre could explain why the bishopric was transferred there from Dorchester-on-Thames

York

DAVID A. HINTON

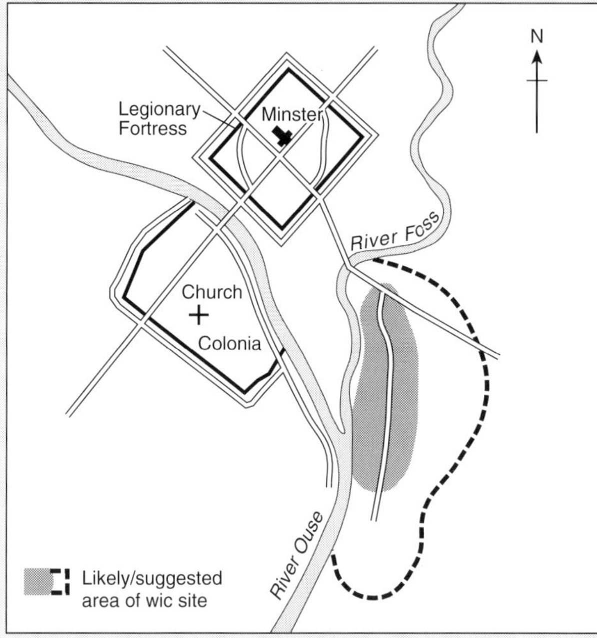

Anglian York, showing roads and streets possibly in use by the mid 9th century. The later Coppergate site was south of the fortress, between the Ouse and the Foss (after R. L. Kemp, Anglian Settlement at Fishergate*).*

Roman York consisted of the fortress on the north side of the River Ouse, and the *colonia* on the south, with some extramural settlement and cemeteries. The site of the fourth-century bishop's church is unknown; the present Minster overlies the barracks.

Within the *colonia*, a stone building next to the main street had rough cobbles and beaten earth as its final floor surface, a graphic illustration of declining standards at the end of the fourth century. Continuing change is shown by the build-up of 'dark earth' composed of decaying plant material, the throwing of rubbish into abandoned buildings, some traces of timber structures where stone would have been used before, and evidence of cultivation where previously there had been courtyards. The street was narrowed, though not left entirely unmaintained, and a wood-lined water-channel was kept fairly clean for a time before it silted up. How long this sort of activity continued into the fifth century is impossible to measure, as the coin sequence stops after AD 402, and such pottery as there is cannot be closely dated.

Within the fortress, civilian use seems to have taken over from military, but a small masonry tower was added to the western defences. Unlike seventh-century churches, it was built entirely of freshly quarried stone, without any blocks taken from Roman ruins. It could be late Roman, or it could have been constructed for a 'king' taking control of the area in the fifth century, before building in mortared stone ceased to be an option. That York remained some sort of authority centre, as perhaps did Canterbury and some other towns, would explain both why there are fifth- and sixth-century cemeteries grouped around it, and King Edwin's determination to have himself baptized there in the early seventh century. His successors probably used York as the minting place for the few gold coins that they issued.

The church built for King Edwin has not been found. It may have been in the Minster area of the fortress, where grave-markers show that there was at least a cemetery for important people in the seventh century. The Roman basilica had lost its roof by then, and soil had been dumped in it. The bones of piglets and lambs suggest that stock was being bred in the shelter of its ruined walls. Pottery and other things of the fifth/seventh centuries had probably not been brought from very far; there is nothing exotic about them. Nevertheless, the bones may represent the residues of feasts held to entertain visitors who assembled at York on special occasions, to whom the king offered the best and most tender meat.

A scatter of finds in the *colonia* shows that there were people using that area in the eighth and ninth centuries, where there was also probably another church; but the most intensive occupation has been

York's 'Anglian Tower' is built up against the Roman wall (on the left). It became engulfed by the earth banks later piled up to strengthen the heightened wall, and was rediscovered in the 1970s. Its date is not certain, but the stone used in its construction suggests that it was built very late in the Roman period rather than in the 7th century.

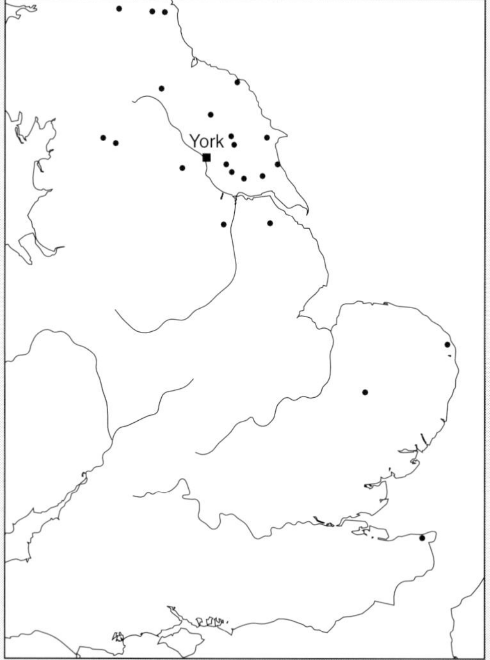

Distribution map of 8th-century Series Y sceattas, *silver coins probably minted in York (after D. M. Metcalf,* Thrymsas and Sceattas*).*

The 'Coppergate helmet' was found in a pit in which it had been hidden around the middle of the 9th century, when it was already two or three generations old. The inscriptions on the metal bands that cross over the top of the head ask for prayers for Oshere, presumably the name of its first owner.

found outside the Roman walls, on the north bank of the River Fosse, just above where it joins the Ouse. Presumably here there was a shoreline uncluttered by Roman masonry, where boats could be hauled up to be unloaded. Excavations have found traces of timber buildings, what are probably property divisions, and perhaps a metalled street like those in contemporary sites elsewhere. Pits had been dug and filled with rubbish.

The coins found at Fishergate show that occupation began in *c.*700 and died out in the 840s/60s. The animal bones indicate people with a very different lifestyle from those around the Minster; not for them choice and tender lamb and pork, but tough and less succulent beef and mutton, with less variety than later townspeople could hope to enjoy. Nor does pottery suggest that they had access to much in the way of imported luxuries, though through their hands may have been passing the sorts of goods that the richer parts of society wanted, notably wine. They were also involved in various crafts—metalworking, textiles—though the volume of production is hard to assess.

Fishergate was probably the site of the *wic* indicated by the name Eoforwicceastre; Alcuin called York an *emporium*, so he knew it as a trading place. Eighth-century silver *sceattas* from all over England and north-west Europe were lost, so coins were being used. There may have been a mint, producing the series of *sceattas* which seem from their distribution in southern Northumbria to have been York products.

The *wic* may have succumbed to Viking raids, or simply have been unsustainable in the troubled ninth century. The deliberate concealment of a fine, but already quite old, helmet in a wood-lined pit at Coppergate suggests turmoil. York was a focus for attacks in 866, and became the centre of the Viking kingdom established ten years later. Burials show the arrival of new customs, and a glass-working hearth shows craft revival. The main surge in activity was from *c.*900, however, and led to the development of tenements and streets in new areas such as that between the Roman fort and the Ouse. The old *wic* did not come back into use for another century, and then only as a burial ground.

in the 660s. The choice of Winchester may have been partly expedient, as the West Saxon hold on Dorchester was slipping, and partly because missionaries deliberately sought old Roman centres, to claim the mantle of Rome. There is no other direct trace of royal involvement in Winchester until King Alfred's reign, but the rich female burial 250 yards north of the Old Minster demonstrates that there was at least an aristocratic interest in it by the end of the seventh century. Some towns perhaps had secular enclosures as well as churches—Bassishaw and Lothbury in London are the *haga* of the Basingas and the *burh* of King Hlothere of Kent (673/4–85). Both of these are in the western part of the City, near St Paul's. A palace originally for the kings of Essex before control of London passed to Kent might be envisaged within the Roman fort in the Cricklegate area, with the bishop's church established in *c.*604 at a respectful distance.

King Aethelberht's existing interest in Canterbury probably brought Augustine to it; Queen Bertha already had a chapel there, one possible site for which is extramural St Martin's, another St Pancras. The royal donation of a *mansio* need not mean that there was a standing structure worth giving the missionary, but implies a property with recognizable boundaries. Traces of a seventh-century church have been found recently below the present cathedral, and presumably that was built by Augustine; to the west, outside the walls, he established a monastery. The role of the Church in towns was thus re-established, even if the first archbishop was not able to set himself up in London as had been hoped.

The *emporia*

The infrequency of early Anglo-Saxon objects within the walls of Londinium suggests minimal occupation there, and the new bishopric did not cause an immediate upsurge in activity. By the end of the seventh century, however, London had again become an international trading place. Upstream to the west of the City, pottery, coins, and other finds now suggest that the Lundenwic referred to in late seventh-century charters was beside the Thames along what is now the Strand, in a belt of occupation for which the earliest positive date is 679, achieved from dendrochronological dating. The place was successful, and the Royal Opera House site shows that it expanded inland, a street with side alleys being superimposed over a scatter of earlier features, including a grave. Remetalled at least ten times, the street was lined with tenement plots, containing buildings.

London's overseas contacts were mainly with the Rhine mouth and north France; pottery, glass, coins, and quernstones are the principal evidence, though wine can be assumed, and also probably silks and spices from even further away. Exports would have included mundane agricultural by-products—wool, cloth, leather—and the product of successful raiding parties, slaves. In its heyday, the site covered some 150 acres, with streets and houses; if a household averaged five people, a total population of between 5,000 and 10,000 can be envisaged.

More is known about another trading place, Saxon Southampton, or Hamwic. The 100 or so acres of that site have not had as many deep cellars and other intrusions affecting it as has London, making recognizable a grid of gravel streets, with timber buildings set in their own compounds, not densely packed as in a later town. Small cemeteries, rubbish pits, and wells are the other frequent features. Occupation began later than in London, but within a couple of generations of

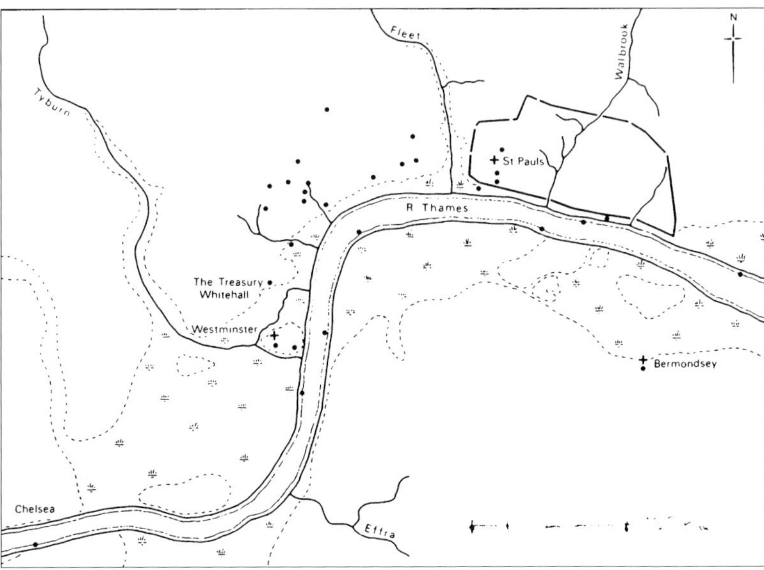

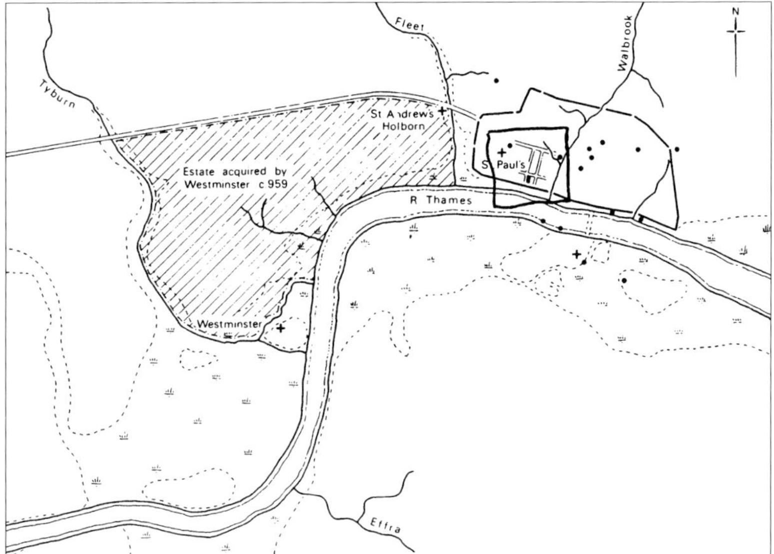

Find-spots of 7th- to 9th-century objects show the area of the mid-Saxon trading zone of Lundenuric*; excavations in the Covent Garden neighbourhood have revealed buildings, streets, and a substantial ditch that was probably dug in the 9th century as a defence against the Vikings. The lower map shows how the City area came back into use in the late 9th century, but only the grid of streets south of Cheapside seems to have been developed initially.*

*c.*700 the town was thriving, with occupation spread over an area that would allow a population of perhaps 2,000–4,000. Domesday Book suggests that late eleventh-century Wessex had a population of a little over half a million, presumably a considerable increase since the eighth century. The *wic* may have housed about 1 per cent of the kingdom's people, therefore.

Two other English *wic* sites have been located, below present-day Ipswich, and in the Fishergate area of York (see cameo). There are references to another at Fordwich in Kent, and place names ending in '-wich' have led to speculation about

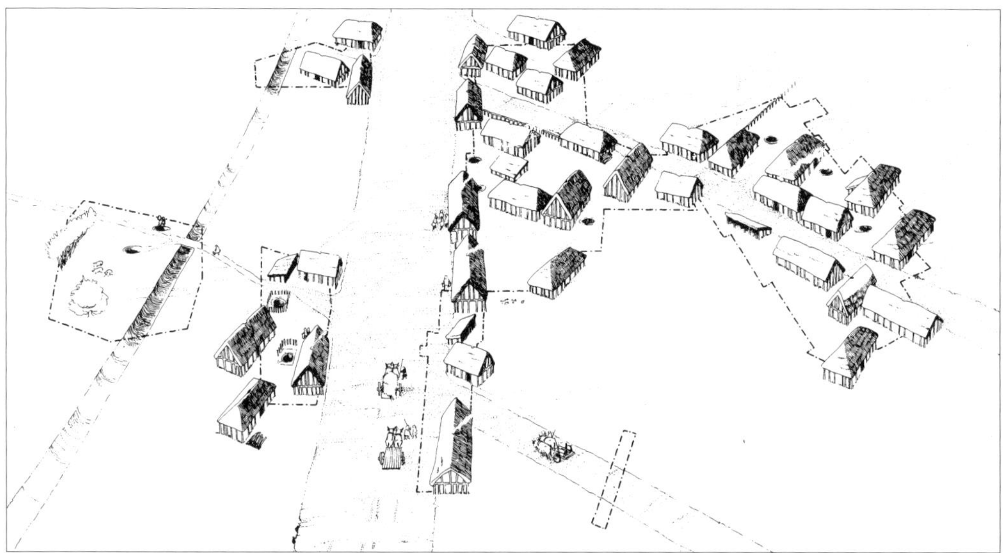

A reconstruction of the streets and buildings found in excavations in part of Hamwic, Saxon Southampton.

many others—Dunwich, Harwich, and Sandwich, for example. Unfortunately, the name has a range of meanings. The four where there have been excavations have many things in common; all are where sloping beaches gave sheltered places for boats to be pulled up onto the shore; all have streets that suggest deliberate layout, not haphazard growth; all have a density of use that outstrips rural sites, as well as a range of imported objects; all have evidence of craftworking.

Apparent dissimilarities may result merely from the availability of different sites. Until recently, Hamwic was the only one known to have had a perimeter ditch and bank, though it was not very substantial, and did not last for the whole life of the settlement. Over 50 yards of a two-yard deep and four-yard wide ditch have now been excavated in London, however. The idea that the *wic* sites were 'open' to prevent them challenging royal authority in the territories in which they developed must be set aside. Early supervision is suggested at three of them by burials with glass palm-cups, indicating at least the wealth and feast-giving ability appropriate to royal reeves; London had a *wicgerefa* by the 680s.

Southampton is downriver from Winchester; if the king of Wessex had an interest in the latter, he may have wanted the former to service it. Sutton Hoo and Rendlesham are not far from East Anglia's Ipswich; the City of London had the interest of the kings of Essex, and later of Kent, Wessex, and Mercia; King Edwin of Northumbria was involved in York. Kings not only wanted what merchants brought, prestigious objects to offer their followers and wine to entertain them, but also toll payments. What is known about the places from documents inevitably stems from the Church: properties acquired in London by bishops and monasteries, and exemptions from tolls on boats using the port, or incidental mention of Southampton as a *mercimonium* in a saint's life. Their development is synchronous with that of formalized political units, with which the Church worked to secure its protection and interests.

The *wic* sites had to be supplied with food, as there were too many inhabitants to be self-sufficient, and animal-bone studies show that they were not farmers, going out each day to till local fields. Elderly cows and sheep provided the bulk of the meat, probably plentiful but tough. There are slightly more younger animals in the first phases of Saxon Southampton than later, but even then the pattern is not what would derive from a normal farm breeding-stock. Even pigs, which can be reared in urban backyards, were mostly fully grown; if they were being kept in the town, they were brought in as piglets to mature. There was little variety: a few fowl and geese, and fish, particularly easily caught eels and flatfish, with a few deeper-water herrings, cod, and other larger species. In the ninth century, the animal bones show more skilful butchery, evidence perhaps of a specialist trade developing.

This evidence can be interpreted in two ways; the animals might be the driven-in surpluses of royal food-renders—what the kings did not consume themselves—or they could result from deliberate production for the market, with local farmers already beginning to participate in a supply system that required more frequent exchange than annual tribute payment. Around London, pollen changes suggest seventh-century and later clearance for agriculture. This was only partly stimulated by the new demand, however, since the produce was not all going into the *wic*—spelt wheat was grown, but is not found in the town. Southampton's grain must have come from further away, because the local heaths are not suitable for cereal cultivation. This would have diffused any market effect, and would not be separable from the general intensification of production that marks the mid-Saxon period. The food eaten in the *wic* sites, and the quality of the metalwork, suggests people who were adequately provided for, but who did not have a rich lifestyle.

The only commodity that was being imported and was in regular use at rural sites was the Mayen lava quern-stones; very few imported pottery sherds are found. The metal objects made in the new towns were not different from those made elsewhere, and may not have been intended for more than internal sale, nor is there evidence that the textile workers had specialized skills that took their products further afield. The exceptions are coins and in one case pottery, the distinctive product of kilns in Ipswich. It was distributed around most of East Anglia, with some going further afield to London, Kent, Yorkshire and the East Midlands. Distance was not the only limiting factor, however, as there is relatively little in Essex, which suggests trade restrictions between adjacent kingdoms.

Coin distributions are very comparable to that of Ipswich ware. The number of some types of the small silver pennies now termed *sceattas* that are found at and immediately around the *wic* sites indicates that they were minted in them, though no dies or other direct evidence have been excavated. A fantastic bird is a distinctive design associated with Hamwic; it is found almost exclusively in Wessex, though there are so few coins outside Southampton that the local economy cannot have been using money for everyday exchanges. Coins with the name of the king of Northumbria, sometimes also with that of the archbishop, are clearly York products; very few have been found south of the Humber. The only ones with a place name are from London, but *sceattas* probably from London tend to be more widespread than those from the other three known *wic* sites, reflecting its border position, so that it was tied in with, and its control sought after by, several competing kingdoms. Ipswich is a little less clear-cut; there are many East Anglian *sceattas*, and a range of possible mints. The only archaeological evidence for a *wic* at Sandwich, Kent, is the distribution around it of a particular type of *sceatta*.

a) *Distribution map of Ipswich ware pottery (after K. Wade, in B. Hobley and R. Hodges,* Rebirth of Towns in the West*), and* **b**) *distribution map of two 8th-century* sceatta *series; only one of Series H Types 39 and 49, minted at Hamwic (Southampton), has been found north of the Thames, whereas Series R, perhaps minted at Ipswich, seems not to have been allowed to travel south. Comparison of the latter with Ipswich ware pottery indicates that there was a trading network within East Anglia from which Essex, a rival kingdom, was vitually excluded (after D. M. Metcalf,* Thrymsas and Sceattas*).*

The *sceatta* coins have many designs that cannot be attributed to particular mints, and many may have been struck by itinerant moneyers, as well as by some who were presumably unlicensed and produced bad copies and plated forgeries. Their production died away in the 760s and later, and coin use must have fluctuated even if there was not a total hiatus before the silver penny was introduced. Currency circulation developed fitfully, unsupported by an urban network. No later eighth- or early ninth-century foundations have been identified that are on the same scale as the four *wic* sites, although a number of excavations and finds suggest that trading was taking place, at churches, royal centres, and perhaps at periodic fairs.

Some royal estate centres, like Tamworth with a watermill complex, were processing what must have been large quantities of grain and other renders, and went on to become towns in later centuries, but they show no trace of urban populations contemporary with Hamwic or Lundenwic. Several grain-driers have been excavated in Stafford, which in the tenth century was to become a shire capital, presumably usurping Tamworth, which became a border town. Another later shire centre was Northampton, where a seventh-century and later complex suggests a major royal centre and church. In Hereford, a large grain-drier gave way to an area of buildings and gravel spreads before being covered by the probably ninth-century defensive bank. The gravel might be a street surface, or just yards, however, and density of occupation, in terms of pits and objects, does not seem to have been on the same scale as in the *wic* sites. Hereford, of course, had the stimulus of a bishopric, and similar information could probably be expected from a number of other places with churches, such as Worcester, Bath, or Chester. At the last, a substantial masonry building may be a Mercian church, though an earlier post-Roman date cannot be excluded, but sunken-featured buildings have been found only outside the Roman walls. Gloucester has evidence of use, but it is primarily of stabling.

Traces of Hereford's insubstantial buildings were found because they were protected by the defences which had originally destroyed them. In normal circumstances, such vestigial evidence is unlikely to survive, and in areas where little pottery was being used, the very presence of eighth- and ninth-century occupation can go unrecognized. But even in pot-prolific East Anglia, it is difficult to find more than limited use of Norwich or Thetford (or a site just to its west), and in Essex Colchester has been well investigated, but has produced nothing between the fifth and the tenth centuries. Canterbury has documentary evidence of ninth-century regulations providing for a two-foot eavesdrop between properties, as well as references to *burh*-dwellers, which suggests considerable development; but it is scarcely visible in the archaeological record, of which there is less rather than more than of the fifth. It remained a mint, however.

The ninth-century North European trading system was disrupted by the Vikings; even though their destruction of places has been exaggerated, those who depended on overseas commerce would not have been able to operate securely. Lundenwic and Eoforwic may have been in trouble in the 830s, Hamwic by the 840s, though a tail of coins shows that abandonment was not immediate. Nevertheless, these sites had all but gone, apart from churches in some of them, by the end of the ninth century. Their disappearance may have held back developments that depended upon them, such as hinterland farms and embryonic market sites, but they were not so structured into their kingdoms that they caused the collapse of entire social structures. Even coins could still be minted without them.

A New Dynamic?

facing page: Because Wareham declined in the later Middle Ages, the map drawn in the 1780s is probably not very different from how it would have appeared in about 1100, after the Norman castle had been inserted. The earlier, Saxon, banks remain, and much of the street system probably dates from the same period. As in the 18th century, so in the earlier period there would have been many undeveloped areas inside the enclosure.

The Vikings were both raiders and traders, fully aware of what trading places were like, even if their own sites like Hedeby, Ribe, and Birka were not quite on the scale of a Dorestad or a Hamwic. York did not flower immediately after the Viking takeover of 866, but growth after *c.*900 was remarkable (see cameo), as it was in Lincoln. The Roman walls of the forts at these places probably first attracted the Scandinavians to use them as power bases. New sites were also used: Stamford was a late ninth-century defensible enclosure, set up either against or by the Vikings, a nucleus outside which a market developed.

The defended places used by the kings of Wessex are recorded in lists which also say how many hides belonged to each one. Collectively known as the Burghal Hidage, these lists show a remarkably sophisticated system of accurate measurement, and an ability to get together men who would construct, maintain, and garrison the forts. Winchester's Roman walls may have provided the base measurement, since the 2,400 hides that were allowed for their upkeep would have

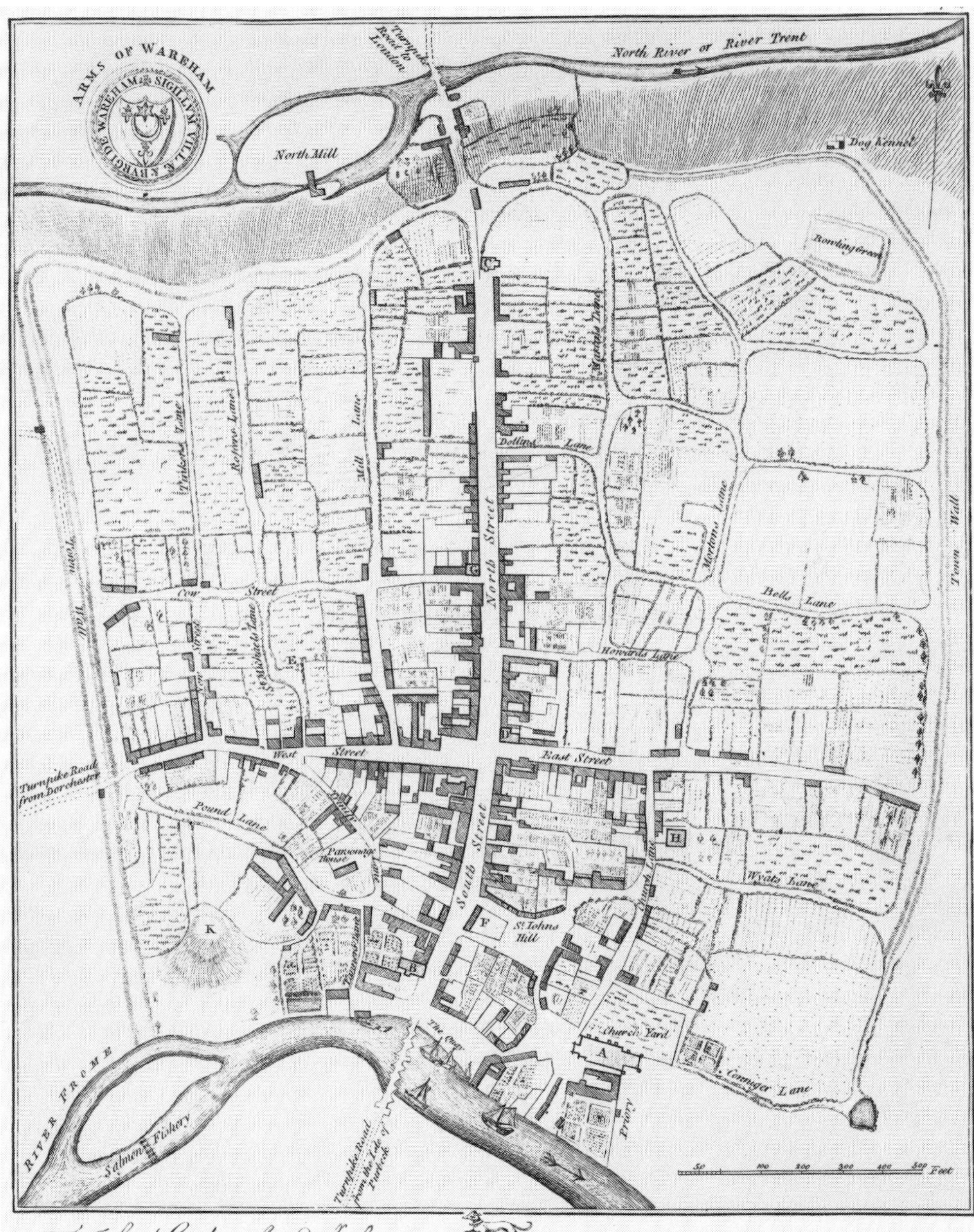
Arms of Wareham
North River or River Trent
Turnpike Road to London
North Mill
Dog Kennel
Bowling Green
Tinkers Lane
Roffers Lane
Mill Lane
North Street
Dollins Lane
Mortons Lane
Bells Lane
Town Wall
Cow Street
Howards Lane
West Street
East Street
Turnpike Road from Dorchester
Pound Lane
Parsonage House
South Street
St. Johns Hill
Wyats Lane
Church Yard
Conniger Lane
Priory
River Frome
Salmon Fishery
Turnpike Road from the Isle of Purbeck
50 100 200 300 400 500 Feet
To John Calcraft Esq.r this Plan of Wareham, is humbly inscribed by The Author.
A. St. Mary's Church.
B. Trinity Church.
C. St. Martin's Church.
D. Town Hall formerly St. Peter's Church.
E. Formerly St. Michael's Church.
F. Formerly St. Iohn's Church.
G. Formerly Allhallow's Chapel.
H. Dissenter's Meeting House.
I. Alms House.
K. Formerly the Castle.

supplied the same number of men, and four were needed for each *gyrde* (= rod, pole, or perch). At 16½ feet per pole, 2,400 hides were enough for 9,900 feet of wall; the actual length has been measured as 9,954 feet. An earth bank and ditch around a site that had no Roman predecessor, such as Wareham, could be assessed for hidage by the same formula. Wallingford was the only other fortress assessed for as many hides as Winchester; it has a largely extant bank and ditch around three sides, with the Thames, and perhaps a bridgehead, being the fourth, making a total length of *c.*9,150 feet. Intriguingly, 2,400 hides almost exactly provide for this if a different length is taken for the pole—15ft 3ins, an Old Saxon measurement, perhaps used in Mercia not Wessex, as the south bank of the Thames was for a time under Mercian control.

Several of these new places, such as Wareham or Oxford, though not Wallingford, had known churches, and often earlier signs of royal interest, but can be fairly certainly said not to have been urbanized. Gates and fords in the middle of their defensive lines served an internal street pattern based on a central crossroads. The regularity of these plans, often with side streets and a widening main street for a market place, suggests that some of these features may have been part of the original design, though demonstrating the precise date of the layout of any one is proving difficult. A coin of Edward the Elder (899–924) and a late ninth-century Arabic dirham in one of Winchester's early road surfaces show that there can have been little time between Burghal Hidage and street layout, but in the Brooks area one of the Roman street lines seems to have been used briefly, before a new alignment was superimposed.

Awareness of the potential of enclosed places for trade is shown by the survival of a charter granted to the bishop of Worcester in the 880s or 890s. The borough was to be 'built for the protection of all the people'; the bishop was to have half the profits 'in the market or in the street' except for tolls paid on Droitwich salt, and half the profits of administration, derived from fines and compensation payments, as well as payments made for upkeep of the walls. A northern ditch located in excavations seems to be an extension of an earlier enclosure around the cathedral, and had inside it the market and other streets.

Worcester's is the most explicit statement about market profits, but similar motives may be recognized in King Alfred's 'restoration' of the City of London, after which finds of pottery reveal that occupation did indeed spread back inside the old Roman walls, with the *wic* not reoccupied. Charters referring to a market and a *ripa emptoralis* show a beaching area being created by the end of the ninth century, with Worcester and Canterbury churches having the benefit of the 'urban manors' thus created. Excavation of early surfaces in the area between the River Thames and Cheapside has shown that streets were laid out both for access and to form boundaries. The grid pattern that was formed can be recognized in later maps. Downriver development, and to the north of Cheapside, was to follow later. Alfred proclaimed his control of London by putting its name onto one of his pennies; Winchester, Oxford, Exeter, and Gloucester were also mint-signatures on his coins, probably to mark the central place and the principal border locations of his kingdom—Canterbury was used, but not named, and not to any great extent.

Not all the *burhs* were located in situations where trade could develop, and some of the places that might have been intended for towns never came to very much. What the Burghal Hidage, the Worcester charter, and the London work seem to imply is a system and an intention, an understanding of potential even though it was to take a long time to achieve fruition. It was also an intention to stimulate internal market places, not merely to rely on merchants visiting a few ports. The *wic* sites had served partly to supply kings and churches at places through which their surpluses and war booty could be funnelled, and partly to produce toll income. The system that King Alfred and his contemporaries were instituting was one in which exchange would be less directed, with toll income their main interest. This required a network of towns to provide the market places where the profits of trade could be tapped.

3 The Medieval Urban Landscape, AD 900–1540

Derek Keene

> Gawain regarded the site of the castle, which sat on an arm of the sea, and noticed that the walls and the tower were so strong that they feared no assault. He looked at the entire town, peopled with beautiful men and women, and the tables of the money-changers all covered with gold and silver and other coins. He saw the market spaces and streets all full of workmen engaged in many crafts: one fashioning helmets and another coats of mail, one lances and another shields, one bridles and another spurs. Some furbished swords, while some fulled cloth and others wove it; still others combed it, and others sheared it. Some melted down gold and silver; others fashioned them into fine and beautiful works: cups and bowls, enamelled jewellery, and rings, belts, and buckles. One might well believe and declare that the town held a fair every day, filled as it was with so much wealth: wax, pepper, grain [an expensive dye], ermine and grey furs, and all kinds of merchandise. He gazed on all this, pausing here and there along the way.
>
> An idealized view of a town, in a French or English context (London would have been an appropriate model), evoked *c.*1190 by Chrétien de Troyes in his *Story of the Grail*

Urban landscape is the physical outcome of more or less large numbers of people living closely together over long periods of time. Proximity, facilitating intercourse and the accumulation of social memory, is the essence of town life. In the Middle Ages, as later, people sought the town because it embodied networks of news, information, and credit through which they might find profit as craftsmen, merchants, and suppliers of professional services—or casual employment and charitable relief. The density of the town, and of the social and commercial exchanges within it, was also a source of intellectual, cultural, religious, and erotic stimulation. Though decried by many as inherently dangerous, towns also offered safety through their collective arrangements for defence. As sites from which justice and great estates were administered, many also contained the headquarters of the super-rich, or they served as bases—economic, cultural, and military—from which their interests were controlled. Servicing the needs of landowning magnates and institutions was an important task of medieval towns, both great and small. In return for peace and protection, rulers exploited towns as sources of income, in the form of tolls, taxes, and loans; as sources of power in the form of fighting men and supplies; and as places of assembly in which to legitimate their authority. These functions, in varying combinations, shaped the landscape of medieval towns.

Urbanization in Medieval England

Medieval England was peripheral to the main focuses of trade and culture in Christian Europe. Yet the country became quite highly urbanized, reflecting the evolution of an increasingly commercial and specialized society, within an exceptionally strong framework of governance inherited from the Anglo-Saxon period. At the Norman Conquest perhaps one in ten English people was a town dweller. By 1300, when the population was at its medieval peak, 15 to 20 per cent of people lived in places identifiable as towns. Thereafter, following famine and plague, the total population was much smaller, but its urbanized proportion may have remained about the same until 1600 or later. The process of urbanization was uneven in both space and time. The establishment of towns was an important element in state policies for the organization of defence, marketing, and taxation in the late ninth and tenth centuries, but the actual rates of town growth, as manifest in the expansion of existing centres and the foundation of new ones, may have been greatest in the eleventh century, and again important during the late twelfth and early thirteenth. The Norman Conquest stimulated the prosperity of some towns, but overall had a disruptive effect, as did the civil war of Stephen's reign. After 1300, and more particularly after the Black Death, most towns contracted in size; but the majority of town dwellers became more prosperous and enjoyed more comfortable living conditions, and in many districts urban markets thrived.

Throughout the period individual towns responded in different ways to broad changes in political and economic geography and to the advantages or disadvantages of their situation. Thus, during phases of overall growth, Wallingford lost its wealth and prominence to the regional centre of Oxford and to London-oriented market towns further down the Thames; much of the prosperous eleventh-century port of Dunwich was washed away by the sea; and as London's commercial magnetism attracted the functions of a capital, Winchester lost its earlier high rank as a royal city. Over the fourteenth century, despite the general contraction of the population, some towns, including Coventry and Colchester, appear to have grown in response to new opportunities presented by textile manufactures and developing markets overseas. Colchester thus more than regained the relative wealth it had enjoyed during the eleventh century. There was a continuing shift in national resources towards London and the south-east, reflecting the spectacular growth of the southern Netherlands as a force in the economy and culture of Europe. Port towns such as Bristol or Exeter which could participate in those overseas networks, yet were sufficiently remote from London not to be undermined by its influence, did relatively well. But even newly prosperous

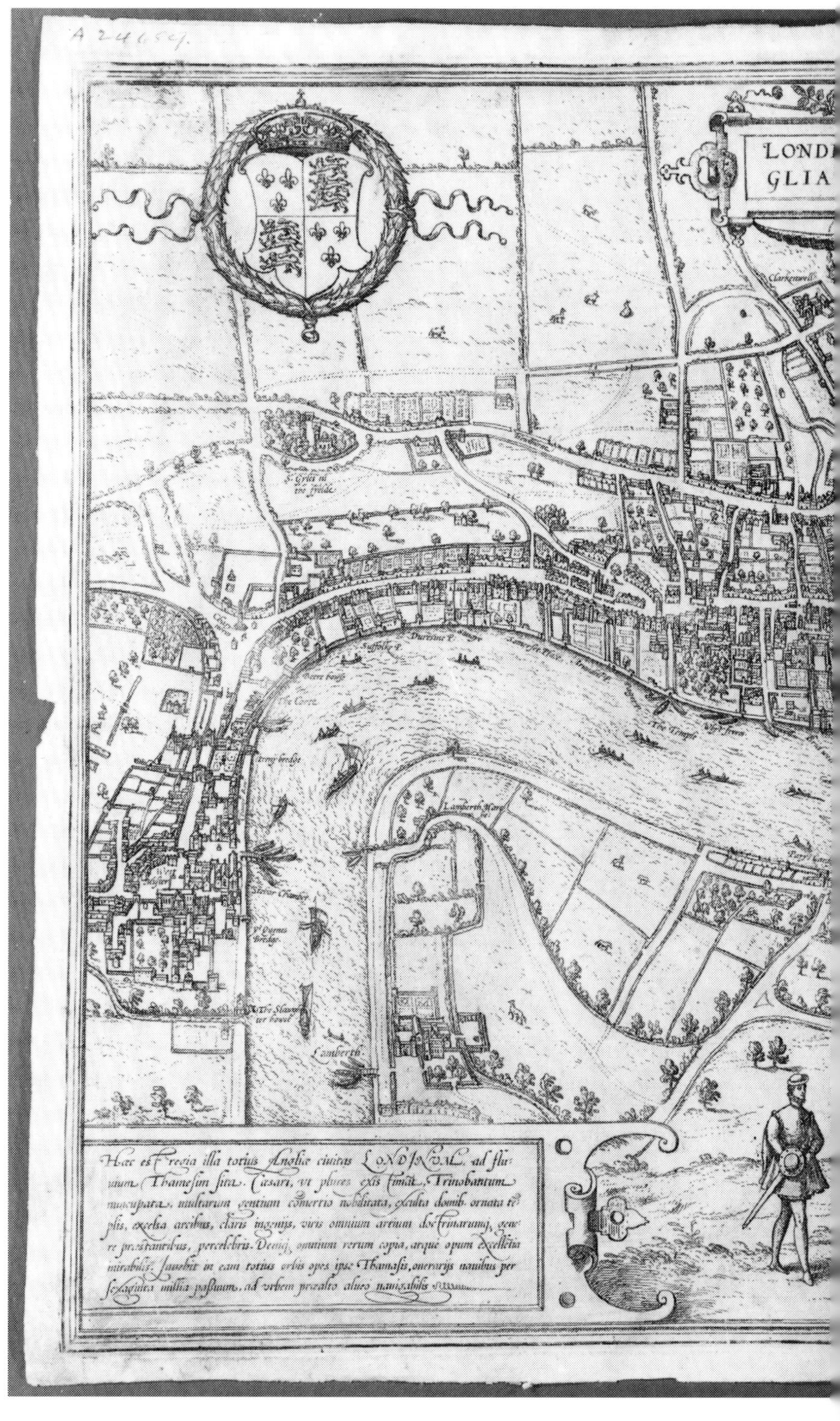

London c.1550, from Braun and Hogenberg, Civitates Orbis Terrarum, *first published in 1572. The extent and density of building were the same in 1300. Dominant features of the landscape included the city wall, which was Roman in origin, St. Paul's Cathedral with its spire, and the river carrying both local traffic and sea-going ships. Open country, much of it devoted to grazing livestock, began within a few hundred yards of the wall, while closer in lay gardens, orchards, and spaces devoted to cattle marketing and to processing cloth. Suburban sprawl was extensive, especially in the direction of Westminster.*

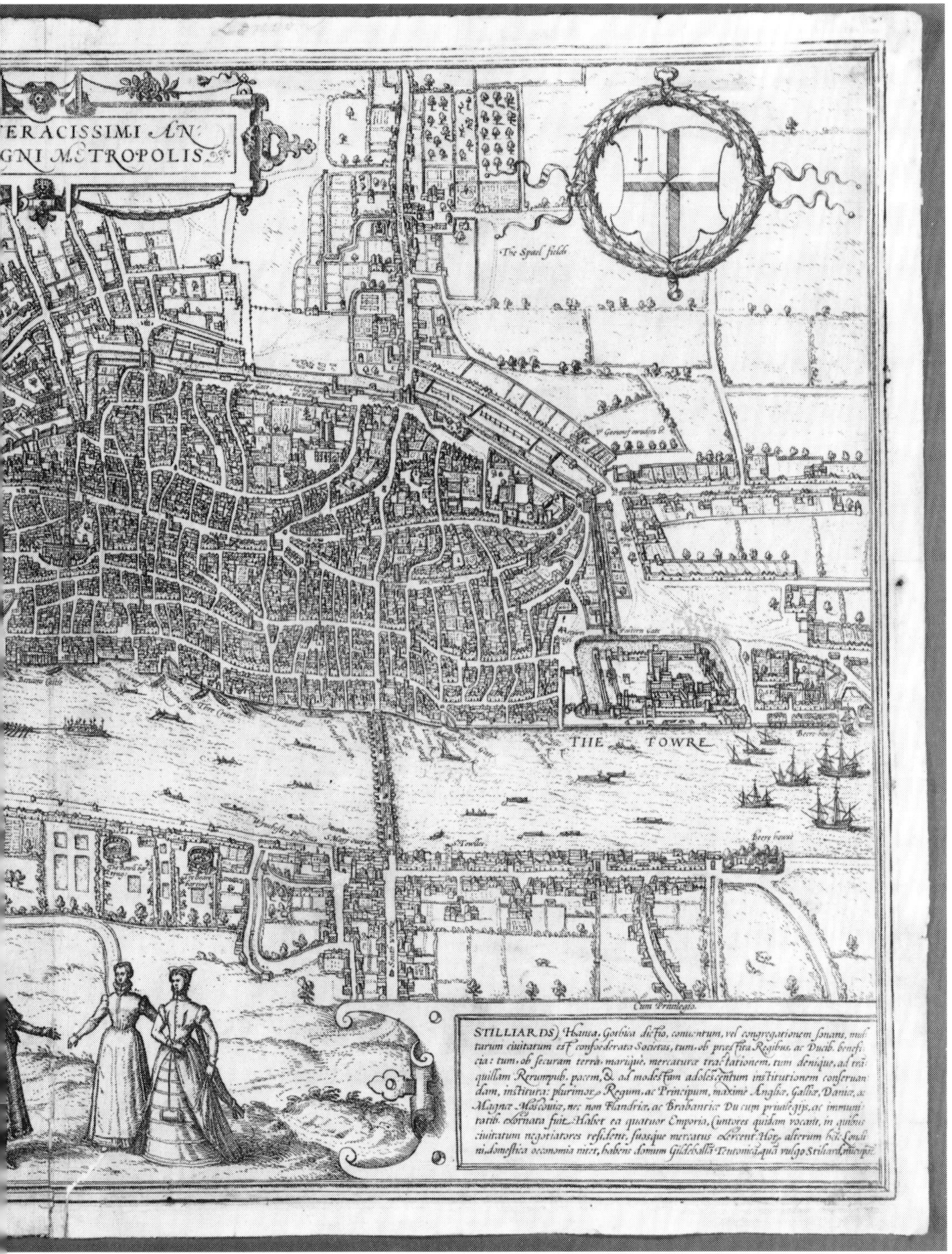
ERACISSIMI AN
GNI METROPOLIS
The Spitel fielde
THE TOWRE
Cum Privilegio
STILLIARDS) Hansa, Gothica dictio, conuentum, vel congregationem sonans, mul
tarum ciuitatum est confoederata Societas, tum ob praestita Regibus ac Ducib. benefi
cia: tum ob securam terra marique mercaturae tractationem, tum denique ad tra
quillam Rerumpub. pacem, & ad modestam adolescentum institutionem conseruan
dam, instituta: plurimorum Regum, ac Principum, maxime Angliae, Galliae, Daniae, ac
Magnae Moscouiae, nec non Flandriae, ac Brabantiae Ducum priuilegijs, ac immuni
tatib. exornata fuit. Habet ea quatuor Emporia, Cuntores quidam vocant, in quibus
ciuitatum negotiatores resident, suasque mercatus exercent. Horum alterum hic Londi
ni, domestica oeconomia viuit, habens domum Gildehallam Teutonicam, quam vulgo Stilliard nuncupat.

towns suffered from the economic difficulties of the mid- and later fifteenth century, and in the last decades of the period few if any towns really prospered. This included London which, in 1500, and for some time thereafter, was still smaller than 200 years before. Despite the expansion of its overseas trade, London's physical growth in the early sixteenth century was sluggish and largely confined to suburban areas, suggesting that impoverishment elsewhere and a narrowing of the basis of its wealth underlay the drift to the metropolis. The landscape of England was perceived to be littered with decaying towns, in the midst of which London shone more brightly than before.

Small towns dominated the late medieval English urban scene. Of a total of 500 or 600 towns (precision is impossible) perhaps 450 to 500 were 'small towns' with populations ranging from about 400 persons to about 2,000. In 1300, about a third of the 'large towns' had fewer than 5,000 inhabitants, another third had between 5,000 and 10,000, and the rest were larger. The twenty largest towns had a marked easterly and southerly distribution: only four lay north and west of a line between the Severn and the Humber. Just two cities had over 25,000 inhabitants, including London with perhaps 80,000. This urban system was unintensive by contrast with some parts of Italy and the Low Countries, where town dwellers represented 40 per cent of the population. Moreover, England's large towns were relatively small and widely spaced. In early fourteenth-century Flanders within a territory measuring less than 60 miles across, there were seven towns each with at least 30,000 inhabitants, while in England the two towns of comparable size were 180 miles apart.

The predominance of a single city, already significant in the tenth century and becoming steadily more salient, also distinguished England from other urbanized regions of Europe. London's role as a capital—the centre of interest for the Crown and governmental institutions which had largely ceased to be peripatetic—was consolidated in the late thirteenth century. This enhanced London's wealth, which was founded on its engagement with commercial networks coursing through northern France, the Low Countries, and the River Rhine. London was a major European city. Especially prominent during the eleventh and twelfth centuries, it was later in the second rank, being about half the size of Paris. Yet while Paris came to outshine London, it was less dominant within France. The political geography of medieval England thus contained elements of a city state.

The geographical distribution of English towns broadly matched that of the population. The urban hierarchy was loosely structured on a regional basis and reflected strong local cultures, notably during the twelfth and thirteenth centuries when several authors characterized English towns according to their products, their ways of life, and the landscapes in which they were set. Under London's impact the urban system became more integrated. The capital engaged directly with many of the 100 or more other towns which lay within about 70 miles. At a greater distance London merchants acted through the larger towns, which also received and transmitted metropolitan styles and forms. These forces weakened the standing of some of the larger towns as provincial centres, such as York in the fifteenth century, but they could strengthen the position of others. At the end of the fourteenth century, one of Coventry's friary churches contained heraldic signs of the leading London citizens of the day, a demonstration of the London orientation of much of Coventry's business. In contrast to London and the provincial centres, most towns had restricted horizons, supplying goods and services to country dwellers within a hinterland of a few miles. The small market town of Ashwell in Hertfordshire served an area measuring about 16 miles by 7; Stratford-upon-Avon, one of the largest of the 'small towns', sat at the centre of a 'main hinterland' estimated at 25 miles by 12; and the comparable territory for Winchester, a town about five times the size of Stratford, measured 75 by 50 miles.

Many towns had specialisms within national or metropolitan frameworks. Numerous small towns in London's hinterland supplied particular commodities to the city's food markets, while others developed crafts which served manufacturing systems articulated through the city. Port towns serviced changing patterns of Norman, Irish, North Sea, or Mediterranean trade. Bristol played a special role in the conquest of Ireland, and periodically York served as a focus of national power in the north, while the frontier towns had a continuing role. County towns made a routine contribution to the governance of the realm. The well-endowed institutions of the Christian Church, albeit drawing their income primarily from rural sources, expressed the role of towns within a universal system of order. The seventeen cathedral cities had a special standing, and a town's endowment of religious houses, friaries, and hospitals was an important measure of its urban culture. Not all such centres of power were equally important for trade, and both cathedral cities and county towns are found among the ranks of small towns. Overall, about half the urban population lived in small towns, and many looked to county or regional centres for the more expensive products which they could not obtain locally. The rich and well-connected regularly went to London, or sent their agents there, as did the bishop of Durham for silks and ornaments in the early twelfth century, and the ladies of Norwich for head dresses in the fifteenth. By the fourteenth century, if not much earlier, many high-quality products from London's workshops were distributed widely about England.

These specialized services and functions shaped the appearance of towns. Thus out of some 500 towns in 1300, only 84 contained one or more convents of the four main orders of friars, whose mission was specifically directed at the burgeoning urban populations. Only a third of those towns contained more than one convent, while only nine, all major centres, had four. Numbers of crafts provide another measure of visible differences between towns. Around 1300 some 175 specialized trades are recorded in London, while Norwich and Winchester, respectively eighth and fifteenth among English towns, had about 70 each. Shrewsbury, wealthy but remote from complex commercial networks, had about 40 occupations. At Stratford-upon-Avon about 30 occupations were named, while in Essex, according to a tax list of 1327, only one of the twenty towns had as many as 17 trades and only five had more than 10.

Medieval towns were generally smaller than their successors of the eighteenth and nineteenth centuries, but they were comparable in their densities of population. In an age when transport was slow and expensive it was necessary to live near the heart of a town so as to profit from its markets and information flows. On the eve of the Great Fire of 1666 London's central parishes, the area of elite commercial residence, contained the highest densities of population ever known in England. In the same district in 1300 the density, at perhaps 170 persons per acre, was only half as great, but still extremely high by modern standards. At that time the density in the High Street area of Winchester was probably more than 90 per acre, higher than at any later date in the city's history, and more than twice the 'dense urban' threshold defined by modern analysts. Outside these areas much lower densities prevailed, and within a few hundred yards of the centre, even of London, open country began. Such contrasts shaped the medieval urban landscape, and, as the fifteenth-century poem 'London Lickpenny' shows, jostling crowds, embodying a culture of commerce and deceit, had a shock impact on country visitors:

> Into Cornhyll anon I yode
> where is moche stolne gere amonge
> I saw wher henge myne owne hode,
> that I had lost in Westminstar among the throng
> then I beheld it with lokes full longe
> I kenned it as well as I dyd my crede
> to by myne owne hood agayne, me thought it wrong
> but for lacke of money I might not spede.

Town Fabric

Some of the most dramatic changes in the urban landscape were apparent in materials and techniques of construction. The early stages of urban growth were marked by the use of materials readily to hand, but by the end of the period there had been a striking evolution from a fabric which was predominantly soft and organic towards the hard, mineral city of today. A town's fabric in part reflected the local occurrence of materials, but was also the product of cumulative investment and infrastructural development over several centuries. That is clear with the use of stone, for the opening of quarries and the carriage of stone were expensive and required systems of labour and marketing. Even when stone outcropped close by, as at Bristol, Oxford, or Shrewsbury, the principal material for house-building was timber, throughout the Middle Ages and beyond. High status structures were the first to be built of stone: cathedrals from the seventh century; parish churches or their equivalent from the tenth century or earlier; castles and town gates from the late eleventh century and town walls (when not of Roman origin) from the thirteenth. York's defensive palisade was not replaced in stone until the thirteenth and fourteenth centuries. Often, stone houses succeeded earlier timber and earthen ones, and major building projects promoted the availability of stone and lime for lesser structures. Stone houses for magnates, merchants, and other town dwellers proliferated from the twelfth century onwards. They indicated status, and provided protection against fire and theft and underground storage spaces more permanent than those of timber: indeed, investment in the first stone parish churches may in part have been motivated by a need to provide security for people and goods. Stone buildings usually occupied secluded sites set back from the street or constituted only the cellars, and so in many urban landscapes were rarely visible features. Stone buildings prominent on the frontage were commonly brash assertions of mercantile success or confident statements of authority.

Developments in timber building were also important. During the tenth and eleventh centuries many houses were of slight construction, often with walls woven of rapidly grown hazel rods. More solid structures of posts and planks, incorporating greater effort and skill, became prevalent during the eleventh century, when many probably had more than one storey above ground. The emergence of timber-framed construction around 1200 allowed relatively cheap buildings to be erected several storeys high. This saved wood, supplies of which, as the crucial fuel resource, came under increasing pressure; and it allowed towns to grow upwards as well as outwards. That in turn facilitated high population densities and newly intensive forms of urban life. There were no later technical developments, before the nineteenth century, which made such a contribution to the attainable height of ordinary domestic and commercial buildings and so influenced the underlying pattern of the urban landscape. After the twelfth century dwellings of less than two storeys were rare except on the fringes of towns.

Framed buildings, especially when set on stone foundations, were more durable than their predecessors, and wall panels of wattle daubed with earth made them relatively fireproof. From the late fourteenth century onwards bricks came increasingly to be used for infilling wall panels, for chimneys, and as a substitute for stone rubble. Bricks seem first to have been employed in towns in eastern England where stone was scarce and which were open to building styles from overseas. Roofing materials also became more durable. Turf and thatch on many tenth- and eleventh-century town houses were succeeded over the next two centuries by oak shingles, slates, and tiles. Fired clay tiles, initially employed where stone slates were most expensive, became more widespread after 1350. Building regulations, apparent from about 1200 onwards in many towns, promoted the use of fireproof materials, including stone party walls; and the devastating town fires which had been common became rarer. The decline in population after 1300 increased the availability of fuel and so facilitated the production of bricks and tiles. Thus the urban fabric in the early sixteenth century embodied more energy than that 500 years before. Street surfaces also became harder, as casual spreads of rubble, boards, or hurdles gave way to deposits of quarried flints, chalk, or gravel. Nevertheless, street maintenance, usually the responsibility of the adjacent householders, was taken seriously from the beginning: in one Winchester side street metalled surfaces built up to a depth of five feet over 150 years before the Norman Conquest.

Urbanization involved the movement of millions of cartloads and boatloads of building materials brought into the town and of rubbish and upcast carried out. Surface relief and the soil composition of sites could change dramatically. Traffic and surface water caused erosion in streets running downhill. Elsewhere, soil could build up rapidly, especially where waterlogging encouraged the preservation of organic materials. Deliberate levelling and infilling were common. At Shrewsbury several parts of the town were terraced to create level sites for housing, while a deep hollow was infilled and the area paved for use as a market place. At King's Lynn marshy ground was consolidated so as to enlarge the settlement. There and at other ports, above all in London between the eleventh and the fourteenth century, river frontages were progressively extended far out into the water. In these constructions too stone walls came to replace timber revetments.

These developments, cumulative and to an extent independent of population trends, contributed to the solidity and comfort of the urban environment, and were accompanied by improved management of streams, surface water, and waste. Better drainage slowed the rate at which ground levels rose, while at Winchester the construction of causeways, channels, and bridges eliminated the 'horrible bog' which was a feature of the lower end of High Street in the early twelfth century. Sewage, ever more problematic as building densities increased, demanded more capital-intensive and long-lasting installations. The wicker-lined latrine pit of the tenth century, which frequently had to be redug in another part of the back yard, was succeeded by the plank-lined pit which was more easily emptied. The stone-lined pit, often serving families on upper storeys who had no access to backyards, became common from the thirteenth century onwards, especially in central areas. Animal litter provided a more intractable problem of refuse removal than human ordure, and piles of stable sweepings often blocked backstreets and alleys. These wastes could be carried out to fertilize gardens and fields, but the economics of transport frequently dictated their dumping in designated areas within the town. Streams and rivers were used to flush away noxious industrial wastes and butchers' offal (cut up so as not to clog the channels), but also to power town mills, to service public washing places and latrines, and as a source of drinking water. From the thirteenth century onwards sanitary codes regulated all these practices, emphasizing spatial and temporal restrictions of waste disposal with a view to maintaining tidy public spaces and access to clean water, while the law of nuisance provided householders with redress against the invasive and polluting habits of neighbours. Supplies of drinking water were often limited and contaminated, and many town dwellers far from flowing water relied on private wells. That was the case in London, where a piped water supply, supplying a public conduit in Cheapside, was not developed until the mid-thirteenth century and, even after it was extended, was used by only a few score households in the heart of the city. There is a contrast between the limited scale of such investments and the provision of channelled and piped water to religious precincts, although in some places town supplies were linked with those to religious houses.

Regional variations in the fabric of towns reflected the local presence of materials, transport costs, and patterns of trade. Even London and Winchester, only four days apart by cart, had different features. In these and other cities reused stone from Roman buildings and foundations was an important resource before the twelfth century. Blue slates, shipped from Devon, were widely used for roofing during the thirteenth and fourteenth centuries at Winchester, but rarely at London. In both cities Caen stone was used for fine work from soon after the Norman Conquest, but otherwise there were plain differences in their sources of stone. Major buildings in Winchester in the tenth century employed stone from near Bath. In the late eleventh century that was eclipsed by shelly limestone from newly opened quarries on the Isle of Wight, until they ran out in the fourteenth. Throughout the period London used ragstone from near Maidstone, readily transported by water; and London's drawing power is indicated by the use of stone from near Boulogne in twelfth-century work at St Paul's and by the periodic use of Yorkshire stone. For cheaper work the cities used ashlar carted from Greensand beds, London drawing on the Reigate area and Winchester on Selborne, in both cases at relatively late stages of their growth. Chalk was not shipped up to London (from below Gravesend) on large scale until the eleventh century and flints even later, but both materials were readily available in Winchester, where they were used from before 900. Loam and gravel, on the other hand, could be dug just outside the walls of London. There were notable differences even in the timber employed: oak, alder, hazel, ash, and beech in both cities, but elm only in London, where imported Baltic timber was also prevalent. At King's Lynn, in a region where wood was locally in short supply, Baltic timber was even more widely used.

The Shape and Extent of Towns

The formal extent of a town, as indicated by its walls or limit of jurisdiction, did not always correspond to its population or significance. Town walls, sometimes inherited from earlier periods, might enclose much uninhabited land, while extramural settlements, strung out along the approach roads, might contain a high proportion of a town's inhabitants. Some towns, such as Cambridge, included within their jurisdiction extensive areas of fields, owned and sometimes cultivated by the townspeople. Even so, defensive and suburban circuits indicate the wide range in the scale of urban landscapes. London was by far the most impressive. By 1200 it had expanded to the modern limits of the City's jurisdiction. Of that square mile, only half (320 acres) was within the Roman wall which, much reconstructed, still served to defend the city. In addition, there were substantial settlements at Westminster and Southwark, beyond the city limits but effectively part of London. To walk from Westminster to Whitechapel, the limits of London's buildings, involved a journey of three and a half miles through busy streets. Comparable walks through York and Norwich, the second cities of the realm, and through Winchester, where straggling extramural development was notable, were of about a mile. Winchester's Roman and medieval wall, enclosing less than half the area within London's wall, contained just over a third of its urban area (which as in a number of towns was divided between two main jurisdictions) and, in 1300, perhaps two-thirds of its population. Even at Winchester's peak, much open space lay within the walls, while by 1500 once densely settled areas had become waste or had been given over to cultivation. Norwich's walls, constructed in the thirteenth and fourteenth centuries and protecting a sprawling city at its medieval peak, enclosed about a square mile, much of it open ground. At the opposite extreme were some new towns founded in the thirteenth century. In Wiltshire, Hindon was established as a parish containing 212 acres, but the urban part occupied only 19 acres, where in 1300 some 500–700 people inhabited houses and gardens ranged along a market street a quarter of a mile long. Many small towns like Hindon acquired distinctively urban features, such as town halls, market stalls, shops, and parliamentary representation as boroughs. Others, despite their formal urban status, lack traces of town life, for which there is more evidence in some villages. Many new villages established at this time were at least as large as some towns and had similar plans.

Investment in town defences reflected the chronological and geographical patterns of warfare, but in haphazard fashion. Influential were the Scandinavian invasions, threats from Scotland and Wales, and the Hundred Years War. Fear of the French meant that in 1400 town defences were most up-to-date near the south coast. Sporadic civil war enhanced the value of walls, which many towns kept in good repair up to about 1500, while at the border towns of Berwick and Carlisle there was substantial investment in defences during the sixteenth century. Most smaller towns and some larger ones lacked defences. The ditch and bank enclosing the large thirteenth-century new town of Salisbury was not a major defence work, although twenty miles away at Southampton the French raid of 1338 caused the defensive circuit to be completed by incorporating stone houses on the waterfront into a wall, at some inconvenience to trade. Town walls, often visible from afar, embodied substantial collective effort and investment, and were a symbol of a town's identity and strength. They were often depicted on

The second seal of the citizens of York, 13th century. Like many city seals, it presents an image of a strongly-defended place, but may not be intended as strictly representational. A tower or castle is surrounded by a wall, possibly a city wall containing three gates surmounted by towers with banners above them.

town seals, although many port communities chose to display ships on theirs. Sometimes, as at Coventry and Norwich, a town wall constructed in stone served as much to express civic identity as to meet real needs of defence. Even more impressive as such statements were town gates. Architecturally elaborate and presenting images of the town's history and allegiances, they were focal points for ceremony, housed prisons and council chambers, and used to display the corpses (or parts of them) of executed rebels. Closed every night at curfew, when streets were patrolled by the watch, gates also symbolized the internal order of towns, while as the collecting points for tolls they represented for many incomers their first contact with town government.

After the twelfth century, England both was more peaceful and experienced lower rates of urban growth than many areas of Europe; hence, the defensive circuits of its towns were rarely extended in the dramatic fashion often evident overseas. Before 1200, however, such extensions were common. Walled or embanked circuits at York, Bristol, Coventry, and Gloucester underwent several phases of enlargement. Oxford's acquired a substantial addition and Northampton's more than doubled in area. At Hereford, in stages between the eighth and thirteenth century, the defended area increased almost fourfold, to over 90 acres. Expansion beyond a small defended nucleus could cause the commercial and administrative focus of the town to shift: at Northampton to the space where streets converged on a former gate, and at Hereford to the broad market street on the outer lip of a town ditch.

The castles imposed on towns in the wake of the Norman Conquest had a devastating impact, destroying streets, churches, and scores of houses. Often they were strategically placed with access to open country, adjoining an existing line of defence, and commanding approaches to the town by land or water. Their purpose was to control the townsmen and to safeguard the king's interests. The imposition of a castle could totally reorient the town. At Norwich the great market place of the new borough laid out for the Normans and Flemings who came with the Conqueror, and placed in the shadow of the castle on the edge of the large existing settlement, became the business focus of the city, a shift encouraged by the siting of the big new cathedral so as to strangle the old commercial centre. At Nottingham the castle occupied a prominence facing the strongly defended pre-Conquest borough. In the intervening space, which may have included a large extramural market, the 'French' borough was established, thus consolidating this area as the centre of the town, the whole of which was later enclosed by a new wall. Castles also served as nuclei for new urban growth, for many were centres of estate administration where produce was collected and distributed. At Banbury the wide market place opens out in front of the bishop of Lincoln's castle, and at Ludlow the High Street, a primary element in the town's plan, leads directly up to the castle gate. In their earlier phases castles could house substantial populations of men and animals and covered areas as large as a town's. Indeed, some small towns originated within castle enclosures, as was the case with Tonbridge, a regional estate centre of the powerful Clare family. With few exceptions, other than in border regions, urban castles lost their significance as royal residences and as centres of military power after the thirteenth century; but as seats of county government they performed important roles throughout the Middle Ages and beyond.

Streets and market places were the framework for circulation and the disposition of houses within towns. As open spaces they were subject to the lord of the town, but in practice tended to come under the collective control of the inhabitants. They could be deliberate creations or emerge by informal custom and use. In numerous towns both processes were present in varying degree. Many acts of town foundation, planning, and extension are recorded, and others can be inferred from regular features in street plans and property boundaries. There was great variety of form. In the larger towns laid out as centres of refuge and trade in the late ninth and tenth centuries, a wide central market street was common, with side streets running off at right angles, but not usually forming a true grid pattern; in addition, lanes served the backs of properties on the market street and both sides of the defences. These elements can be detected in parts of London's complex plan, and at Winchester, Oxford, and smaller towns. Market streets were also often the central or only element in the plans of the small towns founded during the twelfth and thirteenth centuries. At Bury St Edmunds the town outside the monastery gate was more than doubled in size soon after the Norman Conquest when the abbey authorities laid out a grid of streets on arable land: one of these rectangular blocks was devoted to a market place. Similar layouts, adapted to local topography, were deployed in new towns of the twelfth and thirteenth centuries. At Salisbury the bishop's new town, laid out after the cathedral had been moved to its valley bottom site in 1220, had a chequer pattern of streets, although it was some time before the whole of the newly planned area was built over. The block allocated to the market place covered about ten acres, almost a tenth of the city outside the cathedral close. At Salisbury, Winchester, and elsewhere the laying out of the streets involved major exercises in hydraulic engineering, creating and realigning streams and rivers to conform to the new grids. The burgesses of thirteenth-century Bristol were even more ambitious in their realignment of the River Frome so as to improve their harbour facilities.

Few market places were so large as Salisbury's in its original form. Even Nottingham's, later renowned as the largest in England, covered only six acres. The full length of Winchester High Street, the central element in its plan, offered just over three acres of trading space, about the same as Banbury's market place. At Winchester an additional market area was created by encroaching on to the cathedral cemetery. Many towns also had lesser market areas near town gates, both within and without, and extramural livestock markets were common. The two big market places at Lynn, serving tenurially distinct parts of the town, originally opened on to the river, but as land was reclaimed came to be enclosed on that side. London had the most complex set of market spaces, within streets, in enlarged spaces at street junctions, on the river frontage, and outside gates. Groups of markets specializing in everyday commodities such as corn, meat, and fish, were distributed so as to serve different quarters of the city. Specialization within and between market spaces was apparent in the larger towns by the twelfth century and came to be regulated by sets of by-laws designed to promote open dealing, to protect the interests of townspeople and outsiders trading at recognized sites, and to control the itinerant traders. At many of the smaller new towns market places were created by enlarging existing roads or streets, especially at junctions. A common form, as in front of the abbey of St Albans in the late tenth century, was that of a triangle with roads entering at the corners. Traffic was so important to urban prosperity that new towns were commonly sited on or near busy roads and junctions. Almost as often a road was diverted, either informally or by the deliberate act of a powerful lord, to bring business to the town and to the detriment of other places.

These public spaces, though regulated, were not unchanging. In many towns we can trace the addition of new streets and lanes, as the intensity of land use at the centre increased and as settlement expanded outwards. In thirteenth-century London, one 'new street' was a shopping development at the heart of the business district, while another opened up suburban fields between Holborn and Fleet Street. Such processes contributed to an 'organic' pattern of growth, but also involved conscious decisions by occupiers and landlords, and sometimes regulation by municipal authorities. The estate pattern of development, which played such a large part in the expansion of English towns from the seventeenth century onwards, had its predecessors. In 1086 a minor Lincolnshire landlord, Colswein, was said to have built 36 houses and two churches in a suburban part of Lincoln that had been unoccupied before. There were many such developers, both larger and smaller than Colswein. Before the fourteenth century they mostly used their urban estates as sources of rent, the occupants having responsibility for the

The coronation procession of Edward VI passing through Cheapside, London, in 1547; from an 18th-century copy of a contemporary painting now destroyed. Cheapside, the city's principal commercial and processional space, is shown juxtaposed to Tower Hill on the left. St Paul's, with its spire, correctly marks the west end of the street. The large square tower is that of the church of St Mary le Bow. On the street frontage next to it stands the substantial 13th-century stone house of Canterbury Cathedral Priory, in sharp contrast to the timber houses elsewhere in Cheapside. The king is about to pass the Great Cross, erected in memory of Queen Eleanor in 1296, and richly decorated goldsmiths' shops, the upper storeys of which are crowded with onlookers.

buildings; later, as land values fell and as towns adjusted to their smaller scale and to demands for better housing, landlords took a more active role.

Demand for buildings close to the main sites of trade also caused encroachment on to public space, a process which could radically alter the street scene. In many towns the entries to side streets leading off the principal street were reduced to a third of their original width by piecemeal encroachments from stalls or shops, already well advanced by 1100. The formation of religious precincts could, like castle building, dramatically interrupt the street network. Encroachment on to market places was often extensive. At Bury St Edmunds, Salisbury, and elsewhere much open space in the market was lost to rows of shops specialized by trade, which presumably replaced rows of temporary stalls. Sites in the market place were also occupied by public buildings such as market halls, courthouses, pillories, and prisons. Piecemeal encroachment, which made a useful addition to municipal revenues, continued into the nineteenth century through phases of decline as well as growth.

Principles of public benefit informed the management of streets. From the thirteenth century, and doubtless earlier, there were periodic campaigns to

*(**a** and **b**) Speculative housing of the 14th century. The York houses (**a**) were erected in or soon after 1315 along the street frontage of the parish cemetery of Holy Trinity Goodramgate, the 15th-century tower of which is just visible. The two-storey row probably at first contained 11 cottages, each with a ground floor area of about 190 square feet. The surviving houses have been much altered externally, but their timber frame is largely intact. Rent from the houses supported a chantry priest in the church. The row of cottages at Winchester (**b**), revealed by excavation, was erected at about the same date on the corner of Pancras Lane (right) and Tanner Street, next to the parish church of St Mary (left). Each unit occupied about the same area as its equivalent in Goodramgate. The external walls of clay and rubble probably supported a timber frame, while internal partitions were of clay and timber. Three of the units had identical internal plans, with a screen to the left of the door off the lane, a fire behind the screen, and an enclosed area, perhaps for sleeping, in the opposite corner. The unit next to the street, served by a water channel, was probably a workshop. If there was an upper storey, it would have been only partially floored, allowing smoke to escape through the roof. The Goodramgate houses perhaps had a similar internal arrangement. Houses such as these seem to have been occupied by artisan or labouring families. The poor endured much worse conditions.*

maintain the order and integrity of the space within the principal streets, which tended to become encumbered by stalls, fences, lean-tos, jettied upper storeys, projecting cellar steps, stacks of firewood, heaps of rubbish, and the frames used by smiths for shoeing horses, which were a special nuisance near town gates. Often such initiatives anticipated royal visits. During the great reform of London associated with Edward I's accession, the mayor swept away the permanent stalls obstructing Cheapside and provided at least some of the displaced traders with new stalls and a new market house on less central sites. Such incidents hint that the principal streets of towns served as processional routes as well as for ordinary traffic. By the early thirteenth century, the citizens of London certainly used their streets in that way on formal occasions, employing torches, music, and dancing, and decorating their house fronts with rich hangings. In the royal entries of the later Middle Ages, Cheapside played a prominent role, and by then had acquired monuments which formally divided its space and served as settings for pageants. In other towns, crafts and fraternities developed a processional culture, often associated with pageants and plays, culminating in the Corpus Christi procession which served as visible demonstration of the physical and social unity of the town. When such practices began is far from clear, but in cathedral and monastic towns there was a model at least as early as the tenth century in the liturgical processions associated with Easter and other festivals, whose routes and stations came to be marked by stone crosses in the streets and suburbs.

Patterns of Building

The plots of land on which houses were built varied in size and shape. Depths reflected local topography and the street layout, but widths are more revealing. By the early twelfth century the mean width of properties in Winchester High Street was about 30 feet, and wider in most side streets and in the suburbs. In

London's Cheapside in 1300 a common property width was between 20 and 30 feet, and it is possible to identify many properties which in the twelfth century had been around 100 feet in width, while blocks of land laid out at an earlier date were larger still. Contemporary perceptions of a standard urban pattern are indicated by evidence that in new towns of the twelfth and thirteenth centuries plots assigned for building commonly had frontage widths of between 33 and 66 feet. On the other hand, excavations in York, London, and elsewhere have revealed streets which in the tenth and eleventh centuries contained closely packed houses measuring between ten and fifteen feet on the frontage, sometimes with narrow passages between them. This contrast may reflect the social character of different neighbourhoods. At least one street immediately outside the wall of late thirteenth-century London was lined by small houses with ten-foot frontages, each a separate freehold with a narrow garden behind extending back 300 feet to the suburban boundary: their occupants perhaps cultivated vegetables for the city markets. However, it was equally likely that a plot frontage would be occupied by a row of small houses erected by the landlord who controlled the whole plot. By 1300 such rows, erected as single structures (a development perhaps facilitated by framing), were a standard feature of the urban scene. They generally contained no more than four or five units, but were sometimes much longer. Such houses, described as shops in the more commercial and densely settled neighbourhoods and as cottages elsewhere, represented high proportions of the urban housing stock. As land became scarce, they could be fitted into narrow spaces or built as encroachments in areas such as parish cemeteries. A row of cottages erected in a Winchester side alley during the early fourteenth century offered accommodation measuring only sixteen feet square on the ground floor, which was divided by earthen partitions; in addition there was perhaps a partially floored upper storey, allowing the smoke to escape through the roof. Contemporary shop houses in London could rise three, and sometimes more, storeys and accommodate several families. Houses of this type were common in later medieval towns, usually on busy corners and frontages.

In central districts plots and buildings came to be minutely divided, a process which could cause anxiety over the degeneration of neighbourhoods and loss of public revenue. By about 1100 it was noted in several towns that 'good' houses had been replaced by 'poor men'. Subdivision was greatest on the street frontage, where there was competition for trading space. These houses or shops tended to be higher than other buildings on the plot, rents from upper storeys being a means of meeting the high cost of the site. Often a gate on the frontage led into an alley where there might be one or more substantial houses, occupied by merchants or wholesalers who, unlike most shopkeepers, enjoyed the luxury of a yard or garden. Many of these larger houses included an imposing hall, which rose through two storeys and served as the social focus of the household and as the place where important business was done. Sometimes these houses also included rooms above the shops and overlooking the street. In the busiest areas, the rear part of the plot might be occupied by rows of small houses, built new or created by converting sheds or dividing existing houses. Units of accommodation were continually rearranged by joining or subdividing structures. This social flux contrasted with the relative stability of the fabric, the masonry elements of which, such as cellars and party walls, often perdured for centuries. Some plots subdivided in this way remained under the control of a single landlord, who if he lived at the rear might describe the houses on the frontage as his 'rents'. In the busiest neighbourhoods control was fragmented, both horizontally and vertically, generating a complex hierarchy of tenurial and monetary interests and of rights such as those governing access to rear or upper parts of the buildings. Uniformity of demand on frontages, masons' and carpenters' use of standard modules and techniques, and the durability of some structural features, generated physical patterns which were often remarkably regular and obscured the identity of the earlier land units within which they had emerged.

facing page: Housing, sex, and shopping in a 13th-century capital. The painting, from a mid-13th-century bible (made probably in Paris, but possibly in London), tells the story of David and Bathsheba. It contrasts the king's stone house with the wooden house, containing a shop on the ground floor, where Bathsheba is bathing. Narrow doors and shuttered windows, with projecting shelters over them, are described in many 13th-century records of shops. Placing Bathsheba in this setting is a clear allusion to the contemporary culture of shopping, in which the female shopkeeper was a powerful stimulus to trade but ran the risk of sexual assault.

The most visible part of the house was the shop, which in a principal street was primarily for retail trade, while in a side street manufacturing or processing predominated. By the thirteenth century there had emerged a distinctive urban

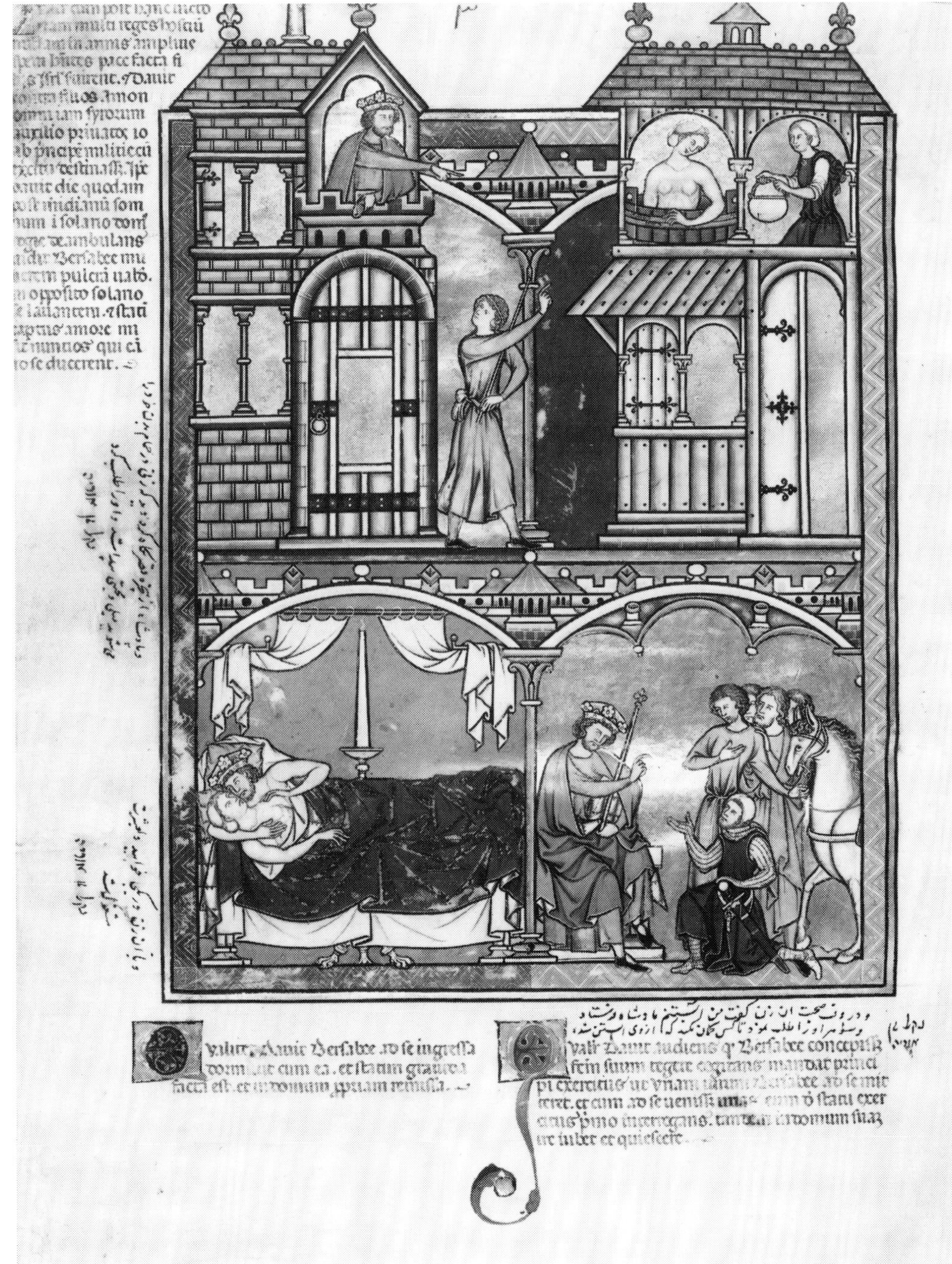

culture of shopping. Display and the desire to consume material goods were juxtaposed with the enticements of sexual exchange and possession. Women played a major role as stallholders and shopkeepers, both on their own account and within family businesses. In the busiest areas during the thirteenth and early fourteenth centuries shops were very small, sometimes with frontages of six feet or less, including doorways, and no deeper than twelve feet, while on corner sites they were smaller still. These shops were partitioned off within larger structures. Many shops may have been lock-ups run by people who lived elsewhere, but so minute were many retailing interests that traders probably often slept in the shop, as was common practice among apprentices at a later date. After 1350, when there was less pressure on space and the incomes of shopkeepers rose, shops became larger, but even in fifteenth-century London side streets shop houses were erected with frontages of less than eleven feet, rising through three storeys over a cellar, while their equivalents in Lavenham, Salisbury, Winchester, or York occupied more spacious sites. Where competition for trading space was very keen, the building immediately behind the shops, which elsewhere might be the hall of a substantial house, was used as a bazaar, providing sites for a score or more retail traders. In the Rows of Chester, and in similar but less extensive structures elsewhere, the demand for retail space was met by accommodating shops and stalls at two levels, on the street and in an upper walkway contained within the building. In these multilevel commercial environments on busy frontages the cellars, to which there was direct access from the street, were often used as wine taverns, high-class establishments for the entertaining which was an essential element in business and municipal life. Cellars towards the rear of properties were probably used more exclusively for storage. The provision of wine to the gentry of the hinterland was an important function of the larger towns.

Many cellars and stone houses surviving from the twelfth century and later were works of architectural quality, and demonstrate the value placed on environments which gave pleasure and attracted business. Timber structures were also treated decoratively, both inside and out. In smaller houses, this might involve the use of symmetrical framing on the façade and simple mouldings in the most important room. More substantial buildings on prime sites were elaborately carved and richly painted, with armorial designs, allusions to the owner's name or craft, and a religious or mythical iconography also apparent on churches and guildhalls. Particular attention was paid to the decoration of gates denoting the residence of important men in large houses off the street. Indeed, all doorways on the street had a special power as signifiers of the household, the primary social unit in town life and one which complemented the public system of order represented by municipal government. The direct presence of houses on the street, reflecting the underlying commercial dynamic and the intensity of land use, was an essential element in the urban landscape. In the case of small towns it probably served to distinguish them from villages virtually identical in plan but where houses were commonly set back behind ditches and fences. In town, house signs were used to attract attention and to serve as landmarks. The first buildings known to have been distinguished in this way were taverns and other drinking places, and the commercial inns which became prominent in busy centres from the mid-fourteenth century onwards. Before then shops were usually identified according to the name of the craft row in which they stood. Afterwards even shops acquired individual names and signs.

Social Topography and Land Use

The visible landscape was thus rich and legible. As Chrétien's portrayal demonstrates, much of its meaning derived from the commercial and social geography of the town, which in turn was shaped by the practice of business, by land values, and by natural topography. Street names tell us that the clustering of trades was recognizable by the end of the tenth century, although such groupings were rarely, if ever, exclusive. Some trades, such as dyers or fullers, had to settle in districts with plentiful supplies of water. Noxious or noisy trades, such as tanners, tallow melters, and several categories of metalworkers migrated, or were pushed, to the periphery. Dealers in high-value or manufactured goods such as spices, textiles, goldsmith's wares, and saddles occupied shops and houses in prime commercial locations on central streets. Such people, like those in provisioning trades, often clustered in specialized rows, because that both made their shops or stalls accessible to customers and facilitated collective supervision. Dealers in complex manufactured items such as saddles, weapons, and personal adornments often coordinated the activities of specialized artisans who made components, assembled, and decorated them. Artisans pursuing different crafts were often to be found grouped in 'communities of skill' in secondary locations close to the entrepreneurs who dealt in the final product. The numerous textile trades were distributed in that way, while some artisans, including wiredrawers and founders, supplied components for many different products. Streets could thus resemble assembly lines.

Social topography was shaped by commerce and production. Shopkeepers and artisans occupied street frontages. Merchants, who required more space but not such constant access to the street, occupied more remote sites. The working poor lived out of the way, in alleys, upper rooms, and the fringes of town. In the larger towns the fringes were perhaps too remote from markets and hiring places for all but the unemployed, the disabled, and those carters, drovers, gardeners, and tanners whose trade suited a suburban environment. Often, the complexity of the markets in labour and goods caused rich and poor to live in close proximity, but in distinctive niches. Even so, neighbourhoods can be characterized broadly according to their social composition. Single women and widows were prominent among the residents of predominantly poor areas. Marginal districts contained concentrations of beggars, especially close to town gates. They were associated with prostitution and related services, including bathhouses. London's thirteenth-century bathhouses were on the river frontage, where they were frequented by the traders, mariners, and porters who crowded the quays, as well as by priests and others from within the city. Later, many town authorities attempted to remove prostitutes from intramural areas, and in the case of London to keep them across the river in Southwark. In those larger cities where landed magnates resided from time to time, their houses were usually on the edge of the built-up area: they valued space, air, and access to open country, and could afford to keep their distance from trade. Extremes of wealth and poverty were juxtaposed.

In some commercial centres those born outside the kingdom formed a significant proportion of the population, perhaps as much as 10 per cent in the case of London. The majority came from the Low Countries and the Rhineland: linguistically close to the English they included labourers and craftsmen as well as merchants, and there was a regular traffic of such people to and fro across the sea.

Normans, Frenchmen, Gascons, and Italians were also present in certain towns. Overall the immigrants settled in neighbourhoods suiting their specific economic interests and wealth. Merchants were perhaps the most conspicuous, but some poor immigrants formed linguistically distinct clusters. In a few towns place names denoted the presence of foreigners, although it was in fairs rather than in towns that street names reflected the origins of traders. German merchants, from the mid-thirteenth century organized through the Hanse of German towns, had enjoyed special privileges in England since before the Conquest and so in a unique fashion came collectively to control houses in Boston, King's Lynn, and London, the latter two of which became small but distinctive enclaves. Between about 1100 and their expulsion in 1290, communities of Jews at some time lived in most of the larger and many of the smaller towns. Their concern with finance drew them to certain districts, where their legal status, need for protection, dietary requirements, and exclusive places of worship caused them to form especially dense clusters. Of all ethnic groups, Jews had the strongest impact on street names, but even within their streets Jews had many Christian neighbours.

Land on the periphery of towns was commonly devoted to the cultivation of crops for which there was a distinctive urban demand or which could not be carried far to market: vegetables, apples, pears, vines, 'industrial crops' such as madder and teasels, and, later, saffron, hops, and woad. Suburban meadows and pasture were valued for grazing cattle and horses. In this same peripheral zone were limekilns and pits for digging chalk or gravel. Closer in were the tenter yards and bleaching grounds used by textile workers. The immediate hinterland was also a recreational territory, used for hunting, gathering, horse racing, and tournaments, and for visiting springs, hilltops, and country shrines. It was in such a setting that William fitzStephen placed London when he described it in the 1170s. As towns contracted during the later Middle Ages such activities moved closer to the centre. Early fifteenth-century Winchester, still a city of 5,000 inhabitants, contained barns within its walls and in the suburbs which were the focal points of agricultural enterprises run by citizens who also had interests in trade and industry. Sheep grazed intramural closes and the city ditch, and damaged the city walls by crowding over them. Animals always represented a large element in urban populations. Butchers kept dogs, for baiting bulls as well as droving cattle, and others kept them for hunting and to guard the house. Many households kept pigs, and some kept oxen, cows, and goats. Pigs which had broken out of their sties were a general nuisance and a particular danger to small children: in crowded central areas pig-keeping was normally forbidden. Poultry was also a common problem, wandering the cornmarket, fouling the streets, and invading neighbours' gardens. Certain neighbourhoods, generally in out-of-the-way backstreets, specialized in stabling horses. The rich organic fabric of towns and their varied microclimates sustained exceptionally dense and varied insect populations, and provided a home for countless rats and mice.

Public Buildings and Churches

Craft, mercantile, and ruling groups in some larger towns already had guildhalls in the eleventh and twelfth centuries. Such buildings were elaborated and enlarged as municipal institutions and communities became more clearly articulated from 1200 onwards, and in some cases they ended up as major monuments. Guildhalls housed fraternal and convivial meetings, as well as those concerned with municipal politics and administration. Larger assemblies of townsmen had designated meeting places, often outdoors in a churchyard. More routine meetings of a town's courts—concerned with debts, by-laws, public order, and property rights—were formally supervised by representatives of the town's lord and were often held in a building associated with the lord's authority. The complexity and fluidity which characterized the structures of power within towns, were mirrored in the use of secular public buildings. Many guildhalls lacked long continuous histories; churches were often used as guild meeting places and for civic ceremonies; and hospitals founded or adopted by civic communities sometimes also housed civic meetings and administration. Thus at Salisbury the routine administration of the town focused on the 'bishop's guildhall', containing a prison, at one end of the market place, while the citizens had their 'council house' at the other. At Winchester the mayor and bailiffs ran the 'king's court of the city', at a building fronting on to the busiest part of High Street, which had once been a gatehouse of the royal palace and was later known as the guildhall or prison of the city, while assemblies of citizens met in the hall of St John's Hospital, at the far end of High Street.

In some towns bridges were among the most important public buildings. London Bridge, with its nineteen arches, drawbridge, chapel, and rows of fine houses, was one of the wonders of medieval Europe, and its reconstruction in the twelfth century was a collective effort which did much to consolidate the communal identity of the citizens. Bristol bridge, constructed as part of the realignment of the River Frome, was of comparable significance in the history of that town.

One of the most striking features of towns large and prosperous before 1100 was their numerous small parish churches, usually founded by landlords, wealthy householders, or groups of neighbours. Even in the eleventh century their towers were prominent on urban skylines. London had over 100 parish churches, the four second-ranking cities about 50, and others in proportion. New ideas concerning church provision meant that even major towns which came to the fore subsequently, such as Coventry or Salisbury, had many fewer parish churches. In those towns the parish churches came to be enlarged on a scale greater than in the older centres. The multiple altars of those spacious churches served the needs of particular groups of townspeople as the multiple churches did elsewhere. With the contraction of urban populations, many small parish churches were lost, except in London, while those that remained continued to be enlarged as before. In cities with powerful mother churches, the parish churches often lacked full parochial rights, most notably rights of burial and a cemetery. In such cases, the dead were generally buried at the common cemetery of the mother church. From the fourteenth century onwards urban parishes became a more powerful force in the articulation of neighbourhood identity, and parishioners sought to extend the rights of their churches, many of which then acquired cemeteries for the first time. Thus, in the life of all towns at the end of the period, parish churches were more prominent than before.

In most large towns parish churches were overshadowed by cathedrals, priory churches, and commonly by friars' churches. The contrast in scale, and hence in the resources which underpinned the two types of building and institution, was probably most extreme during the twelfth century. Cathedral and abbey churches exceeded probably all but the largest castles as urban building projects. In 1300 the aggregate volume of Winchester's 50 or so parish churches could have been accommodated within that of the cathedral, while in London St Paul's, whose height and bulk was a matter of local pride, would perhaps have accommodated about half the city's parish churches. The proportion of ground occupied by religious precincts was very large. At Winchester soon after 1300 the south-eastern quarter of the walled area was taken up by the cathedral precinct and cemetery (including the site of the former royal palace), the bishop's palace, and St Mary's Abbey. In addition, there were two large friary precincts within the walls, plus two more friaries, an abbey, and a college in the suburbs outside the walls, where another college was to be added later in the century. This was an extreme case, but in several lesser cities and towns the prevalence of ecclesiastical space was similar, and even in London religious precincts took up much of the extramural suburbs and a good deal of land just inside the walls. At the two university towns of Oxford and Cambridge from the end of the thirteenth century onwards colleges took over ever larger parts of what had once been populous commercial districts.

During the twelfth and thirteenth centuries townsmen and women played an increasingly important role, along with the crown, magnates, and bishops, in the foundation and support of religious establishments in towns, notably hospitals for the travellers, the destitute, and the sick. Hospitals and almshouses, often on the edge of town, thus became a distinctive element in urban landscapes. Leper hospitals, no less an urban phenomenon, were set well out in the country. Also isolated, but linked with the city, were the hermits and anchoresses who lived on or adjacent to town walls.

The concentration of religious buildings in towns testifies to the power of urban culture to mobilize the resources of a wider society. An important element in that culture was the visible contrast between the accessibility of certain sites of devotion, such as parish churches, and the closure of the walled precincts. In the midst of, and often overshadowing, a busy secular environment, the pursuit of cosmographic and theocratic ideals, isolation from the mundane and the polluted, and reminders of the wilderness, all had a special power.

Urban Penalties

Executions in the market place, the gallows at or beyond the suburban limit, pillories, and prisons, were exemplary signs of urban systems of order and control. Moreover, as centres of wealth and defence, towns were often the select victims of violence and destruction during times of warfare and political trouble. Internal violence also found routine expression in attacks on ethnic and religious minorities, and in conflicts between rival political, economic, and family groups. Violence had special roots in urban ways of life, as the citizens of London recognized soon after 1200 when they claimed to be exempt from taking oaths before certain enquiries on the grounds that 'they are housed closely together and are more crowded both early and late than other people', and that to swear against a neighbour might lead to killing, 'both at their drinking and at other times'. The sole disadvantages of London life, according to fitzStephen, were the frequent fires and the immoderate drinking of fools. Great fires were soon to be contained, but drinking remained and was a universal force in the urban landscape of fear.

The intensity of town life was also the cause of pollution and disease. Practically nothing is known of the normal rate of mortality, but in the larger towns, with problems of water supply and sewage disposal, it was certainly high, and it was possible to maintain populations only by migration from the countryside. Contemporaries remarked about epidemics, but the practice of sanitary regulation shows that a concern for offensive smells and rotten foodstuffs was informed

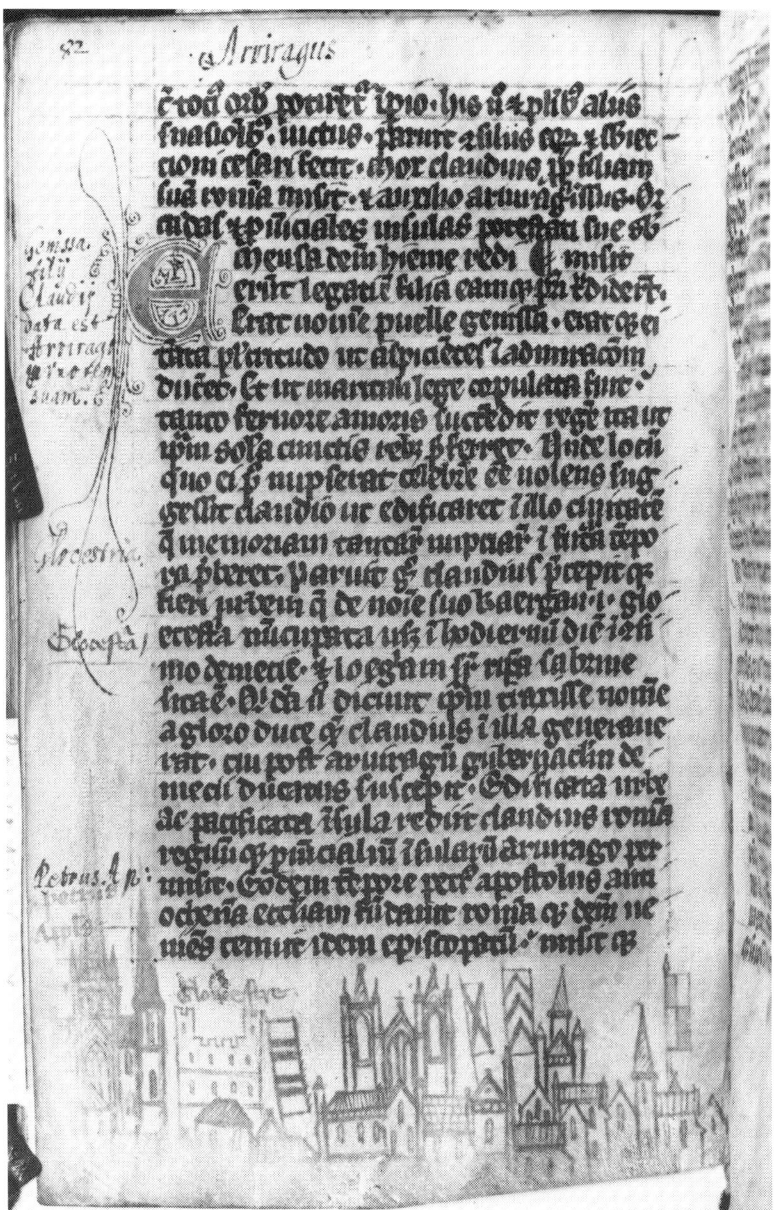

Gloucester in the early to mid-14th century. One of several sketches of British towns added to a manuscript of Geoffrey of Monmouth's 'History of the Kings of Britain'. From left to right, it appears to show the west front of St Peter's Abbey (now the cathedral) with the crossing tower and spire begun in 1222; the strong keep of the castle; and a townscape dominated by church towers and banners.

by a belief that they contributed to the spread of disease. Visual pollution, in the form of blood and entrails and of rubbish deposited in illicit places, was also a common urban problem. There was a concern too for the problem of noise and for the air that people breathed. Firewood, produced commercially within a few miles of the town, was used sparingly, and was not usually seen as polluting, but by 1300 mineral coal was used in some towns with supplies close at hand, especially for industrial purposes such as lime burning. Moreover, London had grown so big that it depended heavily on coal shipped from Newcastle: its smoke and smell polluted the capital and were seen as a danger to health.

Perceptions of medieval towns were thus fraught with a tension between on the one hand their role as sites of opportunity, of beauty, and of social and spiritual order, and on the other their manifest squalor, both material and moral which, though it appealed to many, put body and soul at risk. Universal features of town life, in England these elements of the urban landscape were very largely generated between the tenth and the early fourteenth century and as physical forms or learned patterns of behaviour still underpin the urban landscape today.

4 Early Modern Urban Landscapes, 1540–1800

Peter Borsay

Continuity and Change

The starting-point for any understanding of the early modern townscape is its inherently historic character. Whatever the forces for change in this period, and there were many, they acted on a physical environment that had been formed over several centuries, and whose very existence imposed severe constraints on alteration. The Tudor citizen lived in an essentially medieval town; and in some respects and in some places, the same could still be argued for his Georgian successor. Continuity exerted its influence in a number of ways. The 'natural' landscape was a persistent and intractable element. Hills could not be shifted, nor rivers and shorelines easily restructured; these were the givens—the limitations and the opportunities—with which new development had to cope. It remained a matter of profound importance to Shaftesbury, Shrewsbury, and Brighton that they were respectively hill, river, and coastal settlements. A given of another sort was the underlying morphology of street and plot configuration. This may have been laid down deliberately, or emerged organically, but the odds are that it would have been in place long before the sixteenth century. The ground plan of early modern Hereford, for example, was in essence determined during the Saxon and Norman phases of the city's development. Inherited also were patterns of corporate and individual landownership, which could severely restrict the scope for large-scale modification of the urban form. Potentially the most malleable feature of the landscape was the stock of buildings, but even this proved surprisingly durable. Property demolition was a radical and expensive proposition. A more practical option, where change was desired, was to modify an existing structure, perhaps in the case of a house refronting the façade, but leaving the less prestigious and public areas untouched. Even where a building became functionally redundant, as with monasteries after the Reformation, some of the original fabric could be retained and put to other uses. So at Malmesbury the nave of the abbey was converted into the parish church, and in 1542 Leland reported of the claustral buildings (purchased by a local clothier), 'at the

Assembly Rooms (1731–c.1733), York. Designed by Lord Burlington, the leading artistic patron of the day, its colonnaded 'Egyptian Hall' was among the most advanced Palladian buildings in the country, and confirmed York's status as the social capital of the North.

present tyme every corner of the vaste Houses of Office ... be fulle of lumbes to weve cloth yn'. At York the residence of the abbot of St Mary's became the headquarters of the Council in the North, and after its dissolution in the 1640s served a mixture of functions, including that of school and assembly rooms.

Physical continuity owed something to the well-established structure of the urban system in England. Intensive expansion of towns during the twelfth and thirteenth centuries, and then the dramatic collapse in population after the Black Death, ensured that there was a more than adequate stock of urban centres to service the requirements of early modern England. Between 1500 and 1800 there was little need, with a few exceptions, to add new settlements to the 600 or so towns which were inherited. A consequence of this was that growth, where it occurred, was usually accommodated within or attached to a pre-existing urban form, with the inevitable constraints that this imposed. Also inherited was an established hierarchy of centres. At the apex was the national capital, London; below were a series of provincial capitals—Norwich, Bristol, Newcastle, Exeter, and York—followed by a corpus of regional centres, such as the county towns; at the bottom lay the mass of small market towns and ports that made up the vast bulk of the system.

This hierarchy, particularly among its upper echelons, possessed an inherent resilience. However, powerful as were the forces of continuity, they faced similarly strong pressures for change, which were to have a lasting impact on the urban landscape. Urbanization was a pervasive influence. In the 1520s between one and two in ten of the population of England lived in towns; by 1800 this had risen to almost four in ten. Many of the centres involved were, by modern standards, only tiny places. But this could hardly be argued of the most important single engine of early modern urbanization, London. Between 1500 and 1800 it was transformed from a modest European city of around 50,000 inhabitants (or 2 per cent of England's population) to a global capital of almost a million souls (or 10 per cent of the country), ranking alongside Edo (Tokyo) and Peking (Beijing) as the world's three greatest metropolises. London's explosive growth did not of itself upset the urban hierarchy in England; it simply reinforced the status quo of the capital's dominance. However, from the late seventeenth century a shake-up was underway in the traditional urban order, as—well before the onset of the Industrial Revolution—small but economically dynamic centres such as Liverpool, Manchester, and Birmingham experienced vigorous expansion; by 1750 the trio were already among the top six provincial towns.

Urbanization was the product of a series of economic, social, and political developments, the most important of which was the growing internal integration of Britain, at the same time as the nation's increasing external integration into European and global trading networks. To assess the impact of these changes on the physical form of towns, it is helpful to conceptualize the built environment as a matrix of five landscapes; private, public, economic, cultural, and mental. No claim is being made that these are the only categories that can be deployed, or that each is self-sufficient. Any one building, such as a town hall—with its inner private rooms, its function as a stage for public events, its use for marketing, its accommodation of recreation and ritual, and its symbolic function—might embrace all. But the categories do provide a useful gauge for assessing the impact of change on the template of continuity.

The Private Landscape

For early modern English townspeople there was no easy demarcation between the private and public spheres of their lives. On the contrary, the period saw significant shifts in the boundary between the two. But there were experiences and spaces that were *more* private and *more* public than others. Predominant among the former would have been the domestic realm and its physical seat, the house. It was argued by W. G. Hoskins that under the later Tudors and early Stuarts the domestic fabric, both in town and country, underwent a major reconstruction; what he called 'the Great Rebuilding'. More recent research has demonstrated the existence of a second great rebuild, quantitatively more important, that began under the later Stuarts and rolled into the eighteenth century. It may be more realistic to think of a continuous but phased process of reconstruction, whose impact varied regionally and socially, during which the urban home was subject to three major changes; in organization, building materials, and style.

The late sixteenth- and early seventeenth-century building boom deployed traditional vernacular building practices and materials, with the widespread use of timber framing, wattle and daub infilling, thatch, earth, rubble stones, and jettying—the process by which an upper floor was pushed out over the one below it. However, the interior of the house was fundamentally reorganized, with a shift away from the medieval open hall house, to a much greater subdivision and differentiation of space through the insertion of partitions, ceilings, and staircases. Accompanying this was a growing emphasis on comfort, with the widespread introduction of fireplaces, chimneys, window glass, and curtains, and a growing sophistication in household consumer products. Taken together these trends point to an increasing privatization and commercialization of the household. Outside the home communal contacts declined in significance, while within it a corporate lifestyle was undermined by the greater opportunities for individualized living. These changes can be deduced not only from surviving physical evidence, but also from the inventories drawn up after a person died, which sometimes list in remarkable detail, and on a room-by-room basis, the contents of the deceased's house. So the home of William Wilkox, a walker (cloth fuller) in Worcester, included in 1577 a hall, parlour, four chambers, a kitchen, two shops, and a stable; and among the contents of the property were '5 flower cupps', '4 candlstickes', '3 foote of glas and a frame to it', '1 quission [cushion] and 2 outesides of quissions', and 'paynted clothes' in three of the rooms. Eighty years later a Lichfield apothecary's residence included a hall, parlour, several chambers, buttery, kitchen, dayhouse, brewhouse, barn and stable, cellar, shop, and warehouse; and among his possessions were 8 cushions, 16 books, 6 leather chairs, a looking-glass, 28 pieces of pewter, and 18 spoons.

It was from the late seventeenth century that a range of new building materials—brick, tile, and ashlar or freestone—began to have a major impact on urban housing. Vernacular materials did not disappear overnight, and there was a variety of ruses that could be adopted to ape the new fashions. In 1698 Celia Fiennes noted of Norwich, 'their building timber and they playster on laths which they strike out into squares like broad freestone on the outside, which makes their fronts look pretty well'. She went on to add that none of the houses was of brick 'except some few beyond the river which are built of some of the rich factors [merchants] like the London buildings', an indication of two of the driving forces behind change, the example of post-fire London and the expanding middling orders. The switch to different building materials underpinned a radically new approach to house design, which affected not only the way but also the style in which a building was constructed. In the place of vernacular architecture, with its stress on the local and the pragmatic, came classicism, an international and highly theoretical style, drawn from the Graeco-Roman world, and mediated through the Renaissance. Proportion and symmetry were the underlying principles of the new architectural language, while the five orders provided the basic ornamental vocabulary. Where there was space and money available, owners built anew; where cash was more limited the jettied timber-framed front might simply be ripped off and replaced with an elegant single-plane brick façade, filled with symmetrically arranged sash windows, and adorned with some tasteful classical ornament, such as a pilastered and pedimented doorcase. Over time refronting could transform the appearance of the townscape. Broad Street, Ludlow looks like an archetypal brick Georgian street. Yet though only seven buildings have timber-framed frontages, another 22 are almost entirely timber-framed to the rear, and eight others have incorporated large portions of timber framing into eighteenth-century houses. The spread of classicism was greatly facilitated by the production of printed architectural manuals and pattern-books. These encouraged a standardized approach to design. But although classicism was a universal language it was not a static one, and the manuals were powerful tools in creating and disseminating new stylistic variations—baroque, palladian, rococo, neoclassical (and even a Gothic revival by the later eighteenth century)—by which the wheel of fashion was kept turning.

Ireland's Mansion, the High Street, Shrewsbury (c.1560s). A product of the first 'Great Rebuilding' of English towns, it was erected by a wealthy merchant family who retained part as a town residence, and rented out the ground-floor shops, cellars, and remaining chambers.

Yet fashion, a key element in establishing social norms and codes, is a public phenomenon. Conforming to its dictates necessarily compromised the private character of the house. This would be a willing compromise for most owners since they would be only too aware that parts of their homes functioned as a critical interface with the public sphere. The hall and parlour—and by the eighteenth century drawing room and dining room—might be used to receive and entertain visitors and guests, and would need to be designed and decorated accordingly. Above all, it was the façade that constituted the public face of the house. This was an unavoidable advertisement as to how an owner or occupier wished to be perceived in local society. To possess a frontage that was out of vogue could have a debilitating impact on social position and status. The ornate and exuberant timber carving and patterning on the fronts of Tudor merchants' houses—such as the Ireland's Mansion (*c.*1560s) at Shrewsbury or 225–6 High Street Exeter (probably built in 1567)—were thus a necessary tool in establishing social identity. The transition to classicism accentuated and accelerated the whole process, since the contrast between the old and new styles was so radical. Hence aspiring townsmen tore down the fronts of their vernacular houses with such facility, though leaving the concealed portions to the rear relatively untouched.

The pressure to use domestic architecture to express status varied directly with a citizen's social position. For the poor, and the early modern town contained huge wedges of people in this category, survival rather than social kudos was the priority. Little obvious now remains of the property occupied by this social group, so that it is difficult to recover the nature of the accommodation involved. But in all probability space would have been at a premium, both internally and externally, with the occupants limited to a few rooms, and the premises tucked away in narrow, closely packed alleys and courtyards. The innovations described above would have come slowest to this class of property, which often possessed no more than one hearth and sparse interior furnishings, and witnessed a continued use of traditional building materials that carried a higher risk from dampness, fire, and disease. The onset of rapid industrialization and urban growth in the eighteenth century must have placed pressure on the stock of working-class housing, and, in traditional towns, encouraged the trend towards burgage infilling and the development of court dwellings. In Liverpool court and cellar dwellings were already becoming a problem, but in general it appears unlikely that there was a serious deterioration in the situation before 1800 (even in future shock cities like Leeds), and the classic slum is essentially a nineteenth-century phenomenon. The same cannot quite be said of the suburb. Crudely put, the early modern norm was for the better-off to occupy the urban centre and the poor the outskirts. Evidence of this was provided by the higher levels of mortality suffered by peripheral parishes during Tudor and Stuart plague epidemics, as the richer citizens in the central areas fled the town. But this pattern of social zoning was already being seriously disrupted in post-Restoration London with the emergence of handsome villas on the edge of the metropolis, and the rapid expansion of the West End with its classical terraces and squares. In the eighteenth century such trends can be traced in many of the larger towns, like Bath (Lansdown and Bathwick), Bristol (Clifton), and Newcastle. We are not yet in the world of the classic Victorian suburb, but the centrifugal tendency of the middling orders is already evident.

225–226 (probably 1567), and 227 (mid-17th century), High Street, Exeter. Grand five-storeyed merchant houses, timber-frame in construction, with ornately decorated jettied and gabled façades, designed to demonstrate the wealth and prestige of their owners.

Eighteenth-Century Bath

PETER BORSAY

Bath was one of the boom towns of eighteenth-century England. In 1700 it was a small urban centre of between 2,000 and 3,000 people. By 1800 it possessed 33,000 inhabitants and was about the tenth largest town in Britain. In 1700 it had the appearance of a well-built but vernacular Cotswold town, its compact physical form largely contained within medieval walls, the whole tucked into a loop of the Avon. By 1800 the old city was but one fragment of a settlement whose suburban limbs had sprawled northwards into the surrounding hills of Lansdown, and had recently crossed the river to establish a new residential district—Bathwick—to the east. Initially the driving force behind development was the provision of polite medicinal and recreational services, as Bath became the leading spa in Britain. But during the later Georgian period, when the city's population expanded dramatically, it shifted from being primarily a resort for temporary visitors to a place of permanent fashionable residence. The vast majority of those who constituted Bath's growing population were working people, employed (if they could obtain jobs) in servicing the well-off, or in the emerging industrial sector. The courtyard dwellings and workshops, clustering in the southern and western areas of the city close to the river—some of which, such as Avon Street, were later to acquire the status of slums—were not part of the public image of Bath; nor was much attention paid to the simple terracing constructed to house the more skilled sectors of the workforce. What was part of the spa's consumer profile, and filled the guides and views produced, were textual and visual representations of the spectacular resortscape produced over a century to satisfy the aspirations of the nation's elite. Classicism was the dominant architectural language deployed, but variations in this followed—and sometimes led—the national shifts in style, and by 1800 the Gothic revival was having an impact, particularly in the case of church building. It is the shared vocabulary of classicism, and the repetition of certain built forms—especially the terrace and crescent—rather than the execution of any master plan, which gave the townscape its powerful sense of homogeneity. The architecture which resulted embodied, and enacted, specific aspirations. For consumers multi-dwelling buildings with palace-like façades, such as Queen Square (1728–36) and

the Royal Crescent (1767–74), mixed the Enlightenment public ideal of a corporate lifestyle, with their private ambition to pursue and express status. The elevated terraces and crescents built in the later Georgian period, with their fine views over the city and into the countryside, were also part of a growing urban awareness and celebration of nature. For those designing, producing, financing, selling, renting, and maintaining the buildings the urban fabric

Aerial view of Queen Square (bottom centre, 1728–36), the Circus (1754–8), and the Royal Crescent (1767–74), Bath. Built by John Wood father and son as fashionable residential accommodation, they combined sociability and status, and set the architectural agenda for the city's expansion.

was an economic resource, generating huge flows of capital and income. Architects and residents may also have seen this fabric recreating a vision of the past. Predominantly this would have been one of antiquity, and in particular of Rome. In the case of the Circus (1754–8), modelled apparently on the Colosseum, the connection seemed obvious. However, for its designer John Wood—the foremost architect of early Georgian Bath—the inspiration was also Stonehenge and Stanton Drew, for he believed that in building Bath he was engaged in reconstructing a great ancient British Druidical city founded by King Bladud.

The Public Landscape

Classical architecture may have been used as a vehicle to express social distinction, but it was also widely admired in an urban context for its emphasis upon uniformity. The universal rules and vocabulary of the language, even given stylistic variations, highlighted the qualities shared by different structures. In this sense it echoed the Enlightenment stress on the common perfectibility of man, and can be seen as a means for nurturing a sense of corporate public consciousness. The street acquired, over time, a greater physical coherence, culminating in the development of the uniform terrace. The street had long acted as the basic urban unit of public space, the point at which the private and the communal spheres coincided. In the streets, or in their social annexe the alehouse, neighbours would fraternize and transact local business. The space would accommodate a whole range of commercial, recreational, and ritualistic activities.

Whitehaven, painted by Matthias Read (1736). Developing rapidly from the later 17th century, exporting locally mined coal and imported tobacco, it was laid out to a highly regular plan by the Lowther family, and included one of the earliest provincial squares (centre).

Reproduced by kind permission of Copeland Borough Council and The Beacon, Whitehaven

Moreover, thoroughfares were of course the town's circulatory system, the channels through which the lifeblood of the community—agricultural produce, raw materials, manufactured goods, consumers, and visitors—would be carried to and from the cells of production, service, and sale.

Blockage or damage to the street was the equivalent of an urban heart attack or stroke. Hence town authorities were assiduous in the attention they paid to the condition of thoroughfares. In 1653 the Court Leet at Preston presented several persons who 'fetched sand in the Lane leadinge to the North Moor yate, and have made a great hole to the annoyance of the highway', Anne Ingham who 'hath made middinge or dunghill in the street at the Church gate barres, to the annoyance of the highways', and William Shaw and his mother who 'suffreth his Timber to lye in ye open street, att ye white market, called ye Butter Crosse, to ye Disturbance of Passengers and people wch come to ye market'. Maintaining the street, and safeguarding its effectiveness, was a perpetual headache in early modern towns. Frequently responsibility for cleansing and repair lay in the hands of the householders who occupied the street, leaving the system highly vulnerable to personal whim. All too often the road was seen as a convenient storage space for goods or dumping ground for domestic waste products. What exacerbated the problem was the mounting pressure placed on the intra-urban network by increasing commercial and recreational activity, and the development of larger wheeled vehicles such as the coach. By the eighteenth century action in the medium and larger size towns was a necessity, and a package of measures—involving paving, cleansing, widening, clearance of obstructing buildings, and street lighting—was introduced, albeit in an often piecemeal fashion. By 1800 these measures, which had been emerging over a long period of time, had become absorbed into a self-conscious programme of civic improvement, prefiguring the Victorian obsession with this ideal. Change was facilitated by a flurry of local Acts of Parliament. Some of these established new organs of administration, most notably the improvement commissions. The first was that set up in 1725 for St James's Square in London, the first provincial body that for Salisbury in 1737; by the end of the century 160 commissions had been founded. These changes were not simply of a practical and bureaucratic nature. They also contributed to a redefinition of the boundary between private and public. Many of the new measures effectively shifted direct responsibility for the thoroughfares away from the householder—who would have to pay rates to be relieved of the burden—to bodies accountable to the town. Whereas previously the street had, in a sense, been an adjunct to the adjoining house, it now became more obviously public space, over which individuals exercised few private rights.

The status of the public landscape was further enhanced by the emergence of elements of town planning. As an influence on English urban development planning had been largely dormant since the fourteenth century. The twin thrusts behind change came from the expansion of London and the rise of classicism. Inigo Jones's Covent Garden, erected in the 1630s, was the precursor of a rash of classically designed squares constructed in the fashionable West End of London after the Restoration. The provinces followed suit from the very end of the seventeenth century, with the earliest squares at Whitehaven, Warwick, Bristol, Birmingham, and Manchester. What the square represented was an attempt to subsume the individual dwelling in a larger urban structure, which enclosed a shared interior space. As such it embodied the idea of a corporate architecture.

The logical extension of this approach was comprehensive town planning. After the Fire of London in 1666 a number of schemes were drafted to reconstruct the burnt area to a geometric design aping the ideal of the Renaissance city. These all proved abortive, but the rebuilding Acts imposed simple but important common standards which ensured that a measure of uniformity was achieved. In the

Fire and the Early Modern Townscape

PETER BORSAY

In Britain today fire is not a major urban problem. Minor domestic incidents are a persistent if not necessarily frequent occurrence, and very occasionally these escalate into harrowing personal tragedies. But the conflagration rarely, if ever, spreads beyond the domestic or work unit in which it originates. This was not the case in the early modern period, when fire was a remorseless engine of destruction and creation, capable of engulfing whole portions of a town, and posing a constant and serious threat to people's livelihood. Four factors account for the relative vulnerability of towns at this time. First and foremost were the highly inflammable building materials, associated with vernacular architecture, which were widely in use; timber (for structural framing as well as windows, doors, and internal features), wattle and daub, plaster, and—riskiest of all—thatch, the most common roofing cover. Non-flammable materials were to prove vital not just in discouraging the start of incidents, but even more significantly in preventing their spread. Only with the widespread deployment of brick and tile from the late 1600s did effective fire barriers appear. Second, the close-packed character of urban housing made towns more vulnerable than villages, and the combined presence of narrow thoroughfares and jettying pemitted flames to travel easily across street space. Third, the domestic use of fire, particularly where this involved an open hearth, and the presence in (or attached to) the household of trades which extensively employed fire, such as smiths and candlemakers, posed a major threat. Fourth, very limited piped water supplies allied to primitive fire-fighting services and technology made it difficult to control and contain incidents. A further factor, not peculiar to the early modern town, also played an important part; the weather. Long hot dry summers would turn the urban fabric into a tinderbox, and a high wind could instigate the doomsday scenario of aerial firebombs, as pieces of burning thatch were flung across the town, starting a host of minor fires that gelled into a major conflagration. Large scale incidents were by no means uncommon, in some cases devastating a substantial section of the landscape. Norwich was said to have lost over 700 dwellings in 1507, Tiverton 400 in 1598 (and a further 290 in 1612), Northampton 600 in 1675, Blandford Forum 337 in 1731, and the Great Fire of London in 1666 was estimated to have burnt around 13,000 houses. Whilst the precise details of these claims should be treated with a good deal of caution, there can be no hiding the short term impact of the events. Loss of life was probably rare, but the damage to property, household goods, raw materials, work tools, and premises, could be devastating, disrupting the economic livelihood of the individuals affected—and of the entire community, in the case of an extensive fire—and plunging them into a state of dependence and possibly poverty. The medium and longer term effects are less clear. In the case of a town already in economic difficulties, it could accelerate a process of physical and commercial decline. But in other cases, especially where the fortunes of an urban centre were on the up and finance was easily available, reconstruction could provide a spur to development. There would be heavy investment in the building industry, and where the town took advantage of the opportu-

reconstruction after the Fire of Warwick in 1694 a more concerted plan was introduced, primarily because the local magnate—Lord Brooke at the Castle—placed his full weight behind the scheme. The same was the case at Whitehaven where the Lowther family oversaw the construction of what was virtually a new town, drawing heavily, as at Warwick, on the example of post-fire London. In the eighteenth

Woodcut of the fire at Tiverton in 1612, in which reputedly 290 dwellings were burnt. The illustration shows attempts to control and contain the conflagration using buckets of water to dampen the ignited thatch, and fire hooks to dismantle all or part of the building.

nity to rebuild in the most fashionable manner, then its appeal to well-off consumers, visitors, and residents could be greatly enhanced. Such was the case at Warwick after its major fire in 1694, where—with the introduction of classicism—the image of the town was transformed, prompting Defoe to declare it in his guide 'now rebuilt in so noble and so beautiful a manner, that few towns in England make so fine an appearance'.

century completely new towns were a rarity, but the addition of planned units to existing settlements was not uncommon, ranging from utilitarian schemes like those directed at supplying workers' housing for the naval dockyards (Portsea and Devonport) or an industrial settlement such as Frome (Trinity area), to the grand projects at Bath, Edinburgh, and London. One paradoxical feature of the more prestigious developments was that though they were based on a corporate type of architecture—squares, crescents, and impressive terraces—their public character was severely compromised by their socially exclusive profile. Such spaces were in effect privatized by the upper echelons of urban society.

The flagships of the public landscape would have been those structures and spaces which performed a socio-political function. The quantity and quality of public buildings was an important marker of civic consciousness and sophistication. Over 100 English and Welsh towns inherited medieval walls and gates. Though their value as symbols of civic independence and identity declined, and their upkeep might be neglected (except during a military emergency like the Civil War), it was not until the eighteenth century that a widespread programme of demolition was implemented. By this time they came to be seen as archaic barriers, practically and psychologically inhibiting intercourse between town and region. In the place of fortifications, the principal emblem of civic pride became the individual public building. The years 1500 to 1640 witnessed a burst of activity in the construction, conversion or rebuilding of town halls—over 200 in 178 towns have been identified. This was associated with the wider political moves towards incorporation, external autonomy, and internal oligarchy. The structures built followed a common pattern of an open arcade beneath, which would

Town Hall, Leominster (1633–4). One of several halls built by the master carpenter John Abel. It originally rested on an open arcade, and was located at the busy junction of High Street and Broad Street, but was dismantled and moved in 1861.

normally be used for marketing, supporting a large room or rooms above. Though most halls were modest in scale, some were impressive—such as the timber-framed three-storeyed 'prodigy' halls at Hereford (late sixteenth century) and Leominster (1633–4). The period also witnessed a growing investment in market houses and crosses, reflecting the expansion in internal trade, and in secular almshouses.

From the late seventeenth century, as wealth flowed into towns, there was mounting investment in public buildings, in some cases—such as the cloth towns of the West Riding—rising quite dramatically during the later Georgian years. This was accompanied by two trends. First, diversification and specialization of structures, a product of the growing complexity of urban life. So in the field of medical welfare the first hospitals in the modern sense appear in the 1720s and 1730s (Westminster Hospital was opened in 1720, the first provincial voluntary hospital, Winchester, in 1736), followed by the emergence of several specialist institutions by 1800. Fashionable leisure activities, in the early 1700s accommodated predominantly in civic buildings and inns, increasingly established their own specialist premises as the century progressed. Second, public buildings are at the forefront in adopting classical architecture and the new building materials. This points to the prestige function of these structures allied to growing urban aspirations. The baroque town halls erected at Worcester and Warwick in the 1720s, for example, were designed on a lavish scale, with rich classical exterior and interior decoration. Significantly, both contained first-floor assembly rooms, a sign of the extent to which the urban leaders now sought to align civic life with that of the rural gentry. When York built its handsome classical Mansion House in the 1720s, it was as the equivalent of an urban 'country' house, in which the mayor could live for the period of his office, entertaining both his fellow leaders and visiting gentry, and asserting the city's credentials as part of the same status system as the rural elite. However, to return to the earlier paradox; greater investment in civic buildings, though it enhanced the public landscape, also—by generating greater physical barriers between the populace and their rulers—further privatized places and spaces of power.

The Economic Landscape

In early modern England the worlds of work and business were ones which cut across the private and public spheres. Though there can be no easy way of measuring the position, it is arguable that the largest single field of employment was servicing the domestic household; caring for children, preparing food, cleaning, washing, tending to domestic animals, and suchlike. The trend away from the open hall house towards more divided, specialized, and heavily furnished interior spaces, probably increased the volume of work in the home, and led to its concentration in certain areas, such as the kitchen, rather than others. Moreover, since women—domestic servants, daughters, and wives—were the primary deliverers of household services, then there may in addition have been a trend towards the spatial separation of the sexes in the home. The household was also the location of the majority of the town's manufacturing output. Inventories leave detailed descriptions of the raw materials and working tools to be found in the home, and sometimes list the specialized rooms and buildings devoted to the making and storage of goods. Thus a Worcester weaver of the late sixteenth century had 'in the shope ... 2 lomes and foure geres [part of the mechanism of a hand loom] and 4 tournes [spinning wheels], a warping-bare and a scarve and a narowe lome'; the premises of a pewterer and bell founder of the same city contained a 'ware howse', 'sadware shoppe', 'casting shope', 'working chamber', 'potte howse', and 'bell howse'. After the Fire of Warwick in 1694 George Harris could record among his household losses; 'in the swingall hous [a building in which flax was beaten] brakes [instrument for crushing flax] and bords', 'in the hovil black fate [vat] and dying tubes', 'flax in the rufe', and 'spun yarne, sheats and thride'. Non-family members may have been employed in these premises, but the predominant locus of urban production remained the house, and the range of outbuildings to its rear. Even in late eighteenth-century Leeds, newly built fashionable terraces occupied by wealthy woollen merchants and drapers contained, behind their domestic accommodation, warehouses and workshops. By this time, however, factories had begun to make an appearance. The earliest was probably Thomas Cotchet's three-storeyed silk spinning mill built on the banks of the Derwent at Derby in 1702; and its impressive five-storeyed successor, erected by John Lombe in about 1720, which contained water-powered machinery with over 25,000 wheels and almost 100,000 movements, and employed over 300 workers. The application of steam power towards the end of the century had a crucial impact in concentrating factory production in the town, while the techniques of construction were radically altered with the introduction of iron-framed mills—the first was the Ditherington flax mill built at Shrewsbury in the 1790s.

It is easy, from a post-Industrial Revolution perspective, to look back on towns as simply places of manufacture. However, agriculture—directly or indirectly—was a major preoccupation. Towns were surrounded by fields, and in the mass of smaller urban settlements these must have penetrated close to the centre. Citizens such as butchers would have grazing rights and those living on the periphery of the town might be fully engaged in agriculture. The four suburban wards of Warwick each contained over 30 thatched barns in a survey of 1696. That survey also revealed the existence of malting houses and tanhouses, indicative of how important towns were in processing agricultural products. Tanning, a noxious trade requiring access to plentiful water supplies, was usually located on the edge of a settlement; at Ludlow it was concentrated in a street well away from the centre that backed on to the River Corve. Urban malthouses, with their distinctive functional structure, were often located to the rear and at right angles to the main thoroughfares.

Agriculture also had an impact on the urban landscape because of the town's fundamental role in the sale and purchase of goods. A core urban feature was a market place or places. In many towns this might be accommodated in a broadened thoroughfare, or in a triangular space where several roads met. In the larger towns an extensive area could be set aside, such as at Nottingham, Yarmouth, and Norwich. The Great Market at Norwich was subdivided into various product zones, and a complex list of rules and charges existed governing the operation of the area; thus in August 1721 John Ebbotts was given 'leave to sell rabbits 2s a year. He is to have the liberty of the Hall porch in rainy weather.' In fact it was not uncommon for the various markets to spill out beyond the main market place into a wider network of streets. At York in the 1730s the principal areas of sale were Pavement (grains and edibles) and Thursday Market (flesh and leather);

facing page: The Piece Hall, Halifax (1775–8). The most impressive of the 18th-century West Riding cloth halls, it was probably designed by Thomas Bradley, whose grandiose fusion of commerce and culture symbolized the aspirations of Midland and Northern ports and industrial towns.

but also deployed were Coppergate (peas, beans, and oats), Ousegate (barley, herbs), Mickelgate (butter), Foss Bridge (sea fish), Salter Greeses at the east end of Ouse Bridge (fresh fish), and Peaseholm Green (wool). On market days urban streets must have pulsated with a variegated concoction of people, products, and animals—with their attendant sights, sounds, and smells—as the country invaded the town.

The growth in the volume of trade placed a mounting strain on the urban infrastructure. To a degree this was mitigated by two long-term trends. First, a shift away from open stalls to more enclosed and privatized forms of marketing. The inns which lined the principal throughfares and surrounded the market places became increasingly important transactional venues, where bulk products might be sold by sample. A facet of this process was also the development of the shop, with its opportunity for a commodious, exclusive, and personalized form of consumption, and its encouragement of an architectural form to deliver this. London was the leader here, and as early as the 1720s Defoe was warning how 'tradesmen lay out two-thirds of their fortune in fitting up their shops. By fitting, I mean, in painting and gilding, in fine shelves, shutters, pediments, columns of the several orders of architecture, and the like.' Second, there was accelerating pressure during the eighteenth century, as part of the improvement agenda, to clear the streets not only of temporary stalls but also of more permanent market structures that had been intruded into what were originally open spaces. Compensation was provided by the creation of enclosed market areas to the rear of the street, or by the construction of market buildings, some specializing in particular products. Among the most spectacular of the latter were the cloth halls of the West Riding of Yorkshire. Three were erected between 1700 and 1711, and a further eight between 1755 and 1793. The Piece Hall at Halifax (1775–8) cost over £12,000, and comprised a double-storeyed colonnade, with rusticated pillars below and Tuscan columns above, containing 315 rooms, and surrounding an expansive open 'piazza'. It is among the most impressive urban buildings of the period, functional, but also highly symbolic of the rising cultural aspirations of the industrial towns and ports of the Midlands and North.

The Cultural Landscape

Culturally the most striking physical aspect and achievement of the medieval town was its rich array of religious architecture; parish churches, guild premises, chapels, almshouses, cathedrals, and religious houses. Though monasteries and abbeys often occupied a rural location, they were also very much an urban phenomenon, with some of the wealthiest and most spectacular—such as Bury St Edmunds, St Mary's York, Shaftesbury, and Abingdon—situated in or on the edge of towns. Even if they operated as separate or parallel communities to their host settlement, they were unavoidably part of its physical profile. All the signs are that in the later medieval period parish churches were cherished institutions within civic life, and there are many examples of heavy investment in prestige features like grandiose towers and porches—the textile towns of Chipping Camden, Cirencester, Ludlow, and Lavenham, furnish fine examples from the late fifteenth and early sixteenth centuries—with which to impress citizens and visitors.

The impact of the Reformation on this cultural inheritance could be dramatic, but it was by no means uniformly devastating. Legislation under Henry VIII dissolved the religious houses and under Edward VI the chantries and religious guilds. Where a great abbey was vacated and left to ruinate, its fabric sometimes plundered for building materials, the effect was to create a great and decaying hole in the townscape. At Bury St Edmunds, as the Bucks' 1741 prospect makes clear, the location of the abbey took on the appearance of a bomb site. However, claustral buildings could be adapted to secular purposes, and there are many examples where the abbey church—or its richest portion, such as the chancel—was acquired for use by the town as a parish church, as at Bath, Pershore, Tewkesbury, Malmesbury, and Sherborne. A similar process frequently occurred in the case of guild premises. At Stratford-upon-Avon the impressive (largely fifteenth-century) complex of the Guild of the Holy Cross (dissolved 1547) was transferred to the newly constituted borough corporation in 1553, which preserved the almshouses and fine stone chapel, and converted the other buildings into a council chamber and school.

Adaptation provided a measure of protection, but there is no disguising the impact of the Reformation, and subsequent waves of Protestant zeal, on the urban religious fabric. Richly fashioned statuary, shrines, rood-screens, wall paintings, and stained glass were systematically mutilated or destroyed, and the appearance of surviving churches transformed. Whether this constituted cultural impoverishment is of course a matter of perspective. To committed Protestants, and all the signs are that this is what the English had predominantly become by the early seventeenth century, 'papist' imagery and artefacts were a dangerous impediment in the direct relationship between man and God, and the 'stripping of the altars' was a form of religious catharsis and liberation. In line with changing liturgical practices, the emphasis internally shifted away from the chancel towards the nave and the fount of the (now vernacular) word, the pulpit. The construction of pews and galleries, and the erection of a growing body of sometimes elaborate personal monuments (the imagery of the gentleman replacing that of the saint), led to a more segregated and privatized disposition of space for the living and the dead.

Investment in new urban churches or major reconstruction projects seems largely to have come to a halt after the Reformation. However, from the late seventeenth century an accelerating programme of church building was underway in English towns, a response to the growing demographic pressures of urbanization, the demand among the civic elite for a modern religious architecture that reflected their aspirations for status, and the rising tide of wealth flowing into urban centres. The metropolis set the pace with the baroque churches erected as a result of the post-fire reconstruction in the City, the Fifty New Churches Act of 1711 (only a dozen new structures were actually built wholly as a result of the Act), and the huge project to rebuild St Paul's (1675–1711); significantly all three initiatives drew upon wealth derived from trade, receiving finance from a tax imposed on the vast imports of coal into London. Impressive new churches in the provincial towns followed Wren's City models; notable examples are All Saints, Northampton (1676–80), St Philip's, Birmingham (1710–15), All Saints, Bristol (1711–12, 1716), and St George's, Yarmouth (1714–16). Later the pattern was set by James Gibbs's St Martin-in-the-Fields (1721–6), which influenced the design of a surprising number of the 130 or so Anglican town churches built or substantially reconstructed in the provinces during the eighteenth century. Added to their number must be the Nonconformist chapels, the product of the rise of religious pluralism in Stuart England, and the new opportunities for public worship provided by the Toleration Act of 1689. Many of these would be modest in scale, but from early on architectural pretensions were by no means absent, as the surviving Presbyterian Chapel (1711–12) at Bury St Edmunds and Unitarian Meeting House (1699–1700) at Ipswich demonstrate. The latter is dominated not by an altar but a richly carved and elevated pulpit accessed by elegantly curved stairs, indicative of the extent to which the physical fabric of worship had altered since the Reformation to accommodate transformed religious experiences.

One of the most inventive and elegant of provincial town churches of the eighteenth century was the neoclassical St Chad's, Shrewsbury (1790–2), with its circular nave, elliptical vestibule, and commanding three-staged tower. It sat on the western edge of the built town. To one side lay the handsome brick properties of Shrewsbury's fashionable quarter—whose occupants it serviced, and to which it acted as a public symbol of prestige (many squares were built with attached churches for a similar reason). To the east, on sloping ground that dropped down to the Severn, lay the Quarry Gardens, landscaped walks where the town's beau monde paraded. The gardens were laid out in 1719, and were part of a nationwide trend to provide towns with formal public walks and gardens. The earliest were probably those laid out on Moorfields and at the Inns of Court in early seventeenth-century London, followed after the Restoration by the prestigious walks in St James's Park. Early examples can also be found in the provinces—the raised tree-lined bank which forms the core of the Pantiles at Tunbridge Wells was constructed in 1638—but it was from about the 1690s that the fad swept the larger towns and resorts. Commercial pleasure gardens began life in the 1660s, dotting the periphery of the capital. In the eighteenth century the most celebrated were Vauxhall and Ranelagh, multifaceted emporiums of pleasure that provided models which were exported to towns such as Norwich, Birmingham, and Newcastle-upon-Tyne. Private domestic gardens also flourished, and when taken with the emerging interest of the wealthy middling orders in suburban residence, would seem to suggest a declining commitment to urban culture as such. But though it is certainly true that nature held a growing fascination for well-off townspeople, it was very much an urbanized form of nature that they hankered after, one in which the rural world was sanitized and idealized, and in which the landscape was a source of pleasure rather than work.

After the Restoration there was a marked trend towards towns becoming places of pleasure, devoted to servicing the needs of the gentry and expanding middling order for sociable leisure. London and its West End led the way; indeed the capital's size and importance ensured that throughout the early modern period it was the forcing-house of developments in commercialized public leisure. From the late seventeenth century, the provincial capitals and county centres followed the lead set by the metropolis. Moreover, a whole new category of town emerged devoted to the provision of medical and recreational services, the resort. Initially spas pioneered the new development, but from the 1730s and 1740s they were joined by the seaside town. The core elements of the new urban recreational culture were drama, music, reading, assemblies, walks, clubs, and horse racing. At first, where these activities required indoor venues, the tendency was to make use of inns and suitable public buildings. But before long specialized structures were built; theatres—in London the first of these date back to the late sixteenth century, including the Rose, the Swan, and the Globe—assembly rooms, commercial and institutional libraries, and (in smaller numbers) concert rooms and race grandstands. Bath, for example, possessed purpose-built assembly rooms from 1708 (with attached gardens), Stamford from about 1727, and York from 1732. The last of these, designed by the leading aristocratic patron of the arts Lord Burlington, was—with its famous colonnaded Egyptian Hall—among the most advanced Palladian buildings in the country, and helped confirm York's role as the social capital of the north.

Assembly rooms were socially exclusive spaces, intended to separate the polite minority from the plebeian majority. The pastimes of the latter were accommodated in altogether humbler and less formalized surroundings. Before the Reformation, church and churchyard would have represented important venues. With new notions of religious propriety pertaining, popular leisure was forced into the street, market place, and alehouse. The last of these was an institution rich in practical and psychological functions, if generally modest in architectural pretensions (in plan it was often no more than an ordinary dwelling house), whose numbers grew rapidly in the century before the Civil War. Protestantization effectively killed off traditional religious open air ritual. But secular public ceremonial—such as that associated with coronations, military victories, and mayoral inaugurations—expanded, sharing the town's thoroughfares with a bewildering range of more popular pastimes, including calendrical celebrations (like May Day and Whitsuntide), sports (such as football and animal baiting), skimmingtons or rough ridings, and riots. Imprinted on the physical streetscape was a cultural topography, which dictated the course of a procession, charivari, or bull-running, or determined where a bonfire would be lit on Midsummer's Eve, where alcohol would be distributed on a day of public celebration, where a maypole was erected, and so on. Because all levels of society deployed, in one manner or another, the street as a cultural locus, then there was considerable potential for friction. This may be reflected in political demonstrations and riots. It could also be seen in the eighteenth century in urban authorities' street improvement programmes which, transport benefits apart, were an attempt to enhance civic middle-class control of public space and popular culture. The long-drawn-out and bitter battle to banish bull-running at Stamford, which began in 1788 and took half a century to achieve its objective, is testimony of the extent to which the street had become contested space.

The Mental Landscape

One occasion which filled the streets with colourful spectacle and noise in early modern Norwich and York was mayoral inauguration day. What shaped the pattern of each event was a customarily determined processional route, which linked together indoor venues and outdoor spaces. In early eighteenth-century York the mayoral procession began at the mayor elect's house, moved on to the old mayor's dwelling, then to the council chamber on Ouse Bridge, thence to the Guildhall—where the formal transfer of power would occur—before a lengthy perambulation along specified streets, during which there would be a stop to drink wine at the Pavement Cross, ending up at the new mayor's house for a feast, and a final visit to the old mayor's residence for further refreshments. The procession at Norwich opened and ended in the same fashion as at York, but in between there were visits to the Cathedral, the Free School, the Guildhall, and the New Hall for a sumptuous feast. The landscape traversed on these occasions was a palpably physical one. But this would have had little significance were it not overlaid with a mental landscape, stored in the collective memory of the participants—spectators and performers—which invested the hard places and spaces with social and political meaning. Cerebral space was not static. Much of the mental map of the late medieval town had been a function of the religious culture of the time. The loss at the Reformation of the great processions and plays that accompanied festivals like Corpus Christi and Whitsuntide involved a reorientation of perceptions of the landscape, that came to focus more on secular political and social culture. Ritual routes now looked more to servicing the needs of civic elites, or fashionable society who at the resorts followed a daily routine rigidly tied to specified buildings, walks, and rides.

One factor which transformed attitudes to the mental landscape was the arrival of print, and the growing impact of this on the culture of early modern England. Images of the townscape need no longer remain locked in people's brains; there was now a medium through which these could be given material form, and—critically—reproduced for dissemination to others. Three types of representation were created; maps, views, and literary accounts. The only reasonably complete medieval plan of an English town is Ricart's bird's-eye manuscript view of Bristol in *c.*1479. The earliest known complete map of London dates from as late as the 1550s, though in this case it was executed on fifteen copperplates for printing. It was Elizabeth's reign which witnessed the first real burst of interest in urban mapping, and this culminated in the publication of John Speed's *Theatre of the Empire of Great Britain* (1611–12), in which set into his county maps were plans of 73 towns. There followed something of a hiatus, until from the late seventeenth century a new phase of town mapping got underway, providing most substantial centres with one—and in some cases several—dedicated printed plans by 1800. Maps produced during this phase were characterized not only by greater detail and accuracy, but also by a shift towards the modern conception of a two-dimensional plan, as opposed to the bird's-eye view of the Tudor and early Stuart cartographer. This in its turn encouraged the production of a distinct genre of urban views and prospects, the most impressive outcome of which was Samuel and Nathaniel Buck's printed panoramas, produced between the 1720s and 1750s, of over 70 English and Welsh 'cities, seaports, and capital towns'. Engraved reproductions of individual features of towns also proliferated. Many of these focused on antiquarian objects, such as medieval fortifications and churches, but modern structures—like public buildings and fashionable residential blocks—were also well represented.

Views and maps might form part of a published history or guide to a town. This constituted the third area where the advance of a print culture generated urban images—the written account. From the fifteenth century civic annals and manuscript histories were prepared of English towns; but these, like John Leland's early Tudor topographical *Itinerary*, remained in manuscript. Though John Stow's magnificent *Survey of London* was published in 1598, and national and county surveys contained urban material, before 1700 no more than a handful of town histories had made it into print. During the eighteenth century this scenario changed as more and more of the substantial towns acquired published accounts of their past. Newcastle, for example, added to Grey's *Chronographia* (1649), Bourne's *History* (1736), Brand's two-volume *History and Antiquities* (1789), and Baillie's *Impartial History* (1801), the last reflecting a long-term trend towards the production of a more integrated history, geared at the middling orders as a whole rather than the civic elite specifically. From the middle of the eighteenth century there also appeared specialist guides for the spas and seaside resorts, and business and residential directories for the larger towns. At a national level the printed guided tour emerged in the early eighteenth century, the most famous of which became Daniel Defoe's *A Tour through the Whole Island of Great Britain.* First published in three volumes between 1724 and 1726, and reissued in new editions up until 1779, it had a markedly urban emphasis with potted accounts intended to encapsulate the towns described in a textual snapshot. One of the appeals of Defoe's guide was its tour format, since this reflected the growing fashion—made possible by improved roads—for personal tourism. Towns were often an essential part of the itinerary—at this stage places to be visited and admired rather than avoided and derided—and as part of the educational function of these tours the travellers frequently compiled their own diaries, containing cameo descriptions of the places visited. Though these usually remained in manuscript, the form of the accounts produced was closely influenced by the printed guides and topographical works.

The printed urban image, visual or literary, was in part ornament and aide-mémoire; a way of reflecting on and recollecting a place. But it was much more than that. It could also structure perception of the townscape, and influence behaviour within it. Urban images, though often appearing comprehensive, were highly selective in what they portrayed. Whole classes of features could be omitted, others given a boosted profile. Francis Drake's *Eboracum* (1736), which rolls together text, illustrations, and a map, presents York from a predominantly antiquarian point of view, with fulsome descriptions and plates of the city's ancient structures, especially its medieval religious buildings. Produced in a sumptuous format, and subscribed to by the local gentry, it invested the city with historic meaning, and helped turn it into a heritage resource for the rural elite. Significantly, where modern structures were reported on and illustrated they tended to be those associated with polite pastimes; thus there are three plates of the new assembly rooms and one which shows the New Walk along the Ouse. The corporation supported the project morally and financially, partly because the work did contain a good deal of civic documentation; but primarily because they saw the overwhelming economic advantages in creating an image of York that appealed to the county gentry, who had become the city's principal market. Much the same could be said of resort towns. Here the focus in the guides, maps, and views was on the modern water, leisure, and shopping facilties, and the fine architecture. Studiously omitted were references to working-class districts or industrial activity. Such material provided visitors with a preconceived interpretation of the townscape that proceeded to determine the way that they interacted with it. Before the end of the eighteenth century, this process was being applied not just to the man-made landscape, but also to the natural one which surrounded the town. Written and visual accounts, with their picturesque and romantic emphasis, helped to energize visitors' perceptions of a countryside and sea that not long before they might have ignored. In this fashion the mental landscape helped to restructure its physical counterpart.

In the Bucks' prospects of early Georgian towns the old and the new jostle for prominence with each other. The view of Bristol is dotted with the spires of medieval churches; but the Baptist Mills Brass Works, not to mention a forest of ships' masts and the outline of the newly erected Queen Square (*c.*1700–27) are also conspicuous. The Minster dominates the prospect of York, supported by the medieval fortifications and parish churches; but the Mansion House (1725–7), Assembly Rooms (1730–2), Infirmary (1740), and New Walk (1730s/40s) are also picked out in the key. Elements of continuity and change were evident in all towns, even if in one place the old might predominate, and in another the new. In domestic architecture the vernacular tradition continued to be a powerful force well into the eighteenth century. But within that tradition a reordering of the internal structure of the house was underway from the later Tudor period, and from the later 1600s the classical revolution began to have a serious impact on the design of the homes of the more prosperous citizenry. Classicism, conceived in urban-focused civilizations, possessed an inherently public ethos, embodied in the principle of uniformity, and in the practice—increasingly to be seen in

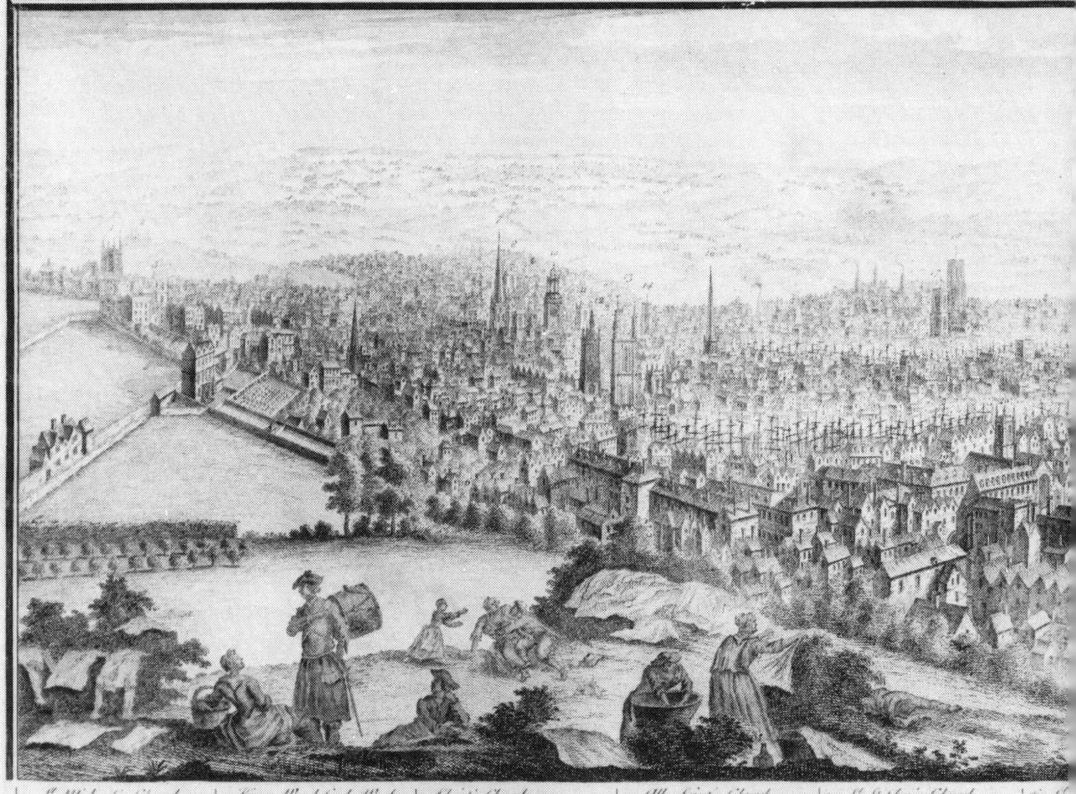

Bristol, 1734, by Samuel and Nathaniel Buck, who produced the first systematic visual record of the leading English and Welsh towns. Elements of change and continuity jostle together, with medieval spires sharing the scene with the newly erected Queen Square.

post-Restoration English towns—of constructing terraces and squares. Street improvement, allied to growing investment in civic buildings, suggested a new public spirit abroad. That is how contemporaries would have liked to have perceived it, as part of an urban enlightenment. But underpinning and undermining the ideal was the hard reality that the engine of urban change was private wealth, whose natural tendency was to promote personal aggrandizement. If the boundaries between the public and the private shifted in the townscape, it was not because the elite became per se more public-spirited, but because sociability became the most fashionable—and therefore most effective—vehicle for the pursuit of self interest.

Throughout the early modern period agriculture remained, directly or indirectly, a major influence on the appearance of towns, and the predominant unit of manufacture continued to be the home and domestic-based workshop. However, the latter part of the period saw a growing rationalization of industrial functions into the town, an attempt to curtail the impact of agricultural marketing on the open streets, and the emergence of the first true factories. William Stumpe's

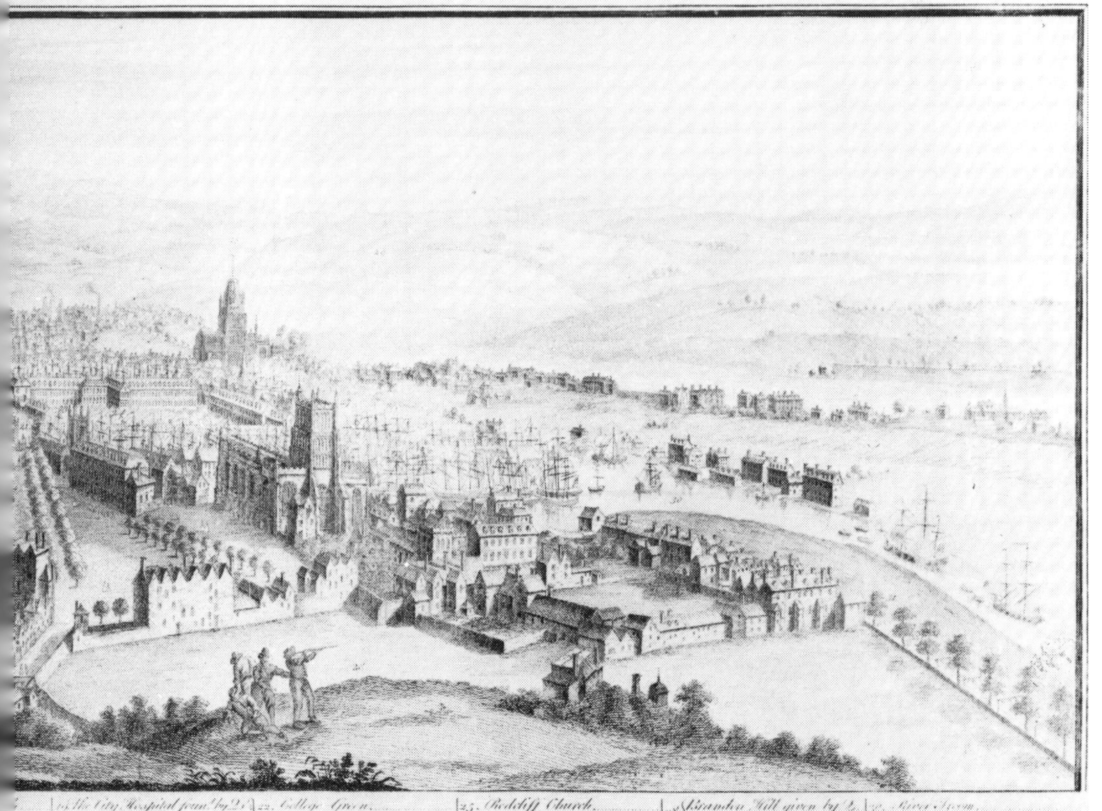

conversion in the 1540s of the monastic buildings at Malmesbury into weaving sheds was hardly a contender here, but it was indicative of the widescale physical damage done to the urban cultural fabric in the wake of the Reformation. Not that all was lost. The Bucks' prospects make it clear that two centuries later much of medieval heritage still remained; moreover, amidst the Gothic spires classical towers were appearing—at Worcester the steeple of the new St Nicholas's (opened 1730) is clearly visible, and All Saints was added a decade later—indicative of a new wave of church building. To this must be added the surge of investment in fashionable leisure facilities—such as the York assembly rooms—a sign of the rising cultural status of towns after the Restoration. Of course, the Bucks' panoramas, strikingly realistic as they appear, should not be taken as a verbatim record of the early Georgian town. Like the histories, maps, guidebooks, and travel diaries that proliferated at the time, they were part of that mental landscape, conveyed through printed images, that did so much to structure attitudes to and behaviour in the material landscape. If past and present competed in the Bucks' vision, it is because there was a growing contemporary consciousness and concern for the traditional townscape, prompted by an awareness but also celebration of the gathering forces of urban change.

5 Modern London

John Davis

Urban history tells us that in the early modern period the major growth centres were ports and capital cities, but that manufacturing centres grew more rapidly during the first phase of industrialization. London in the nineteenth century was not only Britain's capital and her principal port but also, if less obviously, her largest industrial centre. Its growth was therefore prodigious. In the mid-eighteenth century the capital's population probably stood at around 675,000; by the time of the first national census in 1801 it was counted at 959,000; by the end of the nineteenth century Greater London contained 6.5 million people, roughly a fifth of the population of England and Wales.

The development of public transport services, from the introduction of omnibuses in 1829, ensured that London sprawled. Despite its enormous population, nineteenth-century London did not experience the cramming suffered by Berlin or St Petersburg. The verdict of the authors of the *County of London Plan* in 1943—that London's housing problem was due 'not so much to high density as to a general drabness and dreariness'—would have held throughout the nineteenth century. Density was not, by continental standards, a problem; dreariness was accentuated, though, by the sheer scale of the built-up area, which even by the 1830s stretched from Hyde Park Corner to Blackwall and from Kennington to King's Cross. Accidents of tenure and topography meant that this area was not entirely covered. The royal parks and the squares forming part of the planned aristocratic townscape of the West End and of Bloomsbury escaped the advancing bricks. Hampstead Heath in the north-west and Victoria Park in the north-east were protected by statute after public campaigns, to be joined later in the century by several municipal parks. The builders themselves eschewed much of the unpromising east Thames riverside; the eerie Bugsby's Marsh, formed by a twist of the Thames east of the Isle of Dogs and only seven miles from the City, remained, in Charles Booth's words, 'one of the most out-of-the-way spots conceivable' until it was invaded by the Blackwall Tunnel at the turn of the century

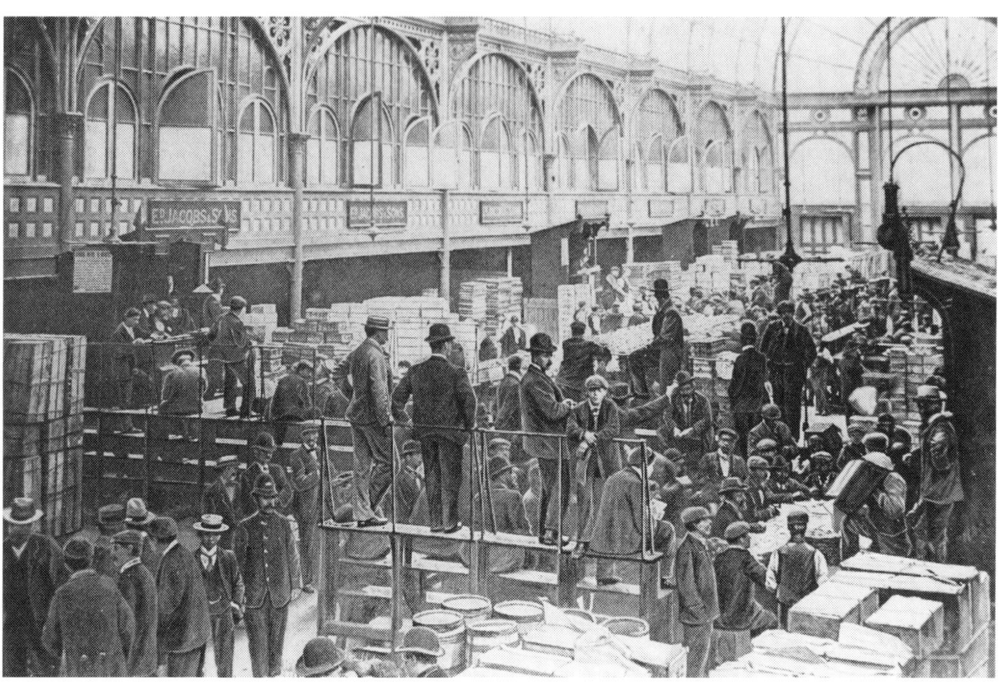

Fruit Auctions at Covent Garden, 1902. The inconvenience of placing London's principal fruit market in the centre of the West End was recognized well before the market's relocation in the 1970s. Even in 1902 it was 'impossible for nearly half the buyers going there to drive up within sight of it'.

(even in the twentieth century it has remained unwanted land, fit only for a gasworks and now the Millennium Dome). Generally, however, the image of a 'province covered by houses', coined by the Royal Commission on the Corporation of London in 1854, was valid.

'One has not the alternative of speaking of London as a whole,' Henry James claimed in the 1880s, 'for the simple reason that there is no such thing as the whole of it. It is immeasurable—embracing arms never meet.' The size of the metropolis, and the high degree of residential segregation within it, meant that few of its inhabitants could comprehend the entire city. London became the subject of successive social investigations produced primarily for the metropolitan market. Their preoccupation was with the capital's poor, viewed initially as a potential menace but increasingly as an object of anthropological curiosity. Those unready to risk entering 'darkest London' in person could instead immerse themselves in a torrent of investigative writing, in the semi-journalistic works of John Hollingshead (*Ragged London in 1861*) and Blanchard Jerrold (*London: A Pilgrimage*), or in the more cerebral but still popular studies of London's industry and poverty by Henry Mayhew in mid-century and Charles Booth at the century's close. Victorian London presented the greatest aggregation of poverty that the world had ever seen. Unsurprisingly, therefore, these poverty surveys received the greatest attention and are still most likely to be read today, but we should not overlook those works which simply attempted to explain how the capital lived and functioned, from George Dodd's analysis of *The Food of London* in 1856, through C. M. Davies's studies of London's religious heterodoxy and R. Mudie Smith's survey of formal religion in 1873 and 1904, to George Sims's meticulous metropolitan anatomy in the three volumes of his *Liv-*

ing London of 1902, far broader in scope than Booth. We are better acquainted with London than with any other nineteenth-century city.

As a result it is possible to analyse the development of the Victorian metropolis as a social and economic organism. The Chicago-school model of urban development, with graded social zones radiating from a commercial core, offers only limited guidance: as in every city but Chicago, it is heavily qualified by circumstance. In the first place, London's central zone has always been bifurcated, with the City of London proper becoming the preserve of first commerce then finance, but the centre of court, parliament, and society remaining in Westminster. The topography of an undulating landscape has disturbed an underlying concentric social pattern: high ground, always fashionable in the polluted city, promoted Hampstead's exclusivity; conversely the hollows of river valleys, likely sanitary blackspots in the Victorian period, tainted otherwise salubrious districts. Booth painted a black picture of the Wandle Valley, where 'building of a vile character' blighted middle-class Wandsworth. Necessary urban infrastructure could disfigure whole areas. Railways, canals, and gasworks encouraged urban blight; where they occurred together, as in the King's Cross/St Pancras complex, or at Kensal New Town in the north-west, they generated social degradation. Landowner preference and estate policy might also distort underlying social processes. The builders of the West End clearly sought and achieved social selection, as did, in their different ways, the trustees of the Dulwich College estates and the managers of the Peabody and other model dwelling trusts. The inventive and tenacious Octavia Hill aimed to improve the urban environment and its occupiers by encouraging her tenants to take responsibility for the state of their homes. Conversely, the unconcern of the Church Commissioners in letting the notorious Agar Town in St Pancras on short leases spawned a shanty town in the 1840s, unpaved and inadequately drained.

Two features above all shaped London's evolution. First, the Thames provided a daunting caesura between north and south. Underused as a transport artery itself, it marked off south London throughout the Victorian period. The court, palaces, parliament, fashion, and finance lay north of the river; the south, by contrast, was 'immense ... in size, ... invertebrate in character', according to Booth, who was not normally given to such language. More detached from the centre than east or north London, it lacked an independent life. Other than between 1843 and 1865, when Marc Brunel's tunnel between Rotherhithe and Shadwell was open to pedestrians, there was no crossing east of London Bridge before the construction of Tower Bridge and the Rotherhithe and Blackwall Tunnels in the 1890s. The communities contained in the twists of the Thames—Rotherhithe, Wapping, the Isle of Dogs—became semi-detached from London, gaining, in Booth's view, a village atmosphere. More important still, though, was the distinction between East and West Ends. As in most large cities in western Europe, the prevailing westerly wind made the West End desirable, though the evolution of the City—on the eastern edge of the central area—into a depopulated fortress of finance accentuated the contrast with the poverty of the crowded 'East End' beyond it. The progressive polarization of west and east was evident to contemporaries as early as the 1820s; by 1875, when the Reverend Harry Jones published his *East and West London*, it was a familiar social phenomenon.

Social segregation was complemented by economic segregation. As London expanded, its distinctive economic profile became clearer—one in which discrete areas came to be devoted to particular specialities, characterized by an ever-strengthening division of labour within trades. The capital's most successful trade—financial services—provides the first and best example. The same consideration which has prevented the dispersal of the financial centre in the age of information technology—the value of face-to-face contact—encouraged the initial concentration of financial services in the Square Mile. In the eighteenth-century City coffee houses served in lieu of offices, but by the 1850s the City housed specialist exchanges and the national headquarters of merchant banks. Proximity to partners and fellow traders was indispensable in a world where speed

The Royal Exchange (Threadneedle Street and Cornhill), c.1885. One of the 'pressure points' of late-Victorian London. The antiquated street pattern of the City left it ill equipped to handle the volume of traffic which its economic expansion generated.

of operation was vital. 'The peculiarity of business here is the amount of running about that it involves', observed the future director of the Bank of England, William Lidderdale, in 1864; pinstriped athletes remained a feature of the Square Mile well after the invention of the telephone. Even as technology weakened the purely functional case for a City location, the promotional value of a City address to a finance house was, if anything, strengthened. John Dunning and E. V. Morgan noted in 1971 that rents fell away quickly beyond the City's north-eastern boundary: 'some firms will pay highly for a "good" address on their notepaper'. Susan Fainstein suggests that failure to appreciate the cachet of a City location accounted in part for the failure of the Docklands Development Corporation to seduce finance houses away from the City in the 1980s. Once established as the monopoly centre of finance in the early nineteenth century, the City underwent a growth characterized by functional specialization, both in the emergence of the specialist exchanges such as the Baltic Exchange of 1858, with concurrent downgrading of the Royal Exchange almost as soon as it was completed, and in the appearance of occupational distinctions within the financial community. Though the City was described as early as 1866 as part of the system of outdoor relief for the aristocracy—like the Empire—the claim really applied only to banking: the distinction between banking and 'mere' stockbroking was an occupational division buttressed by snobbery. Within the stock market the roles of broker and jobber diverged, creating a distinction which would last until 'Big Bang' in 1986.

The mid-Victorian transformation of the City demonstrated—to a degree accentuated by the sheer compression of the financial district—that displacement of the residential population that would gradually come to characterize the entire central area. The City's population fell from 127,000 in 1851 to 26,000 in 1901. The immediate result was the creation of shanty towns on the City fringe as a displaced population crammed into property which was often decrepit and which almost invariably predated the era of strict building control. This was the 'Ragged London' that the journalist John Hollingshead described in 1861, surveying a labouring population squeezed into the arcane courts and alleys that survived from the pre-modern metropolis. In Clerkenwell, where two-thirds of the population depended upon the City for their livelihood, 'some of the passages are so narrow that it is scarcely possible to creep up them'. Fryingpan Alley was worse than anything in Whitechapel or Bethnal Green: 'its entrance is two feet wide—a long narrow slit in the wall—half paved, with a gutter which constantly trickles with sewage . . . The rooms are dust-bins—everything but dwelling places'. Neighbouring Finsbury was characterized by 'low black houses, that look as if they were built as a penal settlement for dwarfs', crowded not only with people but with their dogs, pigs, and chickens. The City overspill crossed the river, swamping what had once been the gentility of Southwark. Hollingshead evocatively described decline of a red-brick mansion in Jacob's Island:

> sunken, decayed, chipped and neglected, let out in tenements, with rowing sculls in its passage, a boat lying high and dry in its yard, and its old gardens covered with courts and huts of the most wretched character. Its over-hanging and hood-like porch is still full of the ancient mouldings, representing clusters of fruits and flowers and containing the date, *in relievo*, of 1700.

In reality the 'Ragged London' that Hollingshead described was a transient community, created by urban transformation and instantly threatened by it.

These slum pockets were magnets to railway promoters and the designers of street improvements, because slum property was cheaply requisitioned and because the appeal of clearing a sanitary blackspot generally augmented the case for redevelopment. The residents of Fryingpan Alley viewed the imminent transformation of the Fleet Valley in the 1860s without enthusiasm:

> [They] are ready to fight for their castle of filth. They dislike the new underground railway that is forming in the neighbourhood, they look upon New Farringdon Street [*sic*] as a Corporation job; and they have got the rude notion that all local improvements put money into the pockets of Government.

The local impact of railway building (with the construction of Charing Cross, Cannon Street, Holborn Viaduct, St Pancras, Broad Street, and Liverpool Street stations between 1864 and 1875, and the complementary provision of what would become the Inner Circle to link them) and of street improvement was enormous, but neither political authority nor aesthetic will existed to effect the kind of planned urban transformation achieved in contemporary Paris. By the mid-Victorian period the Georgian pattern of uniform town houses grouped around squares, which offered the most promising model for holistic reconstruction, had fallen into contempt; the stylistic eclecticism which replaced it encouraged piecemeal development. The complexity of London's pattern of landownership, particularly in and around the City, also worked against 'Haussmannization'. Wholesale rebuilding would have required extensive compulsory purchase and consequently unimaginable expense. The only public London-wide body able to contemplate such action, the Metropolitan Board of Works, enjoyed little popular legitimacy on account of its being indirectly elected and, almost from its inception in 1855, tainted by real or fancied scandals. Some of the street improvements which it did undertake, including the construction of Northumberland Avenue and Shaftesbury Avenue, generated corrupt property deals which eventually led to the Board's downfall in 1889. For these reasons, although the mid-Victorian period saw massive reconstruction of central London, it was a transformation largely effected by private enterprise, largely fuelled by commercial need and by rising land values and largely uncontrolled.

It was nonetheless effective in destroying Fryingpan Alley and the other archaic poverty nooks of Hollingshead's London. In the inner West End the process of commercialization affected all residential property, not merely the homes of the poor. Mayfair and St James's Piccadilly would be virtually denuded of their aristocracy by the 1890s. Ironically, virtually the only new residential developments in the inner West End in these years were built for the deserving poor, as aristocratic landowners donated land to the Peabody and other philanthropic housing trusts. The 'upper ten' moved further west, where a succession of superior developments awaited them. Some proved more successful than others. Belgravia, after a faltering start, was established as an exclusive aristocratic ghetto by the 1850s, but the attempt to encourage high-class flat-dwelling in and around the new Victoria Street failed badly: Booth saw that area as a preserve of high-class prostitutes. Speculative building in South Kensington followed the development of that area as museumland in the wake of the 1851 Great Exhibition. The startling social upgrading of the Cadogan Estate in Chelsea from the 1870s was characterized by the construction of mansions in the newly fashionable Queen Anne style, occupied by, as the *Builder* put it in 1881, 'if not magnificent people, the possessors certainly of magnificent means'. Further north, Notting Hill, Bayswater, and south Paddington became upper-middle-class enclaves, sustaining William Whiteley's sprawling emporium, which boasted 159 departments by 1906, just as the residents of Kensington supported Harrod's.

There was, though, always a social difference between the areas north and south of Hyde Park. The developers of Notting Hill, Ladbroke Grove, and Paddington eventually succeeded in their search for well-heeled families to fill their imposing villas, but they often had to wait: in 1860 the elegant houses of Ladbroke Gardens formed a 'desert of dilapidated structures and decaying carcasses' as they waited for purchasers. The North Paddington fringe of this area was overbuilt, and never fully established itself as a prestigious locale; multiple occupation—the fate of large houses in unfashionable areas—would pitch it into poverty during the twentieth century. Those who sought to re-create Bloomsbury in the outer West End faced, even in the 1860s, competition from suburban developers who could offer detached villas and private space instead of town houses with communal gardens. St John's Wood, 'a forest of villas, of nearly all sorts and sizes', was geographically close to Paddington and Marylebone, but its developers rejected their attempt to recreate the Georgian urban milieu in favour of something more distinctively suburban. Hampstead developed as a distinctly upper-middle-class suburb, consciously preserving a village atmosphere.

As London grew, its suburbs assumed social identities of their own. By the 1860s St John's Wood was recognized as the preserve of authors, journalists, and publishers; Bayswater, Brixton, and Clapham housed bankers and brokers; Dalston, New Cross, and Forest Hill clerks; Kennington and Stockwell City traders. Occasionally such broad-brush contemporary impressions have been refined by meticulous historical research. H. J. Dyos's classic study of Camberwell demonstrated the complex social gradations existing within what appeared a physically homogeneous area: Camberwell contained within a few square miles such 'oases of moderate wealth and respectability' as Peckham Grove, other streets housing the schoolmasters, clerks, and respectable mechanics for whom they were designed, a cluster of very poor streets and the notorious 'citadel of outcasts' that was the Sultan Street slum. Estate policy, the terms of building leases, and the quality of the building itself did most to determine the social fate of any new development.

The variegation of Dyos's Camberwell is a reminder that 'respectable' suburbs generated their own trades and services as well as, often, a degree of light industry. Most Victorian suburbs had their working-class quarters. The bulk of the working class depended, though, on the central area—the City, the West End, the riverside, and the docks—and needed to live near their work. The growth of the Victorian metropolis led to the establishment of the major working-class areas in the inner south and the East End.

The working-class quarter south of the river grew up around the Surrey Docks, the riverside trades, the engineering and other works in Lambeth, and the food-processing factories in Bermondsey. Hollingshead saw the area behind the Waterloo Road as London's nearest approach to a northern factory town—a metropolitan Bolton. Although the comparison was not intended as a compliment, it does capture the 'workman's cottage' quality of that area's nineteenth-century housing which, where it has survived, has now been gentrified. The vulnerability of riverside Lambeth and Southwark to flooding—'the sewage in many places bubbles up through the floors' Hollingshead wrote of the Mint area in Southwark—limited its residential potential, ensuring that London's *rive gauche* remained devoted to warehousing and industry for most of the modern period. In general, though, the working-class housing of the inner south was more durable than that of the East End, despite the intensity of south London poverty. The real centre of urban decay lay in the east.

The City's eastern and north-eastern boundaries have until recently formed an invisible but efficient barrier, segregating wealth from poverty and finance from industry. The City's nineteenth-century depopulation and the consequent crowding of the inner East End accentuated the contrast. What Hollingshead described in the East End was not the world of clandestine courts and alleys lying off major thoroughfares that he had seen in Clerkenwell but discrete working-class suburbs on the very fringe of the City. His account of a street in Bethnal Green conveys the colour of London's poorer quarters, as well as the eclectic consumerism of the London working class:

> there are steaming eating houses, half-filled with puddings as large as sofa squabs, and legs of beef to boil down into a cheap and popular soup; birdcage vendors; mouldy, musty dens full of second-hand garments, or gay 'emporiums' in the ready-made clothing line; pawnbrokers with narrow, yellow side entrances, whose walls are well marked with the traces of traffic; faded groceries; small print shops, selling periodicals, sweetstuff and stale fruit; squeezed up barbers, long factories and breweries, with the black arches of the Eastern Counties Railway running through the midst.

Hollingshead offers a more subtle account of the East End than the usual image of undifferentiated squalor that Walter Besant caricatured in 1900, but by the time Besant wrote, the East End had become the uncontested locus of 'Darkest London'. In fact much of the outer east—Mile End New Town, Poplar, Stratford, and, *a fortiori*, the growing industrial suburb of West Ham—differed little from the working-class areas in the south. It was the inner eastern band, from the St George's, Limehouse, and Stepney riverside through Whitechapel and Bethnal Green to Shoreditch and Hoxton, that displayed the most intense combination of poverty, crowding, and physical decay as the area absorbed a population beyond the capacity of its small and inadequate buildings. With the onset of the agricultural depression in the late 1870s the East End sucked in refugees from, in particular, the hard-hit arable counties of East Anglia. Many migrants gravitated to the docks, which now emerged as a residual employer of casual labour in a city which, with its high rents and other overheads, was otherwise tending to shed labour-intensive industry. By the turn of the century the daily scramble for work at the dock gates produced a regular parade of London's losers:

> criminals not twenty-four hours out of jail . . . vagrants, tramps, doctors whose names have vanished from the register, disbarred barristers, unfrocked parsons, labourers without labour, artisans chronically out of work, soldiers, policemen, shop-keepers—all classes of men who have slipped from their rung on the social ladder and never been able to climb back.

If the docks acted as a magnet for the unemployed, they also served as reception centre for immigrants from overseas, most notably the Russian and Polish Jews fleeing the pogroms in the Russian Empire after the assassination of Alexander II in 1881.

Dock gate scene, 1902. The East End and Surrey docks became the last resort for many of London's workless, offering casual work at very low rates for those fortunate enough to catch the foreman's eye at the beginning of each working day.

At a time when the area's two principal industries—shipbuilding and silk-weaving—had been sharply run down, the East End experienced a population influx more typical of a boom town. The overloading of an already inadequate urban fabric soon became evident to the army of social commentators that invaded the area. A. O. Jay, rector of Holy Trinity Shoreditch, provided Booth with accounts of the houses in the notorious Old Nichol area. In one house in New Nichol Street, for instance, Jay detailed the following:

> Wretched room—windows broken, floor rotten, walls crumbling, eaten alive with bugs, chimney smokes fearfully.
> A vile room. Ceiling quite black.
> Wretched room—paper hanging from ceiling in ribbons—2 large holes in floor. Very smoky.
> Wretched room—walls & ceiling damp & mouldy & room full of dense smoke. Parts of ceiling fallen away.

The East End became the centre of a well-chronicled social crisis in the 1880s which did much to alert Britain's political establishment to the condition of the working class. These years saw press and parliamentary investigations into slum housing, sweated labour, and unemployment, bringing the East End into national politics. It was in these years that Charles Booth inaugurated his Herculean survey of London life and labour, initially focused on the East End, and that the newly created London County Council, under Liberal-Radical control for eighteen years after its inception in 1889, promoted the capital's first experiments in municipal socialism.

The intense political interest in the condition of the East End in the 1880s was prompted by a concern that the capital's poor might represent an insurrectionary menace. By 1900 that fear had cooled under empirical scrutiny. Booth reserved a category in his otherwise dispassionate social taxonomy for those who might be thought a danger to society, but reassuringly calculated their number at only 1.23 per cent of the population of East London; they were 'a disgrace but not a danger'. The tide of charitable enthusiasm unleashed by successive Lord Mayors' appeals in the 1880s ebbed as the fear of metropolitan meltdown receded. The enduring lesson of the 1880s crisis was inescapable, though: that late Victorian London was a city with immense infrastructural problems. The condition of its older housing stock, the prevalence of sweated and casual labour, and the intensity of poverty in what was Europe's richest city, all testified to the problem of accommodating a population of five million in comfort.

Arguably, the social crisis of the 1880s was simply a severe example of the strain inherent in rapid urban growth—a process which encompassed environmental as well as social problems, and which dominated most of the second half of the century rather than merely one nervous decade. The Victorian city had to deal with pollution, disease, and congestion as well as overcrowding and unemployment. Pollution was a serious problem throughout the nineteenth century. The water supply could be improved by statute, though only in response to major crises: the cholera of 1848 led to legislation preventing the drawing of drinking water from the open sewer known as the Thames, while the river's 'great stench' in the summer of 1858 was pungent enough to induce the riparian legislators at Westminster to endorse the building of the main drainage system. Finished in the 1870s, it contributed to London's escaping the cholera which devastated other northern European ports in 1893. Supply nonetheless remained inadequate: in successive drought summers in the 1890s it failed completely in the East End. Even by 1900 piped water seldom ran to more than one floor of a house, and bathrooms were a rarity. The late Victorian poor still washed in public street fountains.

Urban living generated other environmental nuisances which yielded only slowly to public regulation. Throughout the first half of the century two million live animals per year traipsed twice weekly through residential London to their doom at Smithfield, fouling the streets en route and causing the roads around the market to run with blood, until a statute of 1851 moved the livestock market to Islington. Even after that date some of the capital's poorest communities replicated the rural habit of keeping livestock on the premises: pigs were said to outnumber people by three to one in the notorious Potteries, in North Kensington, living under the inhabitants' beds. Victorian London was famously susceptible to smog: the 'Great Fog' of 1886 brought bronchial disease and death to thousands. The problem eased from the 1890s, for reasons which remain unclear, though Booth observed that photographers still moved to the suburbs for cleaner air. Many believed Londoners to be enfeebled by their environment. They could be entrusted, Booth reported, with carrying chicken carcasses at Leadenhall, but hefty countrymen were preferred in milling and brewing. Dearle acknowledged that 'the smart young provincial can generally be sure of a good job' in building. Noise pollution—from street traders, paper sellers, street performers, cabmen and their horses' hooves—was almost taken for granted, though it was intense, and appears to have intensified over the second half of the century.

As the century progressed, the major environmental problem became that of traffic. The expansion of the built-up area did not bring a commensurate decentralization of commerce, with the result that London became a commuter city. The problem merited a Royal Commission in 1905, which heard of the saturation of commuter rail services during the morning peak (then lasting from 8 a.m. to 10 a.m.). The average speed of trains on the Inner Circle, lowered by the proximity of the stations in the City, was a leisurely 11.1 m.p.h. The Commission's suggestion that London's railways should be built with four tracks to allow for fast and stopping trains, as on the New York subway, was sensible but belated. Commuting by road was no more pleasurable. Molly Hughes remembered the tedious bus journey from Canonbury to the West End in the 1870s. The replacement of the 'knifeboard' by 'garden chair' seats on buses was a concession to commuter comfort, but these wider vehicles only exacerbated street congestion. By the time the Royal Commission sat this was an intractable problem, both in the City and the West End, where 2,500 vehicles per hour passed Marble Arch during the day. The Commission was neither the first nor the last public body to suggest street widening and demolition on an implausible scale to solve the problem. Without the funds or the will to rationalize its street plan, London remained congested. In the City, with a medieval street map and very narrow roads, the Corporation banned the construction of tramways—a rational response, but one which increased the volume of traffic. Those taking a vehicle into the Square Mile faced, according to P. F. W. Ryan in 1902, 'pressure that would almost embarrass an Arctic ship'.

Overall, then, the problem of poverty which forced London onto the national agenda in the late nineteenth century is best seen as an aspect of a wider urban problem, rooted in the severe concentration of activity in the core of the Victorian capital, serving both as a residential and a commercial centre. London would 'work' better only when its Victorian constraints had been broken.

Urban growth throughout history has depended upon the logistics of feeding a concentrated population. London finally burst its Victorian limits when bulk rail transport of food and milk made it possible to build over the market gardens and dairy farms on the edge of the metropolis. The expansion of the built-up area went hand-in-hand with the development of the commuter rail services which served it: overground extensions of the underground network in the north and north-west, suburban lines into the main line termini in the south and north-east. Much of this suburban building was aimed at the wealthy. Just as Highbury New Park had been developed in the 1860s to allow the rich to escape the cramped Georgian squares of Islington, so, as early as the 1900s, new houses in Edgware were being advertised with 'room for motor'. But suburban building in this period did not target only high-earners. Archibald Cameron Corbett, one of the least celebrated of the makers of modern London, developed Ilford in the north-east, Catford and Eltham in the south-east, and other areas for the benefit of clerks, officials, skilled workers, shop workers, and their equivalents. The movement of these people into the middle reaches of commuterland provided as much of the impetus for growth as the flight of the rich to the rural fringe. The Governors of Dulwich College found themselves forced by the market to relax building controls on their estate, allowing smaller buildings similar to those in surrounding areas, as the clerical army supplanted the wealthy residents whom the estate had been built originally to attract. In the north-east, those areas served

*(**a** and **b**) Regent Street before and after the demolition of Nash's Quadrant in the 1920s. Harold Clunn believed that 'nobody requires any knowledge of the architectural profession to see at a glance that the new Regent Street is in every way a worthy successor to the old one'.*

by the Great Eastern Railway's suburban services, on which the GER had been obliged to run cheap workmen's trains as a condition of being allowed to build its extension into Liverpool Street in the 1870s, developed as working-class suburbs—Walthamstow, Edmonton, Leytonstone, parts of Enfield.

This expansion accelerated the conversion of the central area to commerce and up-market residential building. Booth criticized the exclusive redevelopment of the Cadogan Estate in Chelsea for its failure to appreciate 'the economic strength of the classes who keep no servants and make no pretence to fashion'. The poor who still lived in the central area were most vulnerable. In an essay on 'Evicted

London' in his 1902 collection, Sims described the process by which a woman had her home literally dismantled around her: 'the roof, the doors, and the windows were removed while she (it is generally a woman) still remained crouching in a corner of the miserable room which contained the chair, the table, the bed, the frying pan and the tub that were her "furniture" '. One man known to Sims suffered eviction four times in six years.

Between 1900 and the 1930s the centre of London was transformed, becoming in essence the city we know today. The process was a piecemeal one, lacking the strategic direction and the architectural unity evident in the nineteenth-century rebuilding of Paris, and as a result it remains largely unchronicled except by the enthusiastic Harold P. Clunn, in his *London Rebuilt* of 1927. Clunn applauded the chief features of the transformation—the straightening and widening of the principal streets, the replacement of three- and four-storey buildings (of the type characteristic of the Victorian centre and still to be seen in, for example, Old Compton Street) by five- and six-storey ones, the supplanting of blackened brick and stucco by gleaming stone. He also welcomed the destruction of such statements of aristocratic exclusivity as the 'high garden walls of grimy black brick' which protected the town houses of the Marylebone Road from the nosy gaze of humanity. In general the transformation of the West End respected wealth more than birth, a fact epitomized by the emergence of the massive emporia lining Oxford Street, beginning with Debenham and Freebody in 1906 and Selfridge's in 1909. As Park Lane acquired what Clunn celebrated as 'a typical American appearance' in the 1920s, the aristocratic mansions around it succumbed to the

Chesterfield House, Stanhope Street. Built by Isaac Ware for the fourth Earl of Chesterfield in 1749, Chesterfield House was one of London's last surviving aristocratic mansions, falling victim to the inter-war modernization of Mayfair only in 1937.

developer. Around 1906 the Duke of Cambridge's mansion on the corner of Park Lane and Piccadilly made way for luxury flats and a car showroom. Devonshire House was demolished in 1918, Grosvenor House in 1927, the Holbein family's Dorchester House in 1929 (for the Dorchester Hotel), Lord Tweedmouth's Brook House in 1933, Chesterfield House in 1935. Steadily London lost its Marais.

This physical transformation of the centre spanned the First World War and was largely unaffected by it. Though London was the target of the first Zeppelin raids, damage to the city's fabric was minimal by comparison with the Blitz. The War's main effects on London derived from its galvanizing impact upon the capital's economy. Many of London's traditional industries—tailoring, boot-making, leather-working—needed little adaptation to military needs, while the small scale and habitual flexibility of London industry enabled others to adapt quickly: Jon Lawrence cites the instant retooling of an umbrella factory to produce gun components. London also benefited enormously from direct government investment in new war-related industries. The area around Woolwich Arsenal in the south-east and the Hayes-Willesden-Wembley belt in the west both grew rapidly. This was an enduring benefit. The west London industrial belt became the greatest concentration of manufacturing industry in southern England between the wars. When the Park Royal industrial area ceased to produce aeroplanes for the RAF it turned out London buses instead. In comparative terms, as Peter Hall has shown, even these developments were based upon small units of production, but the new industries of the west were far less strapped for space than producers in the centre. If the war industries had built upon traditional techniques of small-scale production, both the west London industrial area and the Lea Valley in the north (initially developed by the furniture industry, seeking to escape the pressures of the East End) soon attracted large employers in the new industries of the inter-war years. With the completion of the national electricity grid in the 1920s, industrial location became less restricted by energy supply and more concerned with proximity to the consumer; the motor industry (with the admittedly large exception of Ford's Dagenham plant) was drawn to the west London industrial estates not merely because they had once built tanks and aeroplanes but also because they offered easy access to the car showrooms of the West End. In the 1930s American manufacturers came to west London to work within Britain's imperial tariff wall; the Hoover Building on the A40 survives as the most elegant memorial to this phase of London's industrial evolution. These developments promised, for the first time, to turn London into a factory town.

Thus although the hothouse growth of the war years was artificial, it generated a real momentum, and London was not knocked back by the deflation and unemployment of the 1920s in the way that other industrial centres were. The first volume of Llewellyn Smith's *New Survey of London Life and Labour*, a follow-up to Booth forty years on, charted a one-third rise in earnings since 1890 and inferred that poverty—the problem central to Booth's enquiry—had virtually vanished. Recent reworking of the *New Survey* data has qualified this view; indeed, the case studies from Bermondsey detailed in the final volume (1935) show a pattern of poverty amongst riverside families, dependent daily upon the breadwinner finding casual work, that Booth would have recognized. So did the Pilgrim Trust's investigators, examining unemployment in Deptford in 1936, who found a familiar pattern of sporadic casual work interspersed with long periods of idleness. Beveridge, studying unemployment in the first volume of the *New Survey*, was more circumspect than his editor: London unemployment was 'the normal product of particular industrial methods, not the passing consequence of depression'. It was concentrated, as usual, in the docks, in public works, and, in the 1920s, in building. London escaped the worst effects of the depression, but had not cured her endemic social problems. The capital remained a magnet for those unable to find work elsewhere. After the war it attracted ex-servicemen, while throughout the deflationary years from 1920 it sucked in the workless from the depressed areas. One of them, John Bentley, a victim of the contraction of the cotton industry, told his story to the BBC in 1935. After tramping from Lancashire to London he endured the 'absolute hell' of fourteen consecutive nights on Waterloo Bridge: 'so cold—it was an effort to draw the breath into my body.' He rose from that nadir to pavement artistry on the Embankment and then to newspaper selling, which he considered the first step up from the gutter ('you're back in civilization—you talk to clean people again'). The journalist H. W. Massingham, reviving the ancient pursuit of East End slumming in 1936, discovered the absolute futility of hunting for casual decorating work: 'we not only felt like beggars; we were beggars . . . we were not wanted, were a nuisance, and few employers attempted to conceal the fact.'

London's jobless, though never fewer than 100,000 in the inter-war years, were still a forgotten and fragmented minority, denied the community support that consoled the unemployed of the depressed areas. Working-class politics in inter-war London revolved around housing rather than unemployment. It is the poor quality of the housing stock which emerges most strikingly from Massingham's account of the East End, where the occupiers of verminous buildings, denied sleep by biting bugs, 'got up and waged war on the brutes, armed with long sticks soaped at one end and a jampot of oil'. It was principally on the housing issue that the Labour Party, under Herbert Morrison, finally gained metropolitan power in the 1934 London County Council election. Labour would control the LCC until its abolition in 1965, but there was an artificiality in this hegemony. The dated boundaries of the administrative county now encapsulated, north of the river at least, little more than the inner city. Not only villa Toryism lived beyond the county boundary; so did the prosperous and secure workers of Park Royal and the other western industrial estates, and the self-employed plumbers and decorators who bought the owner-occupied houses built by speculative developers in Uxbridge or Acton.

It was this simple physical expansion of London which, more than anything, relieved the mounting social problems of Booth's day. Before 1914 competition for space produced high ground rents, leading to high house rents, which bore heavily on tenants, and high overheads, which bore heavily on industry. London's expansion allowed the construction of labour-intensive industries on a larger scale than before. Likewise, the LCC's suburban and out-county estates enabled it to get to grips with the problem of social housing, which had defeated it—largely because high costs made low-rent Council housing impossible—before 1914. London's growth also allowed the private housing market to make up for its failure in the Edwardian period. The vast majority of the one million houses constructed within a fifteen-mile radius of Charing Cross between 1919 and 1940 were privately built. A bankruptcy report on two Edgware partners in 1937 who had taken to speculative building after having been a 'maker of silk ties' and a 'gown manufacturer', suggests that housebuilding, like lodging housekeeping in Mayhew's day, had come to be seen as a way of turning small capital into a small fortune. Those who did not go bankrupt generally gave their clients what they wanted. Acacia Avenue has never lacked its critics, but the inter-war outer-London house was usually solid, spacious, and adorned by front and back gardens.

The problem was that, however effective this expansion might have been in mitigating London's problems, the city's relentless growth came to be seen as a threat to the interests of the nation at large. In 1936 Sir Malcolm Stewart, the Commissioner appointed under the Special Areas legislation, expressed the fear that industry's attraction to 'the macrocosm of London' was thwarting attempts to regenerate the depressed regions of Britain. In the following year the Royal Commission on the Distribution of the Industrial Population (the Barlow Commission) was appointed, with the somewhat loaded brief 'to consider what social, economic or strategical disadvantages arise from the concentration of industries . . . in large towns or in particular areas of the country'. The Commission's report does indeed appear animated by the view that large towns in general and Greater London in particular were undesirable. London was 'already too large' and was draining not only industry but also 'social, cultural and civic life' from the provinces; migration trends established during the recession threatened to make matters worse. The Commission recommended that a new statutory authority be empowered to license future industrial development in the Home Counties.

The task of persuading industry not to locate where it wished to locate, and of dissuading the jobless from following industry, was Canute-like. Given the tepid backing provided by the National Government for the Special Areas initiative, little support should have been expected in normal circumstances for this oblique attempt to remedy the failure of Special Area policy. But circumstances were not normal in 1937, when the Commission was appointed, and they were still less normal in January 1940, when it reported. What concerned the Chamberlain government was less London's growing industrial concentration than the increasing proportion of the national population gathering in a city vulnerable to aerial bombing. Among the many influences shaping Chamberlain's appeasement diplomacy in the late 1930s was the belief that the effect of war on London would be catastrophic. The Committee for Imperial Defence estimated that 175,000 Londoners would be killed in the first twenty-four hours of war. In the light of the eventual death toll of 30,000 in six years of war, such projections appear alarmist, but the Second World War *did* bring urban genocide to Dresden and Hamburg, to Hiroshima and Nagasaki. Had German nuclear research proceeded at the pace of German rocket technology, London might have usurped Hiroshima's fate. News of the Germans' success with the V2 rockets led researchers on the Manhattan Project, planning the American atomic bomb, to fear London's imminent obliteration.

It was as well for the Cockney psyche that Londoners knew nothing of nuclear weaponry until after the German defeat: mere high explosive seemed menacing enough. As war approached some Londoners made for the suburbs in the belief that they were safer, and houses unsold since the downturn in 1937 were snapped up. Those who remained in the centre really did fear, after the onset of the Blitz in September 1940, that each day might be their last, if Vere Hodgson's diary of life in Notting Hill is representative. The evacuation of 750,000 school children, 554,000 mothers, and 77,000 other persons in September 1939 was achieved voluntarily, if not smoothly. Gradually, an awareness of the feasibility of survival induced that mixture of stoicism and perkiness that kept London smiling through. 'It is amazing . . . how well our nerves keep on the whole', Hodgson wrote in April 1941: 'if we are bombed then they go a bit; but if we survive the night, we come up bright and smiling the next morning, very keen to exchange notes on the adventures of the night.' Gradually the evacuees returned, many, like the author's mother, preferring the risk of bombing to the certainty of snooty Home Counties' hosts. By May 1944 it was said that Londoners felt guilty not to be sharing the dangers faced by those leaving for the Normandy beaches. At any moment, though, the loss of friends or relatives might destroy an individual's world, and the entire community had to accept the piecemeal removal of familiar landmarks, with no way of knowing when the erosion would end. Hodgson would 'never forget the horror', on the terrifying night of 29 December 1940, of learning that the City was ablaze and that 'they were trying to save St Paul's'. The authorities' decision to concentrate fire-fighting that night on saving the Cathedral was psychologically sound, and Hubert Mason's powerful photograph of the dome looming through the flames has become the enduring image of the Blitz. A less familiar photograph, showing the Lord Mayor's procession of 1945 passing down a flattened

The Lord Mayor's Show passing down Cannon Street, 1945. London's war damage was not on a par with that of Hamburg or Dresden, or even Coventry or Plymouth, but the scars left by the raids on the city in 1940–1 were clear enough even five years later.

EKCO

Cannon Street, provides a corrective reminder of what the City actually suffered. The docks and the East End received comparable treatment: of 24,000 dwellings in Poplar on the outbreak of war only *one* escaped damage.

The harm done to the capital's fabric between 1940 and 1945 provided the opportunity, while the wartime fashion for planning provided the motivation, to produce the semi-planned city that is post-war London. The blueprints were the two major proposals authored by Patrick Abercrombie, the guru of post-war urban planning—the *County of London Plan*, produced for the LCC in 1943, and the *Greater London Plan* of 1944. Abercrombie, Professor of Town Planning in the University of London, had been a member of the Barlow Commission but had refused to sign its Majority Report, which he considered insufficiently comprehensive in its ambition. No such criticism could be levelled at the two plans, which envisaged a holistic redesign of London. The *County Plan* envisaged residential and industrial zoning, the channelling of London's traffic, and even the regeneration of the Thames, 'London's most beautiful and neglected open space'. The *Greater London Plan* envisaged the strengthening of existing powers to create a Green Belt around the built-up area. It also developed the Barlow Commission's advocacy of dispersal without reference to the Special Areas, proposing the establishment of ten New Towns beyond the Green Belt to relieve the concentration of people and industry in the centre.

There was much that was visionary, even Utopian, about the Abercrombie proposals. The County Plan's eagerness to establish designated 'precincts'—the doctors' quarter, the university quarter, the theatre quarter, etc.—now seems almost quaint. The suggestion that the radial roads considered central to traffic management could become 'pleasant parkway[s] along which the Londoner can reach the country' has a hollow ring to today's users of Westway or the Old Kent Road. The objective of providing for 'a greater mingling of the different groups of London's society' now appears beyond the planner's reach. Above all, the view that the 'staggering' cost of redesigning the entire metropolis could be tolerated because extensive rebuilding was necessary anyway showed little awareness of the realities of post-war Britain. What was realized of Abercrombie's vision was what could be achieved by fiat and relatively cheaply: the consolidation of the Green Belt and the establishment of the New Towns.

The policy of building up a Green Belt by public land acquisitions and curbs on development had been introduced by the LCC before the war, but the comprehensiveness of the accomplishment owed much to the near cessation of building in 1939. In fact the limits of the built-up area today lie virtually where they lay on the outbreak of war. However fortuitous its formation, once it was established the Green Belt acquired tenacious defenders in the dormitory towns which grew up beyond it in a process of leapfrog development. It protected these towns from metropolitan encroachment and served, in Susan Fainstein and Ken Young's phrase, as 'a political cordon sanitaire'.

The New Towns, beginning with Stevenage in 1947, were intended to act as agents of the dispersal of industry and population, but their success in both respects has been limited. The New Towns proper, along with the economically similar overspill communities of Swindon, Northampton, and Peterborough accounted for less than 20 per cent of population growth in the non-metropolitan south-east in 1951–66. Those who did move tended to be the skilled workmen required by New Town industries, which meant that the initiative did little to diminish council housing waiting lists, as had been intended. These muted efforts at decentralization were more than offset by the centripetal effects of office building. Between 1948 and 1961 the capital's office space almost tripled—an expansion largely unanticipated by Abercrombie. Hemmed in by the iron girdle of the Green Belt, housing, industry, and commercial real estate competed for space in a constricted metropolis.

The first victim was the holistic conception of the planned city that Abercrombie had bequeathed. Large-scale remodelling of that type, impeded anyway by the weakness of the LCC as a planning authority and by the lack of any single strategic authority for the whole Greater London region, now became prohibitively expensive as the cost of central land escalated. Post-war strategic planning in central London has been limited to attempts to iron out specific problem points, and even these have frequently encountered resistance from local authorities or other interested parties. With the defeat of the proposals to 'rationalize' Piccadilly Circus in 1960, it became evident that the tide had turned against Abercrombieism. When the Buchanan Report on Traffic in Towns, in 1963, contemplated the complete rebuilding of the area bounded by Euston Road, Tottenham Court Road, and Oxford Street they made clear that this was a conceptual exercise. So it was, and so it would remain. In the 1960s the planners turned their attention to the growing housing crisis.

Around 116,000 houses in the Greater London area had been destroyed in the war or so badly damaged as to require virtual rebuilding. Around half the houses that did survive dated from before 1918. Some 30,000 wartime prefabs were handed over to local authorities in 1948; many would still be occupied in the 1970s. Though the population of Greater London fell by 2.7 per cent between 1951 and 1961 as many commuters chose to leapfrog the Green Belt, the number of separate households rose by 1.5 per cent. With the supply of bomb sites becoming exhausted by the mid-1950s, residential building was forced into an unequal competition with commercial development for available space. House prices in London rose by 60 per cent between 1958 and 1963. It was at this moment of upward pressure on London rents that the national Rent Act of 1957 began to unwind the mechanism of rent regulation which had existed since the First World War, and which meant that some controlled rents were barely 15 per cent higher than their 1914 level. This gave an extra twist to the developing crisis, as landlords of privately rented property sought to induce tenants of controlled property to leave in order to gain vacant possession for sale or to realize the full market rent from new tenants. The most notorious of them, Peter Rachman, the owner of run-down property in Paddington and Shepherd's Bush, ousted unwanted tenants by intimidation. The most unwanted tenants tended to be the elderly, with long-controlled rents at very low levels, and young families, who occupied a disproportionate amount of space and exacted most 'wear and tear' upon the property. The need to ensure that neither children nor the elderly ended up on the streets left local authority housing departments at the mercy of landlords who were not generally acting illegally.

As in the 1880s, the housing crisis meshed with other social problems, in this case the growing tension between London's native and immigrant communities. Where Victorian London had been a city of immigrants, from the countryside, from Ireland, or from abroad, the maturing of the metropolis saw the proportion of London-born rise sharply: 62 per cent of the heads of household in the Milner

Holland Committee's 1963 tenant survey were actually London-born. The reversal of this trend had begun in the late 1940s, with the first arrivals from the Caribbean, and a high proportion of the 1.1 million West Indians who settled in Britain between 1948 and 1962 ended up in London. Inevitably they gravitated towards areas of cheap housing, and disproportionately towards the private rental sector. The housing shortage exacerbated the tension existing already in areas where black and white communities collided, exemplified by the race riots in Notting Hill in 1958.

The belief that London's social tensions could be ameliorated by housing reform lay behind the last major public housing drive in the capital, from the late 1950s to the mid-1970s. With little vacant land available, it concentrated upon

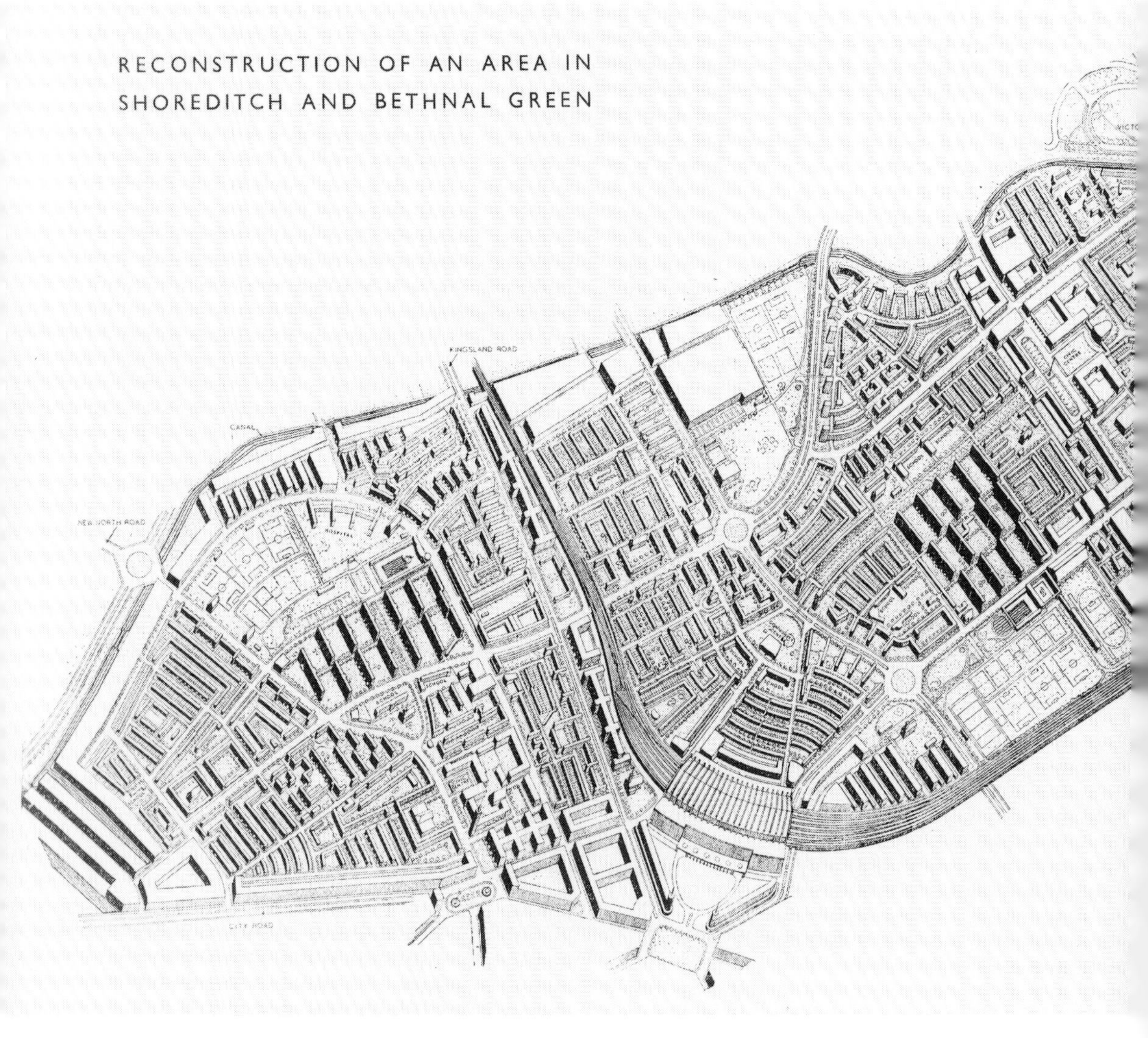
RECONSTRUCTION OF AN AREA IN
SHOREDITCH AND BETHNAL GREEN
KINGSLAND ROAD
CANAL
NEW NORTH ROAD
CITY ROAD

Proposed redevelopment of a 980-acre area of the East End by J. H. Forshaw and Patrick Abercrombie for the London County Council, 1943. The proposal was said to 'embody the character and vitality of a new East End'.

slum-clearance—an increasingly pressing need since much late Victorian housing had been subject to progressive neglect as the end of the standard 99-year London lease approached. Whatever the public health case for clearance, the removal of old neighbourhoods and settled communities for high-density high-rise blocks was often contentious. Young and Willmott's classic study of the destruction of community in Bethnal Green addressed contemporary fears about the process. Their conclusions were not beyond dispute: in comparing a long-established community with one recently thrown together by rehousing, they were not comparing like with like—the sociology of the mature tower block remains to be written. Bethnal Green, whose principal post-war industry appears to have been sociology, was probably over-romanticized as a working-class utopia—this was, after all, the area which nurtured the Kray twins. It is nonetheless clear that slum clearance engendered much insensitivity on the part of the public authorities. Stephen Elkins describes a scheme for local authority flats in Islington being submitted by the Borough Council to the LCC without the residents of the clearance area knowing anything of the proposal. Rehousing sites in Lambeth were said to have been selected 'by a brief external examination from a passing car'. It was in this period that planners' well-meaning attempts to contain the social problems of a crowded metropolis put them at odds with those for whom they planned. What David Donnison has called the 'micropolitics of the city' developed below the level of conventional politics—an ad hoc politics of community-based resistance to threats to the urban environment or amenities from clearance proposals or road schemes. A 'Homes Before Roads' Party contested the 1971 Borough Council elections.

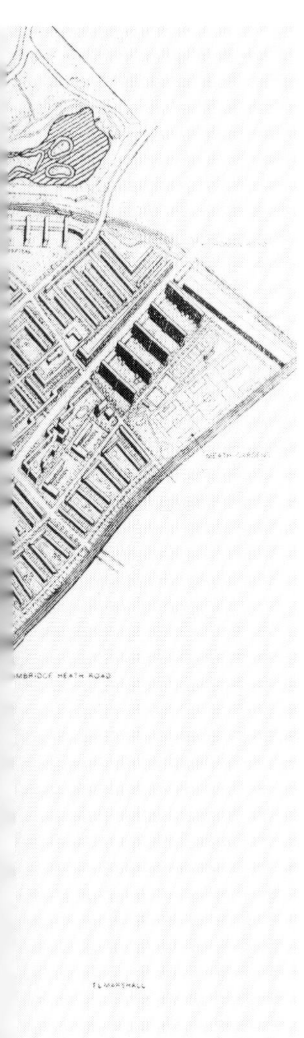

Planners' heavy-handedness with 'the people' perhaps compensated for their increasingly evident weakness in relation to commerce. After the failure of central government attempts to regulate office construction in London in the 1960s, property development in central London has proceeded rapidly, checked only briefly by the repercussions of the 1973 oil shock. Planners schooled in the Abercrombiean tradition of benevolent despotism were ill equipped to haggle with Mammon: 'education won't prepare you for the experience of having a megamillion pound individual sitting across from you who will break your legs', acknowledged the Westminster Director of Planning in the 1980s. By then some developers yearned for a more dirigiste public authority to curb the developers' tendency to overbuild. With the abolition of the GLC in 1986 and the hands-off role of the Department of the Environment in the Thatcher years, however, no strategic authority existed to counteract the Borough Councils' eagerness to compete with each other for office developments. In an industry prone to overcapacity, office supply frequently ran ahead of demand—'London needs another office block like it needs another plague', was the slogan of the campaign against the Coin Street development in north Lambeth in the early 1980s—but the explosion of the financial services sector in the 1980s ensured that the property industry never permanently overextended itself. Underwriting the London property boom of the 1980s were commercial rental levels second only to those of the similarly constricted Tokyo.

Commercial expansion on a scale unknown before 1945 intensified the pressure on metropolitan space, and lay at the root of two of the principal features of the modern London economy—spiralling house prices and the collapse of manufacturing industry. The completion of the Green Belt ensured that the inter-war response to housing demand, the steady expansion of the built-up area, was not possible. It is true that residential London now straddles the Green Belt—Peter Hall defines the London region as stretching from Basingstoke to Chelmsford, Bishops Stortford to Horsham—but from the 1960s the cost and discomfort of the daily commute from such places have deflected many back into the centre. 'Large areas of London have been rediscovered in the last ten years, and settlement has followed discovery', the Milner Holland committee was told in 1965. 'A classical pattern is repeated: the expansive pressures for *lebensraum* are leading to the middle-class colonization of new districts on the fringe of traditionally desirable ones, ... [and] extremely high prices are being charged for houses which for years ... have been rented by working-class families.' In March 1964 the Committee was given by the Leader of Lambeth Council a description of gentrification which could be applied as well today:

> As sociologists you will be aware that the trend amongst the pseudo-intellectuals was first towards Chelsea, then it moved to Fulham and then Hampstead, and then it got into photographers' premises and what have you on the river. Then suddenly North Lambeth became rather the thing. Cleaver Square was a classical example. Some solicitor invested trust funds and so on, and gradually built the place up into respectability. You close the basement, put a girder across to hold the rest up, you paint the front door yellow and buy a coach lamp for 30/- and it immediately becomes rather, I would call it, lower middle class.

With the liberalization of the housing market in the late 1950s a house price inflation began which, with interruptions in 1973 and 1988, has continued ever since. It created many 'windfall millionaires' through the accident of inheritance, but it has also sharpened the distinction between haves and have-nots in the property world. In the mid-1990s the inner London boroughs still had the lowest owner-occupation rates in England.

Social polarization has been accelerated by the collapse of employment in manufacturing industry. London's high overheads have always burdened her industries; post-war developments exacerbated the effect. Even in the boom years of the 1950s, employment in the Greater London conurbation increased more slowly than in every region but the north-west. London was therefore particularly vulnerable to the pressure upon British manufacturing industry from the mid-1970s. Half a million jobs were lost in London between 1971 and 1984, on top of substantial losses in the 1960s, and manufacturing employment halved again between 1982 and 1994. The recession of the early 1990s proved particularly severe in London, manufacturing employment in the six east London boroughs falling by 23 per cent in 1991–3 alone.

London is coming to exemplify the Thatcherite paradigm that a modern economy can live by services alone. Some have related this development to the striking growth of the financial services sector with the liberalization of trade in the City in the 1980s. Saskia Sassen's 1991 study of the three centres of world finance—London, New York, and Tokyo—argued that these 'global cities' became the control centres for the financing and management of a dispersed industrial sector. Their societies consequently became polarized between a managerial elite formed by the grandees of finance and of its ancillary services—lawyers, accountants, etc.—and an underclass employed in low-wage, low-skill service jobs in restaurants, luxury hotels, and gourmet shops. Sassen's thesis is routinely challenged by students of modern London: her reductionist view of the global city economy ('the "things" a global city makes are services and financial goods') downplays such features as the tourist industry—visitors spent £6.65 billion in London in 1995—and the other elements of economic diversity which have ensured that London has not become a modern Jarrow. The post-war deindustrialization of the *rive gauche* has not devastated the area but encouraged its steady conversion to the service of culture and leisure, with the Festival of Britain in 1951 and the subsequent development of the south bank arts complex, the laying out of the Jubilee Gardens in 1977, the re-creation of the Globe Theatre, the conversion of Bankside power station into an art gallery, and the 'bistroization' of the Oxo tower. Sassen's portrait of developing polarization would, though, command general assent. The success of Abercrombie's proposals to contain London's physical expansion and the failure of his plans for economic decentralization have re-created some of the features of the late Victorian city—the fierce competition for space, the congestion of the city centre, the stark contrast between rich and poor underlined by their often random juxtaposition. Income polarization has increased since the 1970s: average per capita income stood 22 per cent higher than the national average in 1992 but 1.5 million Londoners were eligible for Income Support in 1996 and five of the ten most deprived local authority wards in England lie in Greater London.

The London of the millennium is the product of the complex political, economic, and social forces described above. Its development emphasizes the unpredictable nature of urban evolution in those cities—the overwhelming majority—which are not the product of a single grand design or authoritarian vision. The Victorians, in rejecting Georgian urban rationalism, preserved the random layout of central London and endowed it with the stylistic eclecticism which it still displays. Victorian London had no defining style; indeed, if central London has a predominant style today, it is probably the neoclassicism of the inter-war years which, for all its monumentality, is oddly anonymous. The high cost of central land has tended to push large-scale design experiments into peripheral and residual areas—the modernist utopia of Thamesmead, for instance, and the more engaging postmodern montage in the redeveloped Docklands.

Away from the centre a greater degree of visual uniformity presents itself, though the impression of monotony is superficial. London has its stretches of dreary post-war mass-housing, particularly in the traditional working-class areas of the East End and the inner south-east, but the weakness of the London County Council as 'strategic' housing authority in the early post-war period ensured that the inner ring never became a single belt of high-rise, high-density estates during the years when such building appealed as a solution to housing shortage. Instead London's housing stock continues to be dominated by the 'by-law' terraces of the late Victorian period and by inter-war semi's. Aerial photographs of London's suburbs, whether Victorian or inter-war, tend to support the charge of monotony often levelled at them, but the reality of these areas' construction, with many small builders and a weak or non-existent planning regime, made uniformity impossible even there. Beyond the inter-war suburbs lies the Green Belt, still largely effective in confining the metropolis to its 1939 limits. The dormitory towns within and outside it, though inescapably tied to the London economy, do not consider themselves—and thus are not—metropolitan.

Increasingly the pattern of London life is one of shifting social configurations within a relatively settled urban fabric. The pattern of middle-class colonization of former working-class areas identified by the Milner Holland Committee and other observers in the 1960s has spread with every upswing in the property cycle. Former working-class 'cottages' in Spitalfields, North Lambeth, Clapham, Greenwich, Islington, and parts of Hackney and Brixton have been gentrified. Other suburbs have gained diversity with the outward movement of London's immigrant communities. The 1991 census, the first to ask about ethnicity, identified 33 separate non-British communities of 10,000 or more in London. Turkish groceries in Grove Park; the complex of Japanese shops, food halls, and restaurants at Colindale; the proposed Jewish *eruv* in Hampstead Garden Suburb; and, above all, the magnificently crafted Hindu temple in that epitome of suburbanity, Neasden, all testify to London's evolving ethnic topography.

Today the scope for change in the capital's physical fabric appears limited. So far as residential property is concerned, the last thirty years have seen a pronounced change of public mood in favour of the preservation and rehabilitation of the elderly house. Reaction against the inhumane effects of large-scale slum-clearance lay behind the provisions of the 1969 Housing Act providing indiscriminate grants for renovation. Most of these grants disappeared into developers' pockets, but the tide of demolitions was stopped. Since then, a buoyant property market, supported even in lean years by the Green Belt restrictions and by the trend to owner-occupation, has ensured that almost any 'period' property can be profitably renovated. Rehabilitation has also rejuvenated some of the least promising public housing estates, but it is in this area that medium-term change to London's housing stock appears most probable, as the problem of life-expired post-war estates becomes unavoidable. They will have few defenders.

If rising property prices worked to preserve residential property, the rich returns to office development since the 1950s have posed a continuous threat to London's non-residential landmarks. Even here, though, a heightened concern for urban preservation, and a more vocal conservationist movement have made the demolition of these landmarks more contentious and difficult. Again the turning point came with the reaction against modernism during the 1960s. The contrast between British Rail's gratuitous demolition of Hardwick's Euston Arch in 1962 and its inability to destroy Scott's St Pancras in 1969 makes the point. By 1975 Simon Jenkins could feel confident that 'the fight for the relics of the pre-twentieth-century West End is almost won'; his judgement has since been largely vindicated. The defining episode of the 1980s was the very public battle between one developer, Sir Peter Palumbo, and the conservation lobby—including the Prince of Wales—over a premier site not in the West End but in the City, on the corner of Cheapside and Queen Victoria Street. It ended, certainly, in a defeat for the conservationists, but Palumbo's victory, secured only after substituting a gimmicky Stirling design for an undistinguished and *déraciné* effort by Mies van der Rohe, has been a Pyrrhic one. Developers lacking Palumbo's clout and contacts tend to shun controversy, or at least to avoid demolishing buildings with articulate supporters: the City's most conspicuous experiment in postmodernism has occurred on the unloved expanse of London Wall. After two centuries of piecemeal transformation, by the market and by the planners, London would appear to be approaching the stationary state.

6 Temples of Commerce: Revolutions in Shopping and Banking

Michael Winstanley

As we enter the twenty-first century, the continued vitality of the town centre as the prime location of financial services and shopping facilities is increasingly portrayed as being under threat. During the last two decades a sprawling, specialized 'out-of-town' landscape has emerged of supermarkets, retail warehouses, and shopping malls which are home to many of the retail outlets previously associated with towns' core commercial districts. Advances in information technology are tempting firms to abandon expensive, centrally located offices. The facility to transfer money or dispense cash electronically are reducing the need for retail banking premises on the high street. Such developments reflect a growing realization on the part of property developers, commercial enterprises, and retailers that town centres are overly expensive, inherently inflexible, even potentially redundant, incapable of adapting to the changing patterns of work and shopping and more rapid and diverse forms of communication.

Whereas the migration of manufacturing and bulk warehousing to purpose-built industrial estates has generally been welcomed as lessening pollution, eliminating eyesores, and providing opportunities for urban regeneration in the form of new residential accommodation or leisure facilities, and the potential to relocate office work has been supported as a way of reducing inner-city congestion and regional imbalance, the apparent threat to urban retailing has aroused strong emotions and given rise to a variety of schemes to preserve, even enhance, the importance of the 'traditional' high street. However, those charged with revitalizing central shopping areas face major problems. The costs and inconvenience of restructuring invariably outweigh those involved in the development of virgin sites on the outskirts. The outskirts are also more accessible from the major road network and offer considerably more car parking. Conservationists' pressure to preserve much of the existing street layout and physical fabric of older buildings is a further constraint. The wholesale demolition and redevelopment which characterized the 1960s and 1970s, therefore, are now regarded as prohibitively expensive and cultural anathemas. Rather there is an emphasis on the conversion and adaptation of redundant buildings to retain the architectural integrity of the urban landscape.

The irony of preserving them would not be lost on those who erected them; they had few qualms about demolishing premises which were not suited to the needs of modern commerce, or of employing architectural designs and building materials alien to the vernacular heritage of an area. The establishment and development of most town centres owe their *raison d'être* to commerce, and we need to remember that much of what is today considered as 'traditional' is relatively new, having been created largely during the last two centuries. Current developments in retailing, banking, and services, therefore, and their impact on the commercial role and appearance of the town centre, must be considered in the context of a history of continual adaptation and restructuring, both within and between towns in the urban hierarchy.

It is a story which involves consideration of a wide range of complex, overlapping themes—economic, technological, financial, legal, political, and cultural—operating at local, regional, national, and even international levels. Of paramount importance have been changes in the scale, composition, and location of demand for commercial services. These have rarely been uniformly manifested across the country. Before the early nineteenth century, growth was primarily concentrated in the prosperous south-east. London's banking role was clearly exceptional. Emerging spa resorts such as Bath or Cheltenham, fashionable seaside resorts like Brighton, and most county and market towns south of a line from the Severn to the Humber witnessed accelerating investment in new retail facilities. Further north and west, the dispersed nature of a population more reliant on pastoral farming, combined with uncertain and poorly paid employment in manufacturing and mining, restricted investment in commercial premises to a smaller number of administrative, trading, and social centres. As the pace of industrial development quickened from the 1820s, the new towns of the north exhibited dramatic changes: the enhancement of covered market provision; the introduction and rapid diffusion of co-operative retailing; the emergence of neighbourhood shops and proto-suburban shopping centres; and the expansion of provincial banking and mutual savings institutions. By the last quarter of the century, however, the potential for further expansion and innovation was once again more evident further south. Between 1850 and 1914, London expanded its role as the premier national and international financial market and administrative centre, creating an unprecedented demand for office accommodation and banking facilities. The wealth generated by this, combined with a new transport system, promoted the wholesale rebuilding of the capital's shopping districts, especially department stores providing fashionable clothing, household furnishings, and jewellery. Demand from the lower-middle class in suburban Middlesex, Essex, Surrey, and Kent created opportunities for the expansion of large-scale food and clothing multiples and variety stores. Although J. B. Priestley exaggerated for literary effect, there is much to recommend his contrast in 1934 between 'nineteenth-century England', the larger part of the Midlands and the north, with its fried-fish shops, good class drapers, confectioners, and corner shops, and the 'new post-war England' which he identified as he re-entered London, 'a large-scale, mass production job, with cut prices' which could 'almost accept Woolworths as its symbol'. These regional variations have proved remarkably resilient, but they have been progressively eroded from the 1950s by substantial improvements in standards of living, increasing consumer mobility, and the remorseless advance of a national market dominated by a shrinking number of major retailers.

Commercial premises have also changed markedly in appearance and function. Widening access to world markets, the development of mass production, processing, and packing, have simultaneously expanded the range of consumer goods and foodstuffs on offer while reducing the range of jobs performed on retail premises. Cheap, reliable forms of energy in the form of gas and later electricity, have allowed for the remodelling of interiors and extended the hours during which business transactions could feasibly and safely be effected. New building materials and methods—plate glass, reinforced steel, concrete—have transformed the external elevation and revolutionized the use of internal floor space. This increase in scale has been accompanied by a severing of the link between the domestic and business spheres which characterized the premises of the eighteenth-century shopkeeper and banker. The significance of architectural innovation and aesthetics has been muted in shop design where fashion and purpose have been more pronounced influences. Shop frontages have been so frequently altered that even the largest firms have rarely attracted designers of national repute. The joint-stock banks, however, sought to project an image of enduring security through building in bastardized 'Renaissance' and 'Classical' styles. In more recent decades, some larger concerns have experimented with modernist and latterly postmodernist architecture but, with notable exceptions such as Lloyds of London, they have remained imitators rather than initiators of fashion, with style invariably subservient to features concerned with location and functionality.

Entrepreneurs' ability to raise capital and to obtain possession, as either owner or secure tenant, of prime commercial sites on which to develop their businesses has been of cardinal importance. The concept of limited liability enabled businesses to overcome the constraints inherent in dependence on personal sources of credit, partnerships, and reinvested profits. From the late nineteenth century, banks, insurance companies, and commercial property developers were increasingly willing to provide mortgages, loans, debentures, or leaseback arrangements, or to take on the roles of developer and landlord, because they viewed investment in prime commercial sites and premises as offering the potential for relatively high, secure returns and long-term capital appreciation. As in other sectors of the economy such as agriculture, however, they were sometimes balked by patterns of landownership. In many urban areas this was fragmented and led inevitably to incremental, unplanned, and piecemeal change. Gaining possession of sufficiently large blocks of land within an environment conducive to the operations of large-scale business has always been an expensive and protracted process. Businesses have often been assisted, however, by the activities of the state, both local authorities and central government, which have intervened for a variety of financial, strategic, and environmental reasons. Occasionally, government agencies have acted both as property developers and landlords. More commonly, they have worked in partnership with private landlords and property developers, functioning as facilitators and regulators, by invoking legislative powers to demolish narrow, congested streets, unsavoury housing, or polluting manufacturing premises and replace them with broad, central thoroughfares suitable for intensive commercial development. In the twentieth century, as the costs of central restructuring have increased and the car has transformed the mobility of customer and employee alike, developers have pressed for access to peripheral green field or reclaimed industrial sites. The state, intentionally or otherwise, has abetted this switch in emphasis by the construction of trunk roads and motorways and by regional rejuvenation policies which have encouraged development on derelict industrial sites, although in professed policy it has displayed an ambivalent attitude and now increasingly seeks to restrict out-of-town retailing. Although market capitalism has undoubtedly been the major determinant of the urban commercial landscape over the last two centuries, therefore, its development has also been a political process as well.

Local authorities' attempts in the late eighteenth century to establish tighter control over the urban environment were primarily concerned with what today would be called 'town centre management' and reflected twin desires to eliminate nuisances and promote amenities. Improvement commissioners and municipal boroughs gradually acquired powers through a series of local Acts to light, pave, and police central thoroughfares, and to prevent obstructions to the passage of pedestrians and vehicular traffic alike. Increasingly, they extended their ambitions to effecting dramatic alterations to street patterns, seeking to demolish what were then regarded as unsightly old buildings which could not be converted to modern usage and imposing uniform building lines and regulations. The results of these initiatives were similar to the effects of enclosure in agriculture. They transformed the medieval landscape which still characterized most provincial cities and larger towns into something recognizably modern, sweeping away the intimacy of mixed residential quarters and small-scale businesses while facilitating their replacement with warehouses, banks, and retail outlets owned by larger businesses that had the funds either to develop them or to pay the high rental values which they commanded.

The pace of such improvements accelerated during the nineteenth century, spreading initially from London and select resort towns to larger trading centres such as Newcastle, Liverpool, Manchester, and Bristol and subsequently to prosperous, expanding industrial towns lower down the urban hierarchy. London's Regent Street was laid out after an Enabling Act of 1813 which set up commissioners with special borrowing powers to purchase land and to recoup their investment by selling long leases. It was followed by New Oxford Street in the 1840s, Victoria Street and Southwark Street in the 1860s, and Shaftesbury Avenue and Charing Cross Road in the 1870s and 1880s. Dale Street in Liverpool and Market Street in Manchester were both first widened in the 1820s, while in the 1830s Newcastle's Grey Street set new standards of taste and refinement, rapidly establishing itself as the retail and banking centre of the city. The property booms of the late nineteenth century encouraged Leeds, Manchester, Glasgow, Cardiff, and a range of other cities and smaller towns to contemplate whatever further improvements their borrowing powers would allow, primarily to enhance investment in central commercial districts. It was during this period that Joseph Chamberlain launched Birmingham's civic improvements, laying out wide boulevards and a new street, Corporation Street, which was intended to make the city 'the retail shop of the whole of the Midland counties of England'.

The transformation of the market—that most 'traditional' pre-industrial commercial activity—was an integral part of most of these schemes. In the late eighteenth century, most markets were still conducted in the open streets or market square. The nature of their trade was heavily dependent on supplies from neighbouring agricultural hinterlands. Wholesaling and retailing were temporally, rather than spatially, delineated by a mixture of custom and market regulations. Traders variously exposed their wares for sale. Some simply spread them on the ground. Others sold from sacks, baskets, panniers, or carts, but relatively substantial traders deployed trestle-tables or covered stalls. Permanent protection from the elements was limited to butchers' shambles or partially covered accommodation provided under old dual-purpose market-and-town halls like those which still survive in many smaller market towns, and was usually reserved for dealers in corn and dairy produce. The seasonality, unpredictability, and varied nature of trade, however, meant that manorial or corporate authorities were generally reluctant to invest in more substantial premises even if they had the wherewithal and land to do so.

As trade increased from the late eighteenth century, however, this provided both problems and opportunities for market owners, traders, and customers. There were regular complaints that streets were so densely thronged with carts, stalls, and people as to become impassable, threatening the viability of other forms of commercial activity, while posing physical and, allegedly, moral dangers to pedestrians. Congestion resulted in traders spilling out beyond appointed sites for conducting business into other parts of town or public houses, leading to prosecutions for unlawful trading by market owners and complaints from customers that regulations governing transactions were being flouted. Customers and traders alike objected to being exposed to all weathers. Market owners struggled to enforce regulations and to collect tolls and dues. Markets appeared increasingly chaotic and in need of rationalization, while their shanty structure affronted civic dignity and pride. Critics of Manchester's markets in the 1830s berated them as a straddling array of 'unsightly wooden erections covered with tattered canvas' which were not what 'a town of great wealth and magnitude might be expected to possess'. As concerns about public health gathered momentum in the 1840s, the insanitary nature of market operations also featured in the 'Health of Towns' debate. Markets, however necessary and profitable, were rapidly degenerating into public nuisances.

Different private and public agencies sought to capitalize on this situation by providing more appropriate facilities. By the mid-nineteenth century there had been significant investment in corn exchanges, particularly in eastern and southern England, where the more substantial market towns vied for a share of the important cereal trade. Fifteen towns in Lincolnshire alone acquired new exchanges between 1847 and 1857. These were often elaborate structures in Italianate or Elizabethan style, largely funded by private companies or public subscriptions from local property owners and shopkeepers who stood to benefit from the prosperity it was hoped such edifices would bring. They served a dual purpose, providing shelter for farmers and dealers on market days and, for the rest of the time, venues for public functions such as concerts, balls, or lectures. This option was not a feasible solution to problems posed by the buoyant trade in livestock. Cattle markets were traditionally held in the open, with animals of all descriptions being driven through the streets before being tethered or penned for sale. As trade increased and became concentrated in fewer centres, congestion and public health hazards obliged market authorities to relocate livestock markets out of town, preferably close to a railhead. New markets were established at junctions like Crewe to exploit the convenience of their central locations. By 1900 the haggling and personal negotiations associated with earlier forms of dealing had also been largely replaced by regulated auction marts. The result of these changes was that, except in the smaller market towns, agricultural wholesaling had been largely removed from the streets.

The most intractable problems were those associated with the ubiquitous, retail markets in industrial towns and cities. These functioned as major sources of perishable foodstuffs for the working class throughout the century and as outlets for cheap manufactured goods. Given their acknowledged problems, it is perhaps surprising that the streets remained their dominant venue in major centres like Nottingham, Leicester, Northampton, and Norwich. Even in Birmingham, which had erected a market hall in 1833, street trading continued to thrive. In most expanding towns, however, there were vigorous efforts to provide covered accommodation, particularly for trades such as butchery and fishmongery and the products of the 'small industries of the farm', especially poultry, butter, and cheese. Old corporate boroughs in the south-west, reinvigorated by prosperity brought by mining, were among the pioneers in this, the market town of Helston in Cornwall erecting stone-built premises behind its new town hall in 1837. Elsewhere, a spate of voluntary and individual initiatives enjoyed patchy success. Private capital was responsible for a new covered market in Leeds in the

Arcadian Retreats

MICHAEL WINSTANLEY

Covered, pedestrianized shopping arcades, built off major thoroughfares, were among the major urban commercial developments taking place between the mid-1870s and early 1930s, and exemplify many of the broader trends in retail provision during the period.

The prototypes were small select developments catering for a rich, fashion-conscious, leisured class. The Royal Opera and Burlington Arcades in London (1817, 1818) drew their inspiration from Paris, and were laid out as part of the Crown and Burlington estates. Thereafter, arcades in London enjoyed mixed success, and the concept spread only slowly to the provinces, primarily to prosperous commercial cities such as Bristol (1824) and Newcastle (1832) and resort towns such as Bath (1825) and Cheltenham (1845). They came into their own during the retail expansion in the late Victorian and Edwardian decades. Most of the substantial arcades of that period were built in the industrial towns and cities of the north, Midlands, South Wales, and Scotland, especially those where improvement schemes created deep, concentrated plots of land between major thoroughfares. In fewer than thirty years from the mid-1870s, Cardiff acquired nine arcades, Leeds seven, Birmingham, Glasgow and Manchester six apiece, and Halifax four. Clusters also appeared in prosperous provincial resorts: five in Bournemouth between 1864 and 1892, six in Harrogate in just five years between 1898 and 1902, and two in Southport (1874 and 1896). Other towns with more than one arcade included Oldham (1880, 1898), Colne (1875, 1920), Keighley (1898, 1899), Dewsbury (1895, 1911), Sheffield (1875, 1900), Wigan (1898, 1927), Huddersfield (1880, 1884), Wolverhampton (1904, 1909) Hull (1892, 1894), Leicester (1877, 1899), and Newport (1870, 1893). Inter-war developments were less notable but included several in Greater London and the south, such as Letchworth (1922),

1820s, for the reorganization of Winchester's markets in 1835, for the erection of Oldham's first markets in the 1830s and 1850s, and for the maintenance and expansion of those in Rochdale and Bradford well into the twentieth century. Residents of Hanley in the Potteries resorted to a public subscription in the 1820s, while elsewhere Lords of the Manor took the initiative. The Earl of Derby erected purpose-built premises in Bury in the 1830s but the Mosley family struggled in nearby Manchester to cope with the unbearable pressure on market facilities, erecting new shambles for the butchers and designating separate sites for the sale of potatoes, meal and flour, cheese, cattle, fish, and greengrocery.

The most impressive and enduring structures were the enclosed market halls erected by local authorities in the industrial districts of the north of England, especially in Lancashire and the West Riding. Liverpool Corporation's St John's market on Great Charlotte Street, opened in 1822, established a model which was widely adopted in smaller towns. Supported by cast-iron pillars, flagged throughout in stone, lit by gas, and with over 135 windows for ventilation and natural light, the hall consisted of orderly avenues of stalls, subdivided by commodity, while its interior walls were lined with purpose-built shops, occupied in the main by butchers and provision dealers. Birmingham and Newcastle followed in the 1830s, and the rest of the century then witnessed a flurry of activity as improvement commissions, local boards of health, and municipal boroughs alike sought borrowing powers to purchase market rights and modernize facilities.

Worthing (1925), Great Yarmouth (1926), Brighton (1928), Reading (1929), Hertford (1935), and Maidenhead (1937). Many of these later examples were perfunctory, piecemeal attempts to utilize underdeveloped land between existing properties.

Most arcades were developed by individuals and organizations with pre-existing interests in the area. They included landed families like the Grosvenors in Chester, the Ramsdens in Huddersfield, and the 12th Duke of Norfolk in Glossop; local businesses like the Carlisle Old Brewery Company, the White Swan Variety Theatre in Leeds, and David Morgan's department store in Cardiff; borough councils in Halifax, Nottingham, Rotherham, and Southport; a scattering of estate companies including the New Briggate Arcade Company, the Leeds Estate Company, and the Manchester Commercial Building Company; Leeds Industrial Co-operative Society; and a number of enterprising local men.

Eclectic in style, few attracted designers of any reputation. The most magnificent are the County and Cross Arcades in Leeds, designed by theatre architect Frank Matcham between 1898 and 1900. Arcades made use of a wide variety of building materials: wood, brick, stone, cast iron, steel, sheet glass, and even mass-produced terracotta and decorative tiles to provide novelty and colour.

In many respects these shopping arcades were forerunners of the more comprehensive, covered shopping centres of the post-1945 era which segregated pedestrians and vehicular traffic on a much larger scale. In recent years, new arcades have re-emerged as architectural centrepieces of small-scale redevelopment schemes sympathetic to existing urban landscapes.

© Courtesy The Francis Frith Collection

Accrington Market Hall, 1897. Built in 1868–9 at a cost of £28,300, the market hall was designed by John Doyle of Liverpool, who sought to create a 'living treasure of art' as a fitting companion to the adjacent Peel Institute, a classical structure which was, and is, the town's administrative headquarters. The Blackburn Times *considered that the gold decoration to the roof interior gave the market more the aspect of a concert hall.*

From the 1850s, building technology employed in Caxton's Crystal Palace and new railway termini enabled authorities to transform markets almost overnight from urban eyesores to civic embellishments, ranking alongside town halls in terms of status, size, and architectural ambition. The opening of Bolton's hall (1851–5) was accompanied by public processions and civic celebrations; Accrington's colonnaded stone edifice (1868) was hailed by the local newspaper as a 'living treasure of art', Stockport's open-sided, glass and iron 'umbrella on stilts' (1861) as the embodiment of progressive building technology. The apogee was reached in 1903–4 with the rebuilding of Leeds' Kirkgate market.

Externally, these covered halls overshadowed all other forms of retail provision in their towns. Internally, the shelter, lighting, and security they provided revolutionized market trading by facilitating long, daily opening hours and attracting a diverse cross-section of increasingly full-time professional traders selling virtually everything to wear, use, or to eat. Yet they retained many attributes of open markets in which goods were publicly displayed and available for inspection and prices were negotiable. By 1900 these orderly municipal emporia resembled proto-shopping centres, and on Saturdays and market days in particular they acted as commercial and cultural meccas for the working class in much the same way as fashionable department stores did for the expanding middle class.

Responsibility for transforming the rest of the urban commercial infrastructure remained the responsibility of private enterprise. This proved a slower, more piecemeal process. Even after the erection of purpose-built commodity exchanges in major cities, merchants, manufacturers, and professionals continued to rely on public rooms in taverns, hotels, and coffee houses for business transactions, while rooms in their private homes doubled as offices in which to meet clients, or effect and store the attendant paperwork. Although the Bank of England was rehoused in an imposing edifice in Threadneedle Street by 1734, most of the private London banking houses which dominated the eighteenth-century financial world were modest affairs, consisting of little more than extensions to domestic residences with a small front office to act as receiving or counting room and a parlour to the rear reserved for conducting private negotiations. As late as 1877, the *Builder* could comment that several of the old private banks in London carried on their business 'in the most unpretending of houses', often second-hand premises, and that they continued to rely on their personal

William Cheetham family grocer, Grimshaw Lane, Middleton, Lancashire. An archetypal late-19th-century industrial suburban food shop selling a range of provisions, including heavily promoted, branded goods, especially tea and soap. Note the hams on the wall, Brooke Bond's 'Full Weight Tea' (sold net of packaging), and the youthful assistants.

reputation to attract custom, predominantly from the privileged leisured classes. Specialized retail outlets were equally uncommon before the nineteenth century. Most shops were extensions and adaptations to the front rooms of domestic residences, and often shared a common entrance with the house. Business transactions were conducted through an open aperture on to the street which was shuttered at night, or internally over a rudimentary counter. Stock, like market produce, was frequently displayed on the pavement. Other forms of advertising were minimal, although in the fashionable clothing trades in particular, facilities for the permanent display of goods were gradually being incorporated within the premises, first through the introduction of protruding bays or enhanced frontages of small paned windows inserted into the ground floor of residences, and subsequently by the introduction of plate glass windows framed by wooden, pilaster, or iron columns, which were brilliantly lit with gas flares in the evenings to enhance their value as 'silent salesmen'. Relatively low levels of turnover for many products meant that numerous shopkeepers outside London and select resorts could not afford to specialize, but were obliged to combine apparently incongruous trades such as ironmongery and grocery on the same premises.

The distancing of home from work was severed earliest in case of financial services. London was ahead of the field in insurance, with the County Fire Office's imposing headquarters of 1817 setting standards for others to emulate. Outside the capital, and to a lesser extent other commercial cities, insurance companies' calls for specialist office space were negligible and they continued to rely on local solicitors, newspaper offices, booksellers, and shopkeepers to act as commission agents. In banking, the provincial diffusion of the joint-stock companies from the second quarter of the nineteenth century rapidly eclipsed London's private bankers. These only emerged in England following legislation of 1826 and 1833 but had been legal much longer in Scotland where banks had avoided the full impact of the financial crisis of 1825–6. From the 1830s, joint-stock banks in the English provinces, especially in the north and Midlands, followed the Scots' lead by commissioning the pretentious edifices, loosely based on Italianate styles, on thoroughfares of major towns, often as key features of civic improvements, which served physically to consolidate their corporate identity while projecting a reassuring image of security and status. Savings banks, designed to attract smaller depositors, were also predominantly provincial. According to a parliamentary return of 1852, only a quarter of these occupied purpose-built premises, the rest being housed in other buildings including domestic residences, town halls, and a range of quasi-charitable institutions. Again, most of the specifically commissioned offices were north of Birmingham, particularly in Lancashire, Yorkshire, Cheshire, Derbyshire, and Staffordshire where they were concentrated in newly prosperous middle-sized towns.

After 1861 private savings banks were eclipsed by competition from the new Post Office Savings Banks, but the development of commercial, joint-stock banking showed no signs of abating. The late nineteenth and early twentieth centuries witnessed a series of amalgamations and acquisitions which resulted in the emergence of district, regional, and ultimately national organizations. Although this reduced the number of companies, their chains of branches continued to expand into the inter-war years as they further sought to expand their market shares. Banking enclaves began to appear in parts of Victorian city centres, as in Bristol's Corn Street, Manchester's King Street, and Leeds' Park Row. Bank headquarters were remodelled to reflect their enhanced importance and confidence. Glasgow's and Liverpool's transatlantic connections and confined commercial quarters made them particularly susceptible in the 1920s to the American preference for lofty banking halls and the practice of building high to rent out other storeys for offices. Everywhere corner sites, attracting trade from at least two directions, were favoured as locations. Branches proliferated in middle-class suburbs around London. Even in working-class districts in the North, where mutual savings banks and building societies were major competitors for smaller depositors' funds, banks were tempted to establish small, plain branches. Architecturally, banks built before 1914 exhibited a mishmash of derivative, historically based designs which undermined the earlier consensus about what were considered appropriate styles. Mergers initially stymied prospects of achieving a uniform house style within an organization although Barclays and the Midland favoured an unpretentious neo-Georgian revival for many branches built in the inter-war decades. From 1900 banks were also increasingly sensitive to middle-class conservationist lobbies which were particularly prominent in newly prosperous old towns like Guildford, Hereford, Chester, and York. There, banks retained existing frontages or erected new premises in sympathy with surrounding older buildings. Whatever their façades, however, new premises incorporated the latest building material, construction technology, and decorative materials appropriate to their market and retained an emphasis on functionality.

The expansion of dedicated office space in the nineteenth century was less dramatic, and largely confined to the centres of major cities. Here it was needed to process and store increasingly complex legal and financial paperwork and to provide businessmen with permanent bases close to the centres of commercial exchange where they could be easily contacted. Much of it was initially accommodated in converted houses, in rooms above retail outlets or as part of warehouse developments. New 'chambers' of offices, often with lock-up shops to the street frontages, gradually replaced residences in the centres of Liverpool and Manchester but the trend towards purpose-built accommodation was most noticeable in the City of London where a significant proportion of residences had already been fully subdivided for offices by mid-century. From the 1860s, it became virtually imperative for provincial banks to obtain permanent headquarters in the capital to facilitate clearing operations and this, combined with London's increasingly international role, resulted in a burst of speculative office building. Property values in the City soared in response to demand for prime locations close to the Bank of England and central warehousing. As early as 1864 two property investment companies were formed to capitalize on this by financing the development and leasing of suitable accommodation. Between 1855 and 1905, an estimated 80 per cent of the City's building stock was replaced. Later developments incorporated hydraulic lifts to enhance the attractiveness of rooms on higher storeys of increasingly lofty edifices. Such was the scale of corporate speculative development that by the 1900s there was surplus capacity which depressed future building, other than the replacement of dated stock, for several decades. By this period, typical office or bank employees had ceased to be private secretaries or assistants and had become an army of clerical workers who were needed to effect the manual processing of an escalating volume of data and correspondence.

The significance of corporate funding and the erection of purpose-built premises were also increasingly evident in retailing over the same period in the

(**a** *and* **b**) *Selfridge's, Oxford Street, London, 1920 and 1924. Selfridge's, opened in March 1909, was among the first purpose-built department stores. Major extensions during the 1920s more than doubled its original size. The largest of these involved the redevelopment of a site on the corner of Orchard Street in 1923–4, but further purchases of land to the rear of the stores continued throughout the inter- and post-war years. The gap between the two premises evident in the second photograph was intended for a tower which was never built.*

expansion of department stores and branches of regional and national multiples. The concentration of ownership, however, was far less rapid than in banking. Consumer co-operatives, owned by their members, emerged as serious challengers to corporate firms in some parts of the country. Although small shopkeepers lost ground, they survived in appreciable numbers well into the twentieth century despite many gloomy prognostications from self-appointed retail analysts. Those purveying specialist luxury goods for the aspiring middle class continued to trade successfully on their reputations for personal service, credit facilities, and door-to-door deliveries. Others found a niche supplying the daily essentials for the well-to-do working class as food retailing gradually abandoned the central districts of larger towns in the late nineteenth century.

The most startling manifestation of the growth of large-scale retailing was the city-centre department store. William Whiteley's claim that his store in Bayswater was the first 'Universal Provider' used to be widely accepted, but it is now clear that, even if we disregard the co-operatives' claims, there were many other enterprises, both in London and the provinces, whose credentials as the first department store are equally valid, including Lewis's of Liverpool, Kendal Milne's of Manchester, and Bainbridge's of Newcastle. Harrod's originated as a high-class

grocers and David Lewis's as a cut-price gents' outfitters, but most built on reputations they had acquired as drapers catering for the growing middle-class female market for fashionable but affordable clothing and accessories. Whatever their origins, by the early twentieth century, they all retailed a wide variety of consumer goods including ladies' and men's clothing, footwear, furniture and furnishings, household appliances, foodstuffs, stationery, jewellery, glass, china, and toys.

Major cities, London in particular, had the highest concentrations both of impressive premises and of new limited liability companies; but in the half-century after 1860 almost every provincial town of any substance or reputation could boast at least one 'department' store, usually financed from local capital and invariably situated on a central thoroughfare. Seaside resorts, especially those on the south coast which attracted middle-class clientele, also experienced a rash of investment. Some, like Brown's of Chester, developed an upmarket image, stocking Parisian fashions and claiming to be the 'Harrods of the North', but most pitched their ambitions more modestly to supply an area market.

Physical expansion was initially achieved by piecemeal purchase and incorporation of adjacent properties. Growth, therefore, could be frustratingly unpredictable and expensive. Marshall and Snelgrove were unusually fortunate in acquiring sole occupancy of a complete island site on Oxford Street by the 1870s, enabling them to install an impressive, uniform façade to their premises, whereas most stores in central London still betrayed their origins as agglomerations of shops. For a time developments elsewhere threatened to undermine the West End's reputation as the capital's fashion centre. Street widening schemes assisted stores like Barkers, Derry and Toms, and Pontings in Kensington to expand and unify their frontages, while in Westbourne Grove, Bayswater, the 'Bond Street of the West', the success of William Whiteley's store attracted other proprietors in the 1890s including William Owen, brother of Owen Owen who owned a comparable store in Liverpool, Bourne and Hollingsworth, and Henry Dobb. Elsewhere in the country, store proprietors were among the most enthusiastic advocates, and beneficiaries, of municipal improvements. In 1880 and 1885, David Lewis opened purpose-built stores on Market Street, Manchester and the new Corporation Street in Birmingham. But it was Selfridge's spacious purpose-built store on Oxford Street, opened in 1909, which heralded the arrival of a different concept of shopping. Drawing on his experience of retailing in the United States, Selfridge designed a store with lofty, spacious, uncluttered interiors, while the inclusion of tearooms and restaurants, often with live entertainment, rest and club rooms, a branch post office, hairdressing salon, toilet and washing facilities created a retail outlet which, in his own words, was a 'a social centre, not a shop'. His widely trumpeted success not only confirmed the department store as a key component of high street redevelopments and shopping complexes for the rest of the century, but did much to foster the concept of shopping as a form of leisure rather than a purely functional pursuit.

Investment in shops supplying food and basic household requirements was very different. Although the new by-law terraced houses in working-class residential suburbs and industrial neighbourhoods represented a marked improvement on inner-city slums, they generally lacked adequate food storage facilities, obliging their inhabitants to make small, regular purchases. Limited means of travel dictated that they had to do this in the immediate vicinity of their homes. This opened opportunities for the smaller trader to make a modest living catering for a dispersed, but expanding market. The general 'corner shop' was established as a fixture on many residential streets, while a wide range of specialist shopkeepers, including convenience food outlets such as fish and chip shops, clustered on strategic sites along adjacent arterial roads which cumulatively acquired the status of unplanned neighbourhood or district shopping centres. Although such shops were initially located in converted residences, speculative housebuilders gradually recognized that the financial returns from purpose-built retail outlets on prime sites were significantly higher, and incorporated them into developments, sometimes to the designs of intended purchasers. Most remained dual-purpose, however, the shopkeeper's family living above and behind the shop. This, and their lack of dependence on waged labour, enabled them to maintain long opening hours without incurring extra expenses, while the greater availability of branded, pre-packed, and tinned foodstuffs and household products, supplied on credit by manufacturers and wholesalers through a network of commercial travellers, enabled them to extend their stock without the need for specialist training or considerable capital resources.

In the suburbs small shops were not universally occupied by small shopkeepers. The market was too significant for larger organizations to ignore. In the decades before the First World War the 'co-op' was established as an integral part of most working-class communities in the industrial North and, to a lesser extent, Midlands. The co-operative movement's ideological origins lay in utopian schemes in the 1820s and 1830s, deriving from Robert Owen. It sought to forge an alternative society in which production and exchange were based on mutuality and co-operation, not competition and profit. Initially their shopkeeping was intended to be only a means of raising funds to achieve this end. In 1844, however, a group of co-operators in Rochdale, the 'Pioneers', systematized the principle of redistributing trading surpluses to shareholding members via a regular dividend, an early form of 'loyalty bonus' based on the value of purchases they had made in the previous quarter. Thereafter, co-operative shopkeeping acquired a seemingly unstoppable momentum. Twenty-five years after Rochdale's initiative, societies were successfully established throughout the textile and mining districts of Lancashire and the West Riding, where relative prosperity and the creation of almost self-contained, cohesive working-class communities fostered a sense of collective identity which proved fertile ground for both business and a wider appreciation of the movement's democratic nature. By 1878, membership of co-operative societies had grown to over half a million. By 1891, it stood at 1 million; by the outbreak of war in 1914, 3 million; and by 1939, over 8.5 million. Although societies were formed in most parts of the country, however, certain 'deserts' remained, particularly in

Oldham Road, Rochdale, c.1900. Unplanned, retail ribbon development lining arterial routes emerged to serve adjacent residential neighbourhoods during the late 19th century. This row of converted and purpose-built premises was little more than a quarter of a mile from the town centre, but included a co-operative society store, butcher, ironmonger, draper, tobacconist, and pub.

Enfield Highway Co-operative Society, New Central Stores, 1907. The co-operative movement generally struggled to establish itself in London and the Home Counties but Enfield, with its three branches in Ponders End, Waltham Cross and Waltham Coney and its impressive central store, was an exception. The shop's 'departments' supplied grocery provisions, drapery, hosiery, tailoring, china, glass, hardware, furnishing, books, shoes, bakery, confectionery, and coal. The society also built houses in the area in the 1930s.

inner-city slums and middle-class suburbs, and the movement remained essentially a child of the textile districts, with headquarters based in Manchester.

In its industrial heartland, the co-op's presence was marked. Although stores initially concentrated on a narrow range of basic commodities, primarily non-perishable groceries such as tea and flour, most societies progressively diversified with the intention of becoming universal providers, capable of retailing an enormous range of household goods and services. In the decades leading up to 1914, many of their central stores were redesigned and refurbished on similar lines to their upmarket counterparts, the department stores. Most of their trade, however, was derived from branches strategically located on prime sites in working-class districts, and these still concentrated on purveying unadulterated, good quality 'necessities of life', primarily groceries and provisions, although meat and footwear outlets were occasionally added in adjacent properties. Originally these were either converted houses or taken over from a private shopkeeper, but by the 1900s most of the larger societies' new branches were specifically commissioned to a distinctive local, in-house style.

Meanwhile the Co-operative Wholesale Society, founded in 1863, was developing an integrated system of manufacturing and distribution for virtually every foodstuff and household product. This had no parallel in the capitalist sector. As well as extensive offices and warehousing facilities in Manchester and London, its portfolio of investments by 1914 included flour mills and bakeries; factories producing clothing, footwear, furniture, crockery, tobacco, soap, candles, brushes, polish and a wide range of processed foodstuffs such as jam, biscuits, confectionery, and chocolate; farms and creameries; tea plantations; fleets of steamers; insurance, building societies, and banking facilities; and a thriving undertaking service.

Despite their commercial successes, neither the individual societies nor their co-ordinating agencies such as the Co-operative Union, ever abandoned faith in their original values. They strove to be more than just a shop. By joining a co-op an individual ceased to be merely a consumer; he or she became a 'co-operator' with a potential role to play in the creation of an alternative moral economy built around the principle of mutual improvement. Co-operation was 'lifestyle shopping' with a vengeance, providing members and their families with access to a rich menu of cultural amenities: reading rooms, libraries, educational classes, concerts, festivals, excursions, holiday, sporting clubs, Women's Guilds, co-operative newspapers, and books. The commemorative crockery and jubilee histories of individual co-ops which appeared from the late 1890s, and the speeches and publications of the movement's leaders, exuded a justifiable pride in past achievements. They also portrayed a confidence in the future which ultimately was to be misplaced. Another consumer culture which was consolidating its hold further south during the same period proved more enduring.

Multiple retailers, developing rapidly from the 1870s, shared many of the co-ops' trading characteristics, in that they established networks of branches close to their potential customers, emphasized convenience and value for money, and extended their own chains of supply. In every other respect they were very different. Many remained relatively small-scale attempts by established shopkeepers, particularly grocers, to take a slice of the expanding suburban markets or the trade of neighbouring towns, but, as in banking, these were soon overshadowed by new organizations commanding regional or national chains of outlets. These consolidated their position through a combination of investment in new branches and by merger and amalgamation, especially in the grocery, footwear, clothing, and pharmacy sectors.

Multiples initially relied on aggressive marketing of a relatively narrow range of manufactured products and processed foodstuffs for which there was a guaranteed, mass supply. They kept prices low by restricting choice and eschewing labour-intensive services such as deliveries and credit facilities. Some originated as attempts by manufacturers of factory-produced, consumer products to benefit directly from the expanding working-class market. Singer, an American company, retailed its sewing machines through tied outlets from as early as 1856 and had developed 900 branches by 1938. Footwear manufacturers in the East Midlands, such as Stead and Simpson, George Oliver, and Freeman Hardy and Willis, invested in shops from the 1870s, closely followed by numerous factory producers of ready-made clothing. Jesse Boot, the 'Cash Chemist', had only ten shops in 1883 but over 560 by 1914. Some, like W. H. Smith & Son, who obtained franchises for news-stands and bookstalls on railway stations, diversified into retailing via their wholesale activities. Others were essentially retailers. Michael Marks, joined briefly by Tom Spencer between 1894 and 1903, successfully transferred his concept of the 'Penny Bazaar' from northern markets to a chain of fixed shops during the 1890s and 1900s. Yet others relied on imported foodstuffs. Between the mid-1880s and 1900 Eastmans and James Nelson and Sons both established over 400 branch shops retailing Argentinian and North American beef. Thomas Lipton, who made his name in Glasgow in the 1870s by selling imported hams, bacon, butter, and eggs from Ireland and America before moving on, rather more famously, into tea, had established over 500 shops by 1899. Like the co-operative movement, many of these food retailers diversified into production to obtain consistent supplies and remove the middleman. Lipton again was a force. In 1890 he acquired his first tea plantation in Ceylon and over the next decade opened factories producing cocoa, chocolate, confectionery, jams, pickles, sausages, biscuits, cakes, and sauces. The Maypole Dairy Company followed a similar route, investing in creameries in Britain and Denmark, margarine factories, vegetable oil refining, and the West African groundnut trade.

Many of these businesses originated and expanded in the industrial towns and cities of the Midlands, Northern England, and Scotland, but by the 1890s their prospects for growth appeared significantly better in London and the Home Counties. The pull was most evident in the grocery and provisions trades. Lipton moved his headquarters to the capital in 1891, followed by much of his warehousing facilities and new factories. In part this change in emphasis reflected London's position as the hub of international trade, particularly of imported foodstuffs, its docks' extensive warehousing facilities, and the City's unrivalled importance as a source of capital. But the prospects of the demand created by the capital's burgeoning suburbs were also irresistible. London-based organizations, such as the giant Home and Colonial Ltd with over 500 shops by 1903, successfully tapped into the lower end of this market, while J. Sainsbury, with his emphasis on high-class provisions, established a reputation among middle-class customers who were less concerned with bargains than with quality and service. Although they continued to base much of their appeal on value for money, multiples gradually preferred to project the image of 'family grocers', trading from premises which were larger and more elaborate, both in terms of façade and internal facilities.

The south-east also attracted the attention of multiple retailers in other sectors, when they had exhausted the easy pickings further north and did not relish challenging the co-op and the corner shopkeeper in what had become a cut-price environment. Many seized the opportunity to move upmarket and increase profit margins. Jesse Boot focused most of his efforts between 1901 and 1914 on the south, floating a new company, Boots Cash Chemists (Southern) Ltd., to facilitate his expansion in the region. He also gradually converted his principal stores from basic and cheap drug stores into mini-department stores selling a variety of household goods. Before 1919 Montague Burton's chain of men's outfitters were predominantly located in the industrial districts, but by 1939 these accounted for only half of his 595 shops. He, too, traded up, building a chain of imposing high street premises including a six-storey flagship store on New Oxford Street. Marks and Spencer also participated in the southward drift. In 1907, 80 per cent of their outlets were in the North and Midlands. By 1914 a third were in the London area and London was gradually overhauling Manchester as the firm's centre of operations. Whereas the earlier growth of working-class communities in the industrial districts had created a commercial landscape of small, independent shops and co-op stores, metropolitan suburbs were now characterized by purpose-built shopping districts containing branches of a major multiple.

facing page: Chiltern Parade, Amersham, 1937. Rapidly expanding, prosperous metropolitan suburbs offered excellent markets and investment opportunities for enterprising retailers and commercial property developers. John Sainsbury successfully combined two roles, as here at Amersham, where the firm's development company, Cheyne Investments Ltd, created and controlled an integrated shopping centre around its own retail premises. The contrast with earlier piecemeal growth (see illustration p. 165) is striking.

Retail expansion on this scale necessitated more capital than the reinvestment of profits or the assistance of friends, relatives, and business partners. In the late nineteenth century, the advantages of converting to limited liability appealed to a growing number of businesses. Some local family concerns undertook this step for defensive reasons: not to increase the capital base, but to enable existing assets to be shared between relatives on the proprietor's death without having to sell the business or saddling the member of the family who inherited it with debts incurred by buying the others out. For firms with ambitions to expand, conversion not only reduced the penalties of potential failure but empowered them to raise additional capital through share issues and debenture stock. From the 1890s, the emergence of a national market for share dealing, an active financial press, low rates of interest on government stocks and other forms of savings, all encouraged potential investors to seek higher returns through share ownership. The continuing revolution in retailing was alluring.

Even after incorporation, however, retailers could not be assured of access to sufficient capital to undertake further expansion. Joint-stock banks preferred lending over relatively short periods, so long-term development capital was

sought through other channels. Retailers turned to corporate financial institutions, especially major insurance companies which recognized that investment in shop properties in prime locations could yield a secure income while increasing in value over the longer term. During the early twentieth century, insurance companies became closely involved in financing and managing retail store development, a trend accelerated by cheap money and the property boom of the mid-1930s. Both the Prudential, which underwrote new share issues in Marks & Spencer when it embarked on a policy of purchasing freeholds for store development in 1924, and the Alliance Assurance Co. which provided mortgages to J. Lyons & Co., the catering multiple, obtained representation on their boards. Montague Burton, 'The Tailor of Taste', financed his expansion by purchasing prime sites, erecting smart premises on them, then selling them to financial institutions with long leaseback arrangements. Instead of obtaining a mortgage based on a percentage of the undeveloped value of the property, Burton acquired the full value of the site and continued occupation. Purchasers obtained a guaranteed return in the form of rent, and the prospect of increased capital appreciation once other traders had been attracted to adjacent sites, which were often also developed by Burton. J. Sainsbury adopted a similar policy in the metropolitan suburbs, purchasing a block of land for development as a shopping parade, and then relying on his reputation and presence on the site to attract an appropriate range of specialist shopkeepers to adjacent plots. Equally important were the mutually beneficial relations which large retailers forged with the property development companies that were responsible for financing and building other suburban shopping centres during the inter-war years. These companies wooed well-known retailers by offering them favourable terms for purchase or leasing, safe in the knowledge that their presence would guarantee that other sites could then be sold or let at a higher rent than they would otherwise obtain. By the 1930s London-based commercial estate agents were acquiring information on retail developments throughout the country, to match property developers with retail clients.

Many components of the modern commercial landscape were now in place. Many features were common to other sectors of the economy. Family-run businesses no longer monopolized banking or trade; they were overshadowed by joint-stock banks and chains of multiple retailers which depended on share issues, borrowing, mergers, and acquisitions to fund their growth. Commercial property companies and corporate finance played an increasing role in new developments. Innovations in building technology had transformed the design, scale, and appearance of banks and stores alike. New sources of supply had expanded the range of goods and services on offer. Responsibilities for investment strategy and the day-to-day running of businesses no longer lay with individual proprietors, but were vested in boards of directors and managers respectively. Local authorities' promotion of urban improvements and public transport had enhanced the concentration of consumer durable sales and financial services into town centres while suburban growth had led to the dispersal of much food retailing.

However, as in the industrial sector, change had not occurred uniformly across the country. Smaller market centres with their range of independent shops, still displayed tangible signs of a retail culture rooted in the eighteenth century. Depressed industrial regions in the north clung to a radical, co-operative alternative to the capitalist model of consumer society, and were characterized by municipally owned market halls and numerous small-scale residential shops, all of which had developed during their mid-Victorian heyday. New purpose-built premises were more likely to be found in the centres of major cities, particularly London, and in the suburbs which now enveloped them. Even in such premises, however, conventional assumptions about how retailing should be conducted remained virtually unchallenged. Except in a few department stores, cheap bazaars, and discount stores like Marks & Spencer and Woolworths, the counter still separated customers both from the stock and the staff who served them. Despite the spread of hire purchase as a method of financing working-class purchase of consumer durables, creditworthiness generally remained a matter of the shopkeeper's discretion, while loans and overdrafts still had to be personally negotiated in the banker's private office. Despite the introduction of the telephone, telegraph, and speedy means of postal communication, most financial and retail transactions involved face-to-face interaction. With the exception of central market halls and some pedestrianized shopping arcades, the street remained what it was in the heyday of the open market, both a transport artery and the heart of commercial exchange. Although few traders now exhibited their wares on the pavement, they primarily relied on elaborate street window displays to advertise their wares.

Since 1945 there has been an erosion of regional disparities in shop and, to a lesser extent, office development; and the traditional assumptions about how and where business should be conducted have been undermined. Counter service has been replaced by open displays and self-service. Like many other innovations, this method of selling had its origins in the United States where grocery firms such as Safeway and Food Fare had opened giant stores during the 1930s. In Britain both established independents and multiples alike were initially reluc-

Hull Co-operative Society Ltd., Longhill self-service food store, 1959. Co-operative societies were among the first to recognize the potential of self-service. Ninety percent of all self-service shops in 1950 were co-ops. New outlets, such as this one in Hull, serving a large housing estate, remained in the vanguard of change, but many co-operative societies, especially in older, declining industrial areas, encountered considerable difficulty converting their branch stores.

tant to embrace it for fear of alienating customers. Here the pioneers were again the co-ops, downmarket discount stores often situated off the main thoroughfares in unprepossessing premises, and relative newcomers like Jack Cohen of Tesco, whose branch in St Albans was converted in 1947. Sainsbury's redesigned its Croydon premises in 1950. Thereafter, the practice spread rapidly, first to other grocery multiples, then to most sectors of the retail trade.

Within a decade, it was clear that, as in the past, major restructuring could not be easily accommodated in existing premises. Access to larger sites and corporate finance were again the keys to expansion. With the rapid rise in car ownership, grocery businesses gradually abandoned both the high street and the suburbs, moving to new out-of-town sites to develop self-service supermarkets, preferably close to major trunk routes and with adequate land for future expansion and parking. A small number of successful firms have erected progressively larger stores, and the decades from the 1960s have witnessed the demise of many independent businesses, co-operative societies, and specialist multiples whose capital was tied up in poky, inconveniently situated retail premises or obsolescent production facilities. Some independent businesses have survived as parts of voluntary chains of convenience stores. Regional distinctions still persist, especially in the north where established companies like E. H. Booth's of Preston retain a distinctive upmarket image with an emphasis on quality and local suppliers, and where comparatively new arrivals such as Asda and Morrison's, being largely unshackled by the legacy of investment in outmoded premises, have adopted the northern multiples' original emphasis on price competitiveness. But by the 1990s, a handful of national chains of giant, self-service superstores dominate the grocery sector. These wield financial power to negotiate favourable deals with councils, property developers, and suppliers alike.

Many town centres have also been fundamentally reshaped in an attempt to create a more attractive shopping environment for consumer durables. Like their nineteenth-century predecessors, local councils and central government became acutely aware in post-war years of the threat which traffic congestion, pollution, and underinvestment in retail facilities posed for the viability of their town centres. Concepts of planning design applied in new towns like Basildon and Harlow, proffered an apparently attractive solution—the purpose-built shopping centre. From the mid-1960s, many councils used powers of compulsory purchase to acquire and demolish large blocks of property, selling or leasing these to commercial property developers or financial institutions such as insurance companies. These then laid out covered or partially covered pedestrianized shopping precincts, and provided off-street parking facilities for cars. As in the earlier phase of suburban shopping parades, developers 'anchored' their schemes by offering major national retailers the prospect of acquiring purpose-built premises on favourable terms and conditions. The 1970s witnessed the construction of some of Britain's biggest covered shopping centres, including Brent Cross in north London, Eldon Square in Newcastle, the Arndale Centres in Luton and Manchester, and in the new town of Milton Keynes.

During the property boom of the late 1980s, escalating rents and land values, logistical problems associated with redeveloping previous centres which were deemed functionally and architecturally obsolescent, increasing frustration with councils' financial demands, building restrictions introduced in response to the lobbying of conservationists, and the continuing growth of car ownership, all

The MetroCentre, Gateshead, Tyne and Wear, 1997. The first 'out-of-town' shopping centre in Britain, the MetroCentre was developed on derelict industrial land on the outskirts of Gateshead in the late 1980s. Its 300-plus shops covering over 1.5 million square feet, now regularly attract over 100,000 people on a typical Saturday, the overwhelming majority of whom arrive by car. Such complexes, close to major transport nodes, echo the establishment of markets in earlier centuries, and may ultimately require a redefinition of the current concept of a 'town centre'.

prompted property developers to look for more flexible out-of-town sites, relatively unhindered by planning restrictions, and with convenient access to major motorways. Encouraged by a relaxation of central government's planning guidelines on land use, especially derelict industrial land in 'Enterprise' zones, the mid-1980s saw a spate of proposals for new regional shopping centres located outside existing urban areas. Between 1986 and 1990 the MetroCentre at Gateshead, Merry Hill near Dudley, Meadowhall at Sheffield, and Lakeside in Thurrock all received planning permission. These centres have attracted department and multiple stores retailing fashionable 'lifestyle' products, especially clothing, which are able to command high profit margins. They have also sought to develop a range of other facilities associated with traditional high street shopping such as post offices, banks, eating places, and even leisure amenities. Retailers of bulkier consumer durables and household accessories with lower margins and requiring more extensive floor space—such as electrical goods, DIY products, furniture, carpets, and even toys—have followed a slightly different trajectory, establishing clusters of window-less warehouses in out-of-town locations, with extensive car parking facilities; and these retail or business 'parks' are also now gradually acquiring a range of other outlets, including fast food chains and cinema complexes.

Financial services have been slower to expand beyond their central sites or to relocate regionally. Since the 1950s, the City of London has experienced spectacular redevelopment of central office space by large-scale commercial property companies which has transformed both the skyline and streetscape and spilled out into the old dockland area to the east. As in the past, investment has oscillated between fevered speculation and deep, temporarily damaging recessions brought on by oversupply, after each of which older properties became progressively more difficult to let. While London retains its role as the country's major financial, communications, and political centre, the prospects for continued growth remain buoyant. Nevertheless there are straws in the wind which suggest that its long-term role is changing. Many of the routine labour-intensive and space-intensive activities once associated with it have been relocated to less expensive places, initially to other parts of the south-east but increasingly to the regions. While London's international importance continues to attract demand for offices from foreign companies, it is also true that much of that demand is for what are effectively branch offices.

Elsewhere in the country, apparently contradictory developments are underway. On the one hand, corporate financial premises have become more pervasive on the high street as building societies have shed either or both their mutual and regional origins, and moved from unassuming, functional offices into prime locations. On the other hand, the rationale for retaining what are essentially dispersed, paper-oriented financial outlets has declined as electronic communications and computer technology have generated the capacity to transfer huge volumes of information and money around the world virtually instantaneously. While most financial institutions appear unwilling to abandon either their place in the high street or their London headquarters, recent years have seen the establishment of regional or national data-processing centres in purpose-built accommodation well away from previous locations. Moreover, self-service cash dispensers have diminished another of the high street banks' once labour-intensive functions, and the introduction of 'cashback' facilities, credit cards, and savings accounts by major retailers threatens to erode the barriers which previously existed between the sectors.

So dramatic is the speed and complexity of commercial change that analysts offer widely conflicting scenarios as to what the future holds. Some predict a continuing acceleration of out-of-town development at the expense of the town centre. Others point to projections of expanding demand for consumer goods which suggest that out-of-town stores will be complementary to city centre facilities, increasing rather than displacing retail provision in the country as a whole. Yet others perceive a post-modern reaction against the homogeneity of mass retailing that will ensure a future for smaller centres which have retained their 'traditional' appearance and mix of specialist shops, giving new hope to emporiums like Lancashire's once proud, but decaying markets which are now advertised as a part of the county's 'heritage' attractions. Some even see signs of a rejuvenated producer-retailer sector re-emerging in the proliferation of craft fairs and the tentative re-establishment of farmers' markets.

Whatever the future holds, cultural constructions of what 'traditional' shopping and banking signify will no doubt continue to be redefined. The commercial revolution remains a process that brings far-reaching changes to the urban landscape.

7 The Industrial Town

R. J. Morris

After the King of Saxony visited England in 1844, his physician published a tour diary in which he gave an account of their visit to several manufacturing towns. Dr Carus was

> forcibly struck by the peculiar dense atmosphere which hangs over these towns, in which hundreds of chimneys are continually vomiting forth clouds of smoke . . . What a curious red colour was presented by the evening light . . . The peculiar tint which the country around such a city assumes, cannot be better designated than by the phrase factory tint . . . It would make a pretty picture, if any painter should represent these lofty masses of these square factories, with the much loftier chimneys, between them a couple of Gothic spires . . .

Ebenezer Elliott, ironmonger, radical, and Anti Corn Law rhymer, saw Sheffield as 'the city of the cloud':

> Fire vomits darkness where his limetrees grew
> Harsh grates the saw where cooed the wood dove coy . . .
> canst thou hear the unwearied crash and roar
> of iron powers

Writing to her son Edward Junior when he was away at school in 1824, Mrs Baines reflected the same sense of rapid change:

> Mr Bruce is going to build a large manufactory near Wellington Bridge—when you return you will be surprised at the great number of buildings in that direction—Mr Nussey is building a dyehouse directly opposite Mr Barr's House and on this side of the Baths they are building a waggon warehouse. It is happy for us that we cannot be much injured by the adjoining extension—though I fear we may be annoyed with the smoke.

I am grateful to Dr Trevor Griffiths for generous help and advice with this chapter.

Smoke. Readers of John James's Continuations and Additions to the History of Bradford and its Parish *(1886) are invited to join the horseman looking down on the rapidly growing industrial town. Smoke and factories compete for attention with the parish church representing the old medieval centre. The railway and the quarry for building stone provide key elements of the town's fabric.*

Visitors and residents, kings, radical poets, and letter-writing mothers recognized that something quite extraordinary was happening to many English towns and cities. Central to the process were smoke, factories, and rapid growth.

In 1845, a parliamentary select committee on smoke prevention heard Darnton Lupton, Mayor of Leeds, state

> I lived in Leeds some years ago and the injury to furniture was excessive . . . at the east end of the town are the worst houses consequently the poor flock there; you do not find the wealthy inhabitants living at the east end.

Near to the town 'the vegetation excessively diminishes', whilst in the nearby villages women took in washing from the town where it could never be hung out to dry and stay clean.

The industrial towns were celebrated not just for their machinery but also for the newness of their human organization. The journalist and the tourist had a regular circuit. In Yorkshire they visited the medieval minster at York and then went on to Leeds to see the woollen manufactory of Benjamin Gott at Bean Ing and the flax spinning mill of John Marshall and Sons in Water Lane, Holbeck. The factory was the cathedral of the new economy. *Chambers' Edinburgh Journal*, promoters of rational and moral recreation, and the *Penny Magazine*, purveyors of useful knowledge, were alike entranced 'by the regularity and system observable in such establishments' and by the imposing mixture of steam power, science, mechanical invention, and accumulated capital. Andrew Ure MD was intoxicated by 'the union of capital and science', the 'Napoleonic nerve and ambition [of the employers] to subdue the refactory tempers of workpeople', and the factory children working like 'lively elves' around the spinning frames.

In *Hard Times* (1854) Charles Dickens expressed his deep disquiet over utilitarian philosophy and the factory system. He had visited Preston during the prolonged strike of 1853–54. A demand for a 10 per cent wage increase had been met by an employers' lock-out. Dickens's Coketown was a powerful abstraction which represented the manufacturing town as an oppressive assault on human individuality and creativity.

> It was a town of red brick, or brick that would have been red if the smoke and ashes had allowed it . . . It was a town of machinery and tall chimneys . . . It had a black canal in it, and a river that ran purple with ill smelling dye, and vast piles of buildings full of windows where there was a rattling and trembling all day long, and where the piston of the steam engine worked monotonously up and down.

There was 'a clattering of clogs upon the pavement and a ringing of bells'. The people were 'equally like one another, who all went in and out at the same hours, to do the same work . . . every day was the same as yesterday and to-morrow'.

For many, the processes of forge, furnace, and factory created a sense of terror and excitement. Like the utilitarian and political economist, romantic sensibility was ready for the manufacturing town. Machinery and technology were sublime. They were the destroyers of jobs, of traditional ways of working, of fields and pure air. The factory and the furnace were also hope and progress, the solution to the Malthusian threat of a growing population. By the 1840s, 'the manufacturing town' was a widely recognized category. For Dickens, for Manchester Poor Law surgeon James Kay, for novelist and Unitarian minister's wife Mrs Gaskell, for the visiting German industrialist's son Friedrich Engels, and for many others, they were places of the elemental clash of capital and labour. In parliamentary enquiries, they were places of environmental harshness, of 'dusty and dirty thoroughfares', of 'ditches of stagnant filth', of blocked footpaths and fields enclosed for building, and people 'confined . . . [in] . . . heated factories'.

Reality and Explanation

This forceful presence upon the landscape of Britain had been created by a variety of processes. In 1750, the countryside was full of industrial activity, nailmakers in the West Midlands, edge tool makers in South Yorkshire, and weaving in Lancashire and West Yorkshire. Activity was small-scale and often partially integrated with the farming household. The towns were the organizing centres, with cloth halls, merchants' houses, and lawyers' offices providing finance and marketing. The rural population came into town for market days, the quarter sessions, and parliamentary elections. The countryside had several advantages for industry. Rents and labour costs were lower. The social costs of sickness and unemployment could be spread across households and existing community structures. Industrial activity dealing with high-value and part-processed materials tended to be urban. The finishing end of the cloth trade gathered in workshops behind merchant town houses. Birmingham prospered on gunmaking, enamelled ware, and other high-value metal craft goods. Wolverhampton made the complex house locks whilst the simpler common lock came from the villages nearby. The balance between town and country changed as the intensity of competition and

The Potteries

MARGUERITE DUPREE

The Potteries is a singular example of the urban industrial landscape. Located halfway between Birmingham and Manchester, in the North Staffordshire coalfield, the Potteries was geographically, administratively, socially, and economically distinct from the borough of Newcastle-under-Lyme to the west, moorlands to the north and east, and agricultural land and the Duke of Sutherland's seat at Trentham in the south. Immortalized in Arnold Bennett's novels as 'the Five Towns', the Potteries was actually six towns—Tunstall, Burslem, Hanley, Stoke-upon-Trent, Fenton, and Longton. Though united in a Parliamentary Borough after 1832 and the City of Stoke-on-Trent after 1910, they retain individual identities today. The towns grew in the eighteenth and early nineteenth centuries near the

River Trent and adjacent to seams of high-quality coal essential for the production of pottery.

This area eight miles long and two miles wide has been the primary centre of pottery manufacture in Britain since the eighteenth century. By 1861 the industry had expanded to 180 manufactories or 'potbanks', with 30,000 employees. The Potteries provides an example—almost unparalleled in Britain—of an industry whose location has remained fixed for over two centuries. Even the distribution of potbanks within the district remained virtually unchanged until at least the 1950s, as they formed two groups or lines following the coal outcrops, though a few potworks such as Wedgwood's moved in the eighteenth century from the ridge nearer to the Trent and Mersey Canal, where Twyford's also developed in the later nineteenth century. Likewise, the distribution of potteries manufacturing differing types of ware retained the pattern established by 1830. The bone china side of the industry, having started in the 1790s, developed most rapidly in Longton and Fenton, whereas the older towns of Burslem and Hanley mostly produced earthenware. Subsequently both china and earthenware were made in all six towns, but the concentration of china firms in Longton persisted.

A Potteries town, Longton, in the 19th century. The bottle kilns of the pottery industry created a distinctive urban landscape. Note the potworks in the town-centre, the proximity of housing and countryside, and the low-lying smoke.

Everywhere in the Potteries, the potbanks were set within the most built-up portions of the towns, surrounded by their workers' terraced houses. The potbanks followed a rectangular plan. At the entrance was a porter's lodge and within were sites for clay preparation, ranges of one- and two-storey workshops for shaping and decorating the ware, kilns for firing, and warehouses and offices.

The potbanks gave the landscape a different aspect from that of Lancashire and Yorkshire textile towns. Instead of multi-storey factories and vast warehouses, what dominated the Potteries were the peculiar kilns. Dickens in 1852 thought they resembled 'the bowls of gigantic tobacco pipes, cut short off from the stem and turned upside down', while J. B. Priestley in 1933 described the

> fantastic collection of narrow-necked jars or bottles peeping above the house-tops on every side, looking as if giant biblical characters after a search for oil or wine, had popped them there among the dwarf streets . . . I never . . . quite recovered from my first wild impression of them as some monstrous Oriental intrusion upon an English industrial area.

Yet, pottery was not the only industry in the Potteries. From the outset it was associated with coal min-

MARGUERITE DUPREE

'A view of Burslem' in 1930 by Leonard Brammer (1906–94) who captured the characteristic features of the Potteries' landscape with its concentration of potworks and housing amid open spaces, ironworks, coal mines, and slag heaps.

ing, and by 1850 there were ironstone mines and large ironworks in the same area. This unique combination of industries created an unrivalled density of smoke as well as a distinctive landscape. There was more smoke than Priestley had ever seen, and it 'does not hang well above the towns like a dark cloud, as it does in other industrial districts, but seems to drift heavily just above the roofs'. Smoke from the potworks and houses, and smoke and sulphur fumes from copperas works and especially from the ironworks, contributed to the choking atmosphere. 'Gentlemen who have had residences in the immediate vicinity of the ironworks, have been driven away in consequence of the offensiveness of the calcining of ironstone', observed the chairman of the Burslem Board of Health in 1857. Fifty years later Arnold Bennett remained awestruck by this

> squalid ugliness on a scale so vast and overpowering that it became sublime. Great furnaces gleamed red in the twilight, and their fires were reflected in horrible black canals; processions of heavy vapour drifted in all directions across the sky, over what acres of mean and miserable brown architecture! The air was alive with the most extraordinary, weird, gigantic sounds. I do not think the Five Towns will ever be described: Dante lived too soon.

Not only did the Potteries have an extraordinary visual impact, but its environment made a special assault on the health of its inhabitants. Despite the towns' comparatively small size, abundant employment, relatively high wages, and reasonably good housing, the Potteries had a mortality rate approaching the largest cities'. In 1863 a person living in Stoke-on-Trent had a 25 per cent greater chance of dying during the year than in England and Wales as a whole. In 1880 the statistician William Farr noted that the mortality of male potters was exceeded only by 'the figures for costermongers, Cornish miners and inn and hotel servants'. The high mortality was in part due to respiratory diseases and in part to circulatory disease, as 'the inhalation of the dust induces emphysema and chronic bronchitis, or "potters' asthma" and this in turn gives rise to heart disease'. Not only were potters affected, but the American Consul in Tunstall in the 1870s, bemoaning the 'almost perpetual volume of coal and iron-stone smoke that constantly fills the atmosphere', resigned after eight years when he found his health giving way.

Latterly, gas kilns have replaced the bottle ovens and their smoke; the ironworks and nearly all mines have gone; slag heaps are reforested and marl holes filled in. The tallest building in the area now houses civic offices, and housing estates spread into the countryside. The air is clearer. Yet, the industry that gives the Potteries its name continues to shape its urban landscape.

the pace of technological change increased. That long-drawn-out and somewhat misnamed process the 'industrial revolution' was as much about the increased division and intensification of labour as it was about technology, so that the concentration of populations and producers became more attractive.

Initially the new technologies and forms of labour organization were as much at home in the countryside as in the town. The factories of Richard Arkwright at Cromford and the forges and furnaces of Coalbrookdale were rural. For the employer there were advantages in such places, easy access to water-power and the potential for total control in a relatively isolated community, but such employers not only had the task of hiring and managing labour in the workplace but also had to provide housing, schools, shops, and other services.

Between 1780 and 1850, industry began to come in from the countryside. Those great external income-earning industries of textiles and metal goods which served the expanding markets of Europe, the Americas, and the Far East found several advantages in the town. Supervision was easier and constant. When Benjamin Gott, merchant, gathered his weavers into his 'factory' at Bean Ing on the edge of Leeds, there were few technological gains to be made, but he could ensure the consistency of quality required to compete in demanding and 'distant' markets. Division of labour and specialization were easier. Machine makers like Matthew Murray, who emerged from the workshops at the back of Marshall's linen mill, set up in business independently and exported well beyond the confines of Leeds itself. In the second half of the century, Bradford was served by the nearby Keighley firm of George Hattersley and Son. By 1914, the trade catalogue of this firm was in three languages and boasted of medals in industrial exhibitions in India and the USA as well as in Europe and the United Kingdom.

As a result industrial towns grew rapidly. As the external income-earning industries became more efficient, their markets expanded and the demand for labour increased. Industrial activity required machine builders, chemicals, and financial and legal services. The growing populations required food, clothing, housing, education and medical services, entertainment and consumer goods for every level of taste and income. Each item on the list implied further population growth. This growth both required and stimulated improved transport systems. Canals and railways linked towns with the countryside, with ports and with each other for the supply of food, raw materials, and finished goods. There were also many diseconomies of concentration. Traffic congestion in the main streets and around the new railway stations of the 1840s was frustrating and costly. Disease spread more rapidly in crowded populations. Industrial waste polluted streams. Human waste was so concentrated that all natural processes which might break it down were defeated. Water supplies, especially the shallow pump wells that supplied many houses, became contaminated from overflowing privy systems.

The characteristic English manufacturing town was based upon a merchanting and finishing centre, located in a coalfield area. There was usually a medieval core and a seventeenth-century charter. There were other patterns. Changing agricultural technology and the arrival of the railways stimulated a manufacturing sector in many of the quiet market towns of Lincolnshire in the second half of the nineteenth century. The threshing machine, the steam plough, and the agricultural steam engine were produced in the Stamp End Iron Works of Clayton and Shuttleworth in Lincoln. They exported to Eastern Europe and Russia.

There were very few new manufacturing towns. Middlesbrough was an exception. Here the railways linked coal, iron ore, and a navigable river with the capital and entrepreneurship of the English Quaker network, in the form of the Middlesbrough Owners, and incoming ironmasters like Bölckow and Vaughan. Middlesbrough was a series of interlocking grids like a North American prairie town. East London was a major and often forgotten industrial 'town', taking advantage of the port and of the huge consumer goods market which was London itself. When George Dodd produced his *Days at the Factories* in 1843, it was devoted to East London. He visited a brewery, a vinegar and British wine factory, a sugar refinery, places for making hats, leather goods, soap and candles, the London Marble Works, and a flint glass factory. In East London every level of technology and division of labour was to be found.

The major organizing institution of all this activity with its positive and negative outcomes was the capitalist market. This was not new in the early nineteenth century, but it was increasingly unrestricted by custom. Capitalism here means a system in which the money economy, private ownership, and the search for profit dominated decisions relating to production and consumption. The market proved a powerful information system for coordinating the decisions of many individuals, and price was the most important means of transmitting that information. Migration, housebuilding, decisions to create new factories or purchase machinery, the purchase and provision of food, clothing, and many other consumer items were all guided by the market. The market was a powerful but imperfect means of coordination. The market alone could never have sustained the industrial city or its production. The diseconomies of concentration and the insecurities of trade would have overwhelmed producers and consumers alike. The market was supplemented by a growing bureaucratic economy of regulation, by an increasing number of forms of collective capital and collective consumption, and by the cultural imperatives of domestic and religious moralities.

Population and Life Histories

There was a striking increase in the population of the industrial towns, part of a larger change by which the percentage of the population of England and Wales living in urban places of over 20,000 people increased from 17 per cent in 1801 to 54 per cent in 1891. Manufacturing towns had a disproportionate share in this. Urban population nearly doubled between 1801 and 1851. Of the 212 towns identified by the census, the leisure towns, Cheltenham, Brighton, Bath, and Scarborough, increased the most rapidly, 254 per cent in 50 years. Next came the two groups of manufacturing towns (textiles, 224 per cent; hardware and mining, 217 per cent), whilst the ports (196 per cent), London (146 per cent) and the county towns (122 per cent) were slowest.

The stresses of rapid growth on both physical and social fabrics were focused on particular places and decades. Bradford nearly doubled in size in the 1830s. In Middlesbrough and Merthyr the pace of expansion varied as the incidence of technological change brought advantage to one town and then the other (see Figs. 7.1 and 7.2).

Growth came from both natural increase and migration. Most towns had gained a surplus of births over deaths during the eighteenth century, although the

Population growth rates in Leeds and Bradford per decade.

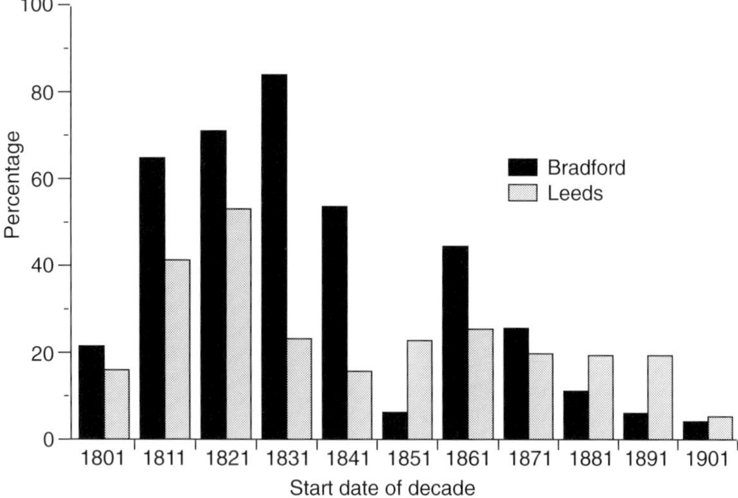

Population growth rates in Merthyr Tydfil and Middlesbrough per decade.

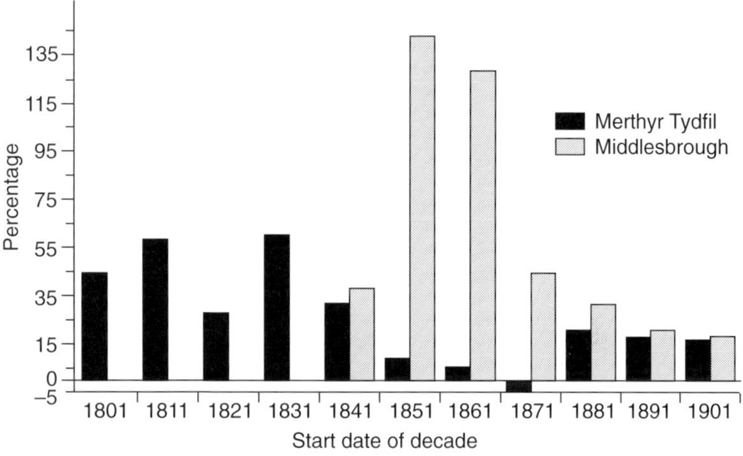

manufacturing towns shared the high birth rate/high death rate pattern characteristic of England and Wales during most of the nineteenth century. Most migrants came from the surrounding countryside. In 1851, only 48 per cent of the population of Preston had been born in the town but, of the rest, 60 per cent had been born within 30 miles. The only significant long distance group were those born in Ireland (14 per cent of the in-migrants). There was long distance migration amongst the middle classes and skilled workers. Middlesbrough was able to draw labour from the declining iron areas of Wales and the English Midlands as well as recruiting unskilled labour from Ireland. The most important reason for migration was the labour market and the cultural pull of the town. Wages were higher. Jobs were available and there was a greater freedom in religion, entertainment, and education than in most rural or small town locations.

Age and gender ratios in Burnley, 1901.

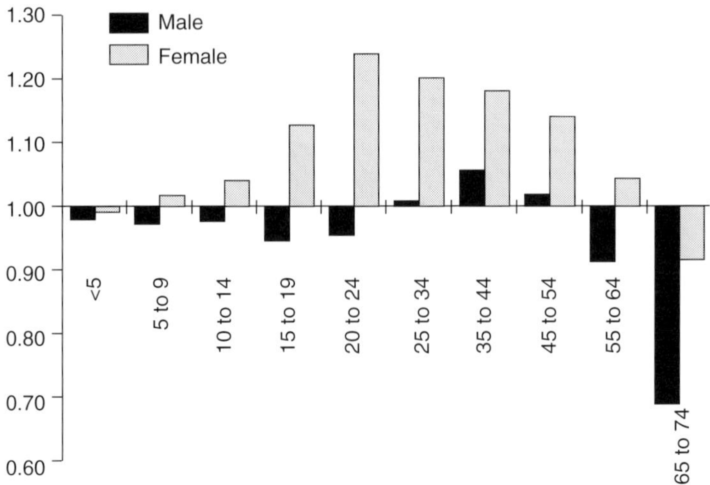

Age and gender ratios in Middlesbrough, 1901.

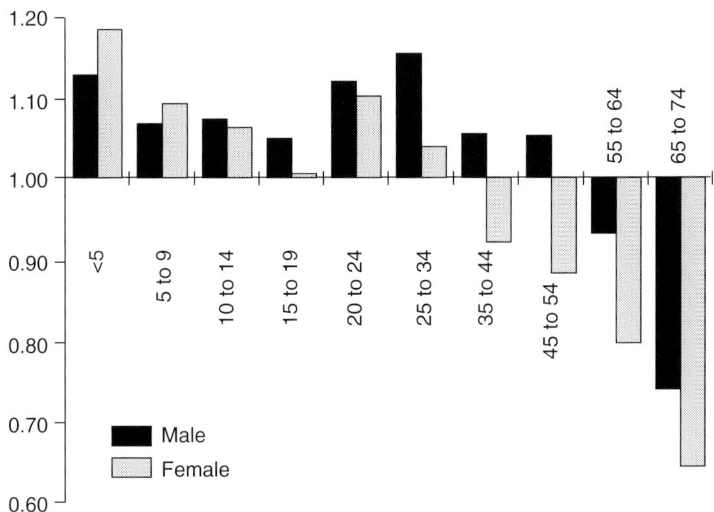

One indicator of the pull of the towns was the manner in which the age, occupation, and gender profile of each town reflected the town's growth, change, and specific demands for labour. In cotton weaving Burnley the gender ratio (women per 100 men) was 114; in Middlesbrough, dominated by iron and steel trades, it was 95. In Manchester, important for commerce and engineering as well as cotton, the ratio was 107, characteristic of the mild female bias found in most European towns. The information in Fig. 7.3 *a-b* comes from the 1901 census and is expressed as the degree to which the age and gender structure of the population varied from that of the population of England and Wales.

Burnley attracted and retained adult female labour. Middlesbrough lost women aged over 30. Even then, 82 per cent of adult women were unoccupied.

The Lancashire cotton industry in 1833: age and employment.

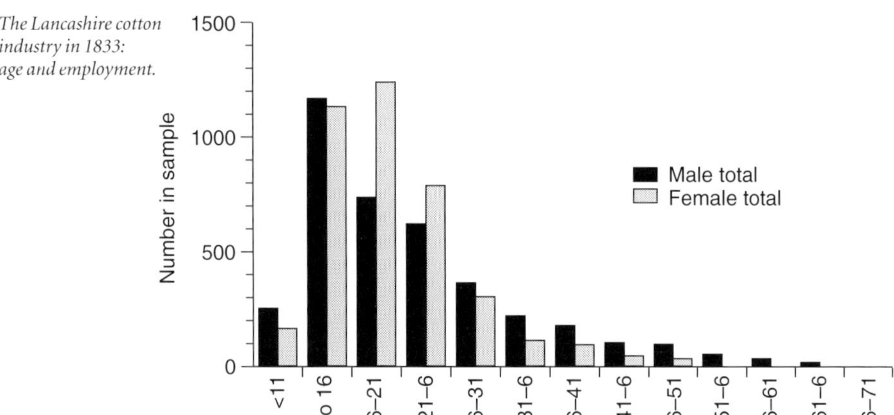

The Lancashire cotton industry in 1833: wages.

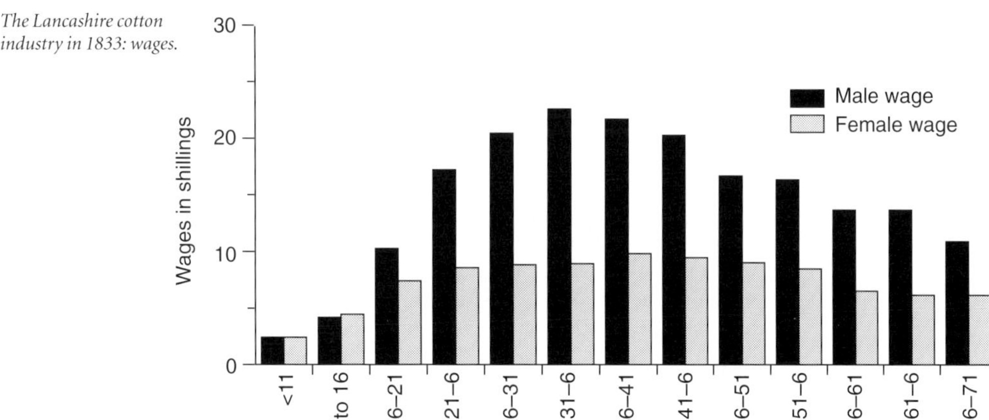

The Lancashire cotton industry in 1833: sickness.

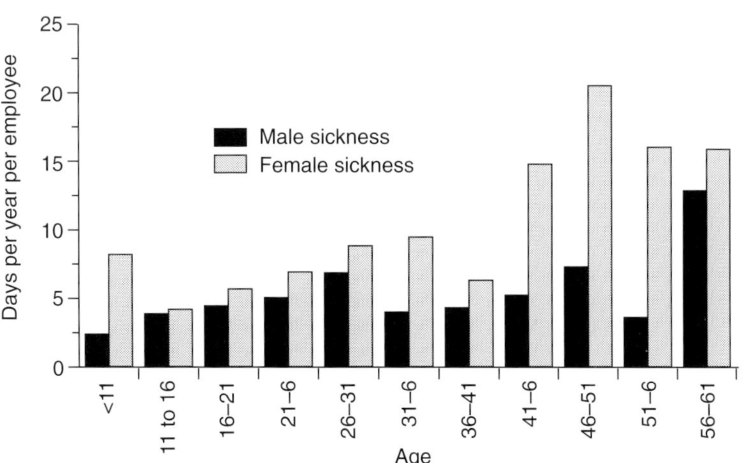

The figure was 47 per cent in Burnley. The large number of children in Middlesbrough resulted from the high birth rate characteristic of workers in heavy industry and from the recent high growth rates in the town, 33 per cent and 21 per cent in the 1880s and 1890s which, like most migration, brought a young adult childbearing population.

So fundamental were the changes which created the early nineteenth-century manufacturing town felt to be, that they became the subject of heated debate. The most important outcome was parliament's decision to regulate the conditions of employment within the textile factories. The information provided for the Royal Commission on the Employment of Children in Factories in 1833 came from a sample of firms which the Commission believed was 'a fair section of the whole'.

Here were outlined key features of the relationship between factories and urban places. Few young children worked in factories but there was a huge army of teenagers and young twenties. Many boys withdrew in their mid-teens to take up apprenticeships whilst the girls stayed until marriage. The rising reported sickness rates reflect the increasing stress of working in the noisy and dirty factory environment. The fall in male wages suggests that stress was met by taking less demanding jobs later in life. The pattern for woollens was similar except that there was a much larger adult male group, and male wages held up for longer.

These figures did not represent a direct confrontation of labour and capital. In an early account of the cotton factories by Edward Baines, the engraved illustrations represent a labour force divided by age and gender. The young boy swept around the machines, whilst women in their teens and early twenties watched the threads for breaks and the adult male spinners guided the semi-automatic spinning frames through their repetitive routine. In the weaving department, young women sat at the loom whilst older male overlookers directed their work. The mills did not function on whole family labour if only because few families had the right balance of age and inclination at any one time; but the authority structures of the family, adult over children and men over women, were carried into the factory to the benefit of the employers. Subcontracting was common. Jane L (a young weaver born of Irish parents in Lancashire) reported that at 18 years she earned 18*s.* a week and employed 'a little helper' for 3*s.* a week.

The graphs present the relationship between factory work and the urban population as a smooth and logical progression. Some individuals worked their way from child labour to adult wages, even to a supervisory position. There were families with two or three generations in the mill, but the biographies of many witnesses to the Factory Commission indicate a more complex relationship between the individual and the urban labour market (see Table 7.1).

Table 7.1.

Date	Age	
1833	51	**Titus Rowbotham**
1782	0	born Macclesfield, Cheshire
1791	9	silk piecer in two places
1796	14	apprentice to cabinetmaker
1801	19	maker and fitter up of machinery with A&G Murray
1819	37	different masters and contract work on own account
1828	46	returned to work for A&G Murray

1833	53	**Richard Wilding**
1780	0	born Kirkham, Lancashire
1794	14	apprentice sail cloth manufacturer
1801	21	Lancashire militia and then artillery (Woolwich)
1814	34	flax spinning mills in Balgony, Ceries and Dundee
1822	42	wholesale provision merchant, Wigan
1829	49	wholesale provision merchant, Bolton; gives up in bad trade
1830	50	warehouseman to Mr Thomasson of Mill Hill, Bolton
1833	38	**Jonathan Ambray**
1795	0	born
1805	10	piecer and scavenger, Stockport; beaten for lateness
1807	12	to Thomas Srimster's 1.5 years; children beaten
1808	13	to Brown's for a year; flogged with a rope; ran away
1809	14	to Marshland's for a year
1810	15	sold muffins in the street
1816	21	helped the dresser in Joseph Lancashire's; scalded in accident
		spinner; 16*s.*
		larger wheel; 28*s.*
		throstle and mule spinner, Newcastle, Staffs; 26*s.*
		candlewick spinner, Stockport; 4 months; 27*s.*
		spinner, Manchester; 6 months; 27*s.*
		provision and drapery shop, 4 years
		death of first wife and failed in business
		spinner, Macclesfield; 17*s.* rise to 26*s.*
		spinner, Manchester; 29*s.*
1829	34	fustian manufacturer; 28*s.* to 35*s.*
1832	37	took up a public house

Common to biographies was a desire to withdraw from the factory and set up a small business, especially a general shop. These lives were dominated by crisis and choice, the urge to get away from poor conditions and physical punishment, the shock of bankruptcy or the death of a wife. Others responded to unemployment, injury, or the desire to take teenage children away from a violent overseer as they sought survival and contentment in the urban labour market.

Oral history provides direct access to the work experience of the twentieth century. Maggie Newbery was born in 1901 in the East Riding of Yorkshire. Her father, a farm tenant, was bankrupted by a bad harvest and cattle disease. The family's response represented that of many rural families over the previous 200 years.

> I suppose we were caught up in the industrial revolution. Our parents decided to give up farming and live in Bradford, where with a large family like ours the children could work in the mills. At least we would be fed and if some of the stories we heard were true our fortune would soon be made.

They went to Bradford by train and the little girl was lost in wonder at the trams and had no idea how the driver 'made it go'. The gas mantle, the water closet, and water tap in the yard were equal urban wonders for the farm family. Playing in the street meant learning new words, although perhaps the hymns of the Methodist Sunday School were familiar. Like many countrymen, Maggie's father became a

carter in the mill, because he could handle horses. Of the eleven children several went into the mill and some of the girls into service. The great variety of urban life enabled each to contribute to a family economy. They lived near the football ground and minded bikes for 2*d.* a time. The sisters in service sent home old clothes and got jars of dripping from the 'big houses'. Aged 12, Maggie was taken on as a half-timer in the same mill as a sister worked; 'all my mother's money troubles would soon be over'. By her late teens she 'wanted to get out of the mill'. Domestic service, 'nice clean work' in the warehouse at Lister's mill, demonstrating Singer Sewing Machines, probationer nurse, and swimming teacher were part of her search for survival and satisfaction in the urban economy. Last in the many waves of migrants were Asian peoples who came halfway across the world. One man who came to Bradford in the 1950s explained: 'the word of mouth thing was quite sufficient . . . even though people would be paid relatively low wages here, that money converted into Pakistan or parts of the Punjab where a lot of the Asians came from sounded an awful lot of money'. In the 1950s, those messages were reinforced by photographs of the newly arrived mill workers, taken at Sandford Taylor's studio in Manningham Lane, often dressed in suit and tie and carrying a briefcase to show their new prosperity.

The by-law back-to-back houses of the 1840s were the result of incipient attempts to regulate the urban environment, with minimum width for the streets and a privy block for every eight houses. Here seen in north Leeds at the end of their life in the 1960s.

Housing

When the ironmaster's wife Lady Bell wrote about Middlesbrough in 1907, she was impressed by 'the rows and rows of little brown streets'. Working-class housing in the manufacturing towns involved an enormous variety of quality, accommodation, amenity, and price, from the one-roomed cellar dwelling to the back-to-back and the terraced through houses with their back yards. This was a direct response to the equally great range of working-class household income. The adult male spinner with several wage-earning children at home needed and could afford a house with two or three bedrooms. The well-paid craftsmen could choose the yarded cottage, whilst the newly arrived casual labourer or the factory worker, whose earnings had been cut by injury or illness, retreated to the damp cellar dwelling.

New arrivals needed to learn how to live in a confined environment. When the Newberys came to Bradford in the 1900s they took a 'one down' with two bedrooms. Counterpanes were used to divide a room for sleeping. They learnt how to light the gas mantle and that water was on tap and not from a pump down the farm yard. They learnt how to use a water closet. The second one down the passage was 'ours'. As members of the family began to earn in the mills, they found a better back-to-back near the football ground for 6*s*. a week. There was a keeping cellar for food and, like many thousands of other women, mother 'set about making the house nice'. The kitchen was cleaned and wallpapered. The floor was scrubbed and rubbed with scouring stone every Monday after washday. The firegrate absorbed many tins of black lead, looked 'warm and cheery', and formed the centre of family life as it did for many successful working-class households. The long narrow stairs, 40 steps from cellar kitchen to attic, were like many which remained in countless childhood memories and tested many ageing limbs. The back-to-back was condemned by public health reformers because of the lack of through ventilation but this evil was not always evident to those who lived there. When the London newspaper the *Morning Chronicle* sent its reporters into the provincial towns in 1849, they found residents in Leeds who considered the back-to-backs 'more wholesome than single ones because they were snugger and warmer. "One heats the other ... like sleeping two in a bed." '

Working-class housing was increasingly separated from the manufacturing workplace. The loomshops which stood above the stone houses of the eighteenth-century Pennine weaving settlements were replaced by the weaving sheds of the mills of the 1830s and 1840s. The overheated and fume-filled rooms which the Bradford woolcombers shared with their families in the 1840s were edged out by the new machines of Listers and others over the next twenty years. At the same time there was little sense of a residential area for working people. School Close to the south-west of the medieval centre of Leeds was stuck between the River Aire and the mill lades. When it was built upon in the 1820s, John Rose took one of the plots out along Neville Street. He built a substantial house and shop on the front of the street. An arched entry led into a courtyard which, by the 1830s, contained seven cottages and a millwright's shop. Here lived his widow and his son who conducted a whitesmith and weighing machine manufactory. This mixed landscape, so hated by later urban planners, was a product of the complex mixture of business and family strategies. In Preston, Bolton, and Bradford the textile mills were surrounded by housing. The Canon Street area of

Middlesbrough was developed from the 1860s adjacent to the ironmasters' district where many of the men worked. The heavy pollution contributed to the high levels of infant mortality and bronchial disease which perplexed the health officials of the 1930s. When Lady Bell crossed the River Tees to her husband's works at Port Clarence, she found 'a colony of workmen live here, actually in the middle of the works . . . every room is penetrated by the noise of machinery, by the irregular clinking together of trucks coming and going, and by the odours and vapours, more or less endurable according to the different directions of the wind, from the works and coke ovens'. She also found many inhabitants 'deeply attached to . . . hard looking shabby ugly streets'. There were many advantages to living by the works, no cold windy walk to work, and no waiting for the crowded ferry across the river. When the fictional Arthur Seaton left his house for a Nottingham bicycle factory in the 1950s of Alan Sillitoe's *Saturday Night and Sunday Morning*, there was 'the factory rumbling a hundred yards away over the high wall'. The noise and fumes of manufacturing were a constant presence for the inhabitants of manufacturing towns. Sound was a key part of the urban–rural contrast which was so important to the English.

The development of elite and middle-class housing followed a related but different path. Between 1780 and the 1820s, many towns saw the creation of a 'west end', closely linked to a nascent central business district and often within walking distance of the new factories. Amid the landscape of squares and terraces with an inward sense of exclusion and order, the appearance of separation from work and the negative aspects of urbanization was an illusion. Behind the elegant red-brick fronts of Park Square in Leeds were the warehouses of their merchant inhabitants and when the south-west wind blew, as it did frequently, the smoke reminded them of local industrial progress. By the 1830s, manufacturing elite families were withdrawing to the hills and fields north and west of the growing towns away from the smoke on which their wealth depended. These were men who could afford a horse, or horse and carriage for their journey to work each day. In Burnley, one branch of the Dugdale family lived at Ivy House near their Lowerhouse Mills and Print Works. By the 1860s, another was hidden away at Rosehill. Here they lived out an Arthurian fantasy. The heads of the king and queen were carved by the main doorway, nearby a coat of arms. A coat of arms and genealogy well researched was a sure sign of manufacturing and commercial success; and given that much start-up capital for industry had its origins in junior branches of minor landed families and that others had married into such families, there was usually something with which to work. Here home and work were truly separated and the adult males would bring back their profits to sustain family and servants and gaze at the staircase stained-glass window with its dreamy romantic lakeland scenes, a soothing contrast to the workplace they had just left, and a reminder of summers in Cumberland or perhaps a wedding trip along the Rhine to Switzerland. The horse-drawn omnibus in the 1850s and the suburban railway and the tram in the 1880s, added to the number who could afford to commute. Social spatial segregation was slow to emerge and never perfect despite the claims of Engels and others. It was late century before the elite villas were joined by rows of substantial terraced houses, little parades of shops, and a new generation of churches and chapels which served the clerk, the schoolteacher, the factory supervisor, the shopkeeper, and the workshop owner who no longer wanted to live over the shop.

Space

There was more to the organization of space in the manufacturing towns than housing, the by-law street, and the middle-class residential suburb. Dominating these industrial towns was a new form of organization of space, often called simply 'the works'.

Contemporary interest and frequently that of the historian has been in the functional logic of work space and its relationship to manufacturing processes. The early textile mills developed in a piecemeal way. Building use changed. Some were multi-occupied with manufacturers sharing a power source and sub-letting space. By the mid-nineteenth century, textile mills were being built with fireproof material. They were more integrated but, except in a few cases, utilitarian in design. In the last half of the century, textile mills grew in size. The double spinning mill made full use of the larger more powerful steam engines. They were multi-storey with a prominent stair tower. The preparation processes were on the ground floor. The weaving shed was single storey with sloping north lights across the roof area. In the cottons especially, weaving was increasingly on separate sites as firms and then towns specialized within the industry. The engine house with the chimney, the warehouse, and the offices—

The Baltic Steel Works in Sheffield was an enclosed and semi-private space, like many referred to simply as the 'works'.

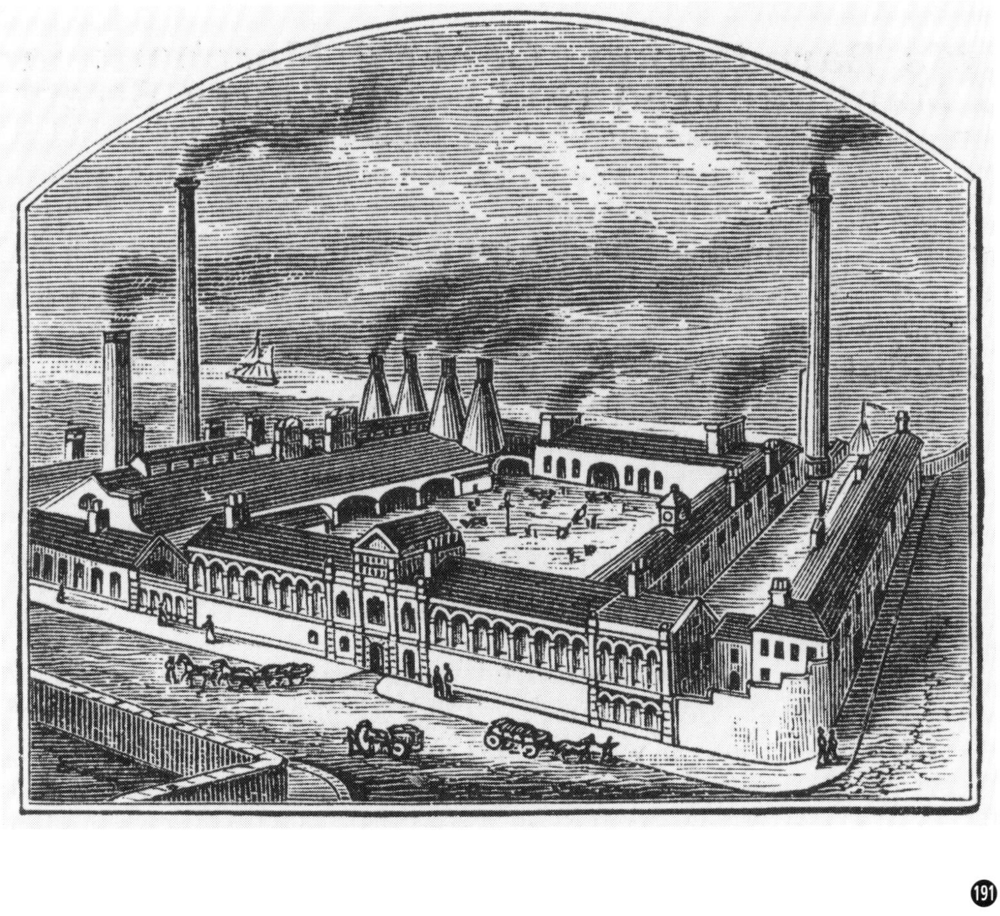

*The blast furnaces and gantries of Middlesbrough (*The Graphic, *1881) were a harsh and dangerous environment.*

often the only building which retained a domestic appearance—were other elements of most sites. The textile mills were distinctive because the whole operation was integrated by the single power source. In other industries the site was integrated by the rhythm and chemistry of the process. Lady Bell was deeply impressed by the physical presence of the iron industry; 'On either shore rise tall chimneys, great uncouth shapes of kilns and furnaces . . . the gloom is constantly pierced by jets of flame from one summit to another'. When the British Industrial Publishing Company produced its promotional review of *The Industries of Sheffield* towards the end of the century, the steel and engineering works which had appeared since the 1840s were detailed in size and the functional organization of space. The Baltic Steel Works at Attercliffe 'comprise melting and converting furnaces, steel forges, rolling and tilting shops, grinding hulls, pattern work and finishing shops, stock and packing rooms, warehouses and a fine suit of offices'. Works in Sheffield and Middlesbrough had yards for storing the coal, iron ore, or semi-finished ingots ready for the furnaces and rolling mills. In Lowry's paintings of Salford and other Lancashire towns, the physical

The Atlas Steel Works in Sheffield rolled the armour plate for the Royal Navy, Illustrated London News, *14 September 1861. There is much evidence of the advanced technology of the rolling mill and furnace here, but notice the importance of dangerous and skilfully co-ordinated sweat and muscle work.*

bulk of 'the mill' dominates his insubstantial ant-like people, as the psychological impact of these accumulations of capital and technology produced a very distinctive artistic style.

Much less is known about the social meanings and social relationships which people created around this space. Streets emptied and filled with the factory hours. At midday, dinner time, those who lived nearby, as many tried to do, would rush home. Others would eat their 'bait' in any space the workforce could make its own, such as the low wall appropriated by the girls in front of the Wigan Mill in Eyre Crowe's painting of dinner hour in 1874. The rush of men and women from the workplace at the end of a shift expressed many of the social forces of industrialization. Boys and girls ganged up as they left the mills, laughing and talking because it was good to be out. The sense of release and anxiety was expressed in different ways in different towns and generations. Delay meant waiting to get the first pint in the pub. By the 1920s, public transport was important for the journey home, and being in the front of the human tide coming from the works meant a seat on the first bus. By the 1930s, the tide was increasingly mounted on bicycles, whilst in the 1950s a growing number of motor vehicles joined the competition to be first to the roadway.

The site of 'the works' was bounded space, with a long frontage to the street, internal yards, and a limited number of controlled entrances. These entrances were the first sign of the authority embodied in this organization of space. Here was the clocking-on machine. When Harry Hardcastle goes blundering into the Salford engineering works in Walter Greenwood's *Love on the Dole* (1933), he is greeted by ' "Hey, what the hell're you doin here?" [by] a tall man wearing

The daily rush of workers from 'the works' was part of the rhythm of time in the industrial city. Here, leaving for lunch, Greenholme Mills, Burley-in-Wharfedale, c.1910.

a badge of authority in the lapel of his coat.' The collective privacy of 'the works' makes its social organization hard to penetrate. Oral history and memoirs all indicate that entry into this world was traumatic with its noise, dirt, dust, and strangeness. The confusing memories of teenage years tend to be buried in later life but the first day at work remained with many men and women 50 or 60 years later: 'The noise was terrifying. I wanted to cry.' They all learnt to use this space. In the mills, the older women guided the doffers along the aisles of spinning machines. In 1950s Nottingham, Arthur Seaton had 'his' lathe. Workers learnt where and when they could have lunch. In the Middlesbrough works, there were cabins for refuge against the bitter north-east winds at break time. These workplaces were spaces of authority and danger. In Drummond's Mill in Bradford in 1913, the overlooker stood at the 'gate' between the spinning frames. Particular places were appropriated in formal and informal ways. The partitioned office was limited to clerical workers. Authority was linked to freedom of movement. The overlooker in the textile mill and the rate checker in the Nottingham cycle factory moved easily around their own department. The proprietor, the 'mayster' would walk around twice a day. Ownership gave the final freedom, the ability to leave and enter the workplace at any time. Learning was about danger as well as authority. By instinct people tried to stand where they would not be caught if one of the straps driving the machinery broke. They learnt the noise a strap made when it was worn and likely to break. This learning was even more crucial around the iron furnaces. For the gantrymen it was a matter of careful balance. Amongst the group in front of the furnace, Lady Bell found 'always a number of men standing round in a state of watchful concentration . . . sudden necessities may arise, of what may be the deadly effect of some swift, dangerous variation, some unexpected development in the formidable material which the men are handling'. Despite the technological achievement involved, much of what happened depended upon manipulative skill, brute force, and the instinctive knowledge built from experience. In the 1860s, at the Atlas Steelworks in Sheffield, the metal plates which made up the new armour plating of Her Majesty's battleships were first heated in a special furnace. They were then manhandled to the huge rollers awaiting them. These gangs of men, like those feeding the furnaces along the Tees, had the help of rails and trucks but the skilful use of sweat and muscle was crucial. At the Atlas Works judgements over the readiness of the plates were made by the furnaceman looking through a small hole in the door. The authority of the workplace was often transmitted by paying such men as a group, but the solidarity of the group was equally enforced by common danger and accumulated knowledge. The social meaning of workplace space was opaque. The intellectuals who studied working-class culture entered only briefly into such spaces whilst those who spent a lifetime there preferred to think of other things, especially when engaged in more repetitive tasks. Fictional Arthur Seaton dreamt over his lathe: 'a present life punctuated by meetings with Brenda on certain beautiful evenings when the streets were warm'. There was no lack of interest or pride in work but it was the machines and the products which mattered rather than place. Martha Heaton at Oxenhope recalled every detail of her spinning frame, made in Keighley with its iron rollers and mahogany boards. Dozens of trades union banners recorded products, tools, and machines as often as they did labour heroes.

Cultural Authority and Place

The manufacturers were a small group but their social and cultural impact was considerable. A few, such as Sir Titus Salt, wanted the total social and cultural domination of their labour force and their environment. In 1853, Salt withdrew from Bradford and established a separate community on a greenfield site three miles from the town. He wanted to escape the cross-currents of urban influence, the physical environment of epidemic and infant mortality, the compromises of elite politics, the threats of radical politics, and the distractions of the cheerful roughness of an alcohol-based leisure culture. Saltaire Mill dominates with its attention-grabbing Italianate façade. By 1871, the 49-acre site had 824 houses, graded to fit the mill labour hierarchy, together with shops, baths, school, institute, hospital, eleven acres of park, and a Congregational church. The result was a capitalist republic with a benevolent dictator. Salt's Liberal, Nonconformist, manufacturing, and profit-seeking personality and power were stamped upon the landscape. The Institute was a flamboyant Italianate *palazzo* building designed to draw the population away from the nearby public houses towards a world of reading rooms, chess, draughts, technical and scientific education, and the drill room for the 39th West Riding Volunteers. There was a superficial resemblance to aristocratic style, the coat of arms, the elite schooling for his sons, the country house a few miles away, and the ethic of authority and obligation. This was no attempt to imitate the aristocracy but rather to elbow them aside and create a new landscape.

Edward Akroyd was a Tory, Anglican, and major worsted manufacturer. Between 1861 and 1873 he fashioned Akroydon, a fragment of Halifax, as an expression of his ideal of the devout industrial squire. His mansion, Bankfield, another Italianate *palazzo*, looked one way towards his mills. Next door was All Souls Church (architect, Sir Gilbert Scott) an imposing Gothic building with a spire 256 feet high, one foot higher than Square Congregational Church, sponsored by his rival Crossley across the valley. The nearby houses were domestic Gothic, designed by a pupil of Gilbert Scott, with naturalistic carvings, such as strawberry and ivy leaves, around the doors and windows. Akroyd was more prepared than Salt to use urban institutions to further his ambitions. The project was designed to encourage the virtue of savings as well as piety. The houses were to be purchased with the help of a Building Society set up for the purpose, supplied with funds by the recently created Halifax Permanent Building Society and guaranteed by Akroyd himself. The initial purchasers of the houses in Salisbury Place had their initials carved over the door, an encouraging expression of individuality within the framework imposed by Akroyd's design and the restrictive covenants signed on purchase.

This paternalist search for cultural and social dominance took a variety of forms. From the 1850s onwards treats, feasts, trips, and celebrations were often linked to the family events of the employer. The family ownership structure of most mills enabled paternalism to identify directly with the individual capitalist, through the walk around the mill, the appearance at the Institute, or the presentation of instruments to the brass band. Effects were often political. As the technologies and working practices of industries stabilized after the mid-century, working people tended to accept their part in the relationship out of a sense of inevitability rather than a sense of fear. The relationship could be hard and manipulative as well as benevolent. Where employers retained some housing, rents were remitted as a dole for loyal and retired workers. Occupants of employer housing were firmly reminded that their children were expected to work in the mill when they came of age.

Most employers allowed the urban economy to supply housing, shops, and entertainment to their labour force. Cultural assertion took the form of cash to the local Mechanics Institution or Technical College, the presentation of land for a park, or the building of an art gallery or public library. In Middlesbrough in 1868, the ironmaster H. W. F. Bölckow financed Albert Park on what was then the edge of the town. At the end of the century in Bristol, Sir W. H. Wills, dissatisfied with the progress of plans for an art gallery, took over. These cases were identified with an individual but cultural assertion was often collective. When the Wool Exchange was built in Bradford between 1864 and 1867, the elite came together as directors and shareholders of a joint-stock company just as they had for the building of St George's Hall in the early 1850s. In Leeds, the elite took the form of a committee of the Town Council using the formidable resources and credit of the municipal rates.

These buildings were part of an elaborate symbol system. The promoters of each building made their choice from a vast scrapbook of architectural styles according to taste, mood, fashion, and purpose. The result was a rich iconography, buildings which were message boards with many meanings, very different from the functional architecture of rural industry and the early mills.

Classical styles were chosen for a wide range of public buildings. Leeds Town Hall (1853–8), with colonnaded front and domed tower, became a definition of what a town hall should be. The references to Greece and Rome involved a sense of civic independence, pride and identity. The Venetian, especially Venetian Gothic, was increasingly important with the dominant series of rounded window heads, often with a touch of foliage on the carved capital. Like the Gothic itself, it was a style which suited domestic as well as public buildings. These choices reflected societies which not only had been successful in trade but also had gained lasting artistic reputations; and that was exactly what the leaders of the manufacturing towns wanted. When the commercial leaders of Bradford decided on building the Wool Exchange, they invited John Ruskin, leading metropolitan intellectual and moralist, to come and advise them. He told them off for worshipping the 'Goddess of Getting-on' and suggested decorating the frieze with pendent purses. The Bradford audience listened with respect and then went on to do exactly what they wanted and built in a lavish Venetian Gothic. Ruskin maybe deliberately missed the point. The Bradford elite had read *The Stones of Venice* (1851–3) in their own way. They appropriated the style of one great trading empire, added symbols of their own history and elite, and continued the trading that made a rapidly growing town. Other choices were experimental. When Marshall's new flax spinning mills were built south of the river in Leeds in 1838, a functional interior was hidden by an Egyptian Temple, a much visited 'wonder of the world'. When factory builders moved away from the functional they tended to prefer the Venetian, with the campanile chimney announcing taste and industry in a variety of landscapes. Gothic was the choice for those who wanted an element of religious-inspired morality, hence its perfection at All Souls Akroydon. Manchester Town Hall (1868–77) was a municipal cathedral to counter the forum-cum-acropolis of Birmingham and Leeds.

There was a wide range of heraldic references which were usually quite specific. Municipal badges mostly went back to sixteenth- or seventeenth-century charters or to the landed families which had founded boroughs in the thirteenth or fourteenth centuries. Leeds Town Hall used the owl of the Savilles and a golden fleece to represent the foundation of the borough and its source of wealth. Middlesbrough had to dig deep for its feudal legitimacy but after a little thought appropriated the lion of the Brus family which had granted Middlesbrough as a cell to Whitby Abbey in the twelfth century. They added battlements for burghal privilege and three ships for the coal trade. At Manningham Mills, Bradford, Lister's produced a gate to the weaving sheds which would have done credit to the park entrance of many landed estates. And then there were the lions, the ultimate heraldic beast representing power rather than any specific Englishness. Lions appeared everywhere. In several places, like Leeds Town Hall and The Square at Saltaire, there were claims that the local lions were rejects from Trafalgar Square, thus gaining metropolitan prestige and the merits of successful bargain-hunting in one blow.

Interior of Marshall's Flax Mill, Leeds from the Penny Magazine, *30 September 1843. This was the utilitarian or 'useful knowledge' vision of industry.*

The cultural power of industrial owners was expressed in many ways. This entrance to the weaving sheds at Manningham Mills in Bradford would have done credit to the gates of a landed estate.

facing page: The elaborate symbol system of Todmorden Town Hall (1866) started with a classical architecture appropriating independence and power from Greece and Rome. The pedimented frieze included Lancashire cotton and Yorkshire machinery and wool, suited to a borough on the boundary of the two counties.

There was no pure imitation in these references. They were drawn inextricably into the world of manufacturing which financed them. Todmorden Town Hall, sponsored by the Fieldens in 1866, was a renaissance classical temple to civic pride but the pedimented frieze was a representation of the place of the borough in the regional and world economy. In the centre were two ladies in classical drapery representing Yorkshire and Lancashire. (The old county boundary ran through the borough.) On the Lancashire side were more ladies with trays of cotton bobbins, whilst tucked into the corner was the Liverpool merchant (with ledger) and the docker heaving the cotton bales. On the Yorkshire side were the suppliers of machinery, wheat, and wool. In Saltaire, the alpaca llama sits proudly over the school entrance as a reminder of the source of wealth upon which the community was based. The expansive headquarters of the Burnley Co-operative

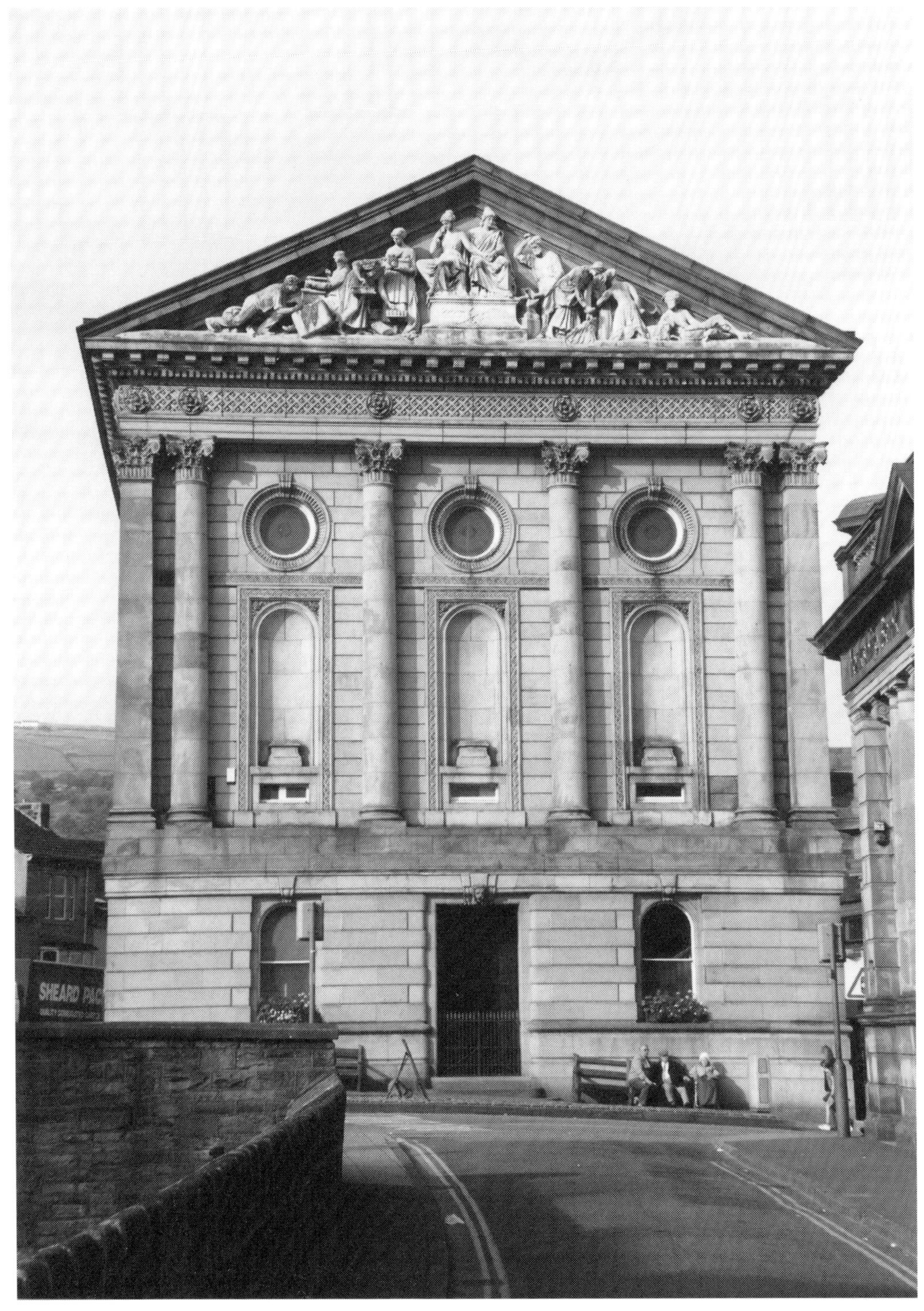

The Italianate bulk of the main mills at Saltaire was characteristic of the monumental nature of much industrial building. This site now sustains a post-industrial existence as the location of a David Hockney art gallery, speciality shops, and an electronics firm.

Society announced its intentions not only with Venetian Corinthian but also with the busy bees of industry and wreaths of English roses and Scottish thistles together with a thoughtful lion who appears to be chewing a cotton flower and a fruitful vine, symbolic reminders of the industrial and the domestic.

The cultural and social authority of these major employers of labour was great but the economic and social structure of the manufacturing town consisted of much more than a few dominant employers. A census of the Lancashire cotton industry in 1841, the end of a decade of sustained investment and technological change, showed that only 25 out of 975 firms in the industry employed more than 1,000 people and that 232 employed less than 50. Within the urban community as a whole the prominence of size was even less. The structure of the economies of the manufacturing town had an important place for commercial, professional, retail, craft, and services, all activities dominated by small units of capital and employment.

Table 7.2. *Occupational structure of the population included in the Trade Directories of selected manufacturing towns, 1834 (percentages)*

	Leeds	West Bromwich	Bilston
Merchants	6.8	3.3	1.0
Manufacturers	22.3	17.4	18.8
Professional	3.0	7.6	7.3
Shopkeepers	30.9	51.1	54.2
Tradesmen	37.0	20.7	18.8

Mid-19th-century Slater's Terrace on the edge of Burnley's Weavers Triangle combined canal transport, warehousing and workers' housing for the nearby Clock Tower spinning mill and the Sandygate Weaving Shed.

The 1851 Census gave fragmentary information on numbers of employers in each region and the number of people employed.

Table 7.3. *Percentage of employers by numbers employed, 1851 Census, North West District*

	350+	100+	10+
All industries	0.73	2.89	13.40
Cotton manufacture	7.41	26.71	54.90
Engine maker	3.48	6.62	28.22
Tailor	0.00	0.00	5.54

Large firms were exceptional. The information on cotton manufacture indicated that an unusual 27 per cent of manufacturers employed over 100 people but nearly half employed fewer than ten.

Time

Time in many forms dominated the life of the industrial city. This clock remained like a ghostly sentinel in the empty weaving shed of Manningham Mills, Bradford.

In the manufacturing town the organization of space and time were closely related. Clocks dominated and the evidence remains. In Middlesbrough the town hall clock still goes, although the dock entrance clock has long ago stuck at half past nine as if marking the withdrawal of industrialization from the original town site. The clock of the old High School, built on land donated by the owners of the Middlesbrough Estate, still keeps good time as does the one in Albert Park, and those on St Peter's Catholic Church at South Bank. This was abstract time

but its reality took many forms. Wages moved with great caution from piece-rates to time rates. Even when formal piece-rates remained, the day was bound around by 'time' and by conventional notions of what 'ought' to be the weekly or fortnightly wage packet. The gates of Drummond's Mill were guarded by the pennyoil man. Early arrival meant that a couple of minutes in bed had been lost. Late arrival meant a fine plus the alley strap awaiting those who arrived after the machines had been switched on. Even for those without clocks the factory towns and townships signalled the passing hours by factory hooters, buzzers, and sirens. Time within the factory was carefully measured. One of the first requirements of the factory inspectors was the keeping of a time book for each employee. Work was repetitive and demanding. In Alan Sillitoe's 1950s Nottingham, Arthur Seaton plays a careful game with the time rate, the rate checker, and his own skill and energy to ensure a wage of around £14 a week. Work study and rate checking had become more exacting since the 1890s with the arrival of so-called Taylorism or scientific management from the United States. This had intensified the day-to-day contest for time.

The dominance of the clock did not eliminate other forms of time. Age was measured not by strength and willingness to work but since 1837 by the birth certificate. As factory and workplace regulation spread, age controlled access to the labour market. There was weekly time, embodied in *Saturday Night and Sunday Morning* (1958). The work of the mill and engineering shop was so repetitive that the minds of the mill girls and lathe operatives were occupied by many other things. The memories of mill girls and many other working people were filled with holidays and weekends, not the details of the workplace. Hiking on the moors above Bradford, 'lads', or music from chapel and music hall filled their heads during work. One advantage of the noise of the mill was that the most tuneless performers could entertain themselves without offending anyone. Then there was annual time which reproduced itself with comforting expectation; the Nottingham Goose Fair, the Lancashire 'wakes' weeks, Bonfire Night, and Christmas. Trips were made into the fields to collect tadpoles in the spring, berries in autumn, or holly for Christmas—a bit of green to bring into the house. Many events tied rural and urban together. Others were part of modern patterns, the annual seaside holiday, day trip, or disciplined stay at the boarding house with the donkey ride, the 'funny' postcard, and the stick of rock before coming home to start saving for the next event. The deep disorientation of the 1970s was closely linked to the disruption of this cycle. There were rarer occasions when historian's time would intervene, local events like the visit of Gladstone or a prolonged strike and, for town after town, the Battle of the Somme and the Armistice.

There was time as progress. This was especially important for towns like Bradford and Middlesbrough which had grown from insignificance to be substantial places. Everywhere quoted population figures. When William Cudworth wrote *Worstedopolis* (Bradford) in 1888, he included not only population but also the number of letters and parcels posted and the number of churches and chapels built. The elites of the manufacturing towns were increasingly busy making their own history. At the start of the century there had been stately antiquarian histories with their accounts of local charities and impressive genealogies for local merchants. There had been short entries in local directories quoting seventeenth-century charters and the foundation of local voluntary associations. By the 1860s, the extent and density of local history were growing rapidly. *The*

Industries of Sheffield, Historical, Statistical, Biographical (*c*.1890) sought a double legitimacy for the town in a mythical past and in current progress:

> It is no modern upstart manufacturing town . . . from time immemorial Sheffield has been associated with the manufacture of cutlery; indeed, there are not wanting historic traditions tending to show that it was relied on by the Ancient Britons to furnish needful weapons wherewith to combat the Roman legions.

When City Square, Leeds was laid out in the 1890s, the Black Prince, to whom mythology attributed the bringing of the wool trade to England, was tastefully surrounded by Joseph Priestley, one time minister of Mill Hill Unitarian Church and representative of science and rationality, and by the company of several ladies whose stone-carved nakedness was steadily covered with the soot and grime of the city. Each town created its own foundation myth. Middlesbrough, with 25 inhabitants in 1801, began with the Quaker 'owners' who cleared a swamp to build a town and continued with the hero ironmasters Bölckow and Vaughan who established the Cleveland iron trade in the 1850s. 'Jacky' Vaughan, an ironpuddler who had joined his skill with merchant wealth, told the guests at a dinner party how he had 'discovered' the Eston ironstone after kicking over a stone whilst shooting rabbits. The story, a mixture of fairy-tale 'good luck' and Smilesean 'self help', delivered with north country understatement, created Vaughan as hero in the identity and justification of Middlesbrough.

The Road to the Post-Industrial Industrial Town

Between 1920 and 1960, the experience of individual manufacturing towns varied. Some places were devastated. Jarrow was a one-industry town on the Tyne where, in 1934, the Palmer shipyard was bought and closed by National Shipbuilders Security Limited, a company formed by the shipyard owners to reduce national capacity. There were towns which paused and fought like Bradford. Some received new inputs like Middlesbrough, where Brunner Mond (soon to be part of the newly formed ICI in 1926) established an ammonia plant and research division on the north bank of the Tees at Billingham. Other economies had an internal dynamic and variety which enabled them to transform themselves in response to the new products and markets of the inter-war period. In Coventry, the decline of ribbon weaving and then watchmaking in the later nineteenth century was replaced by the growth of the bicycle industry, followed by motor-car and motor-cycle production. The transferable skills of labour, plus the support of a growing machine tools industry, attracted entrepreneurs who established firms like Alfred Herbert, Daimler, Hillman, and Triumph which were the basis of post-1920 expansion. Then there were new industrial centres, like Luton or the industrial estates of Slough and the Great Western Road out of London, producing domestic consumer goods. Others diversified. Oxford, long dominated by cultural tourism and the knowledge industry, gained a new industrial suburb at Cowley. Morris Motors produced 2,000 cars there in 1920 and 55,000 in 1925. The Pressed Steel Company established on an adjacent site was one of many suppliers scattered around the old university city.

The 1939–45 war was followed by a period of sustained prosperity and stability during which the industrial towns were the object of detailed total area planning. Industrial and residential areas were separated by zoning. Large areas of nineteenth-century working-class housing were replaced by subsidized local authority housing. Despite well-publicized difficulties caused by poor building standards and social problems, the bulk of the industrial population now acquired basic sanitary facilities such as inside toilets and bathrooms. By the 1960s, most industrial towns were building a road system for mass motor transport. The implementation of the Clean Air Acts reduced bronchial disease and enabled populations to see across their cities for the first time since the 1926 General Strike.

From the mid-1970s, this process came to an end and the manufacturing town was affected by a fundamental process of de-industrialization. Industrial production was being reorganized on a world scale. The control of industrial capital moved decisively away from local or regional family and joint-stock companies towards multi-site and multinational companies disciplined by stock markets, financial institutions, and distant head offices. At the same time the structure of production moved towards services and a wide range of knowledge-based industries, notably electronics. The changing structure of employment in the industrial region of Tyneside (Table 7.4) showed in an extreme form what happened.

Table 7.4. *Percentage of Total Employment on Tyneside by sector*

	1971	1984
Primary	3	2
Manufacturing	37	23
Construction	7	6
Services	53	69
Total employed	398,032	332,139

In general, the reduction of industrial employment took place through a change in ownership structure followed by workforce reductions and the closure of individual sites and branch plants. The rise in services jobs included the establishment of the Department of Health and Social Security benefits centre at Newcastle, providing 8,000 jobs and the Metro Centre, an out-of-town shopping complex south of the river providing 4,000 mostly part-time jobs. Communities were broken and whole strategies of survival developed over 150 years were rendered useless. During the 1980s, the Prime Minister Mrs Thatcher visited Teeside and was pictured in the cleared industrial wasteland of the ironmasters' district. Less well known was her televised conversation with one of the unemployed whom she advised to retrain. She received the, to her, incomprehensible reply, 'But I want to be a labourer, I have always been a labourer'.

The urban clearances of this period produced a reorganization of the landscape as great as anything which had happened since the early nineteenth century. Wartime bombing and total area planning were followed by the impact of a changing world industrial system. The result was a period of deep anxiety and often alienation as communities faced the question of what the 'post-industrial' industrial city should and would be. First there was denial accompanied by clearances and demolition. At the same time communities began to re-engage much like the wayward and intermittent recall of the trauma victim. There were isolated campaigns to save businesses. Industrial buildings were listed for preservation. There were reminiscence projects which sought to capture fast disappearing ways of life long taken for granted. By the 1990s, it was possible to review the post-industrial landscape, and to understand what happened to a manufacturing town when its manufacturing dwindled.

In the late twentieth century manufacturing towns faced a situation very different from the social and economic processes with which they originated in the early nineteenth. The dynamic areas of wealth creation were now in the 'brainware' businesses, design, consultancy, electronics, and entertainment. Manufacturing towns are located in a society which increasingly values 'experience' over accumulation and possession; a society which values identity with the past rather than with the assertively modern and rational. The particularities of place and community are set against globalized structures of power and culture despite, or perhaps because of, the increasing concentration of decision-taking in distant corporate headquarters and financial centres. The impact of such trends upon the ground shows in a variety of ways.

Middlesbrough became not quite a post-industrial city. The area around Middlesbrough Dock and the ironmasters' district is now dominated by the Riverside Stadium of Middlesbrough Football Club, sponsored by Cellnet, thus identifying a local leisure activity with global communication. The surrounding cleared and vacant sites are guarded by pleading notices announcing their readiness for the inward investment of global capital seeking branch plant sites. In Bradford, the Wool Exchange which once traded industrial raw material, became the retail end of the knowledge industry, a branch of a national chain of booksellers. Nearby, the warehouse district is being scrubbed and refurbished. Merchants' House in Peckover Street is across the road from Design House. Both offer modern communications and shared facilities, but the old nickname of 'Little Germany' and the 'prestige' of the ashlar stone warehouses are a positive part of marketing studio and business space. Down the road, Saltaire Mill was taken over in 1958, closed in 1986 but then purchased in 1987 by the Bradford clothing trade millionaire Jonathan Silver. It is the perfect 'post-industrial' mill. Activity in the mill is about lifestyle, creativity, electronics, and 'experience'. It is a place to be and be seen. One tenant, Pace Micro Technology, produces digital satellite receiving equipment. In 1992 the artist David Hockney, whose home was in Bradford, established a gallery at the mill. The path to free admission to the gallery goes through many floors of the mill rented to the retailers of high quality fabric and furniture, designer clothes, and a bookshop. Crossley's Dean Clough Mills followed the same pattern. They were closed in 1982 to be purchased by a local millionaire businessman Ernest Hall. Its major tenants include important service and information processors, insurance, building society, Customs and Excise, as well as a BBC studio, but the personality of the revived site is provided by its function as a design and arts centre with galleries, studios, conference rooms, office space, and a design shop. Tenants range from the Royal Society of Arts, the Quilters Guild, the National Centre for Brass Bands to two sculptors in scrap metal, who inhabit the unrestored west end of the site rent free with a creative energy that is only curbed by the need to stop work when it rains and the water comes through the roof. Across the Pennines in Burnley, the Weavers Triangle promises a familiar variety, hotel development, industrial museums, conference centre, and offices, as well as a marina. This is much more than the museumification of the industrial past. The past is being reused but in a progressive rather than a regressive manner.

8 Transport

John Armstrong

In 1800 about 30 per cent of England's population were urban dwellers; now, in 2000, that proportion is 90 per cent. Both external transport linkages and the internal provision of transport have been crucial to this urban growth.

Living in towns tended to separate the inhabitants from natural sources of food, drink, fuel, and clothing basic to existence. For the majority of urban dwellers growing vegetables or fruit, keeping pigs or chickens, gathering timber and berries from woods and hedgerows, and gleaning from harvested fields were not viable options. These they needed to purchase commercially. Similarly, whereas rural employment had natural rhythms, with lack of daylight or inclement weather restricting hours of work at certain times of the year, urban employment was less seasonal. Machinery imposed a steady application and left less time for home-brewing, baking, or jam-making, again forcing town dwellers to buy these products rather than make them themselves.

Hence the urban centres needed a huge net inflow of the materials from which basic foods and drink could be manufactured: wheat and flour to make the daily bread; barley, malt, and hops to brew beer; and chickens, geese, pigs, fish, sheep, and cattle to provide the protein in an urban diet. All of these had to be transported from the rural areas into towns, alive or dead, in raw or semi-processed form and, as the population of the towns rose and the average standard of living improved, the quantities involved also grew substantially. Thus additional units of transport were needed to carry this increased supply or, better still, new forms of transport were developed to carry larger quantities more quickly and cheaply over longer distances.

It was not only humans that needed feeding. Throughout the nineteenth century and well into the twentieth century, each town had a large horse population for hauling goods from quay or station to factory, and from factory to retail outlet, as well as for making direct retail deliveries such as milk, bread, fish, and vegetables. Wagons, carts, drays, and vans were ubiquitous and each required at least

one horse to draw it. In addition there were horses for passenger travel, mounted individually or pulling coaches and broughams, traps and gigs. England's towns contained a huge non-farming horse population which Michael Thompson has estimated at 535,000 in 1851 and 1.7 million in 1901. About twenty pounds of corn and ten pounds of chaff were eaten each day by each working horse, not to mention the straw litter; and all of this had to be brought into the urban centres from the surrounding countryside. London's animal population was served by 'stackies'—barges loaded high with hay or straw at various East Anglian ports—which sailed round the coast and up the River Thames. Large quantities of oats were also brought to London by coaster from East Anglia, Northumberland, and Scotland. Nor was it only horses that needed feeding. Before strict environmental controls over urban activities emerged, cows were kept in towns to provide fresh milk, and pigs for ham and bacon. These animals also needed feedstuffs brought into the city from rural areas. This cumulatively heavy and bulky material was of low intrinsic value and required transport that was cheap.

An urban population wanted more than food and drink; it also sought heat and light, and as industry became concentrated in urban locations it too needed supplying. By the early nineteenth century coal provided the main source for heat, light, and power. Heat came from coal burned direct in domestic hearths or industrial boilers, light from coal gas production which was developed commercially in the early nineteenth century, and power from coal consumed in steam engines. Coal was heavy, bulky, and low value; therefore it too needed low cost transport or it priced itself out of the market. Thus the collier brig was developed, carrying 200 to 300 tons from the north-east coalfields, which were close to the coast, to the huge London market and the south-east. As the urban population grew so did the demand for coal and the need for additional units of transport.

Urbanization also depended upon large quantities of building materials to construct the houses, factories, and warehouses and the shops, offices, and banks. These all required heavy bulk inputs such as timber, bricks, slates, plaster and for more prestigious buildings, stone and marble. Some few of these could be found locally, if geological conditions were right; for example, in London the excavation for basements often yielded clay suitable for brick-making. Most were geographically specific and needed transporting long distances to the growing urban centres. This was true of the highly prized slates from North Wales, the stone from Portland, and the granite from Aberdeen. Particular cities were fortunate in having a proximate supply of constructional stone, such as Bath and Glasgow, but very few had local timber and much was imported. As the cities grew so did the infrastructural building of roads, pavements, sewers, bridges, and river embankments. All these made additional heavy demands on the transport system: wooden or granite setts for roads, paving stones, bricks for lining sewers, stone and bricks for bridges and embankments.

It is plain from this that urban areas relied on transport to support both their physical structure and their human and animal populations. This was not a one-way traffic. Towns depended on transport to remove material as well as to bring it in. At the most basic level, in an era before large-scale underground sewerage, human waste had to be expelled. Called 'night soil', it was stored locally, then collected by cart to be transferred to river lighter or barge, whereupon it was dumped at sea or used after minimal processing to revitalize farmland. The animal population similarly created much waste, both in stables and stalls and on the public roads. This amounted to about four tons per horse per annum, which necessitated the 'crossing sweeper'—beloved of Dickens—who cleared a path for genteel people through the dung for a small denomination coin. Animal waste was again removed by horse and cart, usually taken to barges where it was shipped to the corn-growing areas for reinvigorating the soil for the next crop. The 'stackies' which brought hay and straw into London often removed the stable and street manure.

Human and animal refuse was not the only waste needing transport. In a coal-burning era much ash was generated. Because domestic fires were not very efficient, among the ashes there remained unburnt material which could be used. Much of this 'breeze' was sold to brickmakers who sifted out the solids and mixed them with their clay, so reducing the quantity of small coal needed to fire their bricks. As in the case of animal manure, one person's waste was another's raw material and a living could be made by transporting the 'rubbish' to those who perceived it as an input. Broken glass was removed as cullet for resmelting in the north-east, and the rubble from demolished buildings either reused locally as hardcore or moved out of the cities for dumping. In brewing, large amounts of malt and hops were soaked in water and mashed to extract their sugars and flavours; but the residue—the draff—was protein-rich and suitable for feeding to livestock, especially pigs. Similarly the extraction of oils from various nuts and seeds left a residue which could be fed to animals as cattle cake. These too needed transporting to the farms from the cities. The key element in the outward transport of waste materials from the cities was, however, the human and animal excretion. This was smelly, liable to spread disease, and, especially in warm weather, deteriorated rapidly, providing a breeding ground for flies, and other noxious insects. In the early to mid-nineteenth century, death rates in cities were much higher than in the countryside and epidemics of cholera and typhus occurred with frightening frequency. Methods of waste-removal were then primitive and inadequate; but without them, the attacks of infectious diseases would have been more deadly. Canal and river barges, combined with the night-soil operator's horse and cart, therefore performed a vital function which allowed the cities to grow.

By 1800 there were four main methods of moving the urban food supply. At the simplest level, where the 'food' was alive and mobile it could walk itself to market. Thus geese and ducks waddled their slow way over long distances from country to town, and were celebrated by the Goose Fair at Nottingham every autumn. Sheep and cattle were also driven from fattening grounds to markets in towns where they were slaughtered, dressed, and prepared for retail butchers. London's Smithfield market was the largest emporium of this trade.

At no greater speed, foods which were immobile and coming from relatively short distances could be brought by horse-drawn cart or wagon, the former carrying up to a ton or two, the latter perhaps coping with up to five tons, but then requiring a team of four or more horses. The disadvantage of horse-drawn road transport was that it was slow, travelling at the normal walking pace of the horse, say three or four miles per hour, and expensive, because the cost of feeding the horse was high; and there were no economies to be gained by increasing the scale of goods carried, because extra cargo meant a duplication of carter, cart, and horse(s).

A more economical way of bringing food into the city, but no faster, was the horse-drawn canal barge or river lighter. It too travelled at near walking pace and with occasional halts while locks were negotiated or weirs bypassed. Despite having a larger capacity—up to twenty tons was usual—it offered less resistance and needed only one horse to draw it. Thus the costs per ton carried were lower and goods could be moved over longer distances. This way, sacks of wheat or malt were brought down the River Lea to London's bakeries and breweries.

Market traffic passing St Nicholas Church in Westgate Street, Gloucester in 1827. Note the sheep being driven, the two pedestrians, one with a basket and the other with a load over the shoulder, and the donkey well-laden with basket panniers. Dogs fighting add to the high noise level of hooves on cobbled streets.

By far the cheapest method of moving large quantities over long distances was by coastal ship. These ranged in capacity from 30 to 200 tons in the early nineteenth century, and were manned by between three and seven sailors. They relied on (the sometimes unpredictable) wind for their motive power but so avoided the expensive horse and kept operating costs relatively low. Also, by virtue of their large capacity, labour costs were lower than horse-drawn road transport. Coasters could sail up many of Britain's rivers and access directly many of the largest cities. Where rivers became too narrow or shallow for a coastal ship, it could offload into river lighters or canal barges so that the cargo continued by the cheapest all-water route. By avoiding quays and wharves the goods did not incur additional charges, and costs were kept down. By these means Cheshire cheese was carried to London, salmon from Aberdeen and Berwick to London, and grain from King's Lynn to the north-east. Coasters were also essential for the movement of intrinsically low value commodities such as coal, sand, lime, slates, bricks, china clay, and salt.

How did these methods of transport affect the early nineteenth-century urban environment? They were crucial in determining where and how towns developed. Many of England's major urban centres developed on wide navigable rivers which allowed easy communication with the hinterland by barge or lighter, and provided external communication by ship to other towns both in the kingdom and abroad. London had the Thames, Bristol the Severn, Liverpool the Mersey, and Newcastle the Tyne. When inland towns developed they were frequently reliant on canal networks, for example Manchester and Birmingham. The shape of the town was also partly determined by transport availability, with towns spreading along the river or coast and remaining relatively compact. Quays and wharves were important centres of trade and commerce. Business districts built up around them as merchants chose to be close to this key transhipment point, and manufacturers with bulky raw materials endeavoured to minimize the carrying distance by the relatively expensive horse and cart.

If these four methods of goods movement were adequate for the first years of the nineteenth century, their weaknesses became more obvious as the size of towns grew. The advent of steam propulsion had an immense impact on interurban transport. It was applied initially in steamboats. Henry Bell's *Comet* in 1812 is usually identified as the first commercial steamboat service in Britain. It plied the waters of the Clyde from Glasgow to Helensbrough carrying passengers, and its example was soon followed by other steamboats on English rivers, such as the Thames, Mersey, and Humber. Within a few years most English rivers boasted steamboat services still essentially for passenger traffic, providing both recreational excursions and longer distance commuting for middle-class clients. The main drawback to the early steamboats was that their engines and boilers took up a large amount of space and, because they were inefficient, they consumed great quantities of coal which in turn required a good proportion of their carrying capacity to be given over to the bunkers. For the first couple of decades they did not carry bulk cargoes but rather high value goods such as passengers, parcels, and post, and perishables such as fish and meat. It was only when improvements in boiler design allowed higher steam pressures and compound engines that they became viable as bulk cargo carriers, such as the steam colliers which distributed coal from the north-eastern coalfields to London and the south-east. From the 1870s triple expansion engines still further reduced coal consumption and made long oceanic trades viable for steam propulsion.

The effect of the early steamboats was to maintain the water orientation of England's towns and cities. Commuting daily from Margate or Southend to the City of London became possible and pleasant in the summer when wives and children might spend their time in a rented seaside villa. The steamboats encouraged a proliferation of piers to allow easy embarkation of passengers, rather than the slower, more cumbersome method of ferrying them ashore by rowing boat. Thus seaside and river piers became common features of the urban landscape. In addition, because steamboats were expensive pieces of capital equipment, their profitable operation depended upon minimizing the time they were not working. This encouraged the development of quays and wharves at which they could quickly load and discharge and also docks and basins which retained water at low tide and allowed ships to enter under most conditions. Cities such as London, Liverpool, and Hull began developing extensive dock systems along their rivers, with locks and enclosed water which allowed uninterrupted loading to minimize turnaround times. Another effect of the greater use of steamships was to seek improved methods of loading and unloading, such as coal drops and hoists, steam-operated (and later electric) cranes, with grabs and scoops, and later conveyor unloading and vacuum methods. These pieces of equipment were often tall and dominated the skyline, equivalent in a more mercenary way to church spires. The other requirement of growing trade, both coastal and overseas, was for accommodation between discharge from the ship and distribution to the merchant or manufacturer. Large blocks of warehousing were built, often along the docks and wharves. Given the value of being close to where the ship was berthed, height was an obvious economic advantage and so multi-storeyed warehouses became the norm with wide doors and hoists to allow easy access for goods on upper floors. These were imposing buildings for their time and had a significant visual impact. Their solidity and size may have raised the public image of the dock company, though the casual nature of most dock employment often had adverse social consequences.

Steam when applied to land transport had an even more radical impact on the urban landscape than did the steamboat. The steam railway arrived a little later than the first commercial steamboat. Two contenders for the title of pioneer are the Stockton and Darlington which opened in 1825 and the Liverpool to Manchester which became operational from 1830. The latter is usually given the title, because it operated with steam locomotives from its inception, whereas the Stockton and Darlington allowed horse-drawn wagons and did not restrict operations to its own trains but permitted other carriers to run over its tracks. Ideally, railway companies wanted their stations and goods yards as close to the centre of the town as possible, as well as having tracks into docks or harbours. For this they needed large quantities of land and railway usage consumed a significant proportion of the total urban acreage by the 1870s. To force the tracks into city centres usually required the acquisition and demolition of existing properties. Railway companies and local councils preferred that these be slum areas and rookeries. They were cheaper to purchase, were likely to cause fewer political problems or protests, and allowed the local authorities to dispose of the least attractive neighbourhoods. J. R. Kellett and H. J. Dyos have shown that railway construction destroyed much residential housing of the poorest sort, which put large numbers of people out of their homes. Because the dispossessed could not afford the time or money to live far from their place of employment, especially given the long working hours of the middle third of the nineteenth century, the net effect of the railways in demolishing property was to worsen the overcrowding nearby and cause adjacent areas to become more insanitary and unhealthy. Similarly, when goods yards or large terminal stations were built, they were often constructed on lands currently in use for low status activities which were unloved by their neighbours and local authorities. London's Agar Town, for example, was a rundown area of unpleasant occupations such as knackers' yards, refuse and rag collection, stabling for costermongers' donkeys, brick kilns, and a gasworks. When, in the 1860s, the Midland Railway drove its tracks through this area and built its terminus, St Pancras, there, it seemed to be clearing an undesirable area; but in practice it was forcing these trades to shift elsewhere and bring other areas down in the social scale.

Gustave Doré print, dating from 1872 showing the railway passing by viaduct above the mean houses of the working class. Notice the symbolism of the train at high level, almost flying above the poor hovels, and the plume of smoke which will add to the dirty and unhealthy environment.

Because railway locomotives performed best on relatively level gradients, they often required to be carried on embankments, viaducts, or some other elevation. By criss-crossing cities at high level railways became visually predominant, as Gustave Doré's prints and the engravings in the *Illustrated London News* make clear. Perhaps, there was a social message to be read from this route taken by the railways. It suggested a superiority, above the overcrowded and mean slum areas which the train crossed at speed and thus with minimal exposure for its passengers cocooned in warmth and comfort. Even if they could afford to use them only occasionally, especially before workmen's fares and cheap excursion tickets became available in the later nineteenth century, the poorer groups in society could not miss their intrusive presence. This was especially true of mainline termini in London and other major cities where stations became much more than buildings with a set of functions such as selling tickets, portering, and carriage cleaning. They were often designed in a fashionable style by architects who included hotel accommodation and a façade which hid the business end of the station. Pinnacles, turrets, oriental palaces, and Doric victory arches were favourite embellishments. These eminences were visible from some distance. They too had a message to impart about the companies which owned them, that they were great industrial powers and possessed the wealth to be ostentatious. Their soaring stations, like Gothic cathedrals, proclaimed permanence and demanded reverence.

Railways played a part in defining urban districts. Because their tracks were built mainly over less salubrious areas, proximity to the railway did not add status. Indeed railway arches, under viaducts, were suitable only for low-grade activities. Two of Doré's prints show them as a shelter for the homeless at night and a workshop for the unemployed during the day. Locations for costermongers' carts and donkeys, scrap dealing, and other such businesses were normal uses. Goods yards created scarcely more prestigious areas. Here was the focus of various activities which required easy access to railway wagons, such as coal merchants, suppliers of building materials, and other bulky trades. Industrial areas often developed around goods yards, with a cluster of businesses reliant on cheap, fast railway transport. Railway tracks also acted as boundaries, defining one zone from another. The expression 'born on the wrong side of the tracks' may have had an American origin, but it also had meaning in England. Difficulties in crossing the railway line dictated directions of travel and where residents shopped, drank, and socialized. They also instilled a sense of neighbourhood loyalty which bound together the inhabitants and made them suspicious of, even hostile to, people from outside their district. In some cases railway lines were adopted as administrative boundaries by school boards, poor law unions, and public health authorities thus reinforcing their physical restrictions by official ones.

There was one more intrusion of the railways on the urban landscape and that was to blacken it. Of course, railways were not alone in their polluting ways. Domestic hearths, factory chimneys, and a host of industrial processes added their quota of smoke to the urban environment. The result was that many towns were thick in fog or smog, as Dickens portrayed in the opening of *Bleak House* (1853) and as was the setting for many of Sherlock Holmes's adventures in the late Victorian period. Given the low level of government control of smoke pollution and the lack of alternative fuels, the hazy conditions on windless days added to the danger and discomfort of urban living, bringing deaths and illnesses from

'Railway Town': Swindon

JOHN ARMSTRONG

Those towns positioned on a railway route were more likely to grow in the nineteenth century, whereas places which the railway ignored tended to stagnate and lose out in relative importance, as did South Molton in Devon and Eccleshall in Staffordshire. This is one measure of the importance of transport connections to urban growth. Transport also played a more direct role in generating urban growth, as railway companies chose locations to base their repair and construction workshops, creating 'railway towns' because such employment predominated. Examples include Ashford, Crewe, Darlington, Doncaster, Wolverton, and even Neasden in north London, but the original railway town was Swindon.

Swindon was a small market town before 1840 when the Great Western Railway decided to site its main manufacturing and repair works there. In 1840 the population was about 2,000; by 1905 the works alone employed over 14,000 men and the total population exceeded 50,000. Swindon's growth was a direct result of the GWR's activity: the company organized the construction of houses which its workers could rent, as well as providing much of the infrastructure in the new town, such as a church and school. It established a doctor's surgery and medical fund, largely financed by the workers' subscriptions, and arranged an annual outing. The company also abetted the establishment of a Mechanics Institute in 1842, and a market hall. All this was in the mould of the paternalistic employer, epitomized earlier in Titus Salt's Saltaire and later in Lever's Port Sunlight and Cadbury's Bournville, in which the employer concerned himself with the social infrastructure because there was no competent alternative. This also allowed the employer to influence the nature of the town, to decide the number and location of pubs, perhaps, or to bring a uniformity of house type to the urban landscape, unusual in other towns where small-scale speculative building produced a variety of architectural styles and embellishments. In Swindon the railway workers' cottages were built by one firm to a common style. They were made from limestone excavated in building the railway, and laid out in a regular design. Now they may appear too uniform and small, but at the time they were perceived as setting a good standard.

In the second half of the century, although the GWR works continued to grow, the company withdrew from housebuilding as local builders were more ready to supply them. This meant a less controlled development. Railway works provided steady employment, with chances of promotion. Both were rare and valued aspects of Victorian jobs and by largely eliminating seasonal and cyclical unemployment, railway workers could afford to pay a little more rent and so slightly better accommodation. However, so successful were the railway works in attracting incomers from all over the country that housing supply rarely kept pace with demand and overcrowding became a problem, with subletting being normal. In 1844 there were on average more than two people per room in the railway cottages. In these early days sanitation and water supply were primitive and the mortality rate was high with the average age at death under 30. In the 1860s more stringent public health provisions and a new water supply company began to bring these problems under control. In the 1860s, too, a combination of continued overcrowding and regular wages led to the establishment of a number of building societies and the possibility of ownership rather than tenancy; and as a result Swindon in 1900 was one of the towns with the highest proportion of owner occupiers in the country.

There were unmistakable drawbacks to living in a company town. If the GWR sneezed, Swindon caught a cold; and loss of employment could lead to loss of housing for the whole family. This made for a docile workforce, one that accepted authority whether in the works or outside it, in one of the many GWR-sponsored 'rational entertainments' and recreations. Alfred Williams's 1915 book *Life in a Railway Factory*, based on Swindon works from the 1890s to the First World War, 'shows a very rigid and unimaginative control' of the workforce by the engineering management.

pneumonia, pleurisy, and other chest and lung infections. The railways added their portion of smoke and steam, making living beside railway lines less pleasant. Washdays were an especial trial as clean clothes were soon strewn with sooty specks expelled from the locomotives. In addition the railways created an auditory pollution as the sound of their steam ejection and whistles, and the vibration caused by their passage, intruded upon houses near the railway tracks. Pauses in conversation became essential. Proximity to a goods yard brought interrupted sleep as the shunting and marshalling of trains took place all night, the locomotives and wagons creaking and clanking into motion or terminating progress with crashes into buffers.

In many ways the operation of railways had a deleterious impact on the urban landscape but it would be wrong to ignore the new social dimension railways introduced to towns and cities. Stations became centres for social interactions, for greeting and bidding farewell, for a lovers' tryst or a business rendezvous, for bustle and hurry, or to while away time between trains. They became regular meeting places and sites of emotional outpourings. Perhaps this was portrayed most poignantly in the David Lean film *Brief Encounter* (1945), based on a Noel Coward play, which was set in a dismal railway station, 'Milford Junction', in real life Carnforth. A host of subsidiary business and social activities became centred in them, from W. H. Smith's newspaper and book stalls to refreshment rooms, toilets, hairdressers, and flower sellers. The railway station also symbolized escape, the promise of exotic locations, whether it be countryside or seaside resort. In this sense they were as important psychologically as practically. They did provide the means for excursions and holidays but equally they were always there. In theory, an escape was quick and easy and this reconciled many to their grimy lot.

So far we have considered methods of transporting goods and people to and from towns; but changes in the ways of moving within urban areas had, arguably, even more dramatic impact on the landscape. In 1800, with the exception of London, most towns and cities were small in extent, perhaps a mile or two square. The predominant method of getting about them was by walking. People lived close to their place of work, both middle and working classes, partly because of the long hours worked and the inability to afford the cost or time to commute. But there was also no cheap, fast means of moving large numbers of passengers. Thus business and professional men frequently lived over their shops or offices, and workers lived within earshot of the factory hooter or bell and sight of the factory clock. Huge numbers of people moved themselves around the city, and foot propulsion was also important for moving goods. Men carried packs, toted sacks and bags over their shoulder, pushed barrows or small handcarts, carried churns and flagons on yokes across their shoulders, peddled from baskets and boxes hung around their necks, and rolled barrels and casks. This was quite practicable while cities remained small and the time taken to walk from one extremity to another was only twenty minutes to half an hour.

Until the 1870s, pedestrianism was without rival for the majority of urban dwellers. Of course the upper classes had their carriages and broughams, and by the mid-nineteenth century lawyers and doctors, merchants and factory masters, quite normally had their gigs and traps to get around the cities. The introduction of the Hansom cab in the 1830s provided a convenient form of casual transport, without the fixed cost of purchasing carriage and horses. But fares were quite high and use of the Hansom was generally restricted to the upper and middle classes. The fouling of the streets from horse droppings may have stimulated the sale of nosegays and lavender water to douse handkerchiefs but was otherwise an inescapably unpleasant feature of the urban landscape. The eventual answer to the equine pollution problem was asphalt surfacing as it sealed the road surface, so preventing the ingress of dung and flies. It was also less slippery, and beasts suffered less harm when they stumbled. The first stretch of asphalted urban road was Threadneedle Street in the City of London in 1869. From then to the end of the century, the asphalting of city streets proceeded apace, with a significant reduction in the fly nuisance and general health hazard. Another benefit of asphalt surfacing was some reduction in the noise levels; but city streets were noisy in any case, with the cries of hawkers and street vendors, the sounds of steam engines and locomotives, the clatter of iron-shod hooves and the rumble of iron-tyred wheels on granite setts or cobbles, and the whinnying of horses or braying of donkeys.

The Ealing to Hanwell horse bus, operating in the late 19th century, acting as a feeder to the underground. Note the small size, pair of horses, and grossly overcrowded top deck, perhaps only so occupied for the purposes of the photograph.

As the size of towns grew, pedestrianism became less practical or efficient. London being the largest English city, it was there that pioneer developments in urban transport often occurred. So it was for the horse bus. The earliest example was one run by George Shillibeer in 1829 from Paddington to The Bank (i.e. the Bank of England). Shillibeer almost certainly got his idea from Paris. The drawbacks of these early horse omnibuses were many. Their capacity, by later standards, was small, seating about twenty passengers. They required three horses to draw them and hence were very expensive, the fare for the whole journey being 1*s*. This was at a time when many a workman's wage was less than £1 per week. Thus it was chiefly the middle and upper classes who could afford to use them. Shillibeer's buses were also slow. The horse-drawn journey of about five miles took between 40 minutes and one hour. This was only a little faster than walking pace and provided a more comfortable means of transport rather than a fast one. This mode of transport was soon imitated by other entrepreneurs and in other cities, but it was a limited form of passenger carriage because size was constrained by horsepower—more capacity meant more horses which in turn pushed up costs and prices.

One solution was to copy the railways and put the coach on metal tracks. This had the effect of lowering the friction between wheel and road and thus the amount of traction power needed. As a result either the number of horses could be lessened or the size of the vehicle could be increased. Either way costs per passenger were reduced. Early single-decker horse-drawn tramcars could accommodate up to 24 seated passengers and as many standing. They were drawn by a pair of horses. Yet, there were drawbacks to the horse tram. Initial costs were higher because of the need to install the tracks. This requirement also caused some resistance, as paving authorities were concerned at the disruption and local traders were uncertain as to whether passing trams would boost or diminish their takings. People living in more fashionable areas resisted tramways because they thought the noise and traffic would reduce the value of their property. In the less prestigious residential streets tramways came to be accepted, especially when the step-rail was replaced in the 1860s by the grooved girder rail which lay flush with the road surface and presented less of an obstacle except for unwary cyclists or the heels of ladies' boots. The first experimental tramways were laid in England in 1859 when William Joseph Curtis ran a service along the Liverpool dockside. This track lasted only a few months but a permanent line was established nearby one year later by an American, George Francis Train. His line ran from Woodside Ferry to Birkenhead, along the banks of the Mersey. It continued in use until the advent of motor buses. Many more were tried in the early 1860s, in Darlington, in the Potteries between Hanley and Burslem, and in West Derby, a Liverpool suburb. The first London tramway was laid in 1861 along the Uxbridge Road from Edgware Road to Porchester Terrace but it was only temporary. London's first permanent lines were opened in 1870 between Brixton and Kennington Church, Whitechapel to Bow, and New Cross to Blackheath Hill. The 1870s saw such a burst of tramway-building in England that by 1876 over 200 miles were operational. In part this was aided by the passing of legislation which made it easier to overcome opposition and to obtain permission to build the tracks. In part it was a consequence of the degree of overcrowding in urban centres which could most easily be solved by spreading out the settled area, which in turn meant an increased need for cheap mass travel.

The horse tram was a great breakthrough in allowing a group, which previously mainly walked, to use intra-urban transport. Ordinary people were newly liberated by the lower fares of the horse tram. Still, there were limitations inherent in the design. The horse remained expensive to feed, was doomed to a short life of perhaps five or six years, and then required costly replacement, as well as expensive stabling and veterinary services. It also remained limited in the load it could pull, thus reducing the potential economies of scale. The answer was to apply mechanical power and so pension off Dobbin. Initially attempts were made using steam. This could be applied directly in the form of a steam locomotive which hauled passenger cars, or indirectly by having a system of steel cables which were attached to winches operated by a stationary steam engine. The first type was pioneered in England in 1876 at Wantage, having been built by John Grantham, though this was of the self-contained type, that is locomotive and passenger car in one vehicle. Although steam traction was popular in the Midlands and north of England it had too many weaknesses to be widely adopted. The noise and smoke nuisance, the legal restrictions inhibiting the employment of steam locomotives on the road, and some well-publicized accidents, all militated against widescale use. Cable-operated tramways were tried in the late 1880s. One short-lived example in London was up Highgate Hill, another up Brixton Hill to Streatham and Kennington. In theory their hill-climbing ability was much superior to the horse trams' but the technical complexities of attaching tramcars to the cables, the replacement of cables, and the problems of constructing junctions made them unpopular.

The winner in this power race came to be electric traction. It was clean, quiet, did not require much space on the tramcar, and was fast accelerating. It depended on a range of technical developments in producing, transmitting, and using electricity, and by the 1880s these were largely in place. The first temporary system in England was built by Werner von Siemens at the Crystal Palace in 1881 and a second was run there for several years by Henry Binko. The first permanent electric tramway in England was opened in 1884 along the seafront at Brighton by Magnus Volk. It is still there. It used the rails as the current conductors, an unsuitable system for most urban areas as the line had to be fenced off for safety reasons. The use of batteries or accumulators was tried, for example at Leytonstone in south London in 1882 and at Gunnersbury in west London in 1883, but was never very successful because the batteries were excessively heavy and bulky, gave off unpleasant fumes, and needed frequent recharging. A safe and easy method of getting the current to the tramcar was eventually hit upon in the form of overhead lines, which fed current to the vehicle via a spring-loaded trolley pole. The inventor of this was a Belgian, Charles Van Deopole, and it was first tried in England at Leeds in 1891 on a line from the city centre to Roundhay Park. This, plus the numerous small but significant technical improvements made by an American, F. J. Sprague, led to a safe, reliable, economical system; and within a few years a boom in tramway electrification took place in all the major English cities. In 1898 there were about 150 miles of electrified tramtrack, and by 1910 over 2,000 miles. The advantages of the electric tram became very evident. Running costs were much lower, because the expensive-to-maintain horse had been eliminated. Capacity was greater, double-deck cars being capable of carrying up to 70 passengers. Both average and top speeds were increased, to about 12 and 20 miles per hour respectively. As a result travel within cities became much cheaper and more rapid at a time when the population was growing fast. Electric trams were crucial to this extension of the urban area without overcrowding.

A street scene on Addiscombe Road, Croydon, in the 1900s. There is not a motorized vehicle in sight, but a couple of hand barrows, horse-drawn wagons, a bicyclist, and of course the open-topped electric tramcar. The street furniture comes out well in this picture.

W.E.BROWN
PELICAN LIFE OFFICE
CHIBNALL
CIGAR TOBACCO
CIGARETTE DEALER
Croydon; George St. F.F.&Co.

Electric trams brought an unparalleled intrusion into the existing urban landscape. The presence of tram tracks had commenced with the horse tram, but electrification caused a large-scale extension of the system and greater degree of complexity. Tram tracks presented a hazard to the heels of pedestrians and to the wheels of cyclists. Much greater was the visual intrusion. The tramcars on average were bigger, nearly always double-deckers; and their overhead wires, supporting poles, and criss-cross cabling added to the clutter of late nineteenth-century streets. There was an embargo on tramways from some fashionable and heritage-rich areas. The other piece of street furniture which multiplied was the tram stop. Stagecoaches usually used inns and public houses as their mounting and alighting places. This practice was also followed by horse buses, though some were willing to pick up en route on demand. Increasingly a formal system of stopping, on which charges were based, was introduced and this meant signalling an official stop by some pole, sign, or similar. One auditory advantage of the electric tram was that it was quieter than the horse tram as the whine from the electric motor was less persistent than the sound of hooves on cobbled surfaces. Above all, it reduced the amount of pollution and allowed a greater dispersal of residential areas from central business districts by providing cheap, quick, and frequent transport.

A pair of open-top London United Electric tramcars at West Ealing c.1905, on their way to Shepherd's Bush. Notice the elegant poles for carrying the overhead power cables, the low level of congestion, and the horse-drawn carts in the distance.

Doncaster High Street in the 1920s, demonstrating a number of forms of transport—the tram in the centre, the motorcycle combination to the left, and both a motor car and a horse-drawn wagon to the right. The street furniture is also clearly evident—tram poles, overhead wires, and lamp posts.

It should not be imagined that traffic jams are features only of late twentieth-century urban life with the mass ownership of motor cars. A glance at some of Doré's prints from the 1870s shows just how entangled animal-drawn traffic could become, even if he exaggerates a little for artistic impact, in the densely populated city centres. Trams compounded this because they were less manoeuvrable, and on occasion they became stuck by an ill-parked wagon or cart. A possible solution to this congestion appeared to be railways inside the cities on dedicated tracks which could not be obstructed by other traffic. As London was by far the largest city in terms of extent and population, so the problems of urban sclerosis were at their most extreme there. London was the location for the first—for many years, the only—English experiment in intra-urban railways. Here the world's first underground railway was opened in 1863: the Metropolitan Railway from Paddington to Farringdon Street, which linked a number of northern mainline termini to the City. Two years later, this reached Moorgate and a number of feeder lines, such as to Hammersmith, were completed. It was followed by the Metropolitan District Railway which opened a line between Westminster and South Kensington in 1868 and within a couple of years had extended this to West Brompton in the west and Charing Cross in the east. This too linked a number of mainline termini and connected to the Metropolitan at Kensington High Street. These early underground lines were built on the 'cut and cover' method in which a large trench was opened and, once the track and tunnel had been built, was then covered over. They mainly followed wide roads, to avoid expensive demolition of property. They also employed steam locomotives, with the drawbacks of such a form of propulsion in a confined space. They were important in allowing rapid, frequent mass transit from mainline stations into the City and West End as well as within the urban area. A significant further development came with the deep-

level tubes built in the early twentieth century by American enterprise and German and American finance. These lines, which are the basis of the present-day Northern, Piccadilly, and Bakerloo lines, were sunk in clay below the level of other services such as water mains and sewers. Eliminating the threat of subsidence to existing buildings made permission easier to obtain and introduced a new concept into urban life, subterranean movement, accessed initially by lifts and from 1911 by escalators. The first escalator was installed at Earls Court station for the Piccadilly Line. Of crucial importance to the success of the deep-level tubes was electric traction. The achievement of workable electric tramways had acted as a spur to the first underground electric railway in the world, the City and South London, opened in 1890. Electric traction obviated the problem of ventilation which steam locomotion had.

Using the underground railway in order to travel to and from work became normal for millions. The great advantage was its reliability. Whatever the level of traffic congestion at the surface, the underground train could get through on schedule. It was crucial in accelerating the shift to metro-suburban living which expanded hugely from the last quarter of the nineteenth century. Other conditions conspired to create this situation. Slow but steady improvements in real earnings gave workers enough to pay a penny or two a day on fares; rising rents in city centres as commercial and business requirements snapped up more property made suburban housing more competitive; special cheap workmen's fares were introduced by many under- and overground lines; and the peace and quiet of the suburbs appealed when compared to the noise, congestion, and smell of inner cities. The tubes also played a social role. Tube stations were identifiable and well known; hence, like railway stations they became places to meet and separate. Being warm and dry, in winter they were preferable places to meet than on the pavement, and many also began to have a range of other services associated with them, newspaper and flower vendors, shoeshines and sweet sellers, telephones and toilets. They became nodal points in the city, where large numbers circulated about them. Sites adjacent became popular for shops because of the large passing trade, and most out-of-town tube stations accumulated a parade of shops around them. Tube stations had their presence clearly advertised. In 1908 the network adopted a common illuminated sign 'UNDERGROUND', with white lettering on a blue background, and tube station names were portrayed on the same bar and circle logo, very similar to the present-day device. This diffused the image of one unified system, and integration was also supported by network-wide tickets and easy transfer from one company's tracks to those of another. Some later suburban 'underground' stations—these were in fact at surface level—on the extremities of the Piccadilly and District lines, were important architecturally. Designed by well-known architects, such as Charles Holden, they upheld the modernist style and projected an image of cleanliness, convenience, speed, and efficiency for the traveller. Thus tube stations came to have a symbolic as well as a functional role for the capital-dweller, just as the mainline railway stations had had. They advertised the unity of the city, the ability to escape from the centre to more rural and peaceful environs, as well as, in a contrary movement, the ease of visiting 'town' to shop, to take in a show, or go to the cinema.

In the twentieth century the most dramatic impact on the urban landscape has been made by the motor vehicle. A rich man's toy in 1900, by the end of the century it totally dominated urban transport, and with it the size, spread, and

Gustave Doré print from 1872, showing, rather exaggeratedly, the urban congestion of horse and foot transport. The train on the London, Chatham & Dover's viaduct, by contrast, is above, literally as well as metaphorically, such delay. It can steam through regardless.

structure of urban living. The presence of the early motor vehicle was first felt in urban settings for it was most efficient for short distance journeys, replacing the horse as a means of moving people and goods. But the triumph of the internal combustion engine was not altogether guaranteed and steam waggons were a real alternative until the 1930s, especially for heavy bulky goods. Electric traction was also tried but never gained much of a market share because of the weight and bulk of the storage batteries. The first motor bus service in the United Kingdom was operated in 1898 in Edinburgh; in 1905 a service was introduced between London and Brighton, and by 1910 motor buses exceeded horse buses in London. Large horse bus operators such as Tilling quickly converted their fleets when more reliable, less vibrating, models became available. The advantages of motor buses over trams were their lower capital cost and lack of disruption, because they did not need the tracks or overhead wires, and they had greater flexibility in switching to new routes, especially in areas where trams had been seen as intrusive, such as in central London and other fashionable locations. The change from solid to pneumatic tyres reduced running costs and also brought down noise levels. Initially motor vehicles had most success in passenger transport, replacing the horse buses because they were much faster and cheaper to operate, and supplementing electric trams by acting as feeders to their termini, as well as conveying people to and from the underground railway stations in the London suburbs. Similarly horse cabs and carriages were soon replaced by motor cabs with taximeters. By the First World War, motor vehicles had largely replaced horses as prime movers for people. The motor vehicles were noisy, smoky, and oily by modern standards, but they produced no manure and their net effect was probably to reduce pollution.

In a similar vein, short-distance goods delivery by horse-drawn vehicle came under attack from motorized road vehicles. The station to factory, or quay to warehouse trade was taken over by motor or

A typical underground station of the inter-war period. Park Royal, designed by Charles Holden and opened in 1936, through its architecture symbolizes the modernity of the tube network. Note how it acts as a nodal point, so attracting a number of retail outlets, including W. H. Smith and Finlays, to capture the large passing trade.

steam lorry. Although expensive to purchase, they were cheaper to run than the hungry horse and, once initial problems were ironed out, had a longer lifespan. They were also capable of hauling larger loads, where multiplication of the number in the team would have been necessary for horse haulage, and of moving at a greater speed. They also took up less room on crowded city streets, motor lorries being shorter than waggon plus horse team. The number of motor vans rose from about 4,000 in 1904 to about 54,000 in 1913, generally predominating in the sector wanting short distance delivery of small quantities. For large loads, especially of bulky lower value goods, the horse remained paramount before the First World War. This created additional problems, because the mix of traffic created jams when slow-moving horse-drawn heavy freight traffic impeded the faster motor van and motor bus, and all were restricted by the electric tram track.

The ownership of personal transport had been confined chiefly to the upper and upper middle strata of society until the late nineteenth century. The appearance of the safety bicycle changed that. It was initially adopted by young middle- and upper-class members of both sexes, allowing them to explore the countryside with a novel degree of freedom. By the 1870s the cost of bicycles had fallen to about £5, hire purchase schemes were being developed to spread the payments, and an active second-hand market had evolved. This allowed working-class ownership of bicycles, not merely for leisure journeys at the weekend but for the mundane journey to work. Bicycles were even more intensively used between the world wars, when industrial estates and ribbon development led to factories being sited on the outskirts of towns. It was quite normal for both sexes to use the bicycle for across-town daily journeys of several miles. Their running costs were low and owners could make a reasonable stab at their own maintenance. The speed attained was several times greater than walking pace and this freed the cyclist to take a more distant job or released time for leisure. In relatively flat cities, such as Portsmouth and Hull, bicycle traffic could reach epic proportions, especially at clocking on and clocking off times.

At the other end of the transport scale, the inter-war period saw the development of commercial aircraft. Initially, the light aeroplanes could use small grass fields and for a while it was believed that every town and city would have its own airfield, just as it had its own railway station. In the 1920s and 1930s there was a proliferation of rudimentary municipal aerodromes, and the sight and sound of planes flying over urban areas became relatively common. Two developments checked this movement towards multiple small airfields and encouraged concentration into fewer and larger regional airports which were usually located well outside the built-up area. One was the increasing size of aeroplanes, followed by the switch to jets which required longer take-off and landing strips. In addition the facilities expected of airports in terms of radar and communications, complex passenger and baggage handling, landing lights and concrete strips made small airports uneconomical or unsafe. Hence out-of-town airports became the norm, such as at London Heathrow, Manchester Ringway, or Luton. The 1960s and 1970s brought protest movements against the visual and auditory intrusion of numerous jet planes overflying urban areas and perhaps expelling partly burnt fuel and residues. This led to objections to runway extensions or terminal expansion to accommodate even greater aircraft, and the unedifying sight of those who were the largest users complaining because jets overflew middle-class suburbs. More

Traffic congestion at Hyde Park Corner, 1937. Notice the variety of motorized traffic—taxis, cars, buses, lorries, and vans—and the complete lack of horse-drawn vehicles at this date in affluent central London.

sophisticated and quieter jet engines, noise abatement regulations, and restricted night flying have made aeroplanes less intrusive. There has also been a move back to small city centre airports, such as London City Airport in the previously unoccupied Docklands; but there are question marks hanging over the economic viability of such ventures and the degree of tolerance of local communities once new housing is located there. The main thrust of airport activity is now emphatically extra-urban but, with the proliferation of shops, restaurants, banks, and other facilities provided by airport authorities, these have become quasi-urban entities in their own right. Moreover, like railway travel previously, flying has quickly been democratized. Though the business and richer classes predominate, ordinary people have taken to the air for 'package' holidays and competitive pressure has reduced prices on many routes, between British cities as well as overseas.

Before the Second World War car ownership was also largely restricted to middle and upper income groups. Even in 1938 there were fewer than two million cars registered, that is one for every twenty-three people. Initially the problem was to keep cars moving on roads which had never been intended for them. This meant some road widening within towns, following the precedent of new roads built in Victorian times, as much to clear unwanted slums as to facilitate transport. Much effort in road building went into arterial roads, and later bypasses to try to remove through traffic from city centres and direct it around key residential or retail areas. Many roads were built during the inter-war period, partly to improve the transport infrastructure, partly to relieve unemployment: among the major accessions were the North Circular road and Western Avenue in London. Before the Second World War Britain built no motorways, but from the 1960s the idea of bringing inter-city motorways closer to city centres introduced a new invasive force into people's lives as many of these urban motorways were built in part on elevated sections. These were comparable to the railway viaducts of Victorian times and had a similar depressing effect on the value and uses of property immediately below or adjacent to them. Another response in the post-war period to the growing problem of motor vehicles in towns was to segregate them from other traffic via cycle lanes and pedestrianized precincts. The former, in theory, allow the cyclist greater safety and the ability to make progress when motorized traffic is jammed, while the latter provide havens for people to shop or stroll. Coventry, in rebuilding the centre devastated by wartime bombing, led the way in the early 1960s in such an approach.

The mass ownership of motor cars truly began in the 1960s. The total registration of private motor vehicles doubled in that decade from about six to twelve million; and it became the norm, in those areas of older housing where there were neither garages nor drives, for both sides of the road to be solid with parked cars. Accordingly, entrepreneurs perceived the potential for dedicated car-parking areas and, beginning with sites bombed flat in the war, companies such as National Car Parks built up sizeable businesses by exploiting this need. This brought a new feature to the urban landscape. Another related innovation was the on-street parking meter. The first were installed in London in 1957 in order to regulate parking and earn revenue for local councils. A close relative of the parking meter was the yellow line, designed to indicate where parking was restricted or forbidden. Thus two more pieces of street furniture were acquired. The meter even gave rise to urban myths, with associated heroes and villains, vandals and fiddlers. In some residential areas councils made additional money by designating street sections as for 'residents' parking only' and by charging an administration fee for the privilege. The net effect of these innovations was to leave most streets packed with parked cars, with meters, with signs on poles detailing parking rules and restrictions, and with an altogether discordant appearance.

The new age of mass motoring has offered unprecedented mobility and freedom to many. Though still more disadvantaged in many ways, even the poor, the old, and the invalid are now more mobile than they once were. However, mass motoring has also brought with it many complications to urban dwelling. The problem of exhaust gases was appreciated only from the 1960s. This has generated campaigns for lead-free petrol and a bias against diesels. Exhaust noise was identified earlier as a problem, especially if the exhaust system was broken or non-standard; and some heavy lorries were inordinately noisy. Regulations to curb this have been applied with increasing stringency but the sirens of emergency vehicles and the equipping of modern cars with 'sound systems' and security alarms, not to mention the common nuisance of tyre noise and door-slamming, have ensured that the motor vehicle remains audibly antisocial. A contingent problem has been the accident rate and safety record. Despite the introduction of belisha beacons, zebra crossings, traffic lights, and other regulating methods, the motor vehicle is a mass killer and maimer. In 1928, there were 7,000 motor-related deaths and over 150,000 injured. These have not decreased. In 1970 there were 7,500 deaths and over a third of a million injuries, though of course the number of vehicles had since soared and annual road worthiness checks, stricter rules on tyre conditions, speed limits, and road improvements had been introduced. As a result of the motor vehicle, once quiet residential streets became dangerous. Children could not be left safely to play in the streets and to make their own way to school or to recreational activities. As people walked less and drove more their social interactions plummeted and became more aggressive. On foot people could exchange greetings, perhaps build up some relationship, or catch up on news or gossip, but isolated inside their metal boxes such communication was limited and other road users were seen as competitors rather than collaborators. The motor vehicle has alienated rather than reconciled.

Separation of traffic types and the reduction of vehicle access have been advanced as possible solutions to ease the motorized domination of the urban landscape, but a different reaction has been to embrace the motor vehicle more wholeheartedly and to build towns around its needs. This is not generally possible, except by an unacceptable amount of property demolition, in existing towns, but new towns offer more opportunities. Several new overspill towns, such as Milton Keynes and Bracknell, have been designed on the assumption that motor vehicles are an integral part of them. Wide dual carriageway roads, large parking areas, numerous roundabouts, good landscaping, and plentiful tree planting programmes have ensured that the motor is catered for and indeed essential to living in these towns, but does not spoil the residential amenities. This is merely one end of the spectrum. Some older towns have had their traffic reduced by motorway or bypass, while others struggle to cope with the insistent invasion. There are current discussions about introducing road pricing, more draconian parking regulations, and higher-than-inflation rises in fuel prices as well as more exhortations to cycle or walk; but the motor vehicle appears totally embedded in the urban landscape in the last years of the twentieth century.

9 Slums and Suburbs: The Persistence of Residential Apartheid

Richard Rodger

During the nineteenth century the inhabitants of England experienced changes to the urban landscape unimaginable to earlier generations. The form, function, mass, and scale of buildings and the spaces around them would have been barely recognizable to their grandparents. Town halls replaced guildhalls, institutional responsibilities overwhelmed philanthropic endeavours to care for the mad, the bad, and the sad, and though pockets of handicraft resistance endured, economies of scale secured the victory of factory over workshop production.

The geometry of the city was radically changed. Irregular pre-modern street patterns yielded to the rectilineal shapes associated with the neoclassicism of Georgian style, reinforced by Victorian building by-laws. The narrow wynds of pre-modern towns produced a porosity in the urban texture through which people could move easily on foot, but by 1900 many of these pedestrian alleys had been swept away in the name of slum clearance and environmental improvement. The multifunctional nature of the street—its 'promiscuity' as a thoroughfare and playground, as the locus of neighbourhood gossip, street games, and child care—conceded supremacy to vehicular traffic. The rash of advertising hoardings that lined the principal thoroughfares informed an increasingly literate society of the delights of consumerism, and a proliferation of street notices prohibited spitting and ball games. Gaslights, bollards, water troughs, and street clocks as well as tram stops and timetables adorned the urban landscape at street level as the century progressed. Street activities and personal behaviour were altered fundamentally by the introduction of such amenities.

All railway companies sought city centre access to gain passenger traffic and freight business. Since several companies punctuated each urban location of any scale or regional significance, and since shared track, stations, and goods yards were exceptional, the resulting spaghetti of railway lines introduced impenetrable cuttings and viaducts and partitioned neighbourhoods. Bridges and underpasses were few; personal communications were severed. Work patterns and worship, shopping and community activities were each transformed by the straight lines and gentle curves of railway installations. 'On the other side of the tracks' acquired a cultural and psychological meaning to add to physical segregation.

Physical barriers were also introduced by the expansion of head offices, warehouses, mills, and department stores. The density and mass of these rectangular blocks often occupied the entire side of a street. There simply was no passage to adjoining streets through such buildings and access was denied by uniformed gatekeepers and intimidating doormen. Security considerations governed the administration of asylums, prisons, sanatoria, workhouses, and hospitals, and walled defences restrained the inmates and kept out the general public. These land extensive developments provided from the public purse on an increasing scale from the mid-nineteenth century swallowed swathes of prime residential land, and as with the provision of gasworks, slaughterhouses, and cemeteries, many institutions were located on the margins of the Victorian city.

To the social conditioning attempted in prisons and workhouses was added the cultural crusade associated with moral instruction, as represented in galleries, libraries, museums, and schools. Institutional building transformed the Victorian townscape not just because of its bulky scale and imposing façades, but also because of a tension between architectural styles in which classical form vied with neo-Gothic. Of equal importance was an era of church building from the 1820s on a scale unprecedented since the Reformation. Ornate spires and elaborate bell and clock towers reached heavenward, transforming the urban skyline.

By mid-century, as industry came into the towns so the chimneys of blast furnaces, of textile mills, indeed of all installations powered by steam, belched smoke into the atmosphere. The smoke-blackened stone and brick of northern and Midland towns was a sombre reminder of the environmental impact of smoke emissions from factories, railway engines, and domestic fires and had a damaging effect on the built environment in addition to the tubercular damage to residents. Air pollution affected the colour and quality of the urban landscape and was a washday curse for those residents in the lee of winds laden with coal dust.

However fundamental all these changes were, one feature of the urban landscape which altered irreversibly was the character of housing. Throughout the country, north and south, town and city, port and resort, whether an industrial or commercial location, the residential segregation of different social classes was ubiquitous. This separation, moreover, was seared on the mental landscape of Victorians as much as it was on the physical landscape.

Congestion and Concentration: The Urban Dimension to Industrialization

Towns have always been the principal locus of industry. During the eighteenth century workshop-based industries, particularly those based on consumer demand, expanded considerably. However, for intermediate products such as iron bars, castings, and machine parts, the cost of water-based sources of energy was a key determinant of industrial location, and such 'proto-industrial' factory developments were frequently found in semi-rural locations.

In response to supply bottlenecks and capacity constraints a series of technological innovations associated with smelting and steam power released industry from its dependence on often unpredictable power sources and resulted in both greater capital intensity and subdivisions of industrial labour. The altered matrix of operating and capital costs changed the balance between inputs of labour, raw material, energy, credit, and distribution costs, and 'a whole network of external economies . . . bound together the areas of regional specialization associated with each great city'. The different factor endowments of individual towns provide a powerful supply side explanation for the specific character of industrialization in a given urban locus. Relationships within and between regional economic systems were redefined based on an increasing degree of specialization which contrasted sharply with the generalist functions associated with eighteenth-century towns.

Towns offered important organizational advantages with cost-reducing implications in three discrete forms: first, in the provision of commercial information; secondly, in infrastructural provisions; thirdly, in the supply of labour.

Towns and cities were the information superhighways of the nineteenth century. Their coffee houses, pubs, and meeting houses were forums to exchange gossip about trade conditions, investment, and work opportunities, where labour might be hired and supplies obtained. Information concerning risk and uncertainty, key variables in business survival, was more fully evaluated where bankers and brokers, merchants and distributors coexisted in close proximity. With distance reduced, the nature and pace of business decision-making were altered. Not to be in touch incurred unacceptable risks for the business community and from the second quarter of the nineteenth century the proliferation of trade directories and journals was indicative of industrialists' recognition of this fact. By the 1840s Trade Protection Societies in over 30 towns and cities had been founded to provide information on the credit-worthiness of local firms, to collate information on bankruptcy proceedings, and to initiate debt collection through the courts on behalf of their members.

Secondly, urban growth stimulated the development of an institutional framework which provided a measure of control in an uncertain business world. Former loose federations of producers and brokers consolidated their mutual interests, forfeiting a measure of independence by forming local banks, Chambers of Commerce, building societies, stock exchanges, and trade associations. This was not entirely novel—there had long been skinners', mercers', and baxters' in major urban centres in pre-industrial times—but the spread of financial and trade-related organizations extended much further down the urban hierarchy during the nineteenth century. The institutional framework was complemented by a private world of social networks established through church and chapel, personal and kinship ties, through Masonic lodges, and overlapping leisure and cultural pursuits.

These networks were buttressed by public infrastructural support. Through town council activity, new roads and sewers were laid, streets straightened and widened to facilitate commerce, and insanitary and red light areas prejudicial to business interests were cleared. Gas and water undertakings were taken into the public domain, and the administration of justice, protection of property, and regulation of markets and street trading increasingly subject to municipal control. Franchises for trams and power generation were granted, and licences of various sorts approved. The official world of urban regulation offered a mechanism for business advantage, charging otherwise legitimate business costs to the public purse (i.e. to ratepayers) and legitimating regulatory codes and public intervention which otherwise transgressed private interests. Towns, and the burgeoning administration they required, offered a way by which business interests could advance their interests while parading civic involvement. While these considerations applied, the business elite represented an important constituency in council chambers.

The third obvious advantage which towns and cities offered manufacturers was as an almost infinite supplier of labour. In the first decades of the nineteenth century, rural emigration followed by a net natural increase was responsible for sustained urban population growth. This reservoir of available labour, certainly amongst the unskilled and semi-skilled, exerted downward pressure on wages and thus reduced manufacturers' labour costs. Furthermore, with the costs of social welfare absorbed by charity and the Poor Law, where it was provided at all, fluctuations in output and pressure on manufacturers' profitability could be met by forcing adjustments on to labour, specifically through lower wages and unemployment, with implications for housing and health.

The Invention of Residential Segregation

The rate of urban population expansion was at its greatest in the first half of the nineteenth century, and the 1820s and 1830s were decades of most intense urbanization. Of the largest cities in Britain, Bradford expanded by 66 per cent in the 1820s; Salford by 56 per cent; Leeds, Liverpool, and Manchester each by 46 per cent; and both Sheffield and Birmingham by over 40 per cent. Older urban centres such as Bristol also participated vigorously in the expansion, as did new resorts such as Brighton. The pace of population growth affected every tier in the urban hierarchy, as was the case for 26 Lancashire towns each of which added about 30 per cent to their population in the 1820s, expanded by another 30 per cent in the 1830s, and then repeated the feat in the 1840s. Specific areas of cities witnessed dramatic transformations. The Liverpool districts of Toxteth, Everton, and West Derby never increased by less than 60 per cent in each census between 1801 and 1851; across the River Mersey, the population of Birkenhead tripled in the 1830s and again in the 1840s. Even before the Great Famine (1845–9), Irish immigration accounted for 5–10 per cent of the population of Bradford, Wigan, and many northern towns, and as much as 12 per cent of Manchester's inhabitants and 17 per cent of Liverpool's by 1841.

The urban population increase in the three decades 1801–31 was greater than the total population of Britain in 1801. In the context of our own times, this would be the equivalent of adding 60 million people to present towns and cities by 2030 and to do so without any planning regulations, building by-laws, or controls in relation to sewage, drains, water supply, or other environmental considerations. It would also involve placing the largest ever building programme in the hands of any individuals who might wish to call themselves a builder, that is, without accreditation, skill, sufficient capital, or experience.

It was in this regulatory vacuum that the excess of families over houses more than doubled in the first half of the nineteenth century. Housing the population increase, mostly of migrants from the countryside and smaller urban centres without benefit of kin and community support, imposed insuperable burdens on an urban infrastructure intended for significantly lower population densities.

Under intense pressure from rapidly increasing numbers of families the housing market functioned in various ways. Most commonly, existing houses were subdivided. This was the simplest solution to housing shortages and the degradation of the urban fabric was instantaneous and progressive. Overcrowding was the inevitable result; disease was rife, and life expectancy in urban areas was commonly under 25 years. Though the cholera epidemic in 1832 was particularly virulent and widespread, outbreaks of the disease were frequent. The use of spaces not previously considered suitable was another short-term response of the housing market which developed into a long-term feature. Cellar dwelling became commonplace in many cities—in Manchester 12 per cent and in Liverpool 20 per cent of the population lived in subterranean accommodation—though less extensive in Midland towns and in Leeds. Lodging houses, initially intended as short-stay hostels for migrants, evolved into long-term accommodation, often for families, with communal living and dormitory sleeping arrangements. Double cellars, flatted tenements, and terraced housing all served as lodging houses and were unregulated until the 1850s. One survey of London in 1854 conservatively estimated about 82,000 residents sheltered nightly in common lodging houses, and in Leeds in 1851, 222 lodging houses in a quarter-mile semicircle from the parish church accommodated 2,500 people at an average of 2.5 persons per bed and 4.5 persons to a room. Shelter, then, was for many no more than sub-let floor space; for an unknown but considerable number, it was a tissue of dens and brothels; for others it was a subculture of railway arches, doorways, and vagrancy. The turnover in rooms and sub-lets was high: in Westminster in 1840 one third of the residents moved every six months. Consequently, the social foundations of neighbourhoods were difficult to establish because of this impermanence among residents.

Where a limited amount of new housing did develop it was often associated with the construction of workshops in the courtyards of existing houses. Behind many shops and houses fronting major thoroughfares were orchards, gardens, and piggeries extending perhaps 50 yards. It was along the length of these plots that developers built workshops and houses; on the opposite boundary they did the same. The effect was to create an inner court of houses facing each other, closed at both ends either by a block of communal privies or by another row of houses. Back-to-back terraces were created when on an adjacent plot another developer deployed the same tactic, using the shared boundary wall of the neighbouring plot to reduce construction costs. No through ventilation was possible in such houses and the repetition of the process created acres of back-to-back housing accessed only by a tunnel or narrow entry at one end of the court. Though back-to-back terraced and court housing constituted about 65–70 per cent of the housing stock built in Birmingham, Nottingham, and Liverpool in the 1840s, the major stronghold was in the West Riding, and in Leeds, Keighley, and Huddersfield, as elsewhere in Yorkshire, it continued at about the 70 per cent level until the 1880s.

The landscape of urban England was transformed in the first half of the nineteenth century by the infilling of central areas and the degradation of existing housing stocks. In place of the winding, narrow streets inherited from medieval

South London terraced housing c.1900. Repetitive, rectilinear terrace-housing reached its peak in the final quarter of the 19th century. Though this was due in part to the introduction of building by-laws from the 1840s, which were compulsory after 1875, it was the economics of housebuilding initially which encouraged grid-iron layouts: simplifying labour-intensive building work to straight lines reduced the costs of foundations, roofs, and piped supplies of water and gas.

and early modern times on which properties had been added occasionally as demand dictated, the economics of building terraced housing imposed a new rectilineal geometry upon the urban landscape from the second quarter of the nineteenth century. The sinuous and porous morphology of the pre-modern town was superseded by the regimentation which landowners and developers introduced as they sought to obtain maximum housing densities. Almost irrespective of the contours of the expanding town or city, grid-iron terraced housing layouts with their straight lines, squares, and rectangles imposed a uniformity and discipline upon the urban landscape. Builders' preferences for straight lines to foundations, brickwork, and roofs, like those of utility companies in the construction of gas, water, and sewage pipelines, were heavily influenced by the need to contain the costs of construction. Maximum productivity from building workers resulted from their familiarity with and solutions for particular difficulties and so small building firms reproduced the same type of accommodation in an effort to restrict costs and increase profits. It was market forces which cloned 'colonies' of terraced housing in the English urban landscape. The interests of landowners, developers, builders, utility companies, and municipal departments often coincided and reinforced the strict geometry of Victorian terraced housing, long before formal regulations were introduced.

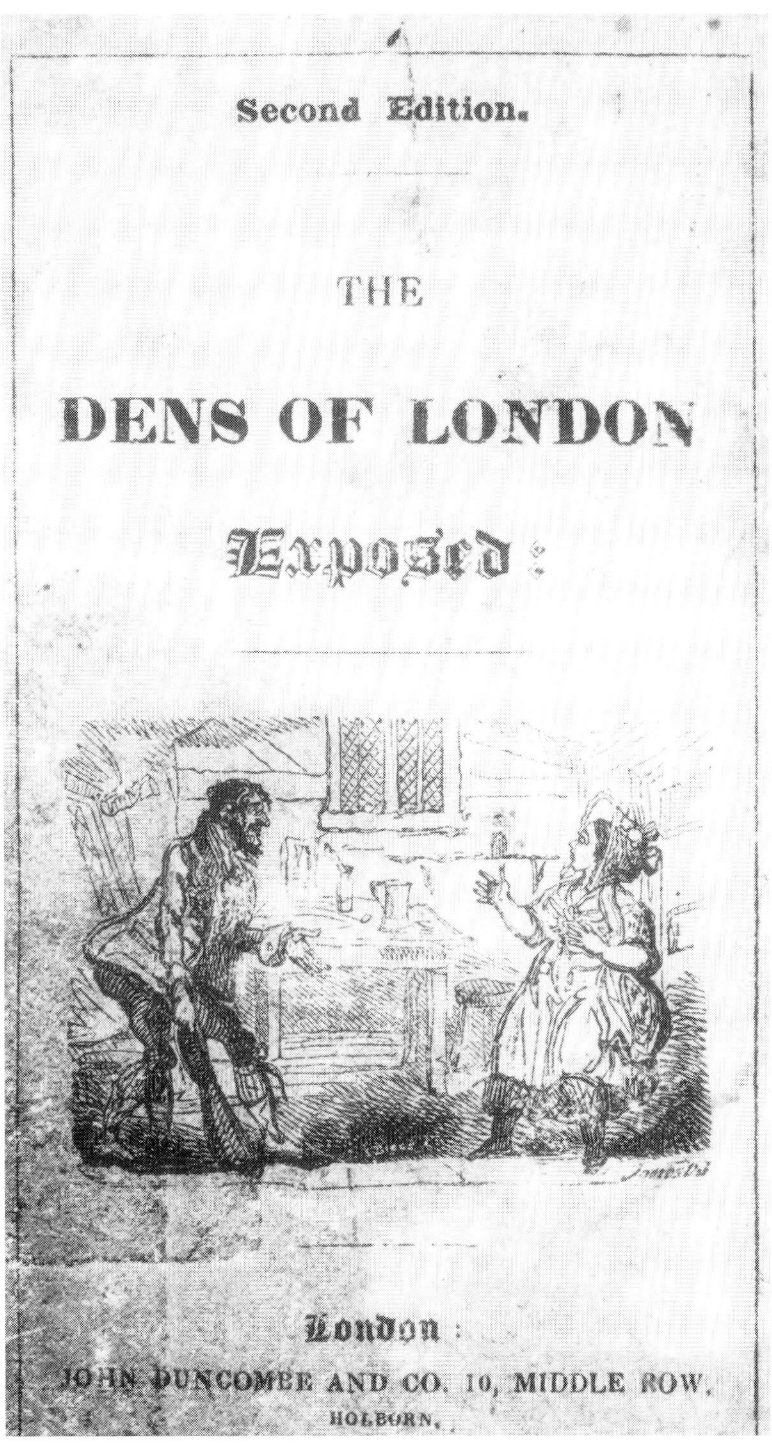

Second Edition.

THE

DENS OF LONDON

Exposed:

London:

JOHN DUNCOMBE AND CO. 10, MIDDLE ROW,

HOLBORN.

'The Dens of London Exposed'. Gentility confronted by poverty is the theme of this pamphlet. In it, and others such as 'One Half of London Made Known to the Other', it was acknowledged that the middle classes knew more about the inhabitants of the Empire than those of British cities, from whom they were socially and spatially segregated.

Figures for the 1840s show population densities in Liverpool of 138,000 persons per square mile; in Manchester the figure was 100,000 persons per square mile, double the level in London where it was 50,000 per square mile. The pace of change and the development of undifferentiated court and terraced housing was an entirely new feature and in terms of design, colour, and materials resulted in homogeneous areas of working-class housing. More significantly, such districts assumed the status of 'no-go areas' for the new middle class, as captured in mid-century pamphlet titles such as *One Half of London Made Known to the Other* or Disraeli's novel *Sybil* (1846). In the late nineteenth and early twentieth century it was this existence of class divisions and 'Two Nations' which informed the thinking of socialists, just as it did that of 'One Nation' Tories, albeit from a different ideological perspective.

The slums or 'rookeries' described by Thomas Beames in 1850 were 'pauper colonies' like 'the nests of the birds from whom they take their name; the houses, for the most part, high and narrow, the largest possible number crowded together in a given space—common necessity their bond'. Disturbing accounts of housing conditions in the first half of the nineteenth century are commonplace. Of cellar dwellings in Manchester, Dr Ferriar commented in 1805 that it was necessary at noon to use a candle to examine a patient, and that the sick 'can seldom afford straw' for bedding. In Durham, another doctor observed 'forty persons half-clothed in ... those wretched dwellings [common lodging houses], three or four lying upon one bed upon straw ... excrementitious matter was allowed to accumulate and lie about the rooms in all directions, the stench being most revolting'.

The language of despair—'the evil is too monstrous for cure by ... superficial means'—was replicated in a flourishing pamphlet literature and in newspaper columns published in the 1840s. The harrowing and debilitating nature of living conditions in central areas of cities was a common concern and reports by medical men assumed weight by virtue of the authors' professional status. Nowhere was this more evident than in the official enquiry by Edwin Chadwick, whose *Report on the Sanitary Condition of the Labouring Population of Great Britain* (1842) became a best-seller. However much this alerted public opinion to housing conditions, it was newspaper sensationalism which in large measure created the slum, a term coined in the nineteenth century. Though insanitary housing was no myth, the 'imagined slum' was. Newspaper sensationalism fed the myth so that in the minds of readers the slum became a reality, thus legitimating private property as a target for public action.

Intervention by civic authorities was one approach towards the control of slums and slum dwellers. The presumption was that moral degeneracy and public health hazards were reversible by the application of minimum sanitary standards. Until 1875, legislation empowered but did not compel municipalities' compliance with minimum sanitary standards. Only gradually and unevenly, therefore, did municipalities address the housing problems posed by slums, first through the requirement to connect to sewers, then by controls on common lodging houses, then through building by-laws stipulating structural standards for new housing, and eventually, through the provision of clean water. From the 1870s slum clearances assumed primacy in the strategy to contain the physical and moral contamination of defective housing. Public health and housing policies were predicated upon improved administrative efficiency and moral instruction for the poorest elements in society.

Farringdon Road Model Dwellings, London c.1850. As models of design and of financial rectitude, philanthropic housing in London and most British cities showed that it was possible to build houses which improved workers' living conditions and produced a 4% return on capital. Much depended on a regular household income and so unskilled workers and their families were excluded by such initiatives.

In parallel, philanthropic organizations such as the Metropolitan Association and the Society for Improving the Condition of the Labouring Classes intervened directly in the 1840s to provide 'model' housing—block buildings which returned a commercially viable 4 per cent per annually to investors and builders—in an attempt to mitigate the worst effects of slum dwelling. Individual benefactors such as George Peabody and Sidney Waterlow carried the philanthropic torch in the 1860s. Collectively, by 1885, philanthropic efforts had housed about 30,000 London families in purpose-built new blocks. Though mainly London based, the Metropolitan formed branches during the 1850s in Dudley, Bristol, Liverpool, and Torquay. A number of independent associations were also formed, as in Wolverhampton, Nottingham, and Halifax. Like earlier factory villages at New Lanark, Styal, and Hyde, the mid-Victorian company-inspired model housing schemes of Salt (Saltaire, Bradford 1853), Wilson (Bromborough, Cheshire 1853), and Ackroyd (Ackroydon, Halifax 1861) provided improved housing in terms of space and amenities to workers, but were conceived as an integral part of factory discipline and labour supply. Locally, these projects and the subsequent Quaker-inspired ones in the last quarter of the nineteenth century begun by Cadbury at Bournville (1879), Lever at Port Sunlight (1888), and Rowntree at New Earswick (1902) transformed the urban landscape in which they were located.

Throughout the nineteenth century the provision of working-class housing was left almost exclusively to the functioning of the market. Where civic and private philanthropic intervention did take place it sheltered behind the convenient belief that administrative changes, model housing, and exhortations regarding moral reform were sufficient to reverse the overcrowded and insanitary housing conditions in which many people lived. Official opinion had adopted the middle-class orthodoxy that poverty was not the cause of 'slum' housing.

To challenge this orthodoxy was to challenge the foundations of the capitalist system itself. Yet the spatial distribution of housing in the nineteenth-century city owed a great deal to inequalities of income and expenditure based on economic relationships. Middle-class rents constituted only 8–10 per cent of household income, compared to 16–25 per cent for artisans and 30 per cent for labourers. Unskilled workers, male and female, were vulnerable to bouts of cyclical and seasonal unemployment which annually affected about one in five of the manual workforce. As for trends in wages, only in the second half of the century and mainly from the 1870s, when international prices for food and raw materials fell dramatically, did the working classes generally participate in sustained real wage gains, long after the period of most intense urbanization had passed. Life expectancy, infant mortality, and the heights and weights as well as the susceptibility to skeletal malformations and nervous disorders in children of all ages were closely correlated with the number of rooms in houses and thus linked to inequalities of income. Anthropometric measurements of army recruits and school children provided conclusive evidence of such relationships.

The endemic nature of poverty was made explicit in the 1890s by Charles Booth's studies in London and later by those of Seebohm Rowntree in York which showed that respectively 30.7 per cent and 27.8 per cent of the population subsisted below a standard sufficient to sustain life at a healthy level. Only at the very end of the century, then, as British economic supremacy began to succumb to German, American, and Far Eastern competition was there a recognition that investment in human capital was connected to economic performance and military power. Once acknowledged as central to national interests, the urban landscape and specifically the quality of housing became a core policy on which elections were fought in the twentieth century.

Yet the inner contradictions of Victorian capitalism were not difficult to grasp. At the simplest level, fluctuations in business were met by hiring and firing unskilled workers. By forcing adjustments in the level of production on labour rather than on capital there were inevitable adverse consequences for the quality of housing affordable by workers. Indeed, for many miners, shipyard workers, and foundrymen their home was contingent upon compliance with an employer's wishes since the company owned their houses. To risk loss of employment was to contemplate the eviction of the family.

The process of suburbanization showed the contradictions of the capitalist system in a spatial dimension. Consciously, and for the first time, new and exclusive middle-class zones were created in the Victorian city. These socially intact areas were in stark contrast to the residential mix typical of the pre-industrial town. Though 'neoclassical' Georgian-style terraces of high-quality housing continued to be built well into the nineteenth century, the detached and semi-detached single family house was almost unknown before it was introduced on the Eyre estate at St John's Wood, London in the 1790s. Developments of a similar kind attempted in Toxteth Park, Liverpool and at Ashted, Birmingham, failed; those in Everton (Liverpool) and Edgbaston (Birmingham) proved problematical until a critical mass of mercantile and industrial wealth was achieved in the 1820s sufficient to sustain the migration to the suburbs.

Improved turnpike roads caused previously discrete villages to be swallowed up just as they permitted new middle-income housing to develop, ribbon-like, along the turnpike, served by improved short-stage coaches and from the 1830s by horse omnibuses. Between these radiating roads, the most common form of suburbanization took place on estates planned by speculative builders in conjunction with landowners. Facilitated by transport improvements, suburbs were a response to land-use zoning since access to the central business district, canal basins, and later to railway sidings increasingly commanded a premium for commercial, retail, and industrial uses beyond the means of private individuals. Moreover, the environmental degradation associated with these uses was a powerful disincentive to remain in the central business district for those with the resources to escape.

The physical and moral environment of urban disease and depravity were increasingly viewed as hostile to personal discipline and social order. In opposing the corrosive effects of urbanism the basic unit of society, the family, was accorded central position. In this crusade, the role of wife and mother was upheld as teacher and monitor of moral values. Based on a code which stressed domestic privacy, sexual separation, social distancing between the classes, and the cultivation of propriety, discipline, and cleanliness, moral rearmament achieved widespread acceptance in Anglican and Nonconformist circles between the 1790s and 1830s. This code rejected street and home arrangements where congestion, communality, noise, and public access damaged self-discipline, extinguished self-sufficiency, or diminished parental responsibility. The suburb, with its tree-lined streets of semi-detached villas and enclosed gardens, was defended by gatekeepers and serviced by domestic staff. The suburb inoculated its middle-class residents against the harsh realities of downtown life.

Privacy and domesticity coincided with the emerging 'separate spheres' in Victorian life since, by the nature of the increasing scale of production and technical complexity, business organization was most appropriately conducted at the plant, not from the home. The resulting separation of work and home isolated men from their families, and though they retained authority based on their earning power, their prolonged absence from home and hearth created a vacuum which was filled by women. How far the working classes were willing accomplices in these shifting domestic patterns and how far they were indoctrinated for purposes of social control remains contentious. What is evident, however, is that changes in the social composition of British cities altered the physical landscape by polarizing slums and suburbs. In some respects this was the product of changing mental landscapes associated with redefined moral priorities, but these in turn produced private, introspective, and self-contained housing and facilitated the acquisition of personal possessions, consumer goods, and eventually household appliances. It was the Victorian separation of spheres and the suburban middle-class lifestyle, therefore, that created the gendered role against which feminist activists have campaigned.

The residential apartheid of British cities which gathered pace in the second quarter of the nineteenth century was not simply a middle-class response to disease and depravity. By obtaining rentier incomes from the central districts and by diverting business profits to suburban development, the middle classes invested heavily in the periphery of towns and cities to the detriment of their centres. Suburbs were themselves the creators of capital, part of a ceaseless search for new investment opportunities and as such provided an integrated self-sustaining capitalist mechanism both before and after 1850. By generating custom for property developers, suppliers of building materials, furnishers, removers, utility companies, and retailing outlets, as well as offering new opportunities for solicitors, savings and insurance firms, surveyors, and a host of financial intermediaries and property interests, suburbs offered a 'bonanza' of new horizons for middle-class employment, profits, and dividends.

An 'ecological marvel' as well as an economic one, the suburb was a spatial device which insulated the middle class against the contagion, both moral and physical, of the degenerate city, both real and imagined. Spun to the outskirts of the city by the centrifugal forces of income and wealth, the social and business elite could direct the political life of the city relieved of the daily problems of survival which confronted those who remained in the city centre.

'Semis' and Housing Convergence

The patterns of residential segregation and the underlying market forces which produced them in the nineteenth century changed little in the twentieth century. As with most items of expenditure, ultimately it was income levels which determined housing choices. However, where unacceptable side effects or 'externalities' impinged on wider interests, civic interventionism mitigated these in the name of the common weal by demolishing dangerous buildings and clearing unhealthy areas using powers assigned to them in various legislative acts in the late 1860s and the 1870s.

Municipal 'improvements' in the late nineteenth century created new design opportunities for an embryonic town planning movement philosophically connected to the garden city movement. Advocates of garden suburbs were not mere idealists promoting utopian visions or a rural idyll, though their planning concepts and design proposals were partially a reaction to the brutalism of urban life and the townscape of Victorian England. Garden suburbs were an attempt to integrate town and country living in a new spatial context and the urban landscape gained new forms as Ebenezer Howard and his disciples sought more generous allocations of space for housing and axial treatments of roads. These design features were realized in Raymond Unwin's plan for the new town of Letchworth, as well as in the garden suburbs scattered around the country, as at Hampstead (London), Wavertree (Liverpool), and Humberstone (Leicester). Their success increasingly influenced the urban landscape by means of a decisive move away from the straight lines of early Victorian terraced housing. Crescents and trees, open spaces and vistas, paired cottages rather than row housing were part of the planning credo which ushered in the twentieth century. Social theorists, clergymen, architects, and 'experts' in a variety of fields, including the emerging town-planning profession, each played a part in shaping public consciousness; and

(*cont. p. 248*)

The Garden City

ANDRZEJ OLECHNOWICZ

The garden city was the idea of Ebenezer Howard (1850–1928), a man brought up in small English country towns—though he also lived in Chicago for four years—and who became a parliamentary shorthand-writer. His only book was published in 1898, entitled *Tomorrow: A Peaceful Path to Real Reform* and revised in 1902 as *Garden Cities of Tomorrow*. He spent the remainder of his life publicizing and implementing his ideas. It is fitting that Howard should have died in the second garden city, Welwyn, and been buried in the first, Letchworth.

Howard summarized his vision in 1919:

> A Garden City is a Town designed for healthy living and industry; of a size that makes possible a full measure of social life, but not larger; surrounded by a rural belt; the whole of the land being in public ownership or held in trust for the community.

Howard did not embrace the anti-urbanism and anti-industrialism characteristic of many late Victorians. He agreed that overcrowded cities were unsustainable, and that the key to this problem was restoring people to the land, which was 'the very embodiment of Divine love for man'. But the town was equally significant as the symbol of society, 'of mutual help and friendly co-operation … of science, art, culture, religion'. In comparison, the country was 'very dull for lack of society'. Only when they were fused in the 'Town-country' would the disadvantage of each disappear, and 'a new hope, a new life, a new civilization' arise. Howard devoted a chapter to the correct principle of a city's growth. His objective was to ensure that the inhabitant was 'in one sense living in, and would enjoy all the advantages of, a great and most beautiful city'. This would be achieved by building a cluster of garden cities, between which there would be zones of country but also rapid transit.

Howard was undogmatic about the layout of the garden city, though he emphasized zoning for agricultural, industrial, recreational, and residential use. Howard saw the 'wards' created by the six boulevards dividing the garden city as focuses for the social life of mixed-class populations. But he repeatedly cautioned that his description was 'merely suggestive, and will probably be much departed from', depending on the nature of the site. The greatest danger was stagnation, not innovation.

Howard was also practical, if over-optimistic, about the financing of the garden city. Purely agricultural land would be purchased with money raised on mortgage debentures at no more than 4 per cent interest. The purchase would be supervised by four trustees, who would hold the land in trust for the garden citizens. The trustees would also collect ground rents based on the annual value of the land. The balance of rents, after interest and sinking fund payments, would be handed over to the Central Council of the new municipality to pay for public works carried out by its various Departments. This would represent a secure and expanding source of revenue.

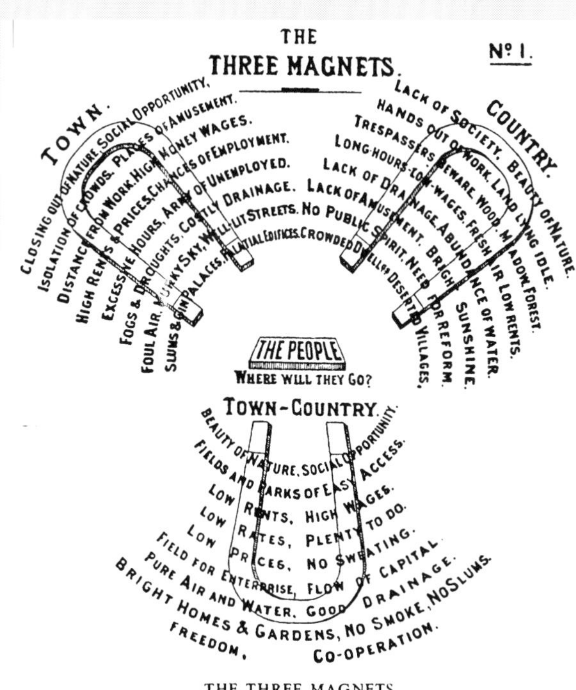

The three magnets.

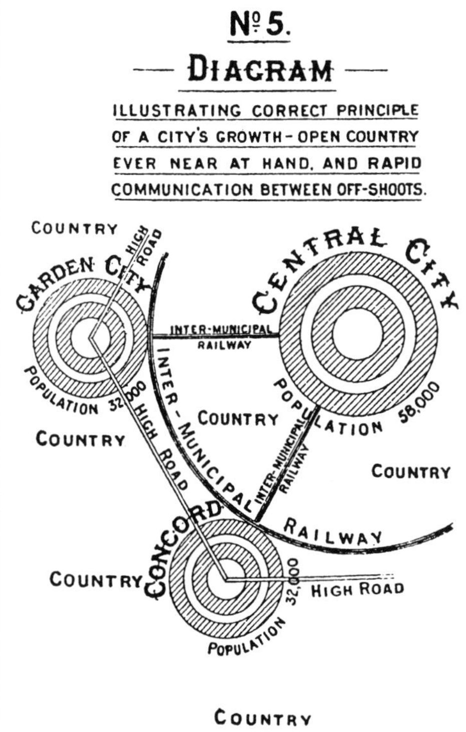

Correct principles of a city's growth.

Howard expressed confidence in municipal enterprise, and expected that its scope was 'probably destined to become greatly enlarged'. Howard held strong ideological objections to the extremes of communism, socialism, and individualism. He condemned, on the one hand, the suppression of all private property and individual effort, and on the other, the view, exemplified by Benjamin Kidd's *Social Evolution* (1894), that the interests of individuals were irreconcilable. As with the 'Town-country', he sought to combine the advantages of both outlooks, while excluding their disadvantages. Municipal action, he believed, united socialism's 'large conception of common effort' and individualism's 'preservation of self-respect and self-reliance'.

Howard took a pragmatic view of municipal enterprise. Its limits would be set by the willingness of garden citizens to pay 'rate-rents', which in turn would depend on the honesty and efficiency of the municipality. Shops and pubs would be municipally regulated to avoid both the waste of free competition and the evils of monopoly. Yet Howard also wished to see philanthropic institutions develop in the garden city to complement municipal action. They would be managed by 'public-spirited people', free from the control of the municipality.

Finally, Howard saw the garden city as the 'true remedy for capitalist oppression'. He hoped that building societies or trade unions would lend workers money to build their own homes. The municipality too might eventually provide funds. This would ensure that the workers' own 'capital' would not be wasted in strikes, but would secure 'homes and employment for themselves and others on just and honourable terms'.

Howard founded the Garden City Association in 1899. True to his emphasis on consensus, it sought patrons from all parts of the political nation: the vice-presidents included Earl Carrington, Earl Grey, Sir John Gorst, George Cadbury, and W. H. Lever. A rural site was purchased in Hertfordshire in 1903, and the First Garden City Ltd. formed to build Letchworth to the plan of the architects Barry Parker and Raymond Unwin. A Second Garden City Ltd. was formed in 1919 to develop Welwyn.

Both garden cities faced financial difficulties. The purchase of Letchworth relied on the generosity of Cadbury and Lever. Falling agricultural prices caused severe problems for Welwyn, which saw major financial reconstructions in 1931 and 1934. The latter resulted in the removal of the limitation on dividends to which Howard had attached cardinal importance. There was clear class segregation at Letchworth, and the Building Trades Workers dismissed garden cities as 'paradises of bourgeois villadom'. Welwyn was not a self-contained township at the end of the 1920s: it had attracted only 32 companies, and its population in 1931 was lower than in 1930 because many residents with jobs in London were forced to leave since they could not afford the combination of rents and travel costs.

Among the wider public the term 'garden city' was used without discrimination. For Howard's most devoted disciples, C. B. Purdom and F. J. Osborn, the villain was Unwin. First, his 1912 lecture *The Town Extension Plan* was credited with undermining the distinction between the garden city and the potentially endless sprawl of the garden suburb. Secondly, his pamphlet *Nothing Gained by Overcrowding* (1912) resulted in the garden city becoming identified with a housing density of 12 to the acre, whereas Howard had suggested a density of between 20 and 28. Equally damaging, many dismissed garden city enthusiasts as cranks. Osborn thought the locals regarded the Welwyn pioneers as 'a bunch of London yahoos'. Betjeman's poem 'Group Life: Letchworth' mocked the fate of the children:

> Sympathy is stencilling
>   Her decorative leatherwork,
> Wilfred's learned a folk-tune for
>   The Morris Dancers' band.

This was not altogether undeserved: Welwyn acquired an Esperanto Society in 1923.

The government provided some funds to support garden city companies in 1921 and 1932. The Unhealthy Areas Committee reported in 1920 in favour of the garden city idea. Howard was knighted in 1927. But the government provided more support for the garden suburb. The Tudor Walters Report (1918) stated that new housing schemes must chiefly depend on 'the belts of undeveloped land on the outskirts of towns'. Likewise, the Marley Report (1955) concluded that '*normally*' [italics added] Satellite Towns, rather than Garden Cities, were the desirable way to proceed. Unwin was the moving force behind both reports.

The one major inter-war development which the Garden Cities and Town Planning Association acknowledged as marking 'a fresh *modus operandi* in starting Garden Cities' was the Manchester Corporation's Wythenshawe Estate. Ironically, Howard may have welcomed Wythenshawe more readily than the post-war New Towns, which are often seen as the triumph of his ideal. For Wythenshawe vindicated his abiding confidence in municipal action, while New Town development corporations were more subject to the central state which he had regarded with misgivings.

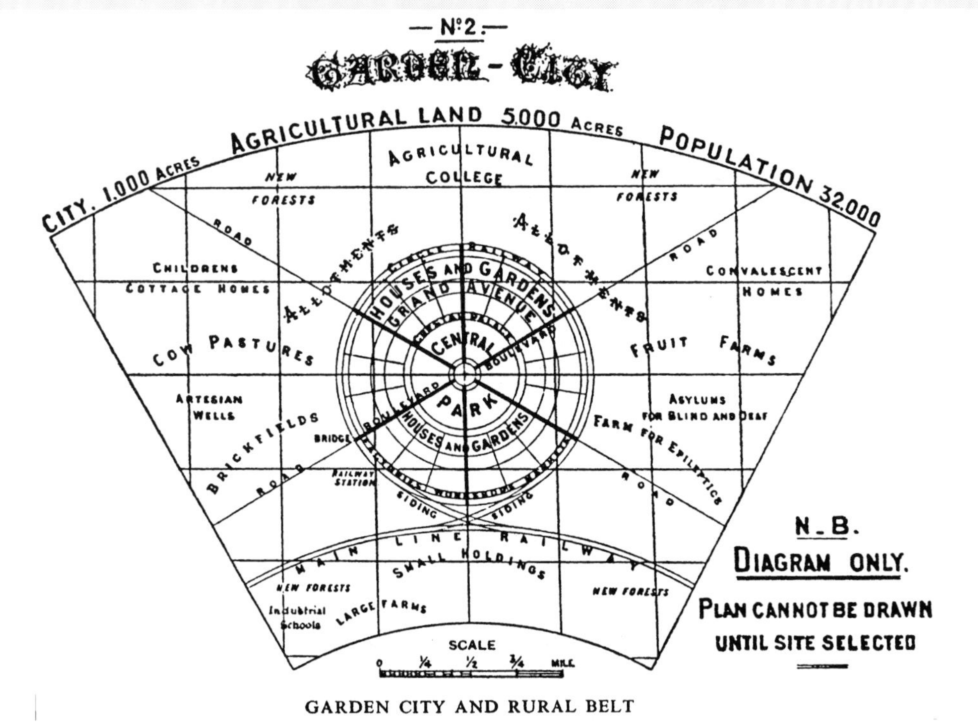

Garden city and rural belt.

model cottage exhibitions at Letchworth (1905), Sheffield (1907), and Newcastle (1908) publicized innovative and economical layouts based on a new landscape of semi-detached housing.

Dozens of local councils experimented in a limited way with garden suburbs. Yet there was a paradox in these cottage-style designs. Based on low densities per acre, garden suburbs simply could not deliver sufficient accommodation to redress the acute housing shortages which existed for unskilled workers and their families. Consequently, municipalities were inclined to adopt the same block-building style as had model lodging initiatives in the 1860s and as continued in London by the Peabody (1881) and Guinness (1892) Estates. So, even though the Boundary Street project designed by the London County Council's new housing department met with critical acclaim from the Architectural Association when its members visited the site in 1900, it was the joinery, sash windows, roof overhangs,

*(**a** and **b**) London County Council housing: Clifton House, Boundary Street 1897 and Totterdown estate, 1903. From its creation in 1888, London County Council was committed to municipal housing. Initially block designs were used, as at Boundary Street (1893–1900), Shelton Street (1894–6), and Millbank (1897–1902). After the scale and mass of such schemes as Boundary Street (1,000 homes, 5,380 residents), the LCC used Part III of the Housing Act 1890 to develop cottage-style, garden-suburb-inspired designs at Totterdown (Tooting) from 1903, White Hart Lane (1904), Norbury estate (Croydon) from 1909, and Old Oak estate, Hammersmith (1911). Over 7,500 houses were built on these cottage estates in 10 years before 1914.*

gable treatments, use of plaster and whitewash, and the moulded corona bricks which capped the chimney shafts that drew their strongest approval. In other words, the charming design detail mitigated the unequivocal reality—block dwellings for Londoners. The *Architectural Review* noted (1905) that there was 'a picturesqueness of disposition as well as a certain refinement of treatment', but a respected member of the Royal Institute of British Architects observed, acutely, 'It is a mistake to praise the LCC . . . for erecting artisans' dwellings while they do absolutely nothing towards providing suitable dwellings for the poorest class.'

Two contrasting visions of the urban landscape emerged in Edwardian London. Block building as at Boundary Street and Millbank presented a practical if retrospective approach to volume building; cottage-style dwellings at Totterdown Fields and Norbury presented a new vision based on garden suburb principles. The difference in approaches centred on building density.

As the civic gospel was extended from a sanitary into a civilizing mission by means of libraries, galleries, and museums, and as tramway operation and electricity generation also increased demands on municipal capital and operating costs, throughout urban Britain the burden on ratepayers rose steadily in the quarter century before 1914. To address this problem major boroughs swallowed up affluent suburbs and incorporated them in their own revenue base from the 1880s. The boundaries of Birmingham, Manchester, Leicester, and indeed most cities were extended; the urban frontier advanced. So at a time when architects and planners presented a new low-density approach to housing, when the London underground and tramways in many towns widened the orbit of settlement, and when municipal intervention to reverse the environmental impact of unrestrained property development was ideologically acceptable, a new vision of the urban landscape began to emerge. In short, the seeds of urban decentralization were sown in the final years of the nineteenth century and the roots of environmental regulation were strengthened through a more systematic approach to urban planning based on social welfare considerations.

Crucially, for several years before the First World War new housebuilding in the overwhelming majority of English towns and cities was only 40–50 per cent of the levels between 1900–5. During wartime all housebuilding ceased except in important strategic locations connected with dockyards and munitions factories. Housing demand outstripped supply. The shortfall in accommodation and wartime inflation produced vigorous campaigns against rent increases, and though the 'Red Clydeside' demonstrations are best known, protests developed in many English boroughs, too, forcing the government to introduce the Rent Restrictions Act (1916). Even in the best-housed English borough in 1911, Leicester, with only 1.1 per cent of its population overcrowded, a newly formed Tenants' Protection League protested against the 'unpatriotic action of local landlords in raising rents during a time of national crisis'. By 1919 Leicester City Council estimated a shortfall of 10,000 houses.

Immediately after the war, with a Communist revolution in Russia still echoing around government corridors, the existence of unemployed and disaffected ex-servicemen together with policemen and miners on strike was perceived as a political threat. An influential book, *The Home I Want*, by R. Reiss, declaimed 'you cannot get an A1 population out of C3 homes'; and having won the 1918 General Election on a slogan of 'Homes fit for Heroes', Lloyd George's government was committed to a programme of social housing, subsidized by the Treasury. The power of Whitehall overwhelmed the power of city hall, and town councils were encouraged to submit proposals to the Minister under the Housing and Town Planning Act, 1919.

It was at this point that the landscape of urban Britain changed fundamentally. Housing projects, once approved, had to conform to a limited number of design guidelines and house types as laid down by the Ministry of Health. At a stroke the appearance of urban Britain was homogenized by the Ministry plans. Warmsworth Road, Doncaster was, and still is, almost indistinguishable from Queen's Drive, Liverpool, or from Coleman Road, Leicester. Throughout the length and breadth of the land, standardized housing units were constructed on the periphery of the pre-1914 city. The designs were largely based on drawings by Raymond Unwin and incorporated the garden suburb style, suitably adapted to take account of cost considerations and shortages of building supplies. The transformation of the urban landscape was achieved indirectly, therefore, through the approvals given by the Ministry of Health for a limited number of designs necessary to secure financial support from the Treasury. Once the immediate fear of insurrection had passed, the Treasury scaled down the 'insurance premium' against unrest, that is, financial support to councils was withdrawn in 1921. Since the 'return to gold' was a central element of British monetary policy in the years before 1925, as its defence was thereafter, then the inflationary effects of public expenditure on housing as in other spheres were rigidly controlled. Interest rates remained at a record peacetime high in support of the Treasury's efforts to improve Britain's export competitiveness. However, when faced with continuing and serious housing deficiencies, modest subsidies were reintroduced. The Conservatives preferred a market-based solution to the housing problem and provided subsidies to private housing projects in 1923; the Labour government extended a financial helping hand to council housing in 1924 but did so on a more limited basis than under the 1919 Act. Ideology was at the heart of housing policy, and the way in which this affected the urban landscape depended largely on the extent to which councils were committed to resolving housing shortages by public or private efforts.

Homogeneity in the urban landscape was influenced by Treasury subsidies. Indeed, with 90 per cent of housebuilding in Liverpool between 1919 and 1923 handled by the council's contractors, standardization was impossible to avoid. Though Reiss had written of A1 populations and C3 houses, by a curious twist of administrative history, it was C1, C2, and C3, or E4 or G3 house types to which councils had to adhere. Tracts of land sufficiently extensive to meeting the housing shortages were unavailable except on the fringes of cities. These were purchased by councils and then laid out along lines consistent with garden suburb principles. Aerial photography still highlights the distinctive spatial characteristics of inter-war council housing; the curves, crescents, and cul-de-sacs of council estates produced whorls on the urban landscape just as distinctive as fingerprints. System building to meet the scale of housing needs and the shortages of both labour and materials produced a further degree of visual uniformity. Even where local variations in building systems did develop, as with the use of concrete in Liverpool, this was only thinly disguised by external rendering. The overall effect was to introduce a new intensity of standardization in the townscape.

The nature of local government housing finance had much to do with the way the urban landscape was shaped. Even after 1924, when local authorities could build as they saw fit so long as they contributed at least 50 per cent of the housing costs from the rates, the tendency was to retain the central features of the Ministry-approved design. However, the infrastructural quality of council estates was weak and visual diversity was limited. The Saffron Lane development in Leicester was typical of many. Garden suburb principles of curves and natural contours were invoked, and straight streets were rejected. The northern or southern aspects determined the room layouts: parlours or larders on the north, living rooms on the south. Some variety was introduced in the detailing for chimneys and windows, and in a variety of rough-cast finishes and roof shapes. But infrastructural provisions diverged markedly from a plan which had promised a shopping centre, library, institute, railway station, three churches, schools, and playground for the 2,000 new houses split equally between brick and concrete construction. The London, Midland and Scottish Railway Company never embarked upon a station; the Working Men's Club was built only in 1935, and the 'pork pie' library at Southfields only in 1939; the lack of shops meant tenants used their houses to sell bread and groceries and thus risked eviction; and despite frequent polls in favour of pubs on the estate, the residents' views were rejected by temperance interests in the council. Throughout the country it was the lack of these amenities that concerned tenants' association meetings, but complaints about defective

structural standards were plentiful too. Cracks in the concrete foundations were evident as early as 1925; since reinforcing rods ran not down the centre of the support columns but to their outside, the result was rusting and fractured surfaces even before the guarantee from Henry Boot and Co. had expired. Over 2,000 houses were completed in three years from the summer of 1924, and though this represented a major increase in the housing supply in Leicester, the short- and long-term consequences of design and materials deficiencies were considerable, not least in the perpetuation of the local name for the estate—'chinatown'—which had nothing to do with immigrants, and all to do with structural faults.

Council housing between the Wars: Leicester, Saffron Lane estate, 1930s. Named 'chinatown' because of the cracks in the walls, the 'Saff' was a system-built housing estate by Henry Boot of Sheffield in the late 1920s. One in every five new houses in England built between 1919 and 1939 looked like this, conforming to approved Ministry designs and Treasury subsidies. Inner-city inhabitants were decanted to estates which lacked amenities and transport connections, and the fabric of which tenants were not permitted to alter without council permission.

If localism gave way in the 1920s to centralizing and homogenizing influences on the fabric of British cities, two further influences reinforced the trend in the 1930s. First, public policy initiatives switched from general housing provision to targeted slum clearance and de-crowding strategies. Inner-city areas were demolished and their residents decanted to the outskirts, often after de-lousing and a ritual burning of some of their possessions. Whereas new housebuilding in the 1920s had added to the built-up area, the policy of the 1930s smashed central areas, obliterated streets and their associated mental reference points for many people, as well as destroying the credit and social networks on which local identities depended. Financial inducements from Westminster were again instrumental in this process.

The second central policy factor was the suspension of the gold standard and sterling convertibility in 1931. No longer were high interest rates required as a precondition for the defence of the pound and, within a few months, mortgage rates which for over a decade had been static at 6 per cent fell to 5 per cent in 1932, and to 4.5 per cent by 1934. This reduced borrowing costs significantly and, together with rising real incomes for those in work, provided an immense boost to private housebuilding and to national economic recovery after 1932 (see Fig. 9.1).

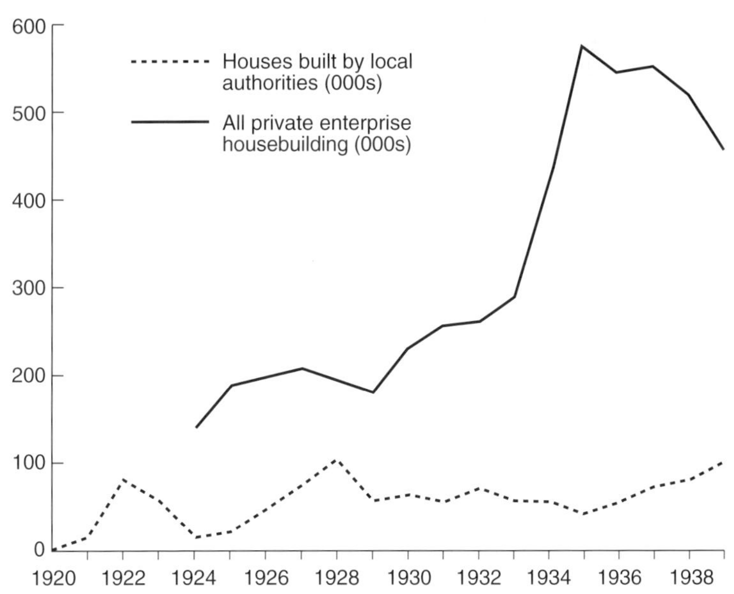

Council housebuilding and private housebuilding in England and Wales, 1920–39.

The Council Estate Community

ANDRZEJ OLECHNOWICZ

Over 90 per cent of the 1.1 million inter-war council houses followed the recommendations of the Tudor Walters Report (1918) and were on low-density estates on the outskirts of towns and cities. The London County Council's Becontree Estate, ten miles from the centre of London and providing 25,039 dwellings for 112,570 persons, was the most spectacular example.

Wide agreement existed among professional and political bodies that council estates must be made into 'communities'. In 1921 the LCC Housing Committee's objective was 'a reasonably self-contained and self-supporting community'. The Departmental Committee on Garden Cities and Satellite Towns in 1935 recommended that 'a town should be the dwelling place of a community; and the conception of "Community" implies personal relations and a proportional presence of all sections of the Community'. Almost all shades of opinion agreed that a 'community' required class mixing. Beyond that, there was little clarity and much wishful thinking.

Although the definition of a community was elusive, many were nevertheless categorical that suburban council estates were not communities. The *Listener* declared in 1938, 'All over the country on the great estates you must picture hundreds of thousands of rather forlorn people, strangers to each other, shyly living side by side.' Publicly reticent civil servants let rip in private: the retired Deputy Secretary of the Board of Education, Sir Edmund Phipps, saw in Becontree 'a gap in our social system, the possibility of a new Pagandom ... likely soon to become a menace to all government'.

A body was formed in 1928 to fill this gap: the New Estates Community Committee of the National Council of Social Service, a powerful and well-connected philanthropic organization. Its solution was to assist the formation of community associations and the building of community centres on all council estates. These would mix classes, restore neighbourliness, encourage the 'proper use of leisure', and conduct 'education in citizenship'. The NECC welcomed State assistance, but was ideologically committed to developing self-reliance among tenants and careful to ensure that 'the dead hand of the State should not replace the live hand of fellowship' according to one of its champions, Sir Wyndham Deedes.

The Tudor Walters Report had recommended 'some form of communal institute or club', and governments readily endorsed such an uncontentious and inexpensive proposal. However, in 1938 when a community centre cost between £5,000 and £10,000, the total government contribution was £930. Even with assistance from local authorities and philanthropic trusts, the NECC's resources were inadequate. By 1939 there were 92 centres; but there were 401 estates of 500 or more houses. Fewer than 2 per cent of tenants on large municipal estates had a community centre.

Only a minority of tenants used these centres. Possibly, their inhospitable appearance deterred people. Mass Observation found that those who did attend 'mainly go there in pursuit of some particular interest, much more rarely for meeting other people or because they feel the need to be an active part of any community'. Where only community associations existed,

The community centre on the L.C.C.'s Downham estate in 1929.

The L.C.C.'s Becontree estate in 1926. New tenants were often overwhelmed by the silence and space of their new environment. Ruth Durant's inter-war survey of the L.C.C.'s Watling estate recorded one woman banging on her neighbour's door: '"Everything is so terribly quiet", said the first woman, still frightened to death'.

they were often divisive as factions of enthusiasts squabbled. On the LCC's Watling Estate, there was open hostility between the Watling Residents' Association and the Watling Association, and even the normally optimistic Deedes wondered whether Watling was ready for a community association. The real trouble was that the whole enterprise was misconceived. It reflected middle-class ideological hostility to the working class. It consequently ignored much that was commonsensical.

It was predictable that new tenants would feel initially strange and uncertain on a low-density estate if they came from the overcrowded inner city. Construction often took years, and it was improbable that community spirit could develop while there was mud in the streets and new tenants were constantly arriving. On Becontree, the first tenants arrived in 1921, but the estate was not completed until 1934. As Peter Willmott indicated

Southwark in 1923: the 'traditional', close-knit, working-class community. One Watling resident told radio listeners in 1938 that in the early days of the estate, 'Quite a number of people got fed up and went back'.

ANDRZEJ OLECHNOWICZ

A Becontree garden in 1927. Starting in that year, the tenant with the best garden received a championship cup from the L.C.C.

in *The Evolution of a Community* (1963), earlier investigators simply left out this critical factor of time. Willmott found that after 40 years, in terms of its patterns of kinship and sociability, Becontree was in part 'the East End reborn'.

It was impossible for these estates to be other than one-class areas. Tenants were selected on the basis of the greatest housing need. Those in greatest need were also usually those in greatest want. Their new life was a continual battle to make ends meet. A study of the Bristol Corporation's inter-war suburban estates found that estate families were not an ordinary sample of the working class: they had an abnormally high number of dependent children, and their standard of living was noticeably below the working-class average. The battle was often lost, and tenants had to remove. In 1928–9, 17 per cent of tenants left Becontree. Such flux made a stable community an impossibility.

With the need to travel often long distances to and from work, most tenants had little leisure time. Many preferred to spend what leisure they had quietly at home. Mass Observation was impressed that 'Most of the people owning a garden treasure it and look after it well.' Local authorities promoted this interest by running competitions with cash prizes; it was a cheap way of being seen contributing to tenants' welfare.

The notion of council estates as 'a gap in our social system' more accurately describes the 1980s and 1990s than the 1920s and 1930s. In 1985 the Report of the Archbishop of Canterbury's Commission, *Faith in the City*, found that 30–40 per cent or more were unemployed on many peripheral council estates, which had become 'local subsistence economies, utterly dependent on state benefits'. In 1995, the Joseph Rowntree Foundation classified 2,000 estates as 'social and racial ghettos', with adult unemployment rates of 60 per cent. From this perspective, the inter-war estates appear as enlightened successes.

Rising real incomes also contributed to the growth of private car ownership and, aided by the spread of bus routes, to an extension of the commuter zone. By these means, therefore, a semi-detached private housing invasion had advanced by the early 1930s, cloning the English urban landscape with only minor deviations locally. Mutant 'stock-broker Tudor' had conquered the English suburbs. The character of bay windows with their painted external beams above differed only in detail from Liverpool's Mossley Hill to Leicester's 'Way' Roads.

Thus, during the inter-war years peripheral estates for both council and private enterprise housing, respectively for working- and middle-class residents, were developed and showed a degree of convergence in their spatial arrangements. The layout of public and private housing estates was based on curved streets, small gardens front and back, and an internal arrangement based on three bedrooms, two public rooms, and a kitchen which perpetuated the Victorian separation of gender roles within the home. The estate layout and room arrangements in English housing converged in the suburbs, although with different tenures (tenancy versus freehold) and by different financial routes (weekly council rents versus monthly building society mortgages). Of course, as local authorities assumed the role of landlord and the ever greater management responsibilities associated with council housing, so they introduced visual elements which homogenized their estates to an even greater extent. Paint colours, door designs, fences, the landscaping of the estates and the absence of trees on them, all reinforced the impression of cloning which resulted from building thousands of homes within very few years. By the 1930s, the centrifugal forces which influenced middle-class suburbanization in the nineteenth century had affected lower income groups and manual workers too.

'Streets in the Sky'

Strong images of the urban landscape in the 1940s persist from pictures of the desolation caused by German bombing. In both Coventry and Southampton 30 per cent of the housing stock was destroyed. Between September 1940 and May 1941, 141 major air attacks were made on 21 British cities. The blitz in London is seared on the memories of survivors and, through oral testimony and film, on those of subsequent generations. Of the 98,000 council houses administered by London County Council only 9,250 escaped unscathed, and 28 per cent were badly damaged or destroyed. Strategic centres of industry and communications such as Birmingham, Liverpool/Birkenhead and Plymouth/Devonport suffered serious physical damage. By contrast, in Bristol just 5 per cent of the housing stock was devastated, and in Leicester, a city of over a quarter of a million inhabitants, only six bombs fell, some harmlessly, during the entire wartime.

Yet the interruption to new housebuilding and the disrepair into which the housing stock slumped because of rationed materials and wartime construction priorities ensured that most towns and cities emerged in 1945 with a backlog of housing demand. 'Temporary' housing in the form of 'pre-fabs'—system-built in factories and assembled on site—was a common and affectionate legacy in the landscape of post-war Britain. Some experiments in the use of non-traditional materials such as steel-frame housing and Swedish-style timber building occurred, but these were of very limited impact on overall housing needs.

Pre-fabricated houses, Leicester, during World War II. 'Pre-fabs' were planned by the Temporary Housing Programme, 1944 in response to anticipated post-war housing shortages. Over 150,000 'temporary' factory-built dwellings were constructed between 1945–9. They had modern galley kitchens and their general design, comfort and convenience won enduring affection from their inhabitants. Until the 1940s, housing design remained the territory of professional (male) architects; pre-fabs contributed to the greater involvement of women in housing design.

Since war damage affected entire regions such as Clydeside and Merseyside, industrial towns such as Sheffield and Coventry, and cathedral cities as well as London, the issues associated with city centre reconstruction stimulated a national debate, permeated also by a social psychology based on wartime solidarity. Thus, housing renewal and city centre reconstruction again possessed a moral and spiritual dimension, albeit in a different context to Victorian times. At one level, since planning helped to win the war, the expectation was that planning would help win the peace too. Lord Simon, a former chairman of the Manchester Housing Committee and Ministry of Health official, stated in 1945: 'If we can tackle the problems of peace with anything like the same sense of purpose, the same devotion, and the same efficiency as we have shown during the war, the Rebuilding of Britain will be child's play.' Because centralization had become increasingly accepted during wartime, the peacetime exercise of state power over housing was assumed not to endanger democratic freedoms and property rights to any greater extent. In short, a new political consensus emerged and was reflected in the groundswell of support in the 1945 election in relation to many areas of social welfare, including housing.

As early as 1941 plans for the reconstruction of London were underway, and it was a flurry of regional plans—the *County of London Plan* (1943), *Greater Lon-*

(**a** and **b**) 'Lost Streets': Leicester 1888 (**a**) and 1968 (**b**). The irregular, porous network of pre-modern streets was swept away in many cities as 1960s town planning proposals embraced 'modernism'. New technologies and building materials were used to produce high-rise concrete buildings, the scale and mass of which dwarfed and isolated surviving areas and communities.

previous page: Southgate Redevelopment Area, Leicester, c.1966. Instrumental in the redevelopment process was the growth of car ownership and the associated construction of inner-city dual carriageways. These smashed through central districts where economically, educationally, and politically disadvantaged inhabitants were usually unable to mount effective campaigns to resist the demolition of their neighbourhoods. As in most major cities, they found themselves rehoused on green-field sites on the margins of Leicester.

don Plan (1945), *Merseyside Plan* (1945), *Clyde Valley Regional Plan* (1946), *West Midlands Plan* (1948)—as well as city plans for Edinburgh, Plymouth, and Hull, all of which had the signature of Patrick Abercrombie upon them, that most influenced post-war spatial arrangements in British cities. A principle common to these plans and enshrined in the Town and Country Planning Act (1947) was the regional context. Population dispersal, therefore, was the means by which issues of unfit and overcrowded housing were addressed and so entirely New Towns were founded. Simultaneously, an arm of the Ministry of Health's Central Housing Advisory Committee emphasized the need for a wider range of accommodation. Specifically this meant more flats than in the 1930s, though the Committee variously recommended housing densities which ranged from 30 per acre in suburbs to 100 per acre for town centres, and 120 for large cities. Building flats was inevitable if these densities were to be achieved, and at 120 per acre some 25–30 per cent of the population would have to become flat dwellers.

The imperative of post-war housing dictated high-density flats. It was a policy objective which affected other key ingredients in the urban landscape—central city redevelopment, ring roads, standardized housing forms, rapid land acquisition, and streamlined planning approval—all of which developments were pred-

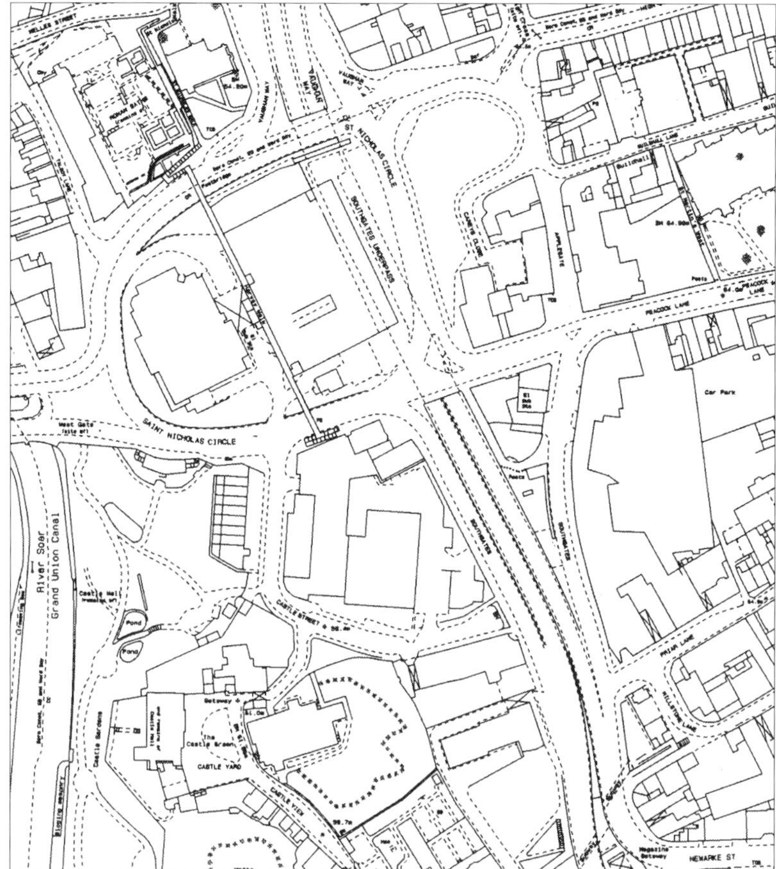

icated upon the dispersed city. The prevailing planning philosophy also legitimated political convenience on occasions, as in Liverpool, where the 'overspill' policy was based on decanting the population to New Towns (Skelmersdale or 'Skem'), existing towns (Runcorn), and to districts such as Huyton outside the city boundary. Simultaneously this altered the fiscal and political bases of the city, as did the 'reorganization' of local government after 1975.

Between 1955 and 1975 almost 1.5 million people (3 per cent of the population) were rehoused from 'slum' accommodation in British cities into high-rise flats (see fig. 9.2). In Leicester, as in many towns and cities, neighbourhoods were demolished, communities destroyed. Impenetrable ring roads divided those who remained, and streets which had existed since medieval times were obliterated. The historic core was destroyed, and the collective memory of areas of the city was lost.

Two factors were instrumental in this re-creation of the urban landscape. First, given the technical and financial complexity required to erect high-rise buildings, dependence on small and medium-sized building firms diminished. Although the trend was underway before 1939 the large-scale contractor prevailed. Whereas in 1935 firms with under 100 employees produced 60 per cent of

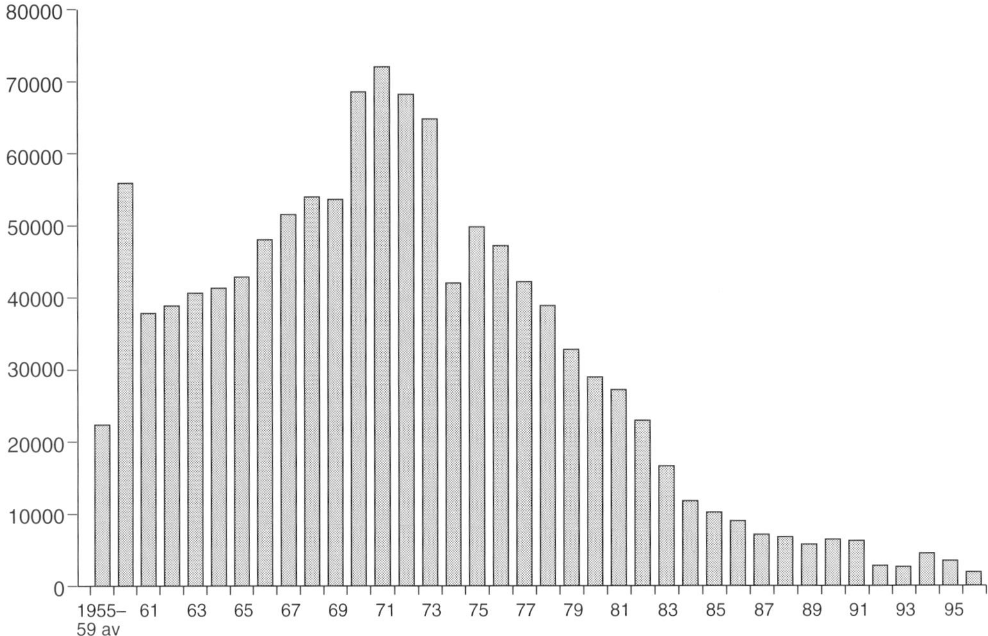

Housing demolition in England, 1955–96.

the output of the construction industry, by 1968 this had fallen to 36 per cent; correspondingly, employment in firms with over 500 employees tripled from 11 per cent to 35 per cent, with the largest five firms—Wimpey (45), John Laing (102), Costain (114), Taylor Woodrow (126), and Bovis (176)—together employing almost 80,000 workers, and highly ranked in respect of their annual turnover (UK-ranked position in brackets). Between 1963 and 1973, the largest seven contractors erected 99,000 or 75 per cent of all high-rise flats built. Large firms dominated the contracts issued by local authorities for high-rise building (Table 9.1). Consequently, accountability was reduced as local control over housing decisions was ceded to the corporate sector.

Table 9.1. *Local Authority contracts for high-rise flats with a single large contractor, 1963–1973, (percentage)*

London boroughs	County boroughs	Municipal boroughs	Urban districts	All authorities
28	45	68	71	54

Secondly, as in the inter-war years, the inducements offered in the form of Treasury subsidies affected the urban landscape. In the post-war era, however, the more generous allowances for flats, and for flats in ever higher blocks, skewed construction towards multi-storey dwelling (Table 9.2). As tower blocks gathered more storeys, so the level of housing subsidy per flat increased—for twenty-storey blocks it was 230 per cent greater than for four-storey blocks. In addition, Ministry subsidies for 'expensive sites' escalated considerably as land prices passed various thresholds. After 1956, this sliding scale was less than 3 per cent of the site costs on land under £20,000 per acre but equivalent to 9 per cent of the site costs where land was over £50,000 per acre. This differential provided further inducement to clear central areas in large cities where land costs were highest and to rebuild using high-rise flats. This was the case in twenty-one London boroughs which together accounted for 38 per cent of all high-rise dwellings built before 1972. Glasgow City Council built more high-rise flats (33,000) than any other single authority. Twelve English authorities outside London—Birmingham (24,013), Liverpool (19,270), Leeds (11,930), Manchester (9,530), Sheffield (8,360) Newcastle (6,170), Bristol (5,450), Warley (4,650), Nottingham (4,300), Wolverhampton (3,770), Hull (3,710), and Bradford (3,080)—accounted for over 100,000 units, equivalent to 25 per cent of all high-rise flats built in England by 1972.

Table 9.2. *Subsidies payable on high-rise dwellings 1946–1965*

	1946–52	1952–6	1956–61	1961–5	1965
house subsidy (£s)	16.5	26.7	22.1	24.0	64.0
flat subsidy					
4 storeys	no high-flat subsidy		32.0	32.0	89.0
5 storeys	but extra £10.50 per		38.0	38.0	95.0
6 storeys	flat on expensive sites		50.0	50.0	107.0
10 storeys	subsidy if 4+ storeys		57.0	57.0	107.0
15 storeys			65.8	65.8	107.0
20 storeys			74.5	74.5	107.0

So quickly did high-rise housing develop that by 1972 it accounted for at least 10 per cent of the public housing stock in 45 local authorities in England and Wales; in nine London boroughs high-rise flats constituted over 20 per cent of the public housing stock, and over 50 per cent in three of them. This transformation in the landscape was also governed by local influences. There was an inverse correlation between high-rise building and both the proportion of owner-occupiers and the extent of open space in the city. However, though the extent of slum clearance was not itself a strong influence on high-rise building, the proportion of poor quality housing in a borough was strongly and positively associated with the building of multi-storey flats. In short, high-rise flats were built in greatest numbers where housing stress was most acute: in the largest cities and London boroughs.

Though some multi-storey private flats were built in the twenty years before 1973, high-rise dwelling became virtually synonymous with council housing and was quickly stigmatized as such. The convergence in the urban landscape towards three-bedroom semis in both public and private house sectors during the inter-war years was rudely interrupted after 1945 and the provision of public sector housing became a highly visible means of perpetuating class divisions. The indicators of social deprivation—unemployment, infant mortality, educational attainment levels, shared amenities, nutritional standards, violence, and drug and alcohol abuse—indicated that England remained 'Two Nations'; in the second half of the twentieth century the peripheral housing estates and tower blocks were just as much no-go areas for the middle classes as Victorian rookeries had been. Housing allocation policies assigned accommodation on the basis of need as determined by levels of social deprivation, and this both implicitly and explicitly perpetuated divisions in society.

Multi-storey living was part of the post-war housing drive to construct more dwellings. It proved deeply unpopular with tenants. High-rise flats were expensive to build—more than 50 per cent greater for flats with six or more storeys than for two-storey houses—expensive to maintain, and expensive for tenants to heat. Lifts were unreliable and, in conjunction with other design features, made shopping, accompanying children to and from school, and similar daily tasks more arduous than for those living in conventional housing. The chairman of one housing authority commented, 'Multi-storey housing represents the peak of man's exercise of power over nature ... but where is the magic?' The detrimental effect of high-rise housing on the social life of inner city areas is difficult to overestimate and one of the most unacceptable outcomes of this phase of public housing. As design standards declined, so litter, graffiti, vandalism, urine, and excrement in the buildings each became more common; inevitably there were adverse effects on the social behaviour of residents.

The distortion of public policy by private corporate interests, that is, by the construction companies and their design teams, led to a backlash against high-rise housing, to a decline in public housing, and to a loss of support for the planning process in general. In short, the failure of the high-rise housing experiment in social terms created a political climate in which centralized decision-making and a reliance on the planning process were undermined. Dismantling the public housing sector in the 1980s was not difficult as a result.

Renewal, Redevelopment, and Rehabilitation

Clearance switched to a policy of improvement in the 1970s as qualitative rather than quantitative issues gained supremacy in the debates over housing provision (Fig. 9.2). The rehabilitation and refurbishment of existing housing stocks represented a decisive cultural shift. This change of emphasis stemmed from man-made disasters, such as the collapse of the multi-storey Ronan Point flats in Newham in 1968 and negative reactions to high-rise flats as a result, and from a change in architectural fashion as lower-density, traffic-free estates based on 'Radburn' principles of design came into vogue. The essentially sound nature of many older properties and the benefits of upgrading them were recognized. These values were enshrined in the Civic Trust (founded in 1957) and the Victorian Society (1959) which extolled the merits of older dwellings and the benefits of housing diversity. Gradually housing improvement was extended from individual properties to entire areas, recognized in Housing Action Areas as set up under the Housing Act 1974. Improvement grants in such areas doubled between 1970 and 1974, though they declined thereafter. Educational Priority Areas, Community Development Programmes, and Neighbourhood Action Projects were initiatives of the 1970s and 1980s which focused on inner city districts with adverse social indicators, especially housing standards. The paradigmatic shift towards housing quality was also intended to encourage local participation in decision-making and housing management and to replace the detached, unaccountable, corporatist provision of the high-rise era. By no means least in this transition in housing policy, was the withdrawal of the subsidy for high-rise housing in 1967.

Environmental issues also came to dominate the housing agenda. The 'Earth Summit' in Rio de Janeiro in 1992 set policies and emission standards to protect the quality of urban life and was an international recognition of environmental values which had been gaining strength in Britain and western Europe for a quarter of a century. To provide safe play areas for the young, sheltered housing for the aged and disabled, amenities for pedestrians and cyclists; to purge the pollution of inner-city rivers and canals; to regenerate natural systems by planting trees and protecting species—these and other locally driven campaigns were closely associated with landscaping and housing quality. One-third of the Urban Aid budget in 1977–9 was devoted to environmental projects, mostly associated with landscaping and planting.

Post-war planning was discredited by public distaste for the distant decisions which delivered high-rise housing and the inner ring road race-tracks in the years 1950–75. Councils discovered the political attractions of small scale and qualitative projects, a trend evident when the Conservative government under Thatcher tightened all public expenditure in the 1980s, especially that for large capital projects such as housing. The embrace of environmentalism by local authorities was a political expedient, therefore, not just in the search for votes but as part of the endemic tension between local and central government policy objectives. In one sense it was a reassertion of local independence in the face of central directives. The landscape of housing from 1979 was entrenched again as part of the broader political and ideological landscape. Municipal expenditures were 'capped' by central government and, as if to flex their local independence, many councils embraced environmentalism, conservation, and refurbishment of their housing stock as the acceptable alternative to the will of Westminster.

Four consequences for the landscape of urban housing flowed from the tight expenditure controls upon local authorities in the 1980s and 1990s. First, new council housebuilding went into rapid decline from 1979 and had virtually ceased by 1986 (Fig. 9.3). After three-quarters of a century, council housing in even the most committed Labour strongholds came to a standstill.

Secondly, to comply with central government directives from 1980, councils were obliged to sell their housing stock on terms very favourable to sitting

Trends in private and council housebuilding in England, 1950–96.

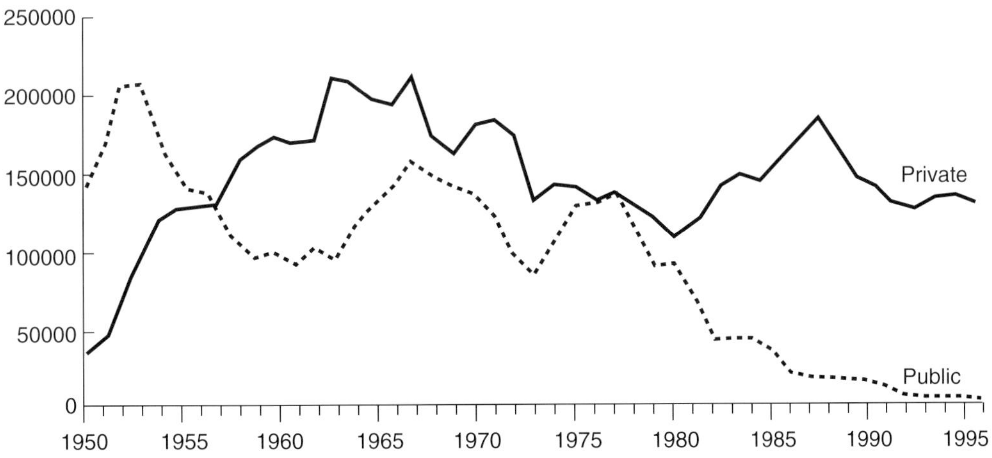

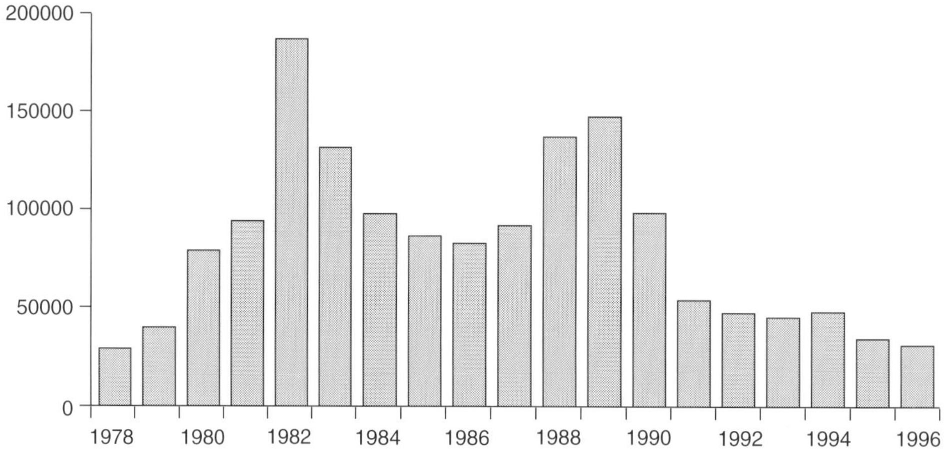

Sale of council houses in England, 1978–96.

tenants who wished to exercise their 'right to buy' (Fig. 9.4). Annual sales of council properties averaged almost 100,000 between 1979 and 1992 and were sold almost exclusively (96 per cent) to sitting tenants. The capital sums generated were not available to councils for reinvestment in new housing, however, though their maintenance bills were reduced.

Tenants bought those houses considered to be most heavily discounted in price. This was socially divisive both within and between council estates as the tenure of otherwise identical properties changed; families and indeed entire estates were stigmatized as unable rather than as simply unwilling to exercise their 'right to buy'. The landscape of council housing changed with the changes in tenure: stone-cladding, neo-Georgian front-doors, PVC windows, and additions such as a garage or conservatory, together with distinctive paint colours, marked out the erstwhile tenant as a new owner-occupier. The homogeneity of council house tenure was altered by the 'right to buy' programme; the visible character of the estates reflected the consumerism of the new owners. But the persistence of large elements of the public housing stock which remained so deeply unattractive to sitting tenants as to be unsaleable, however heavily discounted, indicates that only at the margin was the historical persistence of residential segregation affected. Indeed, the demolition of many high-rise flats and inter-war council estates was probably more influential in countering this than the 'right to buy' policy itself.

Mixed tenure was the third change which was encouraged by the rate-capping of local authorities by central government. Both council and private housing estates built before and immediately after World War II tended to be uniform in terms of their tenure—respectively rented and owner-occupied—and this aspect was strengthened during the high-rise era. However, from the late 1970s housing associations acted as builders and developers alongside private rental companies. Both offered mortgages and leasing packages financed in-house, and in the 1990s such housing developments have also included the local authority as a partner, often on sites cleared of inter-war council housing. This has resulted in mixed housing developments almost unimaginable before 1970 and is one arena in which the long-term divergence of rich and poor, slum and suburb, has been

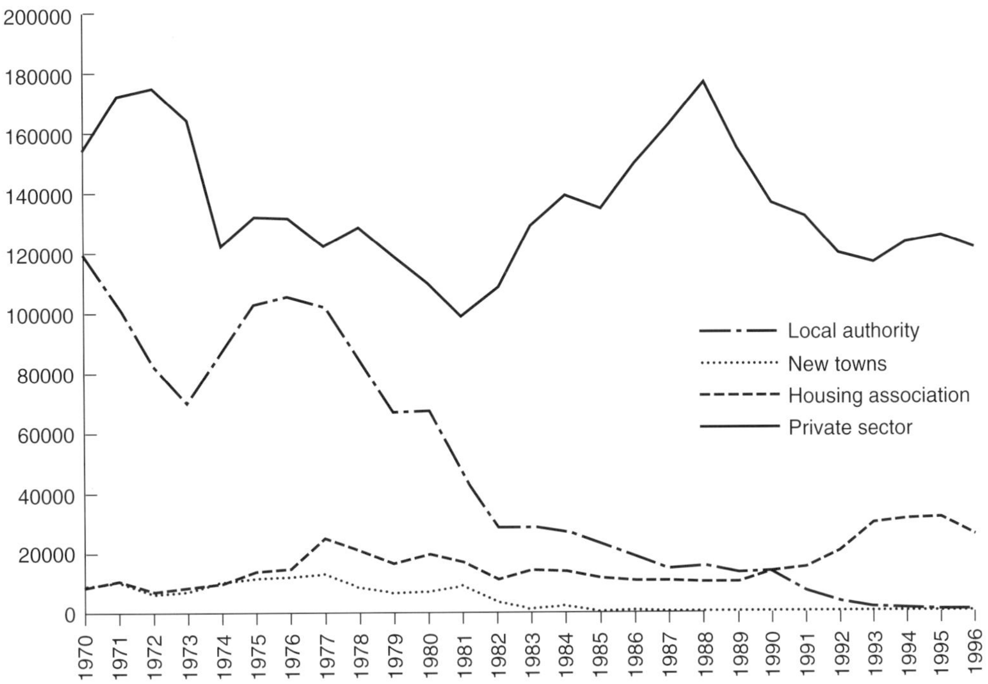

Housebuilding in England, 1970–96.

reversed. However, the scale of such integrated developments should not be overstated. The contribution of housing associations has remained low, although it has more than doubled from an average of 5–7 per cent of all new housebuilding in the 1970s and 1980s to almost 16 per cent in the 1990s.

Lastly, by contrast with the increasing diversity which emerged in the landscape of council housing, standardization developed in new private housing. Barratt's, Beazer Homes, John Wilson, Persimmon, and other housebuilding companies acquired greenfield sites and cloned new homes in the increasingly relaxed atmosphere which existed towards planning during 1979–97. By their planning decisions and transport policies Conservative ministers generally encouraged commuting; its impact on the urban landscape, as well as on that of small towns and villages, was to add a disproportionate number of dwellings in repetitious styles. The honey colour of the Cotswolds was applied nationwide by large construction firms, irrespective of the dominant local colour of stone or brick. The subtle and distinctive hues associated with traditional materials in Yorkshire, north Wales, and the Lothians were rudely rendered redundant as concentrations of yellowish-brick boxes, often with double garages, ubiquitous Georgian windows, and Regency doors have appeared in towns and cities and in the English countryside.

The suburban legacy of the 1980s and 1990s has been to produce housing in a uniform style and colour by national housebuilders to designs known as post-modernist but reminiscent of Lego. By freezing the housing contribution of the public sector, demand for owner-occupier homes has been stimulated. However,

in their pursuit of market share national building companies have had little interest in diversity of design, and the weakened tax base of many local authorities caused by population shifts and central government public expenditure constraints has meant that they have readily granted planning permission, almost irrespective of design. The landscape of housing has been altered drastically as a result. No continental European country has cloned private housing on such a scale in the last quarter of the century.

10 The Pleasures of Urbanity

John Walton

Towns and cities became the sites of an ever-proliferating array of public and private pleasures during the nineteenth century, and the equation between urban living (and urban expeditions) and the kinds of leisure which involve spending, consuming, seeing and being seen, shows no signs of being invalidated a hundred years on. This can be stated despite the penetration of so many lifestyles by 'virtual reality' and the electronic village, building on an earlier set of revolutionary developments in domestic entertainment which made the external environment less relevant and public sociability no longer so desirable. Nor has the new culture of the detached shopping mall, out-of-town leisure centre, or self-contained holiday village—none of which qualifies as urban on criteria which embrace a sense of shared civic culture, a local society which combines production, distribution, servicing, and domesticity, or a participatory political life—yet destroyed the downtown shopping centre or central entertainment district. Although these and related trends (the weekend cottage, the out-of-town football stadium) continue to threaten established town centres with an American destiny of decline, danger, and desertion, the town as centre for shared enjoyment and (usually) safe excitement remains. The conversion of old industrial towns into heritage tourism centres, with new museums, architecture and industrial archaeology trails, cleaned-up mills and sanitized former slums, offers an example of the vitality and adaptability of the urban leisure setting in an age of what Urry has called 'post-tourism', in which the pleasure-seekers enjoy the manipulations which lie behind the transformation of yesterday's working environment into today's temple of titillation. Not that any towns were ever solely consecrated to the gospel of work. The notion that there are 'towns which produce' and 'towns which consume' has always been oversimplified, and we should acknowledge the ways in which leisure in industrial and post-industrial societies was and is both a product and an employer of workpeople. The smokiest of Victorian manufacturing towns also manufactured ways of keeping their work-

people amused and, indeed, intellectually stimulated, from the music hall to the choral society and the geological study group. All these things and more were to be found in late Victorian Burnley, for example, where (fittingly) concerts at the Mechanics (the former Mechanics' Institute) and football at Turf Moor still draw in crowds from the surrounding area alongside the industrial heritage attractions of the Weavers' Triangle in the late twentieth century.

Towns were already making themselves up in their guise as gathering places for pleasure-seekers at the beginning of the nineteenth century. London's theatres, gardens, concerts, shops, assemblies, taverns, brothels, and molly-houses had long made it the nation's entertainment capital for those who could afford to spend time as well as money in this demanding and exhausting setting, at once grimy and glamorous, decorous and dangerous. The rise of a 'consumer society' among the gentry and comfortable middle ranks as well as the aristocracy in the eighteenth century had accentuated existing trends and extended their social range. Lower down the urban hierarchy the provincial capitals and county towns acquired the public pleasure paraphernalia of polite society on an appropriate scale, racecourses included; and below this rank small provincial towns with distinctive hinterlands were generating their own 'seasons', as at Wisbech and Chesterfield and Ulverston, which offered a widening range of consumer goods, exotica, and entertainment and brought together their merchants and professionals with the surrounding gentry and farmers for a season of modest revelry.

By the nineteenth century, again building on previous models, public space was increasingly being set aside and subdivided for purposes of pleasure, display, and consumption, both in terms of special buildings with internal subdivisions (theatres) and of special areas to which notions of social exclusivity were attached (promenades, public walks). Meanwhile, the urban enjoyments of the excluded or marginalized—the rapidly expanding (in many places) working class—were coming under critical scrutiny. This was especially so where they (or their consequences) encroached upon spaces which were also used by the 'better sort'. A developing cross-denominational Evangelical sensitivity to cruelty, irreligion (especially in the form of sabbath-breaking), and loss of control, was coupled with a cultivated aesthetic which gazed in horror on the roughly dressed and unshaven and recoiled from the smell of cheap tobacco and unwashed bodies. All this helped to fuel distaste and dismay in face of the urban crowd on pleasure bent, or the noisy groups which shouted insults at the well-dressed as they emerged from church or theatre in the socially mixed areas of the town centre. Fear of strikes and radical politics added an extra frisson.

The controversies which arose over attempts to regulate and control the time, place, and manner of urban working-class pleasures in the nineteenth century have been particularly attractive to historians. An extensive literature discusses the deployment of coercion (through labour discipline, the privatization of and imposition of rules of conduct on contested space, and especially the interventions of the new police forces from the 1820s onwards), counter-attractions (temperance fêtes, works outings, parks, libraries, Working Men's Clubs), and 'civilization' (the moderating influence of church, chapel, and school on the conduct of the rising generation) in efforts from above to make the recreational behaviour of the urban working class more tolerable to 'polite' society. That sustained efforts were made to recast popular pleasures is undeniable, though the precise mix of motives (humanitarian? religious? self-interested?) is impossible to

Joseph Parry's painting of Eccles Wakes Fair in 1882, showing a decidedly medieval-looking village centre in this industrializing area, and featuring (brandished on a pole) the smock for which young women will later race. Morris-dancers, a gaily decorated horse pulling a rushcart, assorted scuffles, and evidence of drunkenness complete a lively scene, in which the 'rough' and the 'respectable' mingle at close quarters.

recover. That they did not work, for the most part, is also undeniable: the police were too close to the culture they were controlling to do what was expected of them, the consumers of temperance fêtes in the afternoon were all too likely to move on to fairgrounds and pub singing saloons in the evening, and those working-class people who pursued intellectual pleasures and cultivated cleanliness and a calm demeanour usually did so on their own terms, for their own reasons. Arguably the most important middle-class influences on popular urban pleasures came from the entertainment entrepreneurs, often themselves of humble or raffish origins, who with gathering momentum from the 1830s and especially the 1850s set up music halls, sporting activities, popular theatres, and a range of other attractions which in turn came under scrutiny from licensing magistrates who sought to restrain perceived excesses but did not impede the attractiveness of what soon became big business. As the scale and sophistication of urban popular entertainment increased towards the turn of the century, so controversy developed as to how far the providers prospered by giving the punters what they wanted, and how far they exploited their audiences by casting their preferences in a readily satisfied, culturally impoverished and undemanding, and politically quiescent mould. This debate on urban popular leisure has persisted into the twentieth century, as have perceived problems of working-class delinquency and challenges to sensibilities, and disputes over the proper use of public space. Such issues take us through from Irish 'roughs' and scuttler gangs to Teddy Boys, 'mods', and 'ecstasy' culture, with an enduring and increasingly powerful emphasis on aggressively distinctive youth cultures. This has shifted some of the focus of alarm from class to age group. Although the problems have continued to be defined in largely masculine terms, the controversies unfold against and interact with changing urban environments and leisure institutions; and it is these we need now to explore.

The most concentrated development of urban entertainment and related social conflict came in the specialized towns which were emerging to supply pleasure and health to customers from a distance. These were in their infancy in 1800, but grew and proliferated with accelerating rapidity and sophistication during the nineteenth century. They continued this trajectory with sustained vitality until the mid-twentieth century, first changing their nature in many cases

Polite society postures, promenades, and gossips in the sunshine on Bath's South Parade. The formal symmetry of the architecture matches the decorous surface politeness of the conversational groups, and the light gives an almost Mediterranean feel to the relaxed but controlled Georgian scene.

The Graphic *presents a blustery promenade at Torquay in early 1870, with elaborately coiffed and clad ladies predominating, lap-dogs in evidence and a general air of stiffness and formality in the rarefied social atmosphere of this fashionable winter season.*

as they became centres for (often ill-advised and inadequately funded) retirement, then faltering and losing ground in face of changing preferences, foreign competition, and their own inertia from the 1960s and 1970s onwards. In 1800 the most important towns on this model were the spas, with Bath far ahead of its competitors. It was already past its peak as a centre for leisure and conspicuous consumption, and moving over to become predominantly a place of genteel retirement: still a leisure town (albeit with footwear and other clothing manufactures, a radical political tradition, and slums), but a quieter, less raffish and ostentatious one. But the competitors which overtook it in the fashion stakes in the early decades of the nineteenth century (such as Cheltenham, Leamington Spa, and Harrogate) organized their architecture, urban space, and entertainments in similar ways, with their assemblies, concerts, and subscription libraries dancing discreet attendance on the social life of the pump room, and with formal, symmetrical classical terraces providing a shared polite idiom within which to offer equally formal hospitality in a protected setting. Pricing systems, dress codes, and both official and unofficial policing of behaviour kept the visitors and elite residents at a safe distance from those social inferiors who might threaten their conventions and amenities. Masters of Ceremonies imposed at least the outward semblance of mutual respect and politeness on paying customers who were already filtered by the cost of subscriptions and suitable attire, but who might range from old aristocracy to nouveaux riches, with all the social tensions which were so knowingly presented to her readers by Jane Austen. By the mid-nineteenth century this spa culture was in terminal decline as the resorts followed Bath along the path to becoming retirement centres and dormitory towns, although at Harrogate, in particular, the culture of the pump room proved resilient into and through the twentieth century even as the town changed around it.

(*cont. p. 276*)

Scarborough

JOHN WALTON

The south side of Scarborough at the turn of the century, with the Grand Hotel featuring prominently at the boundary between the elevated social tone of the South Cliff and Spa, and the thronged area of popular amusements along the foreshore from the foot of the hotel to the harbour below the castle headland.

Scarborough, a long-established spa resort on the North Yorkshire coast which became a sea-bathing centre from the 1730s and described itself as 'the Queen of Watering-Places' during the nineteenth century, provides a splendid illustration of the ways in which urban space was allocated and contested as the market for leisure developed after 1800. In some ways it might appear almost too perfect, because its topographical divisions came to acquire matching social characteristics and modes of enjoyment; but there was nothing automatic about these processes, which were the outcomes of historical developments, policies and conflicts.

In 1938 Messrs. Adshead and Overfield published a planning report on *The Future Development of Scarborough* which set out the attractiveness of the resort's existing layout. They argued that Scarborough had natural barriers which separated the different classes of visitor, and that although such differences were 'fast disappearing' (a prediction which was to be falsified by events) they needed to be considered seriously in making new provision.

The cliff top at South Bay, and the Spa Gardens and Cliff Bridge which linked this area with the old town, were the preserve of the comfortably-off and socially aloof. The day-tripper 'has not the time, inclination or enterprise to climb up to the South Esplanade or to venture into the Spa', while less-affluent middle-class family parties preferred the North Bay, which provided cheaper accommodation and popular outdoor facilities including concerts, tennis courts, and bowling greens as well as easy access to a sandy beach. Working-class visitors, who were assumed (misleadingly) to be mainly day-trippers, 'seem to concentrate along Foreshore Road and Sandside, where all their amusements are at present provided': they came straight down through the old town from the railway station and the bus parking areas to the

The popularity of outdoor entertainments in Scarborough's Alexandra Gardens, where a lower-middle-class clientele sported prescribed holiday headgear at the resort's North Bay, is here juxtaposed with a view across the Cliff Bridge to the Spa, the centre of polite entertainment, and the South Cliff with its formal terraces and Sunday church parade.

seashore. The old fishing village below the castle, on the promontory which divided the South Cliff from the North Bay, was also tripper territory; and a kind of anthropological excursion was recommended to the select of South Cliff, who were urged that a visit to observe this strange tribe was 'an attraction not to be ignored'. The planners concluded, 'Of Scarborough it may be said that, owing to its natural divisions, it is better able to entertain all classes than any other seaside resort in England'; but success would depend on 'the skill with which the interests and amusements most appropriate for each, are kept reasonably separated'.

Scarborough's use of its 'natural divisions' was a historical product. In 1800 the resort's accommodation was confined to the old town, with higher-class lodgings tending towards the south sands. The Spa was on this side of town and the North Bay was almost unfrequented. It was not until mid-century, after the opening of the Cliff Bridge across the deep Ramsdale Valley had eased access to the Spa and beyond, that upmarket housing development began on the South Cliff and the first terraces appeared on the north side of the castle promontory. The opening of the railway station at the top of the town brought excursionists from the West Riding industrial towns through the old town on their way to the sea at summer weekends, although their preferred route changed with the opening of a new direct road in 1862. But the upper levels of the old town remained the main shopping centre, and the principal impact of the working-class visitors came at their destination, the shoreline by the harbour, where there were stalls and fairground amusements. The opening of an esplanade along the shore to the south had the unforeseen consequence of spreading tripper entertainments, including stalls selling cheap

Scarborough

JOHN WALTON

clothing and jewellery, along the edge of the beach, where bathing itself became a spectacle; and the process culminated in the opening of the orientally decorated underground Aquarium at the bottom of the Ramsdale Valley in 1877. By 1900 this had diversified its popular attractions, with music-hall entertainment, jugglers and ventriloquists, and a female orchestra adding spice to the feeding of fish and seals; and the bottom of the cliff had become a trippers' paradise. The Aquarium itself was not so successful as its Blackpool counterparts. The Corporation bought it up in 1914 but had difficulty in keeping it going: a problem common to many resorts. It was eventually demolished and replaced with a car park; but the work of setting the social tone for the seafront in that area had been long completed.

The old town contained medieval buildings and formed a picturesque object when gazed at from the South Cliff. Its quaintness was not a tripper attraction, though the bustle of the nearby harbour was, especially when the herring fishery catches were landed and the dexterity of the fish-gutting Scottish 'lassies' could be admired. Adshead and Overfield emphasized this setting as a 'special feature of interest', echoing comments which had been made from the turn of the century, and stressing the need to preserve the surviving 'original features' to meet the aesthetic expectations of pleasure-seekers; but they also suggested that the old Ice Factory should be replaced by a Fun Fair which might 'partake of the character of a street of fourteenth-century wooden houses'. This (in its ironic way) futuristic proposal betrayed confusion over the status of the old town as cynosure of the tourist gaze and provider of fun for trippers, confirming that Scarborough's zoning system was not as simple as it looked.

Meanwhile fashionable Scarborough was developing on the South Cliff, where the Crown Hotel and Crown Terrace appeared in the 1840s. The opening of the Valley Bridge improved access just after mid-century, and cliff paths, gardens, and an imposing new church confirmed the area's status. By 1900 the fashion parade after morning service at St Martin's was famous for its ostentation; indeed, the church itself could be regarded as partly consecrated to leisure, with its theatrical High Anglican services. The Spa buildings and grounds, twice redeveloped in the second half of the century, offered high-class music in a tranquil setting; and on the town side of the Cliff Bridge the Grand Hotel of the 1860s, with its exclusive dinners and dances, indicated the upward curve of the social gradient which was to follow. This remained the most clearly defined of Scarborough's social areas. The opening of a bathing pool with extensive spectator accommodation beyond the Spa in 1913 raised fears of social contamination, yet became an outpost of the respectable middle-class families of the North Bay. Only in recent years has this area moved somewhat downmarket, but the quality of its mid-Victorian building and planning continues to set it apart.

During the first half of the nineteenth century a new kind of health and pleasure resort challenged the primacy of the inland spa. The seaside resort was actually an invention of the eighteenth century, when a medical fashion for sea-bathing emerged alongside a revaluation of the sea and maritime landscape as sublime and exciting rather than dismal and frightening. A similar transformation would affect mountain scenery and help to turn the Lake District into a place of literary and tourist pilgrimage, generating modest nineteenth-century urban growth in Windermere, Ambleside, and Keswick. Decaying ports and fishing harbours such as Brighton, Hastings, and Margate were already being resuscitated by the sea-bathing craze by the later eighteenth century, and fresh impetus was given to the seaside spa of Scarborough (see cameo); but after the

The North Bay was a more complicated case. Its development was held back by that of the South Cliff, an early beneficiary of municipal as well as private investment; and the failure of a pier in this area from the 1860s was used as a warning against future investment. When proposals to stabilize the cliffs and build a Marine Drive round the castle were mooted in the mid-1880s there was fierce opposition from South Cliff ratepayers to this investment in a competing area; but the schemes went ahead and were followed by sustained (but always controversial) municipal provision of parks, a Floral Hall, and a boating lake in the Edwardian and inter-war years. The North Bay became dedicated to the lower middle-class family holiday, and the siting of the cricket ground at this end of town reflected this kind of demand. There was nothing socially exclusive about these recreational spaces, which responded to the growing cult of the outdoors in these decades; but there seems to have been a neat match between municipal provision and the tastes of a growing visiting public. This area, above all, set the tone for the growth of Scarborough's holiday season; but it was not achieved without recurrent strife as each proposal met sectional opposition.

What is particularly interesting is the way in which conflicts between different parts of the town, which could have blocked investment, were overcome to enable this balanced and zoned development to take place. Partly this was a matter of strong municipal personalities, who believed in local government's mission to provide amenities to make the town attractive in a competitive world. Alderman Meredith Whittaker and the borough surveyor H. W. Smith are eulogized for their determination in celebratory local literature; but they had to contend with Alderman Pantland Hick, who displayed a principled opposition to local authorities meddling where private enterprise feared to tread, and with councillors who urged that housing improvement for Scarborough people should take priority. There was nothing inevitable about the outcome; and leisure provision for impoverished locals remained deficient (there was, for example, no public library until 1930). Nor should we regard the social boundaries between the different leisure areas as rigid: not only did South Cliff visitors enjoy mingling with the trippers when they so chose, but the seaside environment allowed holidaymakers to reinvent themselves so that actual social status was hard to divine. Thus in 1900 a 'swell actor' might really be a bank clerk, a seeming bookmaker's clerk might really be a peer of the realm, and it could be 'dreadfully difficult' to tell a countess from a board school teacher. Contemporaries had long been aware that social topography was permeable and social identities might have chameleon qualities; and historians do well to remember this too. Scarborough teaches the lesson well, despite the apparent tidiness of its social divisions on the eve of the Second World War.

end of the Napoleonic wars seaside resort growth really began to attract attention. Between 1821 and 1831, in a period of unprecedented industrial growth, Brighton vied with Bradford as the fastest-growing English town, at an off-season census. The 1851 census report identified a group of leisure towns, almost all of them seaside resorts, whose aggregate percentage population growth during the previous half-century was greater than any other category of town; and although the figures would have looked less impressive if more resorts had been included in the calculation and if their initial populations had been larger, the seaside resort as a novel and dynamic kind of town was very much on the map. The spread of the railway network was just beginning to boost demand and extend it among the lower-middle and upper-working classes, and under these influences seaside resorts proliferated remarkably during the second half of the nineteenth century. By 1911 nearly 1.5 million people lived in over 140 English and Welsh seaside resorts, and high levels of migration made for volatile populations and ensured that the experience of seaside living became very widely shared, even without reckoning the seasonal workers and the millions of staying visitors and day-trippers who formed the lifeblood of resort economies. Nor, contrary to some expectations, was seaside resort growth purely a Victorian phenomenon. It continued unabated through to the Second World War, responding to new fashions for informality, sunbathing, and the celebration of healthy outdoor pursuits, which found their niche in established resorts like Blackpool as well as up-and-coming ones like Clacton and Bognor Regis. In the first post-1945 decades, too, the English seaside retained its popularity, buoyed by extra working-class demand as holidays with pay at last became general, and sustained by restrictions on the export of currency for holidays abroad. Visitor numbers grew, but outside Devon and Cornwall what resident urban growth there was increasingly took the form of retirement homes; and resorts ceased to innovate in their entertainments, amenities, and built environment. The stage was set for widespread crisis from the 1970s onwards when competition from the guaranteed sun of destinations in the Mediterranean and then further afield began to erode established markets; and only resorts with strong identities (most conspicuously Blackpool, with its reputation for making working-class people feel at home and entertaining them royally) were able to weather the storm.

The seaside resort became a distinctive kind of urban environment, with peculiar problems and attributes. In contrast with previous maritime settlements, there was a premium on facing the sea and securing vantage points for long views; and away from the original town or village core the quality of housing and social status of residents tended to decline with distance inland. Railway lines running parallel to the coast exacerbated this process, as at Birkdale near Southport. More generally, the siting of the main railway station, through which the overwhelming majority of visitors passed, had a disproportionate impact on the layout of the rest of the town, as the direct route to the sea would be colonized by shops and entertainment premises (especially where a working-class tripper presence was much in evidence) and a central business district would grow up around it. Landownership was unusually important. Resorts were in competition with each other for visitors, and a large seaside landed estate could add to a resort's comparative attractiveness by imposing minimum building standards, insisting on the making up of roads and drainage, planning in the formal ways which attracted the Victorian middle classes, banning public houses and other developments which might attract the wrong sort of visitor (such as fairgrounds on vacant lots and stalls in front gardens), and even giving land for parks and promenades and investing in suitable entertainment amenities such as piers. The Duke of Devonshire's Eastbourne exemplified all these processes.

There were other recipes for success: Blackpool became the world's most popular resort in the late nineteenth century precisely because it was not planned and controlled in this way. Its divided landownership and small densely developed building plots generated warrens of brick-built terraced lodging-houses which were affordable as businesses for working-class people from the 'cotton towns' and provided cheap, unintimidating, even homely accommodation for visitors who might have been ill at ease in less familiar surroundings. It was also hospitable to street stalls and fairgrounds, pubs and cheap eating houses, and the town centre was noisy, lively, crowded, and cheerful. These characteristics helped Blackpool to attract and keep the first generation of working-class holidaymakers from its textile-manufacturing hinterland, who in turn encouraged the investment in pleasure palaces which provided a range of attractions for sixpence, culminating in the resort's famous Tower (opened in 1894) and Pleasure Beach (a product of the turn of the century). In this setting such ventures were enduringly profitable, but elsewhere the summer season was usually too short to allow over-optimistic investors a return on their capital.

By 1900 the attractions of an even more informal kind of seaside development were becoming evident, as bohemian groups among the middle classes (especially of London) colonized cheap marginal land on the fringes of resorts on the south and east coasts and created settlements of randomly assembled converted tramcars and railway carriages, which soon acquired assorted informal accretions, creepers, and garden plots. This trend gathered momentum in the inter-war years, as urban working-class people found this to be a cheap way of enjoying a holiday free from the constraints of the seaside landlady, and it reached a kind of apotheosis in the 1920s in the cliff-top bungalow settlement of Peacehaven near Brighton. The fastest-growing seaside resort of the first half of the twentieth century, Canvey Island, was a collection of chalets on this self-build principle, which provided an alternative informal seaside aesthetic and drove planners to despair. The informal landscape of sheds and variegated greenery which came to characterize the municipal allotment of the early twentieth century, a relaxed enclave for masculine gossip as well as 'rational recreation', showed the pervasiveness of this set of popular preferences.

More orthodox resorts produced their own distinctive kinds of architecture. The substantial terraces and crescents which dominated residential building at the nineteenth-century seaside were hardly distinguishable from similar developments at spas and suburbs inland: the stucco and wrought ironwork of Brighton's Kemp Town in the 1820s was little different from Cheltenham, Leamington, or Nash's Regent's Park, for example. It was the architecture of seaside entertainment that really stood out. Promenade piers proliferated from the 1860s, after a precocious start with Brighton's elegant Chain Pier of 1823. They linked land and sea, culture and nature, the controlled and the wild, to provide a secure promenade and viewing platform as well as a landing place for steamers. Piers soon sprouted eccentric kiosks with extravagant decorative ironwork and oriental pavilions with onion domes after the manner of the Prince Regent's exotic Pavilion at Brighton, as elaborate top-dressing for the mysterious infrastructure of pillars and struts on which they tottered out to the ocean. These peculiar structures filtered out undesirables through admission tolls (although Blackpool's working-class visitors were undeterred) and added music, dancing, and (by the turn of the century) slot-machines of dubious pedigree and taste to the simpler pleasures of promenading, posturing, and conversation. Nearly as distinctive were the Winter Gardens and Aquaria which appeared in the larger resorts from the 1870s, aiming in the first instance at decorous middle-class patronage but in many cases soon moving downmarket. Here, especially, frivolous decorative motifs and eclectic combinations of styles were in evidence along with an extensive use of iron and glass. The culmination of the trend to seaside pleasure palaces arrived with the Tower complexes of the turn of the century, the tallest of which, at New Brighton,

was the dominant motif of extensive pleasure gardens but failed to make the predicted profits. But seaside idiosyncrasies did not end here. The inter-war years saw impressive investment in swimming pools (with imposing classical architecture and extensive spectator accommodation), ornamental gardens, Art Deco hotels (such as the Midland at Morecambe), pavilions (most famously at Bexhill), and fairground embellishments (as in Joseph Emberton's work at Blackpool's Pleasure Beach). Only after 1945 did this vitality begin to fade, as existing premises became shabbier, piers were lost to fires, collisions, and the weather, and Winter Gardens fell into disrepair, while a spreading awareness of marine pollution tarnished the resorts' original *raison d'être.* A seaside heritage revival in the 1980s and 1990s began to turn the tide, but outside Blackpool there was little new to report in architectural terms from these ailing maritime economies.

Local government at the seaside was particularly concerned with the regulation of space, especially where working-class excursionists mingled with their 'betters' in the same resorts. The beach itself, the original focus of the resort activities, posed particular problems. Not only was it an intermediate zone in the sense that people felt free to act in relaxed and informal ways and display parts of their anatomy which were normally hidden; it was also difficult to police, because ownership of the area between high and low tide was often indeterminate and had to be clarified before local government could intervene. Bathing itself could be a headache, because resorts had to satisfy contrasting moralities and expectations, even in the mid-Victorian years, which ranged from a concern to segregate the sexes and conceal all aspects of the body to a preference for nude bathing and an impatience with puritanical interference which embraced clergymen as well as bohemians. As a result rules tended to be stringent on paper but flexible in practice, with bathers ostensibly being confined to the modest discomfort of horse-drawn bathing-machines but usually going unpunished if they avoided these constraints discreetly. By the inter-war years the bathing-machine was in terminal decline and a move to swimming for enjoyment rather than bathing for health relaxed most of the tensions, although these resurfaced in conflicts over the siting of nude beaches from the 1970s. The control of beach entertainment (Victorian 'nigger minstrels' and their Edwardian successors the Pierrots, Punch and Judy, and so on), the licensing and zoning of refreshment stalls, and the generation of revenue from such activities, all involved local government in 'taming' the beach and imposing external order on what had been no man's land. The building of sea defences and promenades, the allocation of land for parks and ornamental gardens, and the policing of behaviour to meet a consensual perception of the needs of visitors and residents in a particular resort setting, all involved resort local government in a long-term project to order, classify, and control urban space and human and vehicular traffic flows. Increasingly the problems were reduced as resorts developed internal zoning systems and visitors of different classes and preferences came to know their place, or behave appropriately in socially mixed settings such as Blackpool's Tower Ballroom. On popular coastlines, networks of resorts developed which could cater for a variety of tastes and whose social identities became known by reputation so that demand could match supply.

Issues such as these were common to all towns in some degree, but they stood out particularly in the seaside resort setting, where the whole identity and economic success or failure of a town might be at stake. Other kinds of town developed recreational areas for differing purposes, with a variety and complexity which increased as the urban scale was ascended. The smallest market towns, such as Horncastle in Lincolnshire, had their precincts of pleasure pathology (as seen by police and magistrates) around the pubs and courts which were frequented by prostitutes and gamblers, especially on market and fair days. Such districts were an almost universal concomitant of urban status throughout the period, but on the lower rungs of the urban hierarchy it was difficult to isolate a more salubrious leisure district, as opposed to particular buildings and precise locations.

Further up the ladder the late-growing Lancashire cotton-weaving town of Nelson, with a population approaching 40,000 by 1914, had well-developed neighbourhoods with their own religious and communal leisure relationships centred on clubs and chapels; but in the late nineteenth century it also generated a sports and leisure complex on the edge of Pendle Water. Here were the football stadium and Lancashire League cricket ground, adjoining Victoria Park; and nearby, in the inter-war years, was the Imperial Ballroom. This part of town provided recreations of various kinds and for various constituencies, although individuals could pick and mix from what was on offer, from band concerts in the park, through cricket crowds of up to five figures in the 1930s when Learie Constantine was playing in the Lancashire League, to dancing and mating rituals at the sixpenny or shilling hops. Pleasure had its place in the town's topography as well as in its daily, weekly, and seasonal rhythms, from the evening out to the annual town holidays, when encounters with Blackpool brought acquaintance with a wider range of commercial pleasures and perhaps helped to change the town's own leisure menu in the longer term.

So might encounters with Manchester, which was a big enough city to develop a range of leisure districts as popular spending power rose and free time expanded from the later nineteenth century onwards. This was the level of the urban hierarchy at which specialist provision might develop in different areas, some serving parts of the city, some catering for a hinterland of smaller neighbouring towns, and some offering higher-order services to a broader regional public. Manchester had a central entertainment area of pubs and emergent music halls around Deansgate by the 1840s, with associations with prostitution and an 'underworld'; it had suburban pleasure gardens, the longest-lived of which was Belle Vue with its dancing platforms, tableaux, firework displays, and curiosities of the animal kingdom, by the second quarter of the nineteenth century; it was able to sustain two top-class professional football teams from the late nineteenth century, where Nelson only had a brief inter-war moment of glory in the League's lower divisions, despite an impressive stadium; it became the headquarters of the county's cricket team, and an imposing sporting complex arose where cricket and football adjoined at Old Trafford; and the Hallé Orchestra and Miss Horniman's theatre drew in aficionados of the arts from a wide radius, with special late trains by the turn of the century to return outlying patrons to the bosom of their families. Where shopping in Nelson was a workaday affair, confined to a few unpretentious central streets, late Victorian Manchester had its department stores and a central shopping district which catered for the emergence of shopping and strolling as a leisure activity in its own right, especially but not exclusively for women. Here, as in the resorts, was an environment in which new identities could be tried out and the pleasures of anonymous self-projection could be sampled.

Manchester's Belle Vue pleasure gardens offered elaborate tableaux of great events, accompanied at appropriate times of day by fireworks and music, on an island in its lake. Here working-class audiences could see, in 1919, a reconstruction of the destruction of Mons in the war that had only so recently ended.

In this respect the Victorian provincial cities were echoing developments in London itself. The metropolis was a pleasure capital as well as the centre of imperial government and administration, and a great commercial emporium and manufacturing centre. Its West End, which had been long in the making, brought together a heady Victorian combination of theatre and music-hall district cheek by jowl with a prestigious shopping area and a cultural district of art galleries and museums. A neighbourhood colonized by gentlemen's clubs was nearby, together with parks which contrived to combine the public and the highly fashionable. These were highly formal recreational townscapes featuring classical and Renaissance architecture and manicured green spaces with geometrical patterns in their layout, but they could be penetrated by the less tidy and ordered, and a prevailing unease was made manifest when, for example, working-class protesters against restrictive Sunday trading legislation disrupted the after-church fashionable promenaders in Hyde Park in 1855. Moreover, part of the attraction of the West End (for that louche male middle class which is too often obscured by historians' obsession with the theme of respectability) was the availability of prostitutes from the nearby 'rookeries' and dubious purlieus of Soho. The most successful courtesans notoriously participated in the Hyde Park promenades, and their presence made it more difficult for late Victorian ladies to claim the privileges of

the strolling *flâneuse*, window-shopping, inspecting others, and displaying their command of fashion and material resources. By the late nineteenth century department stores and cafés provided protected environments where women from the comfortable suburbs or from out of town could meet sociably without their lack of male encumbrance being misinterpreted, but their command of the wider spaces in which these enclaves were created was to be a gradual conquest of the twentieth century. The seaside resorts, which were more carefully policed and less attractive to predatory men, probably provided the safest public spaces for middle-class women wanting pleasurable relaxation.

Urban recreational spaces for the middle and upper ranks, in London as elsewhere, were increasingly being divided and protected along gender as well as class lines by the later nineteenth century. Suburbs were chiefly female during the day, reserved for domestic pleasures such as exchanging calls, bridge, and tennis; public commercial recreations disproportionately male. The working class, which developed its own public recreational spaces, had conventions of its own. Every town of any size had, by 1900, developed its 'monkey rack', variously named in different localities, where the young of both sexes strolled on Sunday evenings in groups and courtship contacts were made. There were also more occasional processional routes which took people beyond their neighbourhoods: the Whit walks of the churches and chapels through Lancashire towns, and the civic celebrations with floats and marching bands, such as the commemoration of Preston's borough charter every twenty years ('Preston Guild') or the annual Hospital Sundays and other charitable jamborees which proliferated in the summers of the early twentieth century and beyond, ostensibly pulling the classes together in joint celebratory and fund-raising ventures. Much less respectable were the Bonfire Night tar-barrel-rolling festivities in southern English market towns, or the surviving mass football games which, after a transition from problem to curiosity to attraction, still take over the streets on annual days of licence at Workington on Easter Tuesday or Ashbourne on Shrove Tuesday. On the micro-level of daily rather than weekly or annual routines, the access lanes at the back of terraced houses had their groups of lads and young men, exchanging ideas and information, gambling on the toss of a coin, and making contact with the street bookmaker who likewise became an institution in the later nineteenth century. Where such groups frequented front streets, and especially where they congregated outside pubs, they were more likely to fall foul of the police, an important part of whose remit was to 'move on' knots of potentially threatening men who were held to be obstructing the thoroughfare. Wasteland and accessible fields might be taken over for games of football and similar activities, especially where parks and formal recreation grounds were policed so as to discourage whatever was noisy, boisterous, and damaging to lawns and shrubberies. All this was on a very local scale, and gangs defended their territories against outsiders, sometimes, as in Salford at the turn of the century, admitting girls to their ranks; but the women's part in all this, the 'monkey rack' excepted, was generally restricted to chatting on doorsteps and, at an earlier age, to sexual encounters in alleys where a provisional privacy might be found which was denied in crowded homes. But the street and the neighbourhood, punctuated by pubs and fish-and-chip shops, were the public theatres of popular leisure for most working-class people, with occasional excursions to the park; to the market with its naphtha lighting or gas jets casting flickering light on winter evenings, where getting the best possible deal provided its own satisfactions, and the crowds were entertained by cheapjacks and quack doctors; and, once or twice a year, to the fairground and the seaside, by the second half of the nineteenth century.

These features were strongly evident in most towns of any size by the late nineteenth century, and remained dominant into the 1950s. Over the last forty years, and especially since 1980, distinctive recreational areas have emerged in smaller towns and more specialized ones have cohered in larger centres. In part this has been a process of transformation. Defunct commercial and warehouse districts have been colonized by restaurants, nightclubs, galleries, and museums. The bank of a Manchester canal has become the focal point of a collection of leisure businesses targeted at gays, a contested space, sometimes threatening, but novel and distinctive, exhibiting the previously hidden with civic approval and police support. Bradford, the epitome of early Victorian urban malaise, with its festering watercourses, filthy streets, stratospheric mortality rates, and fierce political and social conflicts, has been remade (at several removes) in the post-industrial late twentieth century as a tourist destination, not only promoting the literary landscapes ('Brontë Country') of its hinterland but also concentrating museums, music halls, and ethnic eating experiences into its city centre. Whole sections of town centres have been consecrated to the retailing of particular kinds of goods, shopping for which has itself become a leisure experience; while excursions are run not only to nightclubs but also to the shopping malls, temples of consumerism, carefully themed and embellished, which colonize sites on the urban fringes and are often remakings of derelict former industrial landscapes. These are miniature towns in themselves, but without residents or non-retail and leisure functions, as are the knots of supermarkets, fast-food restaurants, cinemas, and bowling alleys which attract drivers from surrounding towns to motorway intersections, and the collections of furniture and do-it-yourself supermarkets in prefabricated buildings which colonize brownfield bypass sites on the edge of the swollen urban carcases of places such as Wakefield or Blackburn. Access to private transport has become essential to full participation in this ultimately placeless culture, whose architecture makes no concessions to local traditions or landscapes. Although devotees of shopping malls make detailed, even sophisticated distinctions between them, they are a world away from the varied local architectures and public spaces within which earlier generations sought pleasures which could be reached on foot or along the routes laid down by the railways and tramways and buses. The two systems coexist, in heightening tension, as the pros and cons of the relationship between leisure and the private car are now debated again sixty years after the motor trade's original victories in the 1920s and 1930s.

An ironic commentary on all this is provided by the case of Hay-on-Wye, a Welsh borders market town which over the last two decades has become dedicated to leisure shopping in the form of the second-hand book trade, attracting a visiting public which sets a premium on quaintness, old-world charm, good food, and a leisurely pace of life, only to become caught up in controversy over the need to extend its huge central car park to cope with the traffic to a place that is almost cut off from public transport and bears, in spite of its romantic landscape and preferred self-image, some generic resemblance to a shopping mall like Sheffield's Meadowhall or Dudley's Merry Hill. The crucial difference is that Hay is still a living town with local residents who value it as something other than a second-hand book emporium, and it is this that causes the conflicts.

A more sustained theme of the last century and a half has been the multiplication of specialist premises for the dispensing of commercialized enjoyment. The origins of this lie with the construction of assembly rooms, theatres, circulating libraries, and other polite leisure spaces in the eighteenth century, as well as with the inn (with its mixture of functions) and the humble alehouse. The alehouse apart, these earlier developments provided segregated space for an expanding 'polite' society to trade in 'cultural capital': display of accomplishments and resources, appreciation of the niceties of fashionable good taste, and conversation that expressed shared assumptions about how the world worked. Social inferiors could be excluded by anticipated discomfort, the feeling of being 'out of place', as well as by the cost of subscriptions or admission to special events. Such rarefied environments continued to be created after 1800, from John Shaw's Manchester punch club of the 1820s which admitted local professionals and merchants to gossip about business after work over a glass of grog under the eagle eye of the proprietor, through the provincial Athenaeum, Literary and Philosophical Society, or subscription library with its own purpose-built premises, the gentleman's club in London's West End with its comfortable library and residential facilities, and the gambling rooms and sporting clubs which might admit accomplished plebeians who would not be welcome elsewhere, to the golf or yachting clubs of the turn of the century and beyond. Thus were the like-minded segregated by choice from the promiscuous mingling of the urban street, and the better-off found enclaves whose structures and rules excluded (at least in theory) those whose presence might embarrass and annoy. These, like the hotels which gained in pretension and multiplied their specialist services in the railway age, and the department stores which clearly expected certain standards of deportment and sartorial elegance among their customers, provided insulation against the more stressful aspects of urban democracy, just as did the quiet streets, extensive gardens, and domestic tennis courts of outer suburbia and the controlled areas of resorts where piers, promenades, and winter gardens might themselves be segregated by toll and convention.

Where markets needed to be more extensive, spanning a range of tastes and social strata, large elaborate buildings with internal subdivisions might be necessary to accommodate several tiers of prices, comforts, and preferences. This practice had a long tradition in the theatre which, even when most suspect in Evangelical eyes, never completely lost a middle- and upper-class following. The 'gods', especially in provincial towns, might play host to noisy adolescents and 'roughs' whose behaviour might be very different from their 'betters', although a taste for melodrama and spectacle united all. Theatre building revived in the late nineteenth century, with the remarkable gilded confections of Frank Matcham well to the fore, and the creation of a West End theatre district on the fringe of fashionable London.

Specialized urban entertainment sites were also emerging for a working-class market by the 1820s and 1830s. The urban public house was becoming increasingly a working-class preserve by this time, and competition in the larger towns was generating investment in elaborate premises for spirit drinking, the so-called 'gin palaces', before the Beer Act of 1830 freed the sale of beer from magistrates' control and precipitated the opening of (to many contemporaries) an alarming spate of back-street front-parlour drinking places. Established pubs, which could also sell spirits and were regulated by the magistrates, responded to this competition by expanding their recreational activities, promoting sport (which was increasingly being pushed off wasteland by enclosure, by the spread of building, and by stricter policing of the public streets) and the community singing of the 'free and easy'. The latter was to mutate into what came to be known as music hall, by way of an increasingly interventionist role by the chairman, the introduction of a stage and an admission charge, and the rise of professional entertainers. Metropolitan claims for the origins of music hall, based on the opening of Canterbury Hall in 1852, should be taken with a pinch of salt: as in many similar respects, the roots lie in the Lancashire cotton towns, with William Sharples's Star in Bolton leading from the 1830s and combining a museum of curiosities with a programme of singing, dancing, acrobats, and humorous sketches. Relatively good wages for the unattached young in the factory economy boosted such provision elsewhere, with Manchester well to the fore. When London took up music hall in the second half of the century it did so decisively, and it was here that the largest purpose-built premises, with tiered auditoria and prices to match, brought in a middle-class audience alongside the original clientele in a setting where drink and prostitution were pushed to the margins, acts were carefully policed (although innuendo and gesture regularly burst the confines in much-appreciated ways) and an architecture of exotic eclecticism expressed a will to distract from the workaday world. The pub singing room survived into the twentieth century alongside this extravagance of its successors, and the music hall still had to struggle for respectability against temperance campaigners and moral reformers in the 1890s; but, with its successor the palace of varieties, it formed a glittering presence on the urban streetscape and punctuated the working week for millions of adherents until the rise of the cinema and the radio drove it back into seaside and metropolitan strongholds by the 1940s and 1950s.

The music hall also provided an acceptable commercial leisure outlet for working-class women. The pub itself continued to marginalize them. Its architecture became more ostentatious and its interior decoration more floral, heavy, and opulent as the nineteenth century proceeded, at least where new premises in attractive locations were at issue; and interiors became subdivided, with some bars being open to all-comers, and others, 'lounges' and 'snugs', being consecrated to particular groups with some pretensions to superiority: skilled or supervisory workers, bowler hats rather than cloth caps. To be compatible with some measure of respectability a female presence usually had to be consigned to one of the outer bars, with husbands in the masculine republics elsewhere buying drinks to be passed through into purdah. Even the dismantling of boundaries over the last twenty or thirty years has left most pubs as uncomfortable spaces for women most of the time, especially unaccompanied ones, although the new idioms of the roadhouse and the 'by-pass Tudor' pub of the inter-war years, with their art deco furnishings, may have been more welcoming.

Commercial spectator sport, another largely masculine activity, developed in close relationship with the pub. Innkeepers had vested interests in horse racing, which brought affluent punters and racehorse owners to what were often small towns for the race weeks, even before the railways helped to broaden the market; and the drink interest, a natural ally of a gambling-oriented sport against moral reformers, was prominent among the promoters of enclosed courses and grandstands as more socially inclusive crowds needed to be regulated, entrance fees collected, and special places demarcated for the better-off to display themselves in comfort. Lower down the social scale the pub became the unofficial organizational centre for working-class off-course betting when it was made illegal, and this continued from the Victorian and Edwardian legislative attacks on street betting to the legalization of betting shops, which themselves became distinctive urban masculine leisure enclosures replete with the odour of strong tobacco, in 1960.

Publicans were also prominent, alongside and increasingly taking over from the middle-class apostles of muscular Christianity, in the development of football as a commercial proposition. As the new forms of rule-bound, time-bound, and spatially corseted football made headway from the 1860s in urban settings, the scope for charging admission for matches which put the pride of localities at stake drew entrepreneurs and seekers after social prominence into investment in grounds and the payment of players. First (as with so many innovations) in the Lancashire cotton towns, then in other industrial and metropolitan districts, the football stadium became the focal point for an increasingly working-class crowd on the Saturday afternoons which since mid-century had been progressively released for leisure pursuits. Here again, there were segregated areas for those who wanted more comfort and could afford to pay a little extra; and stadium architecture was becoming a distinctive genre by the turn of the century. As teams concentrated urban patriotism (reinforcing and perhaps creating in new quarters the civic pride that went with town halls, public parks, and municipal services), so the stadiums generated their own aura or mystique, becoming almost secular temples, as the scramble to acquire pieces of turf when clubs moved to new sites on the urban fringe at the end of the twentieth century bears witness. Cricket followed this path in the northern industrial towns, but not on the same scale; and in the inter-war years new stadium sports like speedway and greyhound racing emerged. Less obtrusive was the Victorian rise and sustained popularity of angling, the most popular of participant sports, with its lines of male competitors huddled along urban canal banks and sluggish rivers, and its own culture of championships, prizes, skulduggery, and betting.

The intersection between sport and civic pride, which professional football (perhaps illogically) came to epitomize, was not confined to the spectator sports of (predominantly) working-class men. In the resorts, especially, it came to be associated with providing a full menu of outdoor attraction for middle-class visitors and affluent residents, most obviously in the inter-war years when golf courses, bowling greens, tennis courts, bathing pools, and other sporting accoutrements of the healthy outdoor life proliferated under competitive municipal auspices. But in all but the most philistine urban settings a movement towards the municipal provision of healthy amenities and 'rational recreations' can be traced from the 1830s at least, overlapping through the Victorian and Edwardian years with the philanthropic (or manipulative) offerings of urban landowners and large employers. Parks, libraries, museums, and art galleries were carefully regulated spaces, designed to promote the decorous pursuit of health, the appreciation of selected aspects of the natural world, and an awareness of the 'high culture' of literature, scientific information, and the arts. These were filtered by the professional staff and municipal committees, classified so as to present preferred stories about the evolution of humankind and the glories of the British Empire, and presented statically under formal conditions which demanded quiet, restrained, untactile behaviour. These municipal leisure spaces, with their formal (often classical) architecture and zoned layouts, have continued to pursue this agenda until very recently, and departures from it still provoke controversy.

Alongside this municipal and philanthropic provision the urban working class began to create its own leisure buildings, as well as taking over the Mechanics' Institutes of the second quarter of the nineteenth century and the Working Men's Clubs of the 1860s and opening them out to embrace the provision of novels and recreational (as opposed to vocational) classes and the enjoyment of beer and indoor games. Chartists had found difficulty in obtaining meeting rooms in the 1830s and 1840s, but by the turn of the century radical meetings could be accommodated in Co-operative Halls, Oddfellows' Halls, Clarion Clubhouses built for socialist cycling groups, and an array of similar premises which came out of the working-class culture of voluntaristic mutual assistance and gave space for billiards, choral societies, libraries, and a range of other activities beyond the tutelage of paternalist employers and gatekeeping municipalities. After the 1867 Reform Act the two established political parties set up their own clubs for working-class supporters and hangers-on as well as more opulent town-centre premises for the comfortably-off, and here as elsewhere the entertainment provided often became an end in itself, transcending nominal political loyalties, especially where the Conservative Club provided the best billiard table in town. In the same way the churches felt constrained to offer recreational activities of a safe kind, including sport (where Sunday School leagues became very important in many urban settings); so urban leisure activities increasingly invaded the premises of organizations whose main or ostensible aims were sometimes subverted by the pleasure preferences of those who took what was on offer but rejected (however passively) the political or denominational baggage that was supposed to accompany it.

The Odeon cinema chain provided sumptuous modernist surroundings in which filmgoing could become a special event, with tea beforehand and a sense of occasion which might be lacking in the routine visit to the flea-pit. This enticing representation highlights space, light and smooth architectural lines in keeping with the elegance of the cars parked at the portals.

The trend of the last thirty or forty years has been away from these Victorian models, based on municipal and employer paternalism, working-class participatory mutuality and evangelicalism. Commercial provision straightforwardly for profit has increasingly predominated, on a model anticipated by the music hall and then the dance hall and cinema, with the impressive art deco buildings of their expansive years still punctuating urban landscapes, though often put to different uses such as bingo. The new specialist buildings of the 1960s onwards, the bowling alleys, skating rinks, discotheques, and nightclubs, and the themed restaurants which have emerged as eating out has become assimilated to the pleasure principle by ever-growing numbers of people, have been overwhelmingly provided on the profit model. Even the new football grounds and transformed football clubs have taken this route, as restrictions on the profits to be made from the sport have evaporated and the relations between clubs, shareholders, and supporters have been transformed. Here as elsewhere in late twentieth-century urban society, the prevailing model has been that of the limited company, as alternative provision for urban leisure has atrophied. Meanwhile quotidian rhythms of leisure have also altered the urban environment, as city centre streets and leisure premises remain busy with revellers and even shoppers into the small hours of the morning and the status of top city for clubbing oscillates between the provincial capitals; while Sunday has been freed for the full range of leisure activities, provoking questions about the cultural forces which inhibited this for so long. Expanded leisure time has also found expression in the privacy of the home, with the comforting routines of television, the wilder shores of choice from the video rental shop, and the sophistication of domestic musical reproduction. The transformation of urban leisure which took place over the second half of the nineteenth century created a set of institutions and locations which sustained their predominance and kept a distinctive ethos into the second half of the twentieth century, assimilating new growths like the cinema into the existing system. What we see now is a second urban leisure revolution, which invades all but the most secluded urban environments.

11 The Public Face

Geoffrey Tyack

facing page: Hilltop Methodist Chapel, Burslem, Staffordshire. Nonconformist chapels played a sizeable role in the religious and cultural life of the Pottery towns in the 19th and early 20th centuries, and their buildings vied with the potbanks themselves as dominant features in the urban landscape. Hilltop was built in 1836–7, to the designs of Samuel Sant, son of a local builder, on the site of a Sunday School that had been ejected from the premises of the local Wesleyan Methodists (the chapel later became affiliated to the United Methodist Free Church). The brick building, in a dignified classical style, is entered through a Doric colonnade; the three-storeyed side elevation reflects the galleries inside the main part of the building and schoolrooms underneath.

In 1700 almost all provincial towns were still dominated by medieval buildings: churches, cathedrals, or castles. Grand public spaces were relatively few, the more recent public buildings—town halls, schools, almshouses—unambitious. Major changes took place in the larger towns during the eighteenth century, and especially after 1750. The dissemination of classical architectural ideas and the replacement of timber by brick or stone as a building material changed the appearance of countless streets, a process which was encouraged by improvement schemes carried out under local Acts of Parliament. The picturesque 'middle rows' which blocked many thoroughfares were swept away, markets removed from streets, medieval walls and gates demolished, narrow timber bridges replaced by new bridges of stone. Sometimes completely new streets were cut through densely built central areas to open up vistas and improve the circulation of traffic. And in all towns of any size new public buildings were erected to cater for the increasingly diverse needs of the inhabitants: not only town halls and schools but also assize courts, prisons, merchants' exchanges, hospitals, asylums, workhouses, assembly rooms, and theatres.

The impulses behind this spate of building were secular and rationalist. England possesses no Würzburg, Nancy, or Noto to celebrate the eternal glory of a triumphalist Church or a hereditary ruler. The State did not play an important part in urban building, even in London. No new Anglican cathedrals were built in the eighteenth century, and few of the new parish churches, dignified though they often are, are as impressive or as numinous as their grander medieval predecessors. Nonconformist places of worship were without exception smaller and plainer. The mercantile, manufacturing, and professional elites who governed the towns fell far short of the landed gentry and aristocracy as patrons of magnificent building projects. There was no tradition of magnificent civic building in England such as was to be found in the independent, or once-independent, towns of Germany, northern Italy, and the Low Countries. Real grandeur—as distinct from restrained dignity—was achieved only when the landed elite and their clients were directly involved in urban projects, either as promoters or, in effect (as in Bath and Oxford), as consumers. Elsewhere the most impressive urban ensembles were the county governmental complexes—assize courts, prisons, and the like—built on the sites of the medieval castles at York and Chester. Here the landed class appeared as wielders of power, dispensers of justice, and guarantors of the social order, positions which they maintained well into the nineteenth century.

1800–1870

It was only with the emergence of a richer, more powerful, and more self-confident urban elite in the nineteenth century that England's larger provincial towns could begin to rival their continental counterparts in civic grandeur. Meanwhile their appearance was permanently changed by rampant economic growth and an unprecedented rise in population. Visitors to Manchester in the 1820s and 1830s were both fascinated and appalled by the cotton mills and warehouses which surrounded the central districts, the factory chimneys belching

out smoke and the warehouses dwarfing the mean houses of the industrial workers huddled within their shadow. Alexis de Tocqueville remarked in 1835: 'Everything in the exterior appearance of the city attests the individual powers of man; nothing the directing power of society. At every turn human liberty shows its capricious creative force. There is no trace of the slow continuous action of government.'

For many of Tocqueville's English contemporaries the roots of this civic malaise lay not so much in the lack of government as in the failure of the churches to rise to their obligations. England's churches had been built to serve an overwhelmingly rural society but, as the urban population grew, large numbers of people found themselves cut off from the close physical presence of institutional religion. At first much of the initiative for new church building was taken by the Nonconformists, and especially by the Methodists. Most towns already contained one or more Nonconformist chapels in 1800, but many were little more than 'upper rooms', tucked away behind street frontages. Methodism grew especially fast in areas where the Anglican parochial structure was weak, and here chapels made a significant mark on the urban landscape that can still be seen today, as in the Five (actually six) Towns of the Potteries and the tin-mining towns of the far south-west, like Camborne in Cornwall. Early nineteenth-century Nonconformist chapels were invariably classical in character, their interiors taking the form of galleried auditoria, with a reading desk and pulpit at the far end and an organ above. It was common to build an elementary school alongside the chapel, thus providing, along with the Anglican schools which began to be founded at about the same time, the basic infrastructure of primary education. By 1851 half of the churchgoing population went to non-Anglican places of worship; and in many towns Nonconformists greatly outnumbered Anglicans.

The Anglican response was sluggish at first. This was in part because of the rigidity of the parochial structure: until 1843 an Act of Parliament was needed before a new parish could be formed. Some wealthier parishes circumvented this difficulty by establishing new chapels-of-ease; and 'proprietary chapels'—speculations funded by pew-rents—flourished in London and the fashionable spa towns. These developments did little for the urban poor, and it was widely believed, especially in the tense years after 1815, that unless churches were built in the expanding areas of towns the Church, and with it the established order of society, would come in danger from the encroachments of Dissent and secularism. Therefore in 1818 £1 million was voted by a still unreformed Parliament towards the building of new Anglican churches in the poorer districts; this was supplemented by another £500,000 in 1824. The resulting 214 'commissioners' churches' established an unmistakably Anglican presence in what are now the inner suburban areas of most English towns of any size. Many were classical, though with towers and Grecian porticoes to distinguish them from Nonconformist chapels, but some were Gothic, such as Holy Trinity, Bordesley, Birmingham (1820–2). Now deconsecrated, this rather forlorn building stands, like many other churches of its date and type, in an inner-city landscape of roads and tower blocks.

With the growing influence of the Tractarian or Oxford Movement and its architectural offshoot the Cambridge Camden Society, founded in 1839, Gothic gradually displaced classicism as the universal architectural style of Anglicanism. It was also adopted by the Roman Catholics, and it was the Catholic convert

A. W. N. Pugin who, in *Contrasts* (1841), produced the most eloquent visual indictment of the industrial town when he compared a 'Catholic town' of 1440 with its counterpart of 500 years later. In the hands of Pugin and his many followers Gothic architecture signified a rejection not only of 'pagan' classicism but also of the utilitarian pursuit of wealth. Thereafter Gothic became more than simply a style; it was part of a moral and cultural crusade.

St Walburge's Roman Catholic Church, Preston, Lancashire. This spectacular building, adjoining the London–Glasgow railway, is a monument to the revival both of English Catholicism, especially in Lancashire, one of its old heartlands, and of the 'Middle Pointed' Gothic promoted by A. W. N. Pugin and his followers. It was built in 1850–4 to the designs of Joseph Aloysius Hansom, in a working-class area to the west of the town centre; the spire, over 300 ft high, is one of the tallest in England. In the background is the tower of the Anglican church of St Mark, designed by the local architect E. G. Paley and built in 1863–6.

The new zeal for Gothic can be seen in the rebuilding of town centre churches like the parish church at Leeds, England's fourth largest provincial town. Here the vicar, Walter Hook, replaced the ancient but much rebuilt and pew-encumbered building with a new church of 1838 designed as a setting for the sacramental worship favoured by the Oxford Movement, with a deep chancel for the performance of the liturgy and stalls for a surpliced choir. More commonly, existing parish churches were extensively restored, as at Stafford in 1841–4, where George Gilbert Scott ruthlessly purged the building of post-medieval accretions and introduced the pews, ornamental floor tiles, and dark stained glass which survive today.

It was in suburban areas, and in the resort towns, that the Anglicans and the Roman Catholics made their greatest impact on the Victorian urban landscape. Between 1831 and 1911 the number of Anglican worshippers increased faster than that of the Nonconformists, and between 1835 and 1875 an average of 96 new Anglican churches were consecrated each year. State funding was no longer feasible after the 1832 Reform Act, so the resources had to come from private individuals and from the collective efforts of bodies like the Incorporated Church Building Society, established in 1818, and the church-building societies of individual dioceses. The new churches formed the focal points of a gradually expanding mosaic of urban parishes, each served by its own resident parson, usually with an elementary school on a nearby site. Meanwhile the number of Roman Catholic churches tripled in number in the second half of the century, following large-scale Irish immigration and the re-establishment of the Roman Catholic bishoprics in 1850, and in some towns, especially in the north-west, they made a greater impact on their surroundings than Anglican churches.

The pattern of church building owed much to local patronage and tastes in churchmanship. Brighton, whose population rose tenfold to 77,693 between 1801 and 1871, became a stronghold of the most 'advanced' Anglo-Catholicism largely through the efforts of Henry Michell Wagner, vicar of Brighton, and his son the Revd Arthur Douglas Wagner, who inherited his substantial fortune. The elder Wagner's first foray into church building came in 1824–8, when he built St Peter's church in the North Steyne, an open space laid out by Improvement Commissioners at the entrance to the town from London; the architect was the young Charles Barry and the style Perpendicular Gothic. Twenty years later, in 1848, Wagner erected the church of St Paul, West Street, in a poorer neighbourhood near the town centre, employing his son as priest in charge and R. C. Carpenter, 'the Anglican Pugin', as his architect. The style here was the purest 'Middle Pointed' Gothic, favoured by the Tractarians, and critics of ritualism poured scorn on 'the Sunday opera at St. Paul's'. A. D. Wagner later went on to build four more churches in the poorer districts inhabited by the growing numbers of people employed in Brighton's burgeoning service and manufacturing industries, and he played a major part in the building of a fifth. Some of these churches vie with the finest ecclesiastical buildings of the Middle Ages. St Bartholomew's, built to the designs of Edmund Scott in 1872–4, rose up above the surrounding sea of artisan cottages in the hinterland of the fashionable Regency terraces like a vast brick ark, four feet higher than Westminster Abbey, and its shadowy interior can compel admiration even from the most determined sceptic.

Church and chapel building also flourished in small market towns. Interdenominational rivalry often played a part in determining the outcome, as in

Abingdon, a town of 6,251 inhabitants in 1851. Here there were two medieval parish churches, and there was also a long-established Nonconformist presence which manifested itself in the building of handsome new chapels, first by the Baptists in 1841 and then in 1862 by the Congregationalists. Like many of the churches of 'Old Dissent' in the mid-nineteenth century, these were classical buildings, with dignified temple-like frontages to the street. But when the Methodists came to build their chapel in 1845 they opted for Gothic, and Gothic was chosen for a second, and much grander, Methodist chapel of 1875, serving the inhabitants of a new middle-class suburb, Albert Park, where an Anglican church had been erected ten years earlier. Thus the heterogeneous nature of the religious life of the town was manifested in the architectural character of its churches.

New schools, like new churches, were seen as essential in the early nineteenth century if urban society was to maintain its cohesion. The two organizations which did most to provide elementary education—the British and Foreign Schools Society (founded in 1808) and the National Society (1811)—both had strong religious links, the former to the Nonconformists and the latter to the Anglicans. Under legislation passed by the Whigs in 1833, government grants for building were made available to the two societies, and with their help elementary schools were provided in ever-greater numbers in the expanding working-class districts of all English towns. In Nottingham, a town whose population rose from 28,000 in 1801 to 74,000 in 1861, there were thirteen elementary schools in 1835, five of them run by the Anglicans, six by Nonconformists, and two by the Roman Catholics. By 1870 the number of schools had risen to 36, of which 22 were under Anglican control; and elementary education was deemed to be available for all who needed it. The schools of this period were usually unassertive in their architectural character, with classical elevations gradually giving way, especially in the Anglican schools, to Gothic, a good example of which is the attractive red-brick school by G. E. Street next to his new church of All Saints in the suburb of Boyn Hill, Maidenhead, built in 1854–7. Here the school and the adjacent parsonage and schoolmaster's house combine to present an image of an organic community under the beneficent shadow of the Anglican church: a medieval ideal in modern guise.

For the urban middle class—perhaps a fifth of the population—there were the long-established grammar schools and recently founded 'proprietary' schools which could offer a more varied form of education. Most of these schools were rebuilt, usually on new and more spacious sites, in the course of the nineteenth century. The classical style was often chosen for Nonconformist-backed schools like the porticoed Leicester Proprietary School, built in New Walk, an area of middle-class housing to the south of the town centre, in 1837—and it was surely no accident that the Anglicans had chosen Gothic for their own school, the Leicester Collegiate School, a year earlier. By the 1830s the Greek Revival was becoming a lost cause and it was Gothic in its various manifestations which became the quintessential architectural expression of English secondary education, as at Clifton College, Bristol (1860–2), a new proprietary school set up for boys of the professional and commercial middle class. Schools of this kind were usually situated well away from town centres and surrounded by playing fields, allowing the pupils to escape the supposedly baleful influences of the town and to learn the virtues of manly exercise in the open air. Similar concerns caused

Chorlton Union Workhouse, Withington, Manchester. For 20 years following the Poor Law Amendment Act (1834), those of Manchester's paupers who sought 'indoor relief' were accommodated in a central workhouse built in 1793 and housing 1,200 inmates in 1845. This was superseded in the 1850s by two new workhouses on what were then the city outskirts. Chorlton workhouse, which served the poor of the southern half of Manchester, was built in 1856, to the designs of Hayley, Son and Hall, and consisted of a long three-storied brick residential block with an Italianate tower in the centre and a chapel projecting forwards towards the entrance, which was flanked by two substantial lodges and an impressive set of iron gates. An Infirmary (not in the illustration), one of the first in England on the 'pavilion' principle, was added in 1865–6, and the whole complex later became Withington Hospital.

many old grammar schools to migrate to more spacious sites. Thus in 1868 Reading School vacated its old home near the ruins of the medieval Abbey in favour of new red-brick Gothic buildings in a suburban area on the southern fringe of the town designed by Alfred Waterhouse, who later, in 1875, designed the new Town Hall. The presence of such schools helped attract middle-class residents to certain towns and suburbs, thus fixing their social character for the future.

New churches and schools played a part in imposing some degree of peaceful coexistence among the urban population, which by 1851 constituted half the total population of the country. But a degree of coercion was also necessary for the maintenance of social order. Anxiety about crime and unrest was widespread in the first half of the nineteenth century and received tangible expression in the building of new complexes of assize courts and prisons. The Grecian style was employed in some of these buildings, like the Assize Courts at Devizes (1835); but the forbidding face of authority was perhaps more convincingly conveyed in neo-medieval castellated structures like the Courts at Carlisle (1810–12) and Oxford (1839–41), both of them built within old castle precincts, and both proclaiming the medieval origins of the English judicial system. The entrances to the Oxford building are flanked by iron fasces, symbol of civil authority to the Romans. Castellated architecture was also often employed for the external detailing of prisons, many of which occupied sites close to the Courts. These bastilles still cast a blight over towns like Reading, where the prison (1842–4), scene of Oscar Wilde's incarceration, looms up over the main town-centre park and the ruined medieval Abbey in which Henry I lies buried. Later prisons were usually built away from the centres of towns, like Strangeways Prison, Manchester, designed in 1866–8 by Alfred Waterhouse, architect of the adjacent (but now demolished) Assize Courts, and still exuding a sinister air of implacable power.

After the Poor Law Amendment Act of 1834 a second coercive structure was built in all large, and many smaller, towns: the Union Workhouse. The relief of poverty formerly had been the responsibility of the parish, either through cash ('outdoor relief') or within a workhouse, but after 1834 the Poor Law Union became the unit of administration, with the workhouse becoming a means of deterring the poor from seeking public relief, so as to reduce costs and encourage the able-bodied poor to migrate in search of work. The new workhouses were usually built on the edge of towns, where land was cheap, and in some, like those at Tavistock, Tiverton, and Bideford in Devon (1836–7), the 'panopticon' principle was adopted to ease surveillance—a nineteenth-century obsession—and to reinforce the punitive message implicit in the 1834 legislation. After the demise of the Poor Law in 1929, workhouses were often turned over to the local authorities as hospitals and, where they survive, they can still be counted on to depress the spirits.

Hospitals, like workhouses, were a legacy of the eighteenth century and they also grew much larger in the nineteenth. Financed at first by private subscriptions, most hospitals were built on the fringes of towns, like the Royal Berkshire Hospital at Reading, built in 1839. With its impressive Grecian portico this elegant building resembles the country houses of the local gentry from whom some of the funds emanated, and, massively enlarged to the rear, it still serves its original purpose. Hospitals of this kind could not cope with the innumerable ailments of the poor, and for them recourse had to be made first to dispensaries and then to the infirmaries erected in the second half of the nineteenth century by the

Poor Law Unions: the first tangible recognition of governmental responsibility for health care. Poor law infirmaries usually adjoined the workhouse itself, like the Chorlton Union Infirmary at Manchester (1865–6), a vast structure spaciously laid out with five parallel blocks 100 feet apart on the latest approved 'pavilion' principles to allow adequate ventilation—another nineteenth-century preoccupation—and lauded by Florence Nightingale as the best hospital in the country. The larger towns also boasted specialized orphanages and lunatic asylums, like the neo-Elizabethan Winson Green Asylum built, with a twenty-acre farm for the inmates, next to the Borough Gaol (now Winson Green Prison) on the former Birmingham Heath in 1850. This became part of a large institutional complex which also included a workhouse, with its associated hospital, and a separate fever hospital.

Most town dwellers in the early nineteenth century still found their last resting places in grossly overcrowded town-centre churchyards. The growing demand for space for burial, and Nonconformist objections to the Anglican near monopoly of interment, encouraged the development of private cemeteries on the edges of the larger towns. One of the first was at Liverpool, where a Necropolis catering mainly for Nonconformists was opened in 1825. It provoked an Anglican riposte in 1825–9 when St James's Cemetery was laid out in a disused stone quarry by a company which paid a dividend of 8 per cent to investors. It attracted a clientele of local worthies, including William Huskisson, MP for the town and the first man to be killed by a railway locomotive (at the opening of the Liverpool and Manchester Railway in 1830). Similar privately managed cemeteries were opened in Newcastle, Birmingham, Sheffield, Bristol, and Nottingham in the 1830s, some of them with Grecian gateways and chapels. Public provision came only after revelations in the 1840s about the unhealthy state of the older cemeteries. Under the Burial Acts of 1852 and 1857 it became possible to close the old town-centre churchyards and establish Burial Boards funded by the rates so as to allow decent interment for the poor in huge cemeteries like that at Toxteth Park in Liverpool. The Burial Boards were taken over by the local authorities in 1894, and by this time the legalization of cremation, and the opening of the first crematorium at St John's, Woking, Surrey (1885), made it possible to tackle the question of urban interment in a less space-consuming manner.

The Municipal Corporations Act of 1835 changed the character of urban government in England by introducing elected councils with the power to levy rates, in place of the self-perpetuating corporations of the chartered boroughs. One hundred and seventy-eight such councils were now established, and previously unincorporated towns such as Birmingham and Manchester acquired elected councils which controlled municipal property and supervised the local police force. For some time these new town councils existed alongside the Improvement Commissions which had long provided essential local services, but by the 1860s the two bodies had usually merged. This was in part a result of the Public Health Act of 1848 which gave wide-ranging powers to lay down sewers, improve sanitation, impose building controls, and thus to remedy many of the excesses of rapid and uncontrolled urban growth. Already, some of the larger towns had begun to acquire the most essential local utilities such as gas and water. Under successive Acts of Parliament they were also empowered to build public baths (1846–7), open public libraries (1850 and 1855), lay out parks (1859), and lay down tramways (1870). Cumulatively these pieces of legislation greatly

The Civic Buildings of Birmingham

GEOFFREY TYACK

Until the 1830s Birmingham's public services were provided by its Street Commissioners, whose offices were in Moor Street, near the market place, in a plain though elegant classical building of 1805–7. Birmingham was the fourth largest town in England in 1800, and its population nearly doubled (from 60,822 to 110,914) by 1830; yet in comparison with Manchester and Liverpool there was a dearth of distinguished public architecture. With this in mind, some of the leading citizens began to campaign in the 1820s for the building of a hall which could serve as a venue for the triennial music festivals, inaugurated in the eighteenth century and hitherto housed in St Philip's church (now the Anglican Cathedral). A site was bought by the Street Commissioners at the western end of New Street, an area where property was relatively cheap but which was beginning to attract banks and shops. The design, chosen after a competition in 1830, was supplied by Edward Welch and his partner Joseph Aloysius Hansom, who went bankrupt as a result of his involvement in the project but later recovered to achieve fame as the inventor of the eponymous cab and as a designer of Roman Catholic churches. Modelled externally on the Temple of Jupiter Stator in the Roman Forum, its main internal feature is the galleried hall dominated by a vast organ—the first of many in English town halls. Here occurred the inaugural performances of two of the mainstays of the Victorian choral repertoire, Mendelssohn's *Elijah* and Elgar's *The Dream of Gerontius*.

For one writer the building of Birmingham Town Hall represented a 'revival of the age of Pericles', but it did not immediately signal a major expansion of municipal government. Birmingham was incorporated in 1835, but the Corporation took over the powers of the Street Commissioners only in 1851, and for ten years or more after that the 'economy party' was in the ascendant in local affairs. This situation changed dramatically in the 1870s, when the population had grown to over 340,000. Under the charismatic leadership of Joseph Chamberlain, the city—as it now was—became a byword for 'municipal socialism'. A Medical Officer of Health was appointed in 1872—much later than in most comparable cities—the gasworks were acquired by the Corporation in 1874, the waterworks in 1875, and in the same year work began on the building of Corporation Street, a city-centre thoroughfare combined, as was often the case, with a slum-clearance scheme. New public offices were now needed, together with a council chamber and adequate quarters for the Mayor; and in 1874–8 the Council House, a sprawling stone-faced domed building in the Renaissance style, was built overlooking the sloping ground to the east of the Town Hall—later named Victoria Square—to the designs of Yeoville Thomason, grandson of a local button manufacturer. The building of the Council House involved the clearing of more slum property; and when the foundation stone was laid Chamberlain reminded his listeners that 'in the erection of buildings worthy of the population and importance of Birmingham, we are not seeking to gratify any personal vanity or petty sense of self-importance, but are endeavouring to show our respect for instititions upon which the welfare and happiness of the community very largely depend'.

Central Birmingham looking east in 1885. This engraving shows the civic centre of the 'city of a thousand trades' soon after it reached its final form during the mayoralty of Joseph Chamberlain (1873–5). The Gothic-spired Chamberlain Memorial and the smaller memorial to the theologian and scientist Joseph Priestley (1733–1804) are in the centre foreground: other buildings are (clockwise from bottom left) Mason College, the School of Art, the Museum and Art Gallery, the Council House, the Town Hall and, in the right foreground, the Central Library. In the right background is New Street railway station. Mason College and the City Library were replaced by the present Central Library in 1971.

Close to the Town Hall and Council House were the neo-Renaissance Birmingham and Midland Institute of 1855–7, the adjacent Central Library, and the spikily Gothic Mason College (1875), founded by the industrialist Sir Josiah Mason and the nucleus of the later University. Together, these buildings comprised a cultural and governmental 'forum', and with the creation in 1880 of Chamberlain Square, immediately to the north-west of Victoria Square, it became possible to see them as part of a coherent whole. The square is overlooked on its eastern side by the Museum and Art Gallery, with its tall clock tower, built in 1881–5, and in the centre of the square is a Gothic memorial commemorating the mayoralty of Joseph Chamberlain, and designed by his namesake J. H. Chamberlain, architect to the Birmingham School Board, in 1880–1. Another statue, commemorating the eighteenth-century scientist and Dissenter Joseph Priestley, stands nearby, and James Watt has recently been admitted to their company. Thus the values of Nonconformity, scientific rationalism, and activist local government are publicly proclaimed.

The city's further expansion—by 1911 Birmingham had overtaken both Liverpool and Manchester to become the largest provincial city in England—meant that the Council House eventually became inadequate to house the local government staff. In 1912 an extension was built to the north of the Council House and Art Gallery, joined to them by a bridge. Meanwhile, the granting of assize town status was celebrated in 1887–91 by the erection of the ornate 'free Renaissance' Victoria Law Courts at the northern end of the recently opened Corporation Street to the designs of Aston Webb and Ingress Bell. Local government activity continued to grow between the wars, and a new Civic Centre was planned in Broad Street, to the west of Chamberlain Square, near the Hall of Memory, a domed Renaissance building of Portland stone (1923–4) which commemorated Birmingham's casualties in the First World War. Close to the basin at the heart of the canal network which had played so important a part in Birmingham's economy in the early nineteenth century, this was an area where property was cheap, and, after two competitions, a classical design by Cecil Howitt was selected. Work began in 1938, but was terminated by the outbreak of the Second World War with only part of the project (the present Baskerville House) built.

This fragment of Birmingham's projected inter-war Civic Centre now overlooks a large open space, for many years occupied by municipal lawns and flower beds, but now remodelled and renamed Centenary Square. The eastern side is taken up by the brutalist though grimly impressive Central Library of 1971, built to replace the old Central Library which fell victim, along with many of Birmingham's other Victorian buildings, to redevelopment in the 1960s. The Inner Ring Road passes in a concrete canyon immediately to the west of the Library, and the western side of the square is now taken up by the tall glass-fronted International Convention Centre of 1986, built partly out of European Union grants—a building which would look equally at home in Chicago or Kuala Lumpur. It overlooks a realist, mock-heroic sculpture by Raymond Mason entitled 'Forward' (the city's motto). Meanwhile, as part of a scheme framed in 1984, the canal basin has been restored, cars have been removed from Chamberlain and Victoria Squares, and the latter has been adorned with massive neoclassical nude figures by Dhuva Mistry, one of them irreverently nicknamed 'the floozie in the jacuzzi'. A pedestrian route runs from the Convention Centre through the still largely Victorian 'civic forum' to New Street, and as a result the western part of the city centre has acquired a new visual coherence and vitality.

Grainger Street, Newcastle-upon-Tyne, by T. M. Richardson, c.1840. The layout of central Newcastle by Richard Grainger in 1835–9 was the most ambitious redevelopment project in any English provincial town in the early 19th century. The width of the streets and the classical façades bear witness to the wealth and aspirations of a long-established provincial capital, which prospered in the early stages of the Industrial Revolution and which still dominates the surrounding region. The building to the right, with its curved corner based on the temple of Vesta at Tivoli, housed the Central Exchange, together with a news room, coffee room, and meeting room, and the column in the distance, designed by Benjamin Green, commemorates Earl Grey, Prime Minister at the time of the 1832 Reform Act.

increased the potential of local authorities to act in the interests of the town as a whole, and the resulting sense of civic pride was often marked by impressive buildings both for the utilities themselves (waterworks and the like) and for the bodies which administered them.

In most towns the spirit of civic pride first manifested itself in the building of a grand hall for meetings and concerts, sometimes combined with premises for the assize courts or a police station, necessary after the establishment of paid local police forces in 1839. Until the 1850s such buildings were invariably classical in character, like St George's Hall, Liverpool (H. L. Elmes 1841–6). Funded by one of the richest of England's urban corporations, this magnificent structure evoked the grandeur of ancient Rome not only in its porticoed exterior but also in its vast barrel-vaulted central hall complete with a massive organ—soon to be a sine qua non in such buildings—at one end. Here a distinctively urban culture could be celebrated not only in public meetings but also in performances of Handel oratorios by massed choirs and organ transcriptions of popular orchestral works. The building stands to the north-east of the town centre on what had been heathland used for lime-burning, with the main railway station, Lime Street, a close neighbour. In time it became the focus of a civic 'forum', dotted with monuments to national and local heroes (including the Liverpool-born William Ewart Gladstone), and overlooked by other classical buildings built, mostly for cultural and educational purposes, between 1860 and 1900: the Library and Museum, the Picton Reading Room, the Walker Art Gallery, the Sessions House, and the College of Technology.

The provision of new civic buildings was often combined with street improvements, most notably at Newcastle, where the fortuitous presence of a thirteen-

acre tract of undeveloped land immediately to the north of the medieval urban core enabled the corporation to lay out a complex of new streets lined with classical stone buildings, including banks and a theatre, in 1835–9. The focal point of the development is an open space with a stone column commemorating the Northumbrian Earl Grey, hero of the 1832 Reform Act: a symbolic assertion both of local patriotism and of the Whig reforming ethos. The developer, Richard Grainger, gained the backing of the corporation after promising to rehouse the market—a responsibility of local authorities from time immemorial—and the new buildings went up to the designs of the local architect John Dobson, whose sober classicism still pervades those parts of the town centre which escaped redevelopment in the 1960s.

The Gothic style only began to make inroads into civic architecture in the 1860s. By then writers like John Ruskin had trained a new generation of architects to look for inspiration to the secular buildings of medieval Flanders and northern Italy, and for the patrons such buildings conveyed satisfying overtones of 'local self-government'. Gothic town halls make an unmistakable mark on their surroundings, especially when there is relatively little architectural competition, as at Rochdale (1866) or at Barrow-in-Furness (1882–7), the latter a mere fishing hamlet in the early nineteenth century before its expansion as a port for the shipment of iron ore. Often the most imposing feature is the clock tower, which at Bradford (1873) recalls that of the Palazzo Municipale at Siena, evoking romantic associations with the medieval past and serving as tangible focus for civic aspirations.

Victorian civic architecture reached its apogee in the town hall at Manchester, built to the designs of Alfred Waterhouse in 1868–77. It stands on a triangular site formed by the clearance of a congeries of densely packed houses and workshops, overlooking the newly created Albert Square with its canopied Gothic memorial to the Prince Consort. The population of Manchester (including Salford, which had its own local government) rose fivefold to 441,000 between 1801 and 1861, but the social and environmental problems which had made it a byword for urban horror in the first half of the century had been contained, if not solved, by the 1860s and the new building, which replaced a Greek Revival town hall of 1822–5, conveys a spirit of optimism. It housed a much expanded municipal bureaucracy—gas board, water board, city surveyor, town clerk, and their staffs—as well as a council chamber, committee rooms, rooms for the mayor, and a hall for concerts and meetings. The city's sense of its historic mission is proclaimed by the architecture and underlined in the internal iconography, as in the sculpture hall, approached by a majestic staircase, with statues of John Bright and other local worthies, the mosaic floors depicting cotton flowers and bees (for industry), and in a series of didactic historical paintings by Ford Madox Brown which line the walls of the timber-roofed Great Hall. And the tall tower rising above the surrounding warehouses and commercial premises is perhaps the most potent surviving symbol of the Victorian civic ideal.

facing page: Croydon Town Hall. During the 19th century Croydon was transformed from a small market town on the London–Brighton road into a substantial suburban centre with over 130,000 inhabitants by 1900. Though joined to London, Croydon retained a strong sense of its distinct identity, which was celebrated by the New Town Hall of 1892–6 (architect Charles Henman), the existing town hall having been demolished as part of a street improvement scheme. Exuberantly neo-Jacobean in style, it contains a public library as well as municipal offices and a council chamber.

1870–1939

The years between the Second Reform Act and the outbreak of the Second World War were the heyday of 'local self-government'. Towns were given increased powers, starting with legislation of 1875, to clear slums and control new housing

development, and local authorities retained much autonomy in the raising and spending of funds for essential services. By 1900 townspeople made up four-fifths of the English population. About half of all town dwellers now lived in conurbations—a word first coined in this period—around London and the great industrial and commercial cities. These amorphous concentrations of people were made up of a network of satellite towns—many of them old villages, market towns, or small industrial towns—grouped around the central core, and here a new town hall could stand out as the most prominent building in an otherwise architecturally undistinguished neighbourhood. This was the case at Croydon, a market town and commuter suburb ten miles south of London whose population in 1900 was larger than that of any provincial town in England a century before. Here the magnificent neo-Jacobean town hall in 1892–6 was built after its much smaller predecessor had been demolished in a street improvement scheme; and it still proclaims the town's distinct identity, despite the proximity of the capital and the virtual reconstruction of the town centre in the 1960s.

Many other towns, especially in the south and Midlands, were meanwhile being drawn into the modern economy, absorbing growing numbers of migrants from the countryside. Here too a town hall could express a burgeoning civic pride, fostered by the growth of local democracy. The Town Hall at Oxford was built in 1893–7, not long after the granting of County Borough status under legislation of 1888, and the architect, H. T. Hare, succeeded in celebrating the self-confidence of a long-established local authority which had only recently begun to emerge from the shadow of an overweening University. By now secular Gothic had gone out of fashion, and Hare adopted an exuberant version of the neo-Jacobean style for the exterior, while resorting to a lavish Continental-inspired Baroque inside. The influence of Baroque architecture in civic building can be seen even more dramatically in the Town Hall (1904–8) at Stockport, part of the Manchester conurbation. This palatial structure, with its Portland stone façade and its tower inspired by Sir Christopher Wren's churches in the City of London, sounds the note of Edwardian civic pride with appropriately Elgarian pomp.

The face of late nineteenth-century government was also represented by the building of new police and fire stations. At Halifax, like many other towns, the police were housed at first in the Town Hall, but in 1900 they acquired their own headquarters, which they shared with the magistrates' court in an imposing new building complete with a campanile. Fire stations were sometimes equally impressive, above all in Manchester, where the terracotta-clad station in Whitworth Street, dating from 1906, contained flats for 32 families and six single firemen, as well as a laundry, gymnasium, billiard room, library, and children's playroom. Smaller police stations and fire stations were also scattered through the suburbs of the larger towns.

Central government legislation gave important new powers to local authorities in the early twentieth century, notably in education and housing. Local School Boards, founded in 1870, were taken over by the local authorities in 1902, and, in the aftermath of the First World War, the Addison and Wheatley Housing Acts of 1919 and 1924 gave central government financial support to local authority housing schemes. In the inter-war period also, many local authorities expanded their boundaries to incorporate newly suburbanized areas, thus increasing their rateable value. New premises were essential to house the growing armies of officials who administered these expanding municipal empires, and,

Scarcroft Road School, York. Designed by the local architect Walter Brierley in 1896, this impressive building rises up out of an area of small terraced houses just to the south of the town's medieval walls. It was built by the local School Board for working-class children who were now subject to compulsory free elementary education. Like the better-known London board schools, it was constructed of brick and consists of a central block housing assembly halls flanked by lower wings for classrooms. The style owes much to the Arts and Crafts movement, of which Brierley was a notable exponent.

while commercial building languished during the Depression, grandiose blocks of municipal offices, many in a chaste and rather frigid neo-Georgian style, began to rise up in larger cities like Birmingham and Manchester alongside the existing Victorian town halls.

Some towns in the south and the Midlands which escaped the worst rigours of the Depression took the opportunity to build completely new civic buildings in the inter-war years. Norwich and Nottingham both acquired new and much larger town halls, each overlooking the ancient market place, Nottingham opting in 1927–9 for a version of English Baroque and Norwich in 1932–8 for a simplified neoclassical idiom inspired by the Town Hall at Stockholm, much admired by English architects of the period. At Southampton, a city which profited from the transatlantic steamer trade, the town hall of 1929–39 forms part of a new and spacious Civic Centre on an open space called the West Marlands to the north of the walled medieval city, with a public hall or Guildhall, law courts, a Library, a School of Art, and an excellent Art Gallery as well as offices for the local functionaries. The architect, E. Berry Webber, adopted a somewhat bland 'stripped classical' style, very popular for public architecture throughout the inter-war period, and the construction of the complex and its associated approach roads hastened a process under which the city's centre of gravity shifted northwards from its ancient core.

The permeation of government into the lives of the urban population in the late nineteenth and early twentieth centuries can be seen especially clearly in education. The direct involvement of the State in the building—as opposed to the subsidizing—of schools began with the Education Act of 1870, under which locally elected School Boards could levy rates and build non-denominational elementary schools to supplement those provided by the voluntary societies. In Nottingham in 1902 there were 94 Board Schools—including the pre-1870 British Schools which had all been taken over by 1892—and 78 denominational schools, of which 64 were run by the Anglicans and the rest by the Roman Catholics. In a passage in Conan Doyle's story 'The Naval Treaty' (1894) Sherlock Holmes hails the new Board Schools—'those big isolated clumps of building rising above the slate'—as 'lighthouses: beacons of the future, capsules with hundreds of bright little seeds in each, out of which will spring the wiser, better England of the future'. And in many inner-city areas the post-1870 Board Schools are, together with Victorian churches, the largest and architecturally the most accomplished buildings, their design and careful detailing offering the promise of higher cultural values to the inhabitants of dingy streets. As E. R. Robson, architect to the London School Board and author of *School Architecture* (1877) wrote: 'School-houses are henceforth to take rank as public buildings, and should be planned and built in a manner befitting their new dignity.' This advice was taken to heart by architects of the calibre of Walter Brierley in York and by J. H. Chamberlain and William Martin in Birmingham. Chamberlain was a devotee of the doctrines of John Ruskin, and his beautifully detailed red-brick schools still enliven many of the drabber parts of the city today.

An important innovation in later Victorian secondary education was the provision of schools for middle-class girls, like the High School for Girls at Bedford (1878–82), funded by the Harpur Trust, an educational charity established in the sixteenth century, and built to the neo-Jacobean designs of Basil Champneys, an architect well known for his work on the first women's colleges of Oxford and Cambridge. After the 1870 Education Act some School Boards also began to establish 'higher grade' or central schools and technical schools in order to offer secondary education to some at least of the children of the more prosperous artisans, and the public provision of secondary education increased after the Education Act of 1902. In Kent alone new secondary girls' schools were opened in nine towns—Bromley, Dartford, Dover, Folkestone, Erith, Ramsgate, Sittingbourne, Tonbridge, and Tunbridge Wells—between 1902 and 1906, and new boys' schools were opened in comparable numbers. These establishments, many of them offering an academic curriculum on grammar-school lines, were usually set, like the Bedford High School, among playing fields in the suburbs, but their architecture was usually neo-Georgian. Such schools, and their inter-war successors, have provided the setting of secondary education for many English adolescents down to the present day.

Higher, including university, education began to make a significant impact on the urban landscape outside Oxford and Cambridge only in the last third of the nineteenth century. It was then that the first civic or red-brick universities came into being, some of them growing out of earlier institutions like Mason College in Birmingham. The University of Birmingham received its charter in 1900, with Joseph Chamberlain—then Colonial Secretary—as its Chancellor; whereupon it moved out of the city centre to the southern edge of Edgbaston, Birmingham's middle-class suburb par excellence. Here in 1900–9 Webb and Bell erected what were intended to be the first of a series of massive quasi-Byzantine buildings radiating from a central campanile: a bold conception which remains impressive even in its incomplete state. A suburban parkland setting was also chosen for the 'palace of education' erected by University College, Nottingham, out of funds supplied by Jesse Boot, founder of the chain of chemists which bears his name. Work started in 1922 to the neo-Georgian designs of Percy Morley Horder, and the college became a university in its own right in 1948, since when it has expanded greatly on the same site. At Bristol, by contrast, the University remained on a site close to the city centre, from which it expanded piecemeal, culminating in 1919–25 in the erection of the magnificent Wills Tower—one of the last examples of secular Gothic in an English town centre—designed by the local architect George Oatley.

Most higher education in the nineteenth century took place outside the universities. Mechanics' Institutes, the first of which was founded in Chester in 1810, offered part-time adult education in many towns, especially in the industrial Midlands and north, and above all in the West Riding of Yorkshire, where many were rebuilt on a more impressive scale in the second half of the century. Some towns also erected Schools of Art, either out of private funds, like the splendid red-brick Gothic Birmingham College of Art and Design (Chamberlain and Martin 1881–5), or with the help of the local authorities following the Technical Instruction Act of 1889.

Libraries formed another important part of the crusade to inculcate a culture of self-improvement among the Victorian urban population. Subscription libraries for middle-class recreational or intellectual purposes existed in many towns in the eighteenth century, and more were built in the early nineteenth century; but it was only with the passing of the Public Libraries Act of 1850, allowing local authorities to provide libraries funded by the rates, that the first free public libraries open to all were provided in the larger cities. A massive new Central Library was built in Birmingham in 1863–5, and Chamberlain and Martin went on to design a series of beautifully detailed suburban branch libraries such as those at Spring Hill (1891–3) and Small Heath (1893), the latter on a triangular site which also includes a Public Baths. No clearer illustration can be found of the vitalizing late Victorian and Edwardian ideal of *mens sana in corpore sano*.

Following the examples of schools and other public institutions, hospitals were increasingly placed in suburban locations where space was plentiful and fresh air more likely to be found than in grimy city centres. Thus the 800-bed Queen Elizabeth Hospital, Birmingham, was built in leafy Edgbaston (1933–8) and was composed of minimally detailed steel-framed multi-storey blocks designed on a rigidly symmetrical plan and grouped around courtyards to admit the necessary air and light. Buildings like this breathed a modernistic air into the public architecture of the 1930s, and their presence helped to impose the values and demands of mass society onto what had once been quiet and prosperous middle-class Victorian suburbs: a movement which was to accelerate after the Second World War.

As public authorities took on more responsibility for providing the cultural and moral infrastructure of urban life, the role of the churches became correspondingly smaller. Yet paradoxically some of the finest of all Anglican churches date from the late Victorian and Edwardian years, from the magnificent cathedrals at Truro (1880–1910) and Liverpool, begun in 1904 on a site overlooking St James's Cemetery, down to countless churches in the suburbs. There was also great activity among the Nonconformists. Starting in the 1860s the Baptists, the Methodists, and, to a lesser extent, the Congregationalists began building large town-centre churches, often called Tabernacles or Central Halls, designed for revivalist preaching, with space for social clubs below the main auditorium. Many of these buildings are exuberantly detailed, and several boasted prominent towers and spires, like the Victoria Hall in Norfolk Street in the centre of Sheffield (1908) and the Methodist Central Hall at the northern end of the recently created Corporation Street in Birmingham (1903–4). Nonconformist churches also continued to be built in small towns like Henley-on-Thames, Oxfordshire, where Sir Frank Crisp, a London solicitor who had recently built an ostentatious house on the edge of the town, built a striking new Congregationalist church in 1907 in commemoration of his grandfather, a Suffolk man who was imprisoned in 1836 for refusing to pay church rates.

Nonconformist church building flourished until the First World War, but in the inter-war years it was the Anglicans and, to a lesser extent, the Roman Catholics who made the greatest impact. Their parish churches are the only monumental buildings to be found in the outer suburbs of many towns like Wellingborough, where Ninian Comper's exquisitely beautiful church of St Mary (1908–30) asserts the enchantments of the Middle Ages in the most unpromising surroundings. Buildings of this size and stature acted as both a counterweight and a reproach to the insidious values of consumerism and mass entertainment represented by those quintessential inter-war types of building, the cinema and the improved public house.

facing page: Central Plymouth from the air, looking east, 1967. A major dockyard town, Plymouth was an important target for German bombers in World War II, and the central commercial area was devastated in 1941. A plan for rebuilding was prepared by the City Engineer, J. Paton Watson, and the town-planner, Patrick Abercrombie, in 1943, and was carried out largely as intended, in the decade after 1945. No attempt was made to follow the existing street lines; instead a new Beaux Arts*-inspired plan was adopted, with a broad east–west street (Royal Parade) bisected by an even wider pedestrian street (Armada Way) leading from the railway station south to Plymouth Hoe, out of this picture to the right. The Guildhall, a Gothic Revival building of 1870–4 (architects Norman and Hine), can be seen in the right middle-distance; just beyond is the medieval parish church of St Andrew, rebuilt in 1949–57 after extensive war damage.*

1939–2000

In 1939 most provincial town centres retained their Victorian character largely intact. J. B. Priestley had remarked in *English Journey* (1934) that the flavour of modern Britain was best savoured not in the centres of the great industrial towns but in the outer suburbs traversed by new roads and dotted with new electric-powered factories. As suburbanization gathered pace between the wars, the central areas stagnated, their blackened public buildings either ignored or held up to ridicule by architects, reformers, and *bien pensants* attracted by ideas of a cleaner, more hygienic future. And as those who could afford it fled into the suburbs or even the countryside, attracted by arcadian visions, the vital link between the urban merchants, industrialists, and professionals who had preached the 'civic gospel' in the nineteenth century, and the cities from which their wealth derived, began to fray.

By 1980 most English town centres had changed drastically, and in some cases out of all recognition. The initial catalyst was the Nazi blitz of 1940–2 which, by reducing large areas to rubble, set in train a process of rebuilding along what were believed to be more rational lines. The lack of available funds during the immediate post-war era meant that rebuilding was delayed, usually until the 1950s, and the character of the rebuilding varied according to the extent of the damage and the preoccupations of the local authorities whose powers were enhanced by the Town and Country Planning Act of 1947. But there were certain common themes among the architects and city engineers who drew up the plans: the need for better roads, and above all for a Ring Road around the town centre; the introduction of pedestrian shopping precincts; and the need to maintain population densities within the existing urban area so as to prevent the uncontrolled sprawl of the 1930s.

These concerns are epitomized in the rebuilding of the city centres of Coventry and Plymouth, two of the very few instances in which the Luftwaffe presented the post-war planners with a virtual tabula rasa. In Plymouth, a city of 220,800 people in 1939, the plan, framed in 1943, envisaged a new layout of streets inside an inner ring road, with a main east–west street bisected by a broad pedestrian avenue leading from the railway station to the Hoe, famed in national history and myth. At Coventry, too, the layout of the new shopping centre was unrelated to the older street pattern, but here the shops were arranged in a single traffic-free pedestrian precinct—one of the first of its kind in the country—aligned on the surviving medieval spire of the blitzed Cathedral. Both schemes were carried out during the 1950s, after the lifting of post-war development controls, and in both cases the bland and now distinctly faded-looking low-rise architecture reflects the egalitarian and anti-monumental impulses expressed by the City Architect of Bristol in 1941, when he called for 'a good, simple and dignified architecture, cutting out all unnecessary "frills", and spending our money on good, sound hygienic ideas'. This desire, shared by the intelligentsia as well as by town hall officials, to sever links with a discredited past, explains the creation of such banal monuments of post-war public taste as the Broadmead shopping centre at Bristol (completed 1960). It is only rarely, as in Basil Spence's new Anglican Cathedral in Coventry (1956–62)—one of the few genuinely popular public buildings of this era—that a more individualist and creative note is sounded.

The public face of the post-war urban landscape can be experienced in undiluted form in the new towns designed, under the 1947 Act, to absorb much of the urban population displaced from the older cities by slum clearance and the relocation of industry. They were characterized by rigidly applied zoning, pedestrianized shopping centres, and the liberal provision of roads. The tone was set at Stevenage (1957–8), whose pedestrianized central square lies at the heart of the shopping area, enlivened by a clock tower, fountain, and abstract sculptural group: features deemed to be more in tune with the *Zeitgeist* than the frock-coated worthies on pedestals who preside over the public spaces of many Victorian towns. The surrounding buildings—an Arts and Sports Centre, police station, magistrates' courts, College of Further Education, and railway station—are of the clean-cut variety characteristic of the early years of English modernism, featuring large expanses of glass curtain walling. The ensemble proclaims the welfarist ideals shared by most local authority planners and architects in the post-war era.

Elsewhere work continued on the reconstruction of innumerable town centres, even those unaffected by bombing. Local authorities were encouraged by central government to work in partnership with private developers who had been accumulating town centre sites, often at very low prices, ever since the end of the War. With the removal of development controls by the Conservatives in 1954, they were in a position to embark on the largest commercial assault on town centres for fifty years. The role of the local authorities was to provide the roads and car parks needed both to service the shops and offices and to enable the growing number of car-owning voters in the suburbs to exercise what was almost universally believed to be their right to free movement to the city centre. With the number of motor vehicles doubling in the 1950s, and both population and traffic projections moving upwards, it was hard to counter the argument of the influential planner Colin Buchanan that 'If we are to have any chance of living at peace with the motor car, we shall need a different kind of city' (*Traffic in Towns*, 1963).

The final impetus to the rebuilding of English cities came from the architectural profession. The vision of a totally redeveloped city centre, with high glass-clad buildings set amid abundant open space, had seduced radical British architects ever since the publication of Le Corbusier's *The City of Tomorrow* in 1929. By the early 1960s the architectural avant-garde had become the new establishment, and modernist architects found ample employment from public authorities and commercial developers. Not only was modern architecture new and glamorous (for a time), it also had the advantages of cheapness—especially when the lack of carved detail is taken into account—and speed and ease of construction: something which was especially important at a time of full employment and rapidly rising wages.

The results of this alliance of local politicians, property developers, planning officers, road engineers, and architects can be seen in almost every English town. Some, like Worcester and Derby, suffered especially grievously, but few escaped damage on a scale far outweighing that of the Second World War. Even in Oxford, where much of the land was owned by the fiercely independent colleges of the University, the working-class district of St Ebbes, on the fringe of the central shopping area, was flattened in the 1960s to make way for a barren landscape of roads, car parks, a shopping centre, and an office block for the County Council. Meanwhile the resident population was rehoused on a new council estate at Blackbird Leys on the periphery of the city, reinforcing that tendency towards spatial segregation which had been a feature of urban development throughout England since the early nineteenth century.

The building of new roads was often accompanied by the construction of offices for the local authorities who planned them. Thus the skyline of Aylesbury, a market town with only 51,000 inhabitants in 1991, is dominated by a brutal twelve-storey concrete office tower reared up in 1963–6 to house the employees of the Buckinghamshire County Council. Edward Heath's local government reforms of 1974 were followed by the building of yet more offices for the growing number of local authority employees. At Reading a new block of civic offices was erected next to an inner ring road in 1976, and the nineteenth-century Town Hall in the Market Place was lucky to escape demolition. Then a massive new Shire Hall for Berkshire was built next to the M4 motorway on the southern fringe of the town, only to become redundant in 1998 when the County Council was abolished under legislation splitting the county into 'unitary authorities'. Bland and impersonal, buildings like these witness both to the growing power of officialdom in the modern world and to the collapse of the tradition of enlightened architectural patronage by local authorities in the post-war era.

A major part in the evolution of the urban landscape in the 1960s and 1970s was played by the agencies of the Welfare State: the National Health Service and the Local Education Authorities. Vast hospitals were built, both on the urban fringe, like Powell and Moya's Princess Margaret Hospital near the M4 at Swindon of 1957–9, and in more central locations like the massive, monolithic Royal Hallamshire Hospital at Sheffield of 1948–79. The impact of such buildings on their surroundings is as great as that of any Victorian hospital or workhouse. School building also expanded, especially after the decision by Wilson's Labour government (1964–70) to pursue comprehensive education; and dour, flat-roofed

The Magistrates' Court, Milton Keynes. The central area of the new city of Milton Keynes was laid out on a hilltop site with broad streets intersecting each other at right angles, flanked by low buildings. To the north of the central axis is a group of public buildings including the Magistrates' Court, designed by John Stewart of the Buckinghamshire County Architects Department and built in 1989–91. Its smooth surfaces and welcoming aspect illustrate the widespread 'post-modern' rejection of the brutal starkness that had typified much public architecture of the 1960s and 70s.

Bauhaus-like comprehensive schools stranded amid acres of grass and tarmac can be seen in every English town above a certain size. Elementary (primary) schools were also built in large numbers, but they were usually smaller and more humane in character.

There was also a large expansion of higher education in the aftermath of the Robbins Report of 1963. New universities were established, usually on the fringes of ancient cathedral cities or in open countryside, and were generously funded by central governments inspired by Harold Wilson's vision of a future shaped by the 'white heat of technology'. Denys Lasdun's buildings for the University of East Anglia at Norwich (1962–8) attracted much attention for their architectural originality, those of the University of York (Robert Matthew, Johnson-Marshall, and partners, begun 1962) for their sensitive integration into the already existing parkland landscape. Much building was also carried out by the older 'red-brick' universities and the numerous Colleges of Technology and Further Education; they were often situated near the central core of the towns they served, and expansion here meant building upwards, as in James Stirling's engineering building at the University of Leicester (1959–63), which became an icon for the younger generation of British architects.

The assumptions which underlay the post-war rebuilding of English towns came under fierce and often justified attack in the 1970s. Some towns still bear the marks of abandoned inner ring roads and first-floor pedestrian routes, and many old buildings scheduled for demolition before the economic collapse following the oil crisis of 1973 gained a reprieve and are now cherished parts of the historic urban landscape. Modernist architecture itself retreated in the face of a new eclecticism in which the styles of the past were revived with various degrees of seriousness and success. In 1973–8, the London Borough of Hillingdon erected a Civic Centre close to the old market town of Uxbridge, already engulfed by the suburban sprawl of outer north-west London. Its red-brick facing, its irregular, picturesque outline, and above all its steep-pitched roofs demonstrated a new concern for detail and appropriateness of scale to surroundings. They also indicate a characteristically late twentieth-century search for meaning through recognizable symbols: something which may be interpreted as a reaction to the increasingly deracinated character of modern urban society. Thus the Meadowhall shopping centre built on the site of an abandoned steelworks at Sheffield is crowned by a metal and glass dome which evokes the heyday of vanished Victorian industry.

The spirit of the contemporary English town, strongly present in places like Swindon and Basingstoke, can be captured in its most unadulterated form at Milton Keynes, the largest and most recent of the New Towns. Here the core of the city centre, laid out on a grid plan and serving a population of over 160,000 people, is taken up by a glazed, modernist covered shopping centre of 1973–9—the modern equivalent of the market place of a medieval town. To the west are offices and a visually rather ineffective domed church for ecumenical use, while public buildings—council offices, Magistrates' Courts, the Public Library—are strung out to the north, with leisure buildings and more offices to the south. Housing estates sprawl over the landscape outside the central area, separated by wide roads, each with its own 'neighbourhood centre', sometimes incorporating an existing village, sometimes a group of new buildings—often in a cosy neo-vernacular or postmodernist mode—comprising shops, primary school, health centre, and occasionally a church. The architectural mood, especially outside the city centre, is cool and understated, resulting in an urban landscape which is inward-looking, fragmented, and unassertive. This is perhaps a reflection of the prevailing values of urban England at the close of the twentieth century.

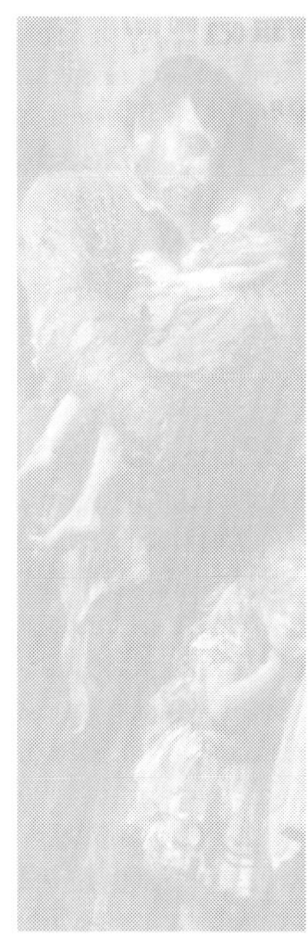

12 English Towns in the Creative Imagination

Stana Nenadic

Art as Understanding

Art as a product of the creative imagination is important for our understanding of the world we inhabit. Great art transcends the specifics of time and place and addresses the constants of the human condition. Popular and ephemeral art provides an eloquent commentary on the societies that produce and consume it. The creative imagination as expressed through art contains within it what has been described as a 'pre-scientific immediacy'—a capacity to say something of importance that cannot be fully expressed in any other form. The message is not always on the surface, but it does exist.

Art—visual, written, heard, or performed—is a valuable and succinct device for understanding the impact of towns in English cultural life, especially from the later seventeenth century when the rate of town growth became so rapid and the implications of new ways of urban living so complex that it was almost impossible to express a response in any other way. The phenomenon of urbanization was one that ordinary men and women struggled to understand. The speed and fluidity of changes within towns in the past three hundred years have constantly outrun the human capacity to make sense of it all. It was easy to know—or believe you knew—a town when you could walk from one end to the other in less than half an hour, or when you could observe the whole from a nearby hillside and recognize the principal personalities of the place because you saw them daily in the streets. This was normal in an England of small towns before the early eighteenth century. People mainly lived in the countryside and they knew that urban living was different. But most imagined that they comprehended the phenomenon well enough to be not too perplexed by towns. This was to change over the course of the eighteenth century with the vast expansion of London and the proliferation of large provincial centres, to become an intense preoccupation giving rise to a remarkable creative response.

The growth of large towns inspired the creative imagination by evoking deep feelings of ambiguity. The formula was a simple one. Towns and cities are composed of buildings, awesome and appalling in equal measure. Towns and cities are centres of people—people in the mass are a source of entertainment and generate innovation, they also provide anonymity. To be lost in the crowd is both threatening and liberating. Towns and cities are centres of power—power is exciting and power is corrupting. Not even today, after many generations of urban living, can it be said that we find the town, both in its concrete reality and in the abstract, a phenomenon with which we are entirely comfortable. The urban landscape has always generated a sense of paradox and continues to inspire the creative imagination.

Given the early and rapid urbanization of England, it is not surprising that artistic and literary creativity has been so dominated by a preoccupation with towns and with the contrast between town and country as binary opposites in a spectrum of human experience. Though most Englishmen did not live in towns before the mid-nineteenth century and few had the leisure to indulge in sustained creative speculations, the potent image of the city had been well entrenched in the popular imagination through religion. The Bible and in particular the Old Testament provided a basis for powerful imaginative engagement with towns, with its images of sin and corruption in the cities of Sodom and Gomorrah and the idealization of Jerusalem as a place of special sanctity. Early popular chronicles in English, such as Chaucer's *Canterbury Tales* (*c.*1387) linking London to the religious heart of England, present another image of the town—as a place of movement, noise, and festivity; a vivid canvas on which a wide spectrum of human behaviour is acted out. Shakespeare developed similar themes in his settings of London and a handful of provincial towns such as Windsor, which were more likely to be places of comedy than the exotic or tragic, peopled by characters that exemplified 'Englishness'—the prosaic, the foolish, the quick-witted, and sometimes the charlatan.

In post-Reformation England, Bunyan's *Pilgrim's Progress* (1678) echoed biblical themes in its striking images of sin and salvation in the City of Destruction and the Heavenly City, where 'behold the City shone like the sun, the streets also were paved with gold, and in them walked many men with crowns on their heads, palms in their hands, and golden harps to sing praises withal'. After the Bible, *Pilgrim's Progress* was the book most likely to be owned and read by ordinary people and it seems likely that the image of London that emerged at much the same time—and was greatly advanced by creative representation in the early eighteenth century—owes much to Bunyan's conceptualization of 'destruction' and 'heavenly glory' as the twin attributes of the idealized city.

City of Destruction

A visual and secular interpretation of the city as a place of problems and sin was first provided by William Hogarth, with his rapidly pirated and therefore widely available engravings of scenes from London life. *The South Sea Scheme*, first published in 1721 in the wake of the financial fiasco of the same name, provided a set of images that were later reworked into popular print sets such as *The Harlot's Progress* (1732), *The Rake's Progress* (1733–5), and *Marriage à la Mode* (1743–5). These were Hogarth's self-termed, 'modern moral subjects'. In emblematic form *The South Sea Scheme* represents a City of London street, with St Paul's in the background, peopled with corrupt clergymen and whores, pickpockets, hypocrites, and dupes, riding the merry-go-round of life and all engaged in the excitement of financial speculation, which is overtly connected with moral corruption and sexual excess.

Hogarth's London was a place of venality, where human flesh could be bought and sold, where men and women could pretend to be what they were not and where social hierarchy was perpetually undermined. Hogarth's London attracted and then corrupted the young. Unable to resist the lure of money and sex, they went mad, were punished, and died of dreadful diseases. There were more prisons and hospitals and scenes of incarceration in Hogarth than in any other English artist of the eighteenth century; and in the popular imagination, these were linked to London. Early eighteenth-century fiction was similarly preoccupied with the dangerous allure and corrupting power of the metropolis. Daniel Defoe's *Moll Flanders* (1722) and *Roxana* (1724) chart the rise and fall of women who have to live by their wits in the city. Though each of the eponymous heroines aspires to be honourably settled in marriage, their only route to this is through trickery and the sale of themselves. It is not surprising that the author of these novels was so preoccupied with the moral character of commerce in all its guises. His *Complete English Tradesman* (1726) is an ethical manual on how to

'City of Destruction', with its biblical overtones, has been a common theme in artistic representations of London. It is a place of corruption, sexual licence, and madness, as portrayed in this satire on the financial scandal which rocked the capital in the early 18th century.

behave and survive in the city for those middle groups in society that emerged with the rise of towns—merchants and shopkeepers. These were the types of people that purchased his novels and hung prints by Hogarth on the walls of their houses. As businessmen as well as artists, Hogarth and Defoe were acquainted with the perils of commercial life London. Hogarth's father was imprisoned for debt and Defoe went bankrupt in spectacular style. For people like them, the social hierarchy was constantly under challenge in a city. Fear of chicanery peppered their experience; financial failure was an ever-present nightmare to parallel the dreams of fortune that cities seemed to offer. Of course, people in the countryside made money and sometimes went bankrupt—but the root of this was trade in the towns and the dominating presence of London. Evoking such themes allowed the popular imagination to accommodate and resolve some of the major dilemmas of evolving urban life. The fact that both the prints of Hogarth and Defoe's novels were swiftly pirated—a type of business fraud that Hogarth sought to prevent—or were translated into popular stage plays, is testimony to the widespread demand for art on such themes.

In the late eighteenth and early nineteenth centuries, English Romanticism fuelled the rejection of towns. Its theorists and popularizers expressed an antipathy to some of the starker tendencies of contemporary life, seeking refuge in an idealized past of humane social relationships and solace in the natural world. Wordsworth and Blake condemned the crushing effects of urbanism on the human psyche and they, along with other poets of the age, launched the first attacks on industrial technology, new commercialism, and scientific rationalism. The cultivation of emotions through artistic creativity and through direct engagement with nature was their antidote to these ills. They sowed the seeds of a deeply rooted aesthetic preference for the unpeopled, rural landscape over the townscape, adding a new layer to an existing distaste for certain aspects of town life. Unwittingly, they also spawned romantic tourism as an industry that would eventually imperil the very thing they celebrated and they stimulated such demand for art in its various forms that it also became a mass-production industry.

Anxiety arising from the destructive character of life in the metropolis has remained a dominant strand in the English creative imagination to the present day. It came to be associated with the evocation of particular urban archetypes—predators and the streetwise, wry observers and eccentrics, the alienated and the victim—all serving to stress the belief that as society became more urban, the individual increasingly stood alone. Urbanization and individualism, two characteristics of the evolving middle ranks, developed hand-in-hand. Samuel Richardson's *Clarissa* (1749) contains the first bourgeois heroine in English literature, who is cast adrift from her family, to make her way in the world, because she won't marry to suit their commercial ambitions. She is duped by Lovelace, an aristocratic villain at home in the brothels and gaming dens of London, who then rapes her in a London boarding house. Even a city church fails to provide her with refuge. Clarissa is not a fool and she is a woman of virtue, but she is also a victim because she is not familiar with the ways of the world which are the ways of the city. English literature thereafter has many such victims and many such predatory Lovelace characters employed to define urban situations of threat and destruction.

Anthony Trollope in *The Way We Live Now* (1874) captured a particular flavour of metropolitan commercial corruption with its sexual undertones, as marriages are made to suit financial ends. To this he added another feature stressing the 'foreignness' of many of the figures that peopled the metropolis. Be it American or European, the foreignness of foreigners in nineteenth-century cities gave them licence to behave outside the rules. They were unknowable, alien, and therefore dangerous. The financier Melmotte in *The Way We Live Now* is a villain whose villainy rests on knowing how to manipulate the institutions and ambitions of the city. His lineage and nationality are deliberately obscured,

Applicants for Admission to a Casual Ward *by Luke Fildes. Social realist paintings of the mid-19th century, which were largely for middle-class consumption, evoked the pitiable life of the poor in great cities, but in terms that also suggested the tenacity of human emotions and community.*

so increasing his evil potency. All we know is that he has lived in the great centres of the world—New York, Paris, Hamburg, and London—and thus he is a villain on an international scale. This was a neat device on the part of the author, responding to an increasingly xenophobic English popular imagination, for transferring the blame for the corrupt and dangerous state of urban society onto the 'other'. As ethnic diversity came to be a more conspicuous part of big city life in England from the second half of the nineteenth century, anxiety about the city

could be dissipated through a new focus on archetypal alien figures, be they Irish or Jews, or Blacks in the twentieth century.

The visual imagination has in many respects paralleled the literary, developing similar themes in response to urbanization. The tone having been set by Hogarth, who exploited the power of the popular print, the language of visual metaphor became more complex in the nineteenth century with the development of mass printing and photography. Hogarth's moral satires on themes such as 'Gin Lane' were echoed in the nineteenth century in the work of George Cruickshank, in particular in his print series on the perils of drink for that central Victorian institution, the family. This was so popular it was translated into a *tableau vivant* for the stage. The grim implications of life in the city found striking visual expression in the 1870s through Gustave Doré's black and white engraved images of the tortured underworld existence of the poor and through photography, notably the publication of *The Street Life of London* (1877). Largely produced for a middle-class audience, these photographs of the capital were paralleled by similar collections depicting other big cities. Though claiming 'documentary' and therefore realist credentials, photographs of this type were always posed to achieve an impact.

The same calculated effect was what the fine arts also bid to achieve from the mid-nineteenth century. Thus the social panoramas of William Powell Frith, embracing rich and poor in conventional urban settings such as railway station or street crossing, and the sentimental portraits of street children by William Daniels and A. E. Mulready, or the urban genre scenes by Thomas Faed. All sought to interpret social difference and extremes of poverty and disadvantage for a middle class who viewed these aspects of urban life as uncomfortable and uncharted territory, darker than remotest Africa. The most forceful single painting of this type was *Applicants for Admission to a Casual Ward* by Luke Fildes, exhibited at the Royal Academy in 1874 and widely engraved thereafter. It was appraised as an honest account of the sordid reality of the city and it became an icon for the problems of the age, translated into urban types within a formulaic notion of lost community—the orphan, the abandoned mother and baby, the wretched drunkard, the elderly father seeking a lost child, and the kindly policeman who tries to keep the wretched mass under control. To our eyes it seems sentimental and 'Victorian'. To the Victorians, it conveyed a powerful truth.

The implied realism of much Victorian art and literature was part of a deliberate attempt to understand the impact of the city on human existence, arising in parallel with the emerging science of social investigation. This realism was manipulated and the documentary form—even in photography—was a visual style reflective of the age and suggestive of a middle-class psychological ambivalence: at home in the city, yet frightened of the urban poor; and desiring to understand and resolve real problems, yet effectively evading them by aestheticizing the phenomena. As the work of Gustave Doré testifies, notably his illustrated book *London: A Pilgrimage* (1872), there was an underlying sinister quality to the urban scene and this was a theme that assumed further prominence towards the end of the century. Doré's city was dark and threatening, edging beyond reality into the supernatural. It was the same space occupied by mythologized figures such as Jack the Ripper and other contemporary fiends, who were the stock subjects of street ballads and 'penny dreadfuls', with their tales of terrible crimes and punishments that found a massive audience among the urban working classes.

facing page: The sinister underbelly of 19th-century urban life, stripped of all sentimentality, is powerfully evoked in such stark images of the poor. Though sensational in his approach, Doré relied on a 'documentary' impact to convey his message.

The more respectable end of this literary response was the sensation fiction of the 1860s and 1870s, best illustrated by the work of Wilkie Collins, with its emphasis on what Henry James called 'those most mysterious of mysteries, the mysteries which are at our doors ... the terrors of the cheerful country-house

The Fictional Detective as Modern Urban Hero

STANA NENADIC

The crisis of modernity in nineteenth-century England was spawned by large technocratic cities, but was manifested in a social preoccupation with the non-technocratic urban underworld of corruption, vice, and intractable poverty. The modern city of the popular imagination, as famously illustrated by the artist Gustave Doré, seethes and suffocates under the weight of human misery. Civilized life is precarious. There are stark distinctions between day and night, good and bad, rich and poor. In the age of 'Jack the Ripper', rationality and the great advances in science and wealth seemed powerless to counter the mystery and dangers of the city. Criminals and profligates were the cause of growing neurotic obsession. This was particularly true in London and among middle-class women, whose hard-won freedoms were often underpinned by anxiety over the sexual threats that they faced when alone in the city. Newspaper surveys and social inquiries such as that of Charles Booth in the late 1880s, seemed to confirm the deep-held fears of moral degeneration and crime flowing from the slums to pollute the respectable world.

These anxieties called into existence a powerful fictional archetype whose purpose was to resolve the dangers of the city. First through novels and magazines, later through film and television, the urban detective, male or female, amateur and professional, became the 'hero' of the modern age. One of the earliest models of the type was Mr Bucket, the stout, middle-aged police inspector created by Dickens in *Bleak House* (1853). An enigmatic figure who occupies the dens of the poor with the same authority as the drawing rooms of the rich, Bucket is ordinary in appearance, yet the effect he has on those around him is extraordinary. With his emotional detachment and intellectual brilliance he sees into documents, places, and souls. Conan Doyle's Sherlock Holmes, introduced in *A Study in Scarlet* (1887), is exemplar of the amateur detective fighting the forces of evil. Like Bucket, he can resolve the problems of the city because these problems are personalized in the form of identifiable malefactors. Not surprisingly, the villains of these popular novels largely conformed to the criminal archetypes of the popular imagination. The London they inhabit is the London of Doré, with the bright open streets of the rich and respectable uncomfortably close to the dark and dangerous underworld of crime. Holmes is a man of the modern world, able to slip effortlessly from one sphere to another by disguise. A super-rationalist, he is abreast of the latest in science and technology, but also suffers the torments of his own fractured psyche. The contradictions of Holmes the man are in many respects the contradictions of the modern city.

Class issues are always close to the surface in detective fiction, providing a mirror to the class dynamic that underpins many problems of modern cities. Police officers like Bucket and his heirs are mainly drawn from the lower middle class. Amateur sleuths like Holmes and his numerous successors, are from a higher social group—gentlemen and sometimes ladies of leisure. The aristocratic inter-war detective-hero Lord Peter Wimsey—the invention of Dorothy L. Sayers—occupies the same social sphere as Bertie Wooster, his contemporary in literature, though the self-effacing wit and metropolitan ennui of the former hides an urge to do good in the world. Where amateur and professional investigate the same crime, the amateurs like Holmes and Wimsey invariably have a better understanding of the criminal mind. This fictional convention reflects a deep-seated and conservative English cultural attachment to the social virtues of the elite. The benefits that were believed to flow from paternalistic relationships between rich and poor had, of course, been undermined by the growth of large and technocratic cities.

Many authors of detective fiction have been scholars who have taken an intellectual delight in the complexity of the crimes they invent. With privileged social backgrounds and superior understanding, their fictional detectives are at home in university towns, especially 'the ancient and noble city of Oxford', which, according to crime writer Edmund Crispin, 'is, of all the towns of England, the likeliest progenitor of unlikely events and persons'. Harriet Vane, the heroine of Dorothy L. Sayers and the eventual wife of Lord Peter Wimsey—introduced in *Strong Poison* (1930)—is, as was her creator, an Oxford-educated Bloomsbury bluestocking who writes crime fiction. In *Gaudy Night* (1935), which revolves around a college reunion, Sayers created an Oxford where murderous malice provides a sinister slant on the educated elite. With gentlemanly leisure a growing anachronism in the second half of the twentieth century, the new breed of amateur sleuth is often an academic. Professor Gervase Fen, the invention of Edmund Crispin, is an Oxford don with Holmes-like eccentricities, who applies his powerful intellectual skills, in such novels as *The Moving Toy Shop* (1946), to uncovering mysterious crimes both in and out of college. Dr Loretta Lawson, a lecturer in English at the University of London, is a young female addition to the galaxy of scholar-detectives, making her first appearance in Joan Smith's *A Masculine Ending* (1986) which is also partly set in Oxford.

The dark undercurrent of civilized life in genteel scholarly communities has also been the dominant theme of Colin Dexter's *Inspector Morse* mysteries, made popular through television in the 1980s. Like many successful detective heroes, Morse stands on the margins of the urban world that he inhabits, the better to understand its problems and resolve them. A professional policeman of uncertain social background, scholarly in his inclinations and brilliant in his reasoning, Morse continues the line of psychologically flawed detective heroes, not only fighting crime but fighting his superiors in the police force that employs him. Anxieties generated by corruption in the system of law and order, especially in big cities, have become yet another twist in the crisis of modernism to be addressed by fictional detectives. Detective Chief Inspector Jane Tennison, heroine of the *Prime Suspect* television series in the 1990s, written by Lynda La Plante, is hard drinking and promiscuous, more macho than the men in the brutal masculine world she inhabits; yet, by investigating crime and resolving the evils of the city which include the crimes of her colleagues, she fulfils the same role in the popular imagination of today as Sherlock Holmes in Victorian London.

Women have been prominent in detective fiction, reflecting the fact that they have always been a large part of the authorship and audience. In the inter-war years, Agatha Christie's Miss Marple, introduced in *The Murder at the Vicarage* (1930), was the most famous of a small army of female amateur detectives, mostly conveyed to a mystery-hungry public through stories in magazines for women and girls. These mainly churchgoing spinster aunts and retired governesses of unimpeachable character were the unlikely vanguard for a feminist appropriation of the power to see into the criminal mind and redress great wrongs through the application of reasoning and science. Recent women detectives, of which there is a growing band, are less likely to be 'ladies' than those of the past and have assumed the male characteristics of fractured psyche and problematic private lives, yet they serve the same purpose in empowering a group who have often felt threatened by modern urban life. In an age where cities are perceived to be dangerous, middle-brow, middle-aged, middle England sleeps more easily at night from knowing that Sherlock Holmes or Jane Tennison are out there, somewhere, in pursuit of crime.

The cerebral Morse, played by John Thaw, and his trusty sergeant Lewis (Kevin Whatley). The Carlton TV Inspector Morse *series used Oxford, dominated by colleges, pubs, and the river, as a living set.*

and the busy London lodgings', which often assumed a documentary style and found a wide audience through magazine serialization and performance on the stage. Sensation fiction and its demotic equivalents spawned three fictional genres that have remained popular—detective and science fiction and novels of the supernatural.

The mixture in an urban setting of the sinister, science, and detection looms large in Robert Louis Stevenson's *The Strange Case of Dr Jekyll and Mr Hyde* (1886) which is set in London. Bram Stoker's *Dracula* (1897) brings an additional dimension of perverted and exploitative sexuality to an account of the evil and supernatural potential that underpins modern society. Made known by repeated interpretations in cinema and television, the Yorkshire fishing town of Whitby is ever associated in the popular imagination with the landing place of Dracula on English soil, arriving by boat at night in the guise of a great dog, and rushing up the steps to the ancient Abbey to take refuge in an unhallowed grave by day and seek out his victims by night. Images of the 'beast' in London—at the heart of civilized and rational society—thread through the narrative and have been repeated in numerous twentieth-century stories of the supernatural.

Heavenly City

The city as problem has been a dominating paradigm within the English creative imagination. Yet, as society became used to large cities and the shock of the new gave way to familiarity, there emerged an alternative set of urban narratives with comic potential and affectionate resonance that signalled an ability to graft onto the city the reassuring structures of stable family and idealized community. William Thackeray's *Vanity Fair* (1848), published at about the same time as the English urban population first exceeded the rural, marks that transition. It is a tale of an opportunistic society, corrupt and banal in equal measure, mostly based in and around London. Villains and victims are there aplenty, but the central figure—Becky Sharp—though she claims from the outset 'I'm no angel', is portrayed with affection. We applaud her resourcefulness as an honest underdog who thrives on her wits. In *Vanity Fair*, the city is folly, but not evil. It is an enjoyable human spectacle; humane and sometimes heavenly.

Dickens produced a whole repertory company of affectionate urban archetypes, spanning the spectrum of mainly London society. These people are well adapted to an urban environment, often servicing its needs, frequently eccentric yet always comfortably familiar. Many of these characters were, and have remained, the wry observers of urban life—direct heirs to Chaucer and the court fools of Shakespeare—moulded by their environment but also transcending it. Their lives might be struggling and mean, but they possess, as did the author, an understanding of the city and its ways and by association an understanding of the human psyche. Sam Weller, the manservant in *The Pickwick Papers* (1837) began the tradition and Boffin the 'Golden Dustman' or Jenny Wren, the crippled dolls' clothes-maker in *Our Mutual Friend* (1865) are part of the same family some thirty years on. Even today, these literary characters occupy a privileged place in the popular imagination. This is partly due to the powerful use of illustration. Our image of nineteenth-century London was created by the first illustrators of Dickens and Thackeray, made available to a wide public through

serialization or contemporary theatrical adaptations and later through film and television. Illustrated magazines, notably *Punch* (founded in 1841), have similarly contributed to an abiding image of the metropolis embodied in a cast of affectionately portrayed urban characters.

Twentieth-century English literature has continued the tradition of wry observers with a focus on London, distilling two classic archetypes—the 'West End Toff' and the 'East End Barrow Boy'. P. G. Wodehouse created an aristocratic world of the inter-war years that linked imagined country houses to Mayfair flats and West End clubs, peopled by bluff retired colonels, hearty fox-hunting aunts, strapping girls who know their own minds, and such drone-like, perpetual bachelors as Bertie Wooster, with his gentleman's gentleman, Jeeves. Jeeves's London is entirely under control—always bathed in sunshine, with smart little roadsters

'Vanity Fair', the term coined by Bunyan in Pilgrim's Progress, *suggests the folly and petty corruptions of life in towns, with its 'jugglings, cheats, games, plays, fools, apes, knaves and rogues'. Becky Sharp, Thackeray's amoral heroine, survives by her wits because she understands the nature of the 'fair'.*

parked at the kerbside and the distant sound of bandstand music floating on the air. He glides effortlessly through the fashionable metropolitan milieu with a perfect understanding of the frailties of humankind and his own sights set on higher things. Like Dickens, this is an alternative, parallel universe in which to escape from the prosaic struggles of ordinary life. Alfie, the eponymous hero of the stage play by Bill Naughton which was also made into a successful film in 1966, is directly descended from Dickens. A Cockney, a small-scale rogue, and an accomplished womanizer, Alfie threads his way through the lowlife of London's East End with consummate ease, evoking a community that transcends inner-city poverty and disadvantage.

Constructing knowable communities in the form of archetypal subgroups or personalized networks linking rich and poor was one way whereby the literary imagination has made sense of the vast anonymity of the city and accommodated some of the broader social and economic changes that wrought instability in England. Jane Austen accomplished this within a narrow social spectrum, as did Anthony Trollope several decades later. Their urban world, which is always organically connected with the countryside, embraced London and leisure towns such as Bath, along with a handful of places with a strong professional and gentry presence—the cathedral towns of Trollope and the navy towns of Austen. Both novelists created fictional towns. Jane Austen's last, unfinished novel was *Sanditon* (*c.*1817), the name of a new seaside resort which sets the scene for the commercialized developments in leisure that both characterize and undermine the social group to which she belonged. Trollope invented the imaginary county and cathedral town of Barchester. The popularity of both writers arises from places and people that transcend time. Poverty, despair, and real human strife are absent. Tension there is, to be sure, but the focus is on the immutable details of human relationships in an environment that accommodates town and country through the creation of a psychological comfort zone, the knowable community.

This technique was applied most explicitly by the mid-nineteenth-century 'condition of England' novelists. *Hard Times* (1854), Dickens's novel of a northern manufacturing town, or *North and South* (1854) by Elizabeth Gaskell, dealing with a fictionalized Manchester, made the urban-industrial landscape acceptable through their focus on minute social interactions that link rich and poor, evoking a traditional moral connectedness which overcomes the alienation of the modern world. A parallel device, signalling a gradual accommodation of urban communal life among the middle classes, was seen in those novels that made town-living attractive through a nostalgic setting in the recent past. Mrs Gaskell's *Cranford* (1853), an early example, is a comic evocation of a small country town adjacent to a great industrial city and dominated by respectably genteel but shabby spinsters. The heaving turmoil of Manchester, with its splendours and poverty, is ever-present in the middle distance, but the ladies of Cranford, based on the Cheshire town of Knutsford, choose to ignore such things.

George Eliot's *Middlemarch* (1871) is the greatest work in English fiction whose name is that of an imagined English town. A small, busy provincial place, intimately connected with the broader currents of national life, it provides a canvas for those quintessential human relationships that transcend time. Its controversies and transitions are the very pulse of English society, precisely evoked at that point in nineteenth-century history—*c.*1830, just before the coming of the railways and the political upheaval of the Great Reform Act—when critical changes, heralding new social formations, came into existence. With its institutions and personalities, Middlemarch is the link between rural, big city, and international life and also between past and present, between Englishness and the great empires of antiquity. Its central characters are bound together through the fabric of the town. Lydgate, the cosmopolitan medical doctor who compromises his ambition; Rosamond, his eventual wife, the social-climbing daughter of a prosperous local businessman; Dorothea, the gentleman's daughter, an idealist out of her time, who makes mistakes and marries foolishly: all are made by their provincial, small-town experience, and all finally settle for a life in London. Middlemarch exemplifies the 'knowable community', a counter to the oppressive phenomena of urban anonymity and industrial blight.

With widespread suburbanization from the later nineteenth century, the English literary imagination gained another comfort zone. The classic comedy *The Diary of a Nobody* (1892) by George and Weedon Grossmith, conjured this to perfection with its straight-faced account of a lower middle-class, middle-aged clerk and his wife, living in a modest brick 'semi' in Holloway. English suburbs have generally evoked a sense of communal safety and retreat, though invariably also linked to images of prosaic family life and pedestrian thinking. True, one of the earliest descriptions of London suburbs, penned by Wilkie Collins in his novel *Basil* (1853: revised and reissued, 1862), hints that the newly made streets, struggling greenery, and status-conscious houses have a mean and threatening dimension. But, generally, the suburbs have been associated in the popular psyche with a timeless innocence and a certainty of values and relationships. It is no coincidence that many of the children's stories that were published in the first half of the twentieth century, such as those of Enid Blyton or the *Just William* series by Richmal Crompton, are either located in the countryside or more often in comfortable middle-class suburbs, with large houses set in spacious gardens and the tennis club just down the road.

One of the most popular English poets of the twentieth century—John Betjeman—is intensely evocative of place, in particular urban places and the lines of communication between them, such as railways and motorways. He is also a poet of the suburbs, delighting in the minutiae of suburban domestic life. Betjeman's towns and suburbs are described as boats on the sea, convoyed together for safety and lit for the night. The modernizing process as manifested in city development is something that jars with the Betjeman psyche. There is a narrowness and a poignancy in the lives of some of his urban types, seen, for instance, in the poem 'Business Girls' (1954); but the urban world he describes is one of comfort alongside a bewildered acceptance of inevitable change.

The image of the familiar, communal city was given added impetus by various trends in artistic representation. At a time when Doré's sinister vision furnished one account of metropolitan life, northern painters, notably Atkinson Grimshaw, were exhibiting hugely popular scenes of industrial cities that stimulated an opposite response. Often nocturnal scenes, or shrouded in smoke and rain, they nevertheless portray a bright bustling in the city centre, with lighted shops and trolleybuses and men and women hurrying through the streets to the securities of home. L. S. Lowry's northern industrial townscapes of the mid-twentieth century similarly sought to represent scenes of the familiar by using the techniques of a child's art to reduce a complex reality into a simplified image that came to occupy a distinct 'comfort zone' in the popular visual imagination. The British cinema of the 1930s to the 1950s achieved an equivalent impact through escapism with an industrial-comic edge. The Ealing comedies and especially the films of Gracie Fields—the mill-girl with guts—or George Formby—the daft lad who always gets the lass—evaded the reality of urban life at an especially bleak time of inter-war unemployment and industrial decline in the north. Through fantasy narratives of individual ambitions achieved and poverty overcome, these films retained a commitment to the knowable working-class community. In the second half of the twentieth century, television soap operas such as *Coronation Street* (first broadcast in 1960) have elevated the working-class industrial community to an archetype of idealized existence equivalent to the nineteenth-century idealization of rural or village life.

These features of popular culture serve to remind us that ordinary working people, living in cities and having to make the best of their environment because they had no option but to remain there, have tended to construct the urban in positive terms that evoked the familiar and the homely. This has been accomplished through a rich tradition of music, song, comedy, and popular theatre—in pubs, in music halls, and latterly through radio and television. In the nineteenth century, glee clubs—formed as part of an English vocal tradition of unaccompanied part-song—and factory brass bands evoked pride in skills and neighbourhoods. Music and song, both serious and comic, have allowed ordinary men and women to make sense of their often difficult existence. The success of the film *Brassed Off* (1996) suggests that when the industry is all gone, the brass band and this type of communal creativity can still hold people together. In places like Manchester or Leeds, a rich popular musical culture, rising hand-in-hand with the growth of their trades, had engendered by the second half of the nineteenth century a quite remarkable breadth of creativity in music, supporting great orchestras such as the Hallé and giving birth to notable composers and fine performers.

Modernity and the Technocratic City

Suburbs tempered the creative response to city life in England. In addressing the fractured quality of experience in the big city, writers in other cultures generated more challenging perspectives on the urban 'problem'. Baudelaire, the French poet writing in the mid-nineteenth century who celebrated the 'ephemeral, the fugitive, the contingent' in everyday Paris and who created the idea of the *flâneur*—the detached observer entirely at home in the city of passing encounters, dissonant exchanges, and ever-shifting crowds—sought to transcend the pursuit of 'knowable communities', accepting that such a fantasy could not exist. For him, the essence of success in modern urban life was not to be found in hopeless endeavours to seek comfort through conventional certainties re-created in an alien context, but rather through embracing the urban as an antidote, a 'salving possibility . . . [providing] relief from one's inner, subjective demons' in a city of strangers and strange things. The writers, artists, and urban theorists of Berlin, New York, or Chicago in the early twentieth century advanced these possibilities, proclaiming the virtues of the 'fragmented self' and the importance of exposure to modernizing forces in cities, which yield a kind of freedom to exist beyond the conventional bounds of society.

The generation from the 1880s to 1920s witnessed the birth and force of European and North American modernism—a cultural movement spawned by the shock of the new as rapid city building and technology came together to cause havoc in societies that were still mostly rural. It was a movement that made limited impact in England before the 1920s. Partly this was due to British insularity and a rejection of things European. Partly it was the product of a longer history of urbanization and modernized industry, whose alienating tendencies had been subjects of English cultural discourse for decades. Rather, attention now shifted towards the countryside, where the technology of capitalist farming was more advanced than anywhere else in the world and where loss of population was seen to have devitalized many communities. The late nineteenth and early twentieth century was thus marked in England by an elegiac indulgence in a romanticized and sometimes sentimentalized rural world. The people and movements involved in this pursuit were entirely urban, but the technocratic city was conspicuous only by virtue of its absence. The Arts and Crafts movement had its foundation in the art schools of industrial cities, but advocated traditional techniques and motifs derived from nature. As a result a number of idealistic and essentially middle-class rural communities were established to practise such crafts. A. E. Housman's wistful poem *A Shropshire Lad* (1896) also promoted this spirit. The Georgian poets, including Rupert Brooke, Edward Thomas, and Walter de la Mare, were London-based but wrote within a pastoral idiom; and novelists such as Thomas Hardy and D. H. Lawrence placed their characters against a largely rural landscape in which the force of nature not machines still held sway. Edward Elgar penned the most powerfully 'English' music of any age and that music evoked a lost rural idyll and the glories of Empire fast slipping away.

Arnold Bennett grasped something of the tensions of modernity through his stories of life in the Midland pottery towns and in London and Brighton—though these were written within the narrative conventions of the nineteenth-century novel. George Gissing, particularly in *New Grub Street* (1891) revealed the bitter competitiveness of modern life for the marginal middle classes. H. G. Wells explored another aspect in his science fiction novels, *The Time Machine* (1895) and *The War of the Worlds* (1897), with their images of parallel existences and fantastic technology. Science fiction has remained a popular genre, imagining a future urban world often in bleakly threatening terms, but also with a subtext that draws on *fin de siècle* images of a lost Eden of Englishness, as in Orwell's *Nineteen Eighty-Four* (1949) or Ray Bradbury's *Fahrenheit 451* (1953). Yet most turn-of-the-century novelists stressed the idea of retreat from the threatening city into the supposed certainties of humane relationships within a rural context.

An elegiac and mythologized yearning for a lost world remained a dominating theme in the English creative psyche and in popular culture throughout the inter-war years and into the present, though there was a brief engagement with modernism to complement that of Europe, in the form of Vorticism, beginning in 1914 with the publication of BLAST: *Review of the Great English Vortex.* Mainly from the pen of Wyndham Lewis, painter and theorist, it was a manifesto for a new movement in art and letters, harnessed to Italian Futurism but with a peculiarly English slant that embraced an attack on such things as the 'pretty-pretty, the commonplace, the soft, sweet and mediocre, the sickly revivals of Medievalism, the Garden Cities with their curfews and artificial battlements, the Maypole

Morris dances, Aestheticism, Oscar Wilde, the Pre-Raphaelites'. Vorticism was a London-centred movement, intellectual and elitist, focused on abstraction and a celebration of the machine, that influenced several strands in the visual arts in the following decades. But far more popular were the paintings of Stanley Spencer, whose evocations of Jerusalem in the Berkshire village of Cookham—a 'holy suburb of Heaven'—depicting biblical scenes enacted in the personalities of an ordinary English village, carried echoes of medieval mystery plays and Bunyan into the inter-war period.

A broad concern with the alienating tendencies of urbanism had re-entered literary culture with the publication in England in 1922 of T. S. Eliot's *The Waste Land*. Though the work of an American with strong European connections and speaking eloquently of the city and the dissonance of urban life in generic terms, Eliot's poetry did this in a manner that particularly suggested London. The impact of socialism and post-war industrial crisis in England, in conjunction with the influence of *The Waste Land*, gave rise in the 1930s to a new preoccupation with the details of working-class life. 'Henry Green' (Henry Yorke), the son of a Midlands manufacturer, produced in his novel *Living* (1929) the first account of the grim predictability of ordinary existence for factory workers, revolving around the monotony and petty respectabilities of family life in the sprawling industrial suburbs. The film *Love on the Dole*, based on the novel by Walter Greenwood, brought to wide audiences the experience of life in north-country towns during the depression. Birmingham featured in the cityscape poetry of Louis Macneice in the 1930s. George Orwell's *Down and Out in Paris and London* (1933) and *The Road to Wigan Pier* (1937)—building on the traditions of Engels and Mayhew—furnished a documentary insight into working-class existence and took investigative journalism into a modern art form which television has made familiar.

The advance of social security, linked to the expanding Welfare State after 1945, did not quell dissatisfactions. On the contrary, it gave rise to a new type of working-class hero, the 'angry young man', born into and fighting against the narrow conventions of industrial communities. John Braine's *Room at the Top* (1957) and Alan Sillitoe's *Saturday Night and Sunday Morning* (1958)—both translated into successful films—caught the type to perfection. In the former, the ambitious Joe Lampton, inspired by war experience, education, and ruthlessness, breaks free of the limitations of his background to rise to the top of a traditional social hierarchy in a bleakly northern manufacturing town. The Welfare State ideal of a meritocracy based on education and the creation in the 1960s and 1970s of a wave of new universities in provincial towns, generated another distinctly English fictional genre, the 'campus novel'. The first was Kingsley Amis's *Lucky Jim* (1954), with the comic 'angry young man' Jim Dixon set against the stuffy conventions of old academe. Malcolm Bradbury's *The History Man* (1975), provided a satire on the hypocrisy of a smug radical in one of the new universities, while David Lodge's *Nice Work* (1988), situated in the fictional University of Rummidge in a large Midlands city and drawing parallels with Mrs Gaskell's novels of nineteenth-century industrial life, introduced an 'angry young woman', Dr Robyn Penrose, a contract lecturer in English Literature, who struggles with the Benthamite imperatives of the late twentieth century and seeks the meaning of life as a single, white female in a post-industrial, postmodern city.

Women, Freedom, and Fantasy

Women and cities are a loaded combination in the popular imagination. Towns have always offered more opportunities for single women than are available in the countryside to work, to find husbands, to buy things, and to sell things. The larger the city, the greater the opportunity. It is not surprising that so many cities, past and present, have had a demographic bias towards a young female population. Yet cities have been dangerous environments for women. Consumerism and the commodification of women's bodies—'sex and shopping' in the modern vernacular—are created in towns and cities. These can empower women as individuals but they also undermine the ideals of moral community. Much of the art and literature of the eighteenth century was unambiguously critical of dangerous female sexuality and the attendant lusting after luxury. These themes have been echoed ever since in cautionary tales, mostly penned by men, of women alone in the city.

Yet women have approached the issue differently. Cities for women are a source of freedom. Life might be fractured, dissonant, and lonely, but when released from the 'prison of expectations' that the family can represent, women are free to find an independent voice, to reinvent themselves if they choose, and to form bonds of affection and community with other women in similar situations. We get a hint of this positive side to urban life through Elizabeth Gaskell, who described in her novels an essence of female collective solidarity. The ladies of *Cranford* (1853) are an 'amazon race' who effectively run the small town and arbitrate on its social affairs. Men have a limited role in their lives. Matters of fashion and the great movements in politics or economy are irrelevant in Cranford because the spinster ladies have decreed them so. The factory girls of Manchester in *Mary Barton* (1848) or *North and South* (1855) walk the streets in gangs, commenting loudly on those they encounter—a real and often shocking experience for many male contemporaries of genteel disposition—and despite the onerousness of their labour, they are comfortable with their life in the city and with their own sense of collective identity. This was a form of empowerment that middle-class women like Gaskell could admire, though it was never part of their own experience. And it has remained a characteristic of female culture into the twentieth century, articulated and frequently glamorized through music hall, film, and television soap opera.

Nineteenth-century women writers also celebrated the liberating potential of the city for women on their own. Charlotte Brontë captured the sense of freedom best when she wrote in *Villette* (1853) 'to walk alone in London seemed of itself an adventure'. *Villette* is also a tale of a tortured and alienated soul, mostly located in bleak urban settings. Yet it is the town and city that spur Lucy Snowe into the search for herself. Virginia Woolf, whose demand in *A Room of One's Own* (1929) was that women have a space in their life for intellectual freedom, not only saw the city as the place in which that freedom might be gained, but was also inspired in her own creative life by her experience of living in the metropolis: 'London itself perpetually attracts, stimulates, gives me a play and a story and a poem, without any trouble, save that of moving my legs through the streets.' Woolf, like the others who formed the Bloomsbury Group, was decidedly a modernist. She embraced the Baudelairian ideal of the detached observer and indulged in the fragmentations, the fleetingness, and the ambiguity of city life to form the

Department stores created districts in town that were devoted to female leisure, fantasy, and consumption. Women's fiction, from the 'silver fork' novels of the 19th century to the 'sex and shopping' novels of our own time, celebrate these features of urban life.

essence of both her literary style and her intellectual preoccupations. Indeed, in the essay 'Street Haunting' (1942) she enumerates the pleasures of being a London *flâneuse*, freely wandering the streets having fled domestic containment.

In the twentieth century, urban fragmentation and the notion of the city as 'palimpsest'—layer upon layer of experience and substance—has been adopted by women writers, particularly those with a feminist orientation, as a metaphor for the modern female condition. This is seen most strikingly in the work of Doris Lessing, notably *The Four Gated City* (1969), a quasi-futurist fantasy partly set in London in which the heroine threads her way through time and streets, seeking a resolution to her own psychological dilemmas. Fantasy, history, and London figure in the popular fiction of Angela Carter, such as *Wise Children* (1991). The agenda here is also the empowerment of women, though this time with an erotic and magical dimension.

For women writers in the nineteenth and early twentieth centuries, the adventure and opportunity of the city was perhaps the equivalent of 'empire' for men: a place in which to get lost and thereby find yourself; a place to make a fortune, take a risk, and indulge a dream; to enjoy the reality of fragmented experiences without submitting to a conventional 'completedness' based on family and community; a place for observing without being always under observation. Gazing, fantasy, and the construction of female identity are closely connected to another aspect of town life that has been dominated by women since the eighteenth century—the art of shopping. The relationship between city centres and consumerism, along with the cultural creation of women as consumers, offered women a certain freedom and confidence within the urban environment. It also determined that the layout of large towns and cities evolved to reflect a feminized agenda, overturning the notion that urban space conformed to binary divisions between public and private, male and female. Streets devoted to female shopping had developed by the late nineteenth century into whole districts, in which the new department stores—palaces of entertainment and employment for women—were a dominating presence.

A fiction extolling the pleasures of consuming was presaged in the later eighteenth century in the novels of Fanny Burney and first came into existence as a distinct genre in the 1820s with 'silver fork' novels, whose concern was with the material paraphernalia and rituals of the rich, mainly in London. Mostly written by minor women novelists such as the prolific Mrs Gore, who enjoyed vast sales among the aspirant provincial middle classes, these novels were notable for providing details not only about how many 'silver forks' were needed to eat fish in fashionable society—along with similar minutiae—but also about the real shops and social institutions where the wealthy were to be found. Vicarious enjoyment of the metropolis and its delights have provided part of the stock subject matter of 'women's fiction' thereafter. Rarely of great literary merit, mostly constructed around conventional notions of gender and status, but always read avidly, 'shopping' novels—and in the late twentieth century, the genre of 'sex and shopping' novels—have been one of the staples of women's escapist entertainment for nearly two centuries.

The confidence of women within certain types of urban public space and the articulation by women writers of a kind of modernist freedom that only the city could offer, generated a new wave of morally laden literary narratives in the later nineteenth century that sought to expose the dangers and in particular the sexual dangers of cities. The development of the West End theatre, with glamorous actresses who were household names and raffish leading men, further fuelled the issue in the popular imagination. The hedonistic mixture of women, luxury consumption, theatre, and the city was connected with another *fin de siècle* cultural phenomenon, decadent aestheticism, as exemplified by the plays and novels of Oscar Wilde or in the drawings and theatre design of Aubrey Beardsley. Affectedly dandified or homosexual and thus inherently threatening to gender norms, and closely associated with French and in particular Paris culture and hence

subversive of 'Englishness' at a time of faltering Empire and xenophobic vulnerability, the aesthetes were entirely at home in the modernist city of dissonances and differences. Urbane, amusing, and iconoclastic—Wilde, for instance, was a feminist—the cultural milieu that was created by the aesthetes, being riddled with contradictions, assumed a city audience of considerable sophistication and tolerance, with a large female presence. Novels like *The Picture of Dorian Gray* (1891) or the play *The Importance of Being Earnest* (1895) represented for those who lived in provincial England, the wit, wealth, and wicked pleasures to be found in London.

Women's popular entertainment in the twentieth century, dominated by fiction and magazine stories and latterly by film and television, has many continuities with that of the past. The safe zone for women is no longer the countryside but rather the suburb, a female space that quickly came to be associated in cultural perceptions with ideals of community and family. More recently it has been the commuter village—the scene of Joanna Trollope's novels or Ambridge in the radio series *The Archers*—set apart from a threatening urban present, but connected with cities as places for shopping and entertainment. The past, including the urban past, has also become an important vehicle for articulating a feminized utopian fantasy at a safe distance from the present. This is seen most forcefully in the popularity of Catherine Cookson, whose novels of life in industrial Tyneside in the nineteenth and early twentieth centuries have topped the best-seller lists and library-borrowing figures since the 1950s and are regularly translated in 'blockbuster' television serials. Though grim urban poverty is part of the Cookson formula, this is always transcended by the energy and enterprise of the heroine, who achieves material success and conventional emotional fulfilment in the form of love and marriage. Heroines change with time and late twentieth-century women's popular stories are filled with successful career women who build industrial empires and make good in a world of men. But they also find their 'Mr Right' along the way. This basic contradiction has fuelled a *fin de siècle* irony among young women today, reflected in the popularity of *Bridget Jones's Diary* (1996), based on a weekly column in the *Independent* newspaper, or the television series *This Life*. Both project the turmoil, ambitions, and loneliness of the wine-bar-haunting, single professional classes of the eighties and nineties.

Visualizing and Celebrating the City

Throughout history, observers have sought to describe the topography of towns in words and images, to render them understandable. As cities became more complex and the contrast between town and country more acute, so the need to describe became stronger. It is only in the later twentieth century, when the whole of English culture has been effectively urbanized and the physical separation of city from city hardly exists in some regions, that we have lost the desideratum to describe, other than in describing the transformation of city centres through gentrification and the architecture of high technology. Indeed, the reverse now prevails—we seek to define a countryside, struggling to survive in the midst of urbanism, through conservation areas, national parks, and green belts.

Description has taken the written form in a number of guises. Tourist literature as a distinct genre first belongs to the eighteenth century. Defoe's *Tour Through*

England and Wales (1722), though inevitably focused on London, well represents the small market towns and cathedral cities that peppered the early eighteenth-century rural landscape, with their prominent church steeples and markets and the bustle of rising provincial prosperity. The next century brought several powerful documentary evocations of the fabric of a single town or city, all inspired by reformist public purposes rather than mere description and observation. A pioneer was Friedrich Engels's account of Manchester in *The Condition of the Working Class in England in 1844* (1845), written while he was still a young man and engaged in business training in the cotton mills of the city. That tradition continued up to Charles Booth's monumental study of *The Life and Labour of the People in London* (1891–1903) and Seebohm Rowntree's anatomies of York, based on surveys that were first published in 1901 and repeated in succeeding decades.

When towns and cities outgrew the capacity to grasp them visually at a single glance, there also developed a need for pictorial representations that embraced the whole of a place and conveyed a sense of reality. Topographical prints of cities were prominent and popular items in print-seller's catalogues from the early eighteenth century. Bird's-eye views and town maps were produced in large numbers to be framed and hung on walls in town and country alike. From the 1780s to the 1850s, painted panoramas of cities, some up to twenty feet in height, which provided the observer with a total view in one circular sweep, attracted massive paying audiences, particularly in London, but also in Liverpool and in county towns like Norwich, where there were large and elaborate buildings devoted to this popular art form. Dioramas, showing a moving image, which

Mill-girls developed a robust, independent street culture which survived in many northern towns into the 1960s. Their catcalling and parading in gangs often scandalized the polite middle classes.

The Impressionist preoccupation with the townscape bathed in moonlight, which evokes the sinister, mysterious, or even the romantic, suggests something of the ambiguity of life in the modern, technocratic city. The single woman here, alone on the pavement, enhances the enigma.

were invented in the early nineteenth century, served a similar demand. Pictures of cities and streetscapes, initially engraved and later photographed, were produced in town guide books from the 1750s and remained popular well into the present century. Albums of photographs were published from the 1840s. The invention of the stereoscope in the 1860s allowed 3-D images of a variety of subjects, including townscapes, to be enjoyed in the parlour. Taken together, these different forms of 'realistic' visual art emerged out of a simple desire to see the totality of a place and to comprehend it. They also provided an alternative to travel—a vicarious experience of something that could not always be achieved in practice, which was later to be served by documentary film and television.

Embracing the totality of a city in its growing complexity had become impossible by the mid-nineteenth century. So the essence was captured through impressions, again in order to render the phenomenon into tameness and familiarity. Ford Madox Brown's street scenes became some of the best-known images of Victorian city life. English urban impressionism of the later nineteenth century was dominated by the paintings of Whistler, whose views of the Thames and its bridges at night provide a powerful and sympathetic sense of the lifeblood of the city. Atkinson Grimshaw's depictions of busy commercial scenes; J. J. Tissot's fashionable city girls in shops and omnibuses; or Lowry's cheerful, 'naive' accounts of industrial life—all found a remarkable popular appeal. In the late twentieth century, the art of Beryl Cook, dominated by the prosaic activities of plump middle-aged women in cities and suburbs and conveyed with an eye to the comic potential of ordinary lives, has a similar standing.

The paintings of all of these artists have been purchased by city authorities and exhibited to wide audiences in most of the big municipal art collections. Urban institutions have long commissioned and owned art; and from the early eighteenth century much of this art sought to mediate public images of the institutions and the cities in which they were located and to celebrate the urban achievement. Canaletto's vision of London as a sparkling jewel of mercantile ascendancy, built upon a teeming river front, was an image of London that was promoted and elaborated throughout the eighteenth and nineteenth centuries. The London Foundling Hospital, one of the great secular charitable institutions—established in 1739 in the first wave of middle-class interest in urban philanthropy as a source of status and esteem—was a major patron of contemporary art. The Hospital's administrators understood the value of public exhibitions for garnering support. They commissioned Hogarth to produce a portrait of Thomas Coram, their greatest benefactor and a wealthy London merchant. This represents, in the iconographical language of the age, the man as a modest and beneficent personality. It shows his trade and the world he was able to dominate through trade. And it celebrates the city in which he had made his mark through enterprise and charity. Portraiture thereafter and in particular the portraits that were commissioned by institutions—showing town council members, scholars and benefactors of the universities, leaders of the chambers of commerce—all employed a well-defined repertoire of visual symbols and physical attitudes. Placed on display in prominent public buildings, such portraits were designed to highlight the power and achievements of cities and suggest the probity of the men at the helm of local affairs.

From the later eighteenth century, views of provincial towns and cities were commissioned by city fathers to adorn their public buildings and to offer locally popular subjects for the engraving trade. These were often based on the conventions of landscape painting, particularly in representations of the new industrial centres such as Leeds or Manchester. The city is usually observed from outside, across fields and the open country, and is safely at a distance where it is tamed by a foreground of conventional pastoral imagery, suggesting an organic relationship between town and country and between the products of farming and the processes of industry. Visual narratives of this type offered reassurance in an environment of rapid urban change, where most people were still country-born. The language of the sublime, commonly used in landscape painting, was also adopted in the early nineteenth century, with images of great buildings and

Images of great bridges spanning rivers are commonly used to suggest the capacity of the man-made city to transcend nature. The Thames, the life-blood of the capital, has dominated depictions of London throughout its history.

manufacturing processes expressed in terms that generated feelings of the awesomeness and spectacular forces at large in the industrial city.

By the later nineteenth century, public art in massive new public buildings provided unprecedented opportunities for a visual articulation of urban achievements. The cycle of twelve wall paintings by Ford Madox Brown for the Great Hall of the new Town Hall in Manchester (1877) was one of the most ambitious visual undertakings of the century. It presented a complex narrative of the history of the city, of its science and industrial enterprise and ended with a celebration of the quintessential Victorian virtues of 'work'. There was nothing to rival this form of visual urban boosterism until cinema in the twentieth century gave scope for films as public relations exercises—normally the 'shorts' before the main feature—to encourage business investment and impress outsiders with the splendours of the city.

Public art collections also provide insights into the ways in which towns and cities were conceived within the creative imagination of those who lived there. Though London housed the great institutions for the national collections of old masters, it was the industrial towns of the nineteenth century that were especially notable for the purchase and display of modern art, both as an act of competitive status-building for the town and in order to make that art available to ordinary people, for their education and cultural refinement. Municipal art collections had been created in most significant towns and cities by the end of the nineteenth century, normally donated by local businessmen. The styles and subjects of these collections, which were mostly focused on contemporary English artists, are revealing. The patronage accorded to the Pre-Raphaelites in Manchester and Liverpool, or to the Arts and Crafts movement in Birmingham, signals a profoundly ambiguous stream of backward-looking anti-urbanism buried deep within the psyche of these most urban and urbane of Englishmen.

Conclusion

The artistic and literary imagination is born out of and feeds into the complex of cultural perceptions that are alive within society as a whole. We are interested in how artists represent and respond to a given phenomenon, because art, literature, or music (indeed, any cultural product of no apparent utility) can be read as a document on the past—as a form of knowledge and possibly the only way of expressing certain feelings and beliefs.

What runs throughout this account of the creative imagination is the paradoxical nature of responses to English towns. This is not surprising in a society and country where rapid change occurred earlier than in other developed nations and where modernity has been embraced in so partial and qualified a manner. Cities and their suburbs may be the environments that most of us inhabit today, but the romantic and nostalgic yearning for an idealized rural or village existence remains one of the dominating forces in popular cultural life. It is reflected in the development of the heritage industry, in the popular response to costume dramas on the television, and even in the ways in which we decorate our houses. We all know of and occasionally may yearn to experience the modern, technological city as work of art—a celebration of urban ingenuity and the power of machines. But we rarely look for this in England. In the United States, Japan, or Germany, perhaps, but not in England. In the popular psyche, England is still a rural place; our towns and cities are intrusions in the Garden of Eden.

Further Reading

Chapter 1

Bédoyère, G. de la, *Roman Towns in Britain* (London: Batsford, 1990).
Boon, G. C., *Silchester: The Roman Town of Calleva* (Newton Abbot: David & Charles, 1974).
Burnham, B. C., and Wacher, J. S., *The Small Towns of Roman Britain* (London: Council for British Archaeology, Research Report 59, 1985).
Johnson, A. S., *Later Roman Britain* (London: Routledge, 1980).
Merrifield, R., *London: City of the Romans* (London: Guild Publishing, 1983).
Millett, M., *The Romanization of Britain* (Cambridge: Cambridge University Press, 1990).
Rodwell, W., and Rowley, T. G. (eds.), *The Small Towns of Roman Britain* (Oxford: *British Archaeological Reports* 15, 1976).
Wacher, J. S., *The Towns of Roman Britain* (London: Batsford, 1995).
Webster, G. (ed.), *Fortress into City* (London: Batsford, 1988).

Chapter 2

Arnold, C. J., *An Archaeology of Early Anglo-Saxon Kingdoms* (London: Routledge, new edn, 1997).
Clarke, H., and Ambrosiani, B. (eds.), *Towns in the Viking Age* (Leicester: Leicester University Press, 1991).
Dark, K. R., *Civitas to Kingdom: British Political Continuity, 300–800* (Leicester: Leicester University Press, 1994).
Hall, R., *Viking Age York* (London: English Heritage/Batsford, 1994).
Hodges, R., and Hobley, B. (eds.), *The Rebirth of Towns in the West* (London: Council for British Archaeology, Research Report 68, 1988).
Kemp, R. L., *Anglian Settlement at 46–54 Fishergate* (York: Council for British Archaeology, Archaeology of York 7/1, 1996).
Ottaway, P., *Archaeology in British Towns: From the Emperor Claudius to the Black Death* (London and New York: Routledge, 1992).
Phillips, D., and Heywood, B. (gen. ed. M. O. H. Carver), *Excavations at York Minster*, i. *From Roman Fortress to Norman Cathedral* (London: Royal Commission on Historical Monuments, 1995).
Rackham, J. (ed.), *Environment and Economy in Anglo-Saxon England* (London: Council for British Archaeology, Research Report 89, 1994).
Rogers, N. S. H., *Anglian and Other Finds from Fishergate* (York: Council for British Archaeology 17/9, 1993).
Schofield, J., and Vince, A. (eds.), *Medieval Towns* (Leicester: Leicester University Press, 1994).
Tweddle, D., *The Anglian Helmet from Fishergate* (York: Council for British Archaeology 17/8, 1992).
Vince, A., *Saxon London: An Archaeological Investigation* (London: Seaby, 1990).

Chapter 3

Beresford, Maurice, *New Towns of the Middle Ages: Town Plantation in England, Wales and Gascony* (London: Lutterworth Press, 1967; 2nd edn., Gloucester: Alan Sutton, 1988).
Blair, John, and Ramsey, Nigel, *English Medieval Industries: Craftsmen, Techniques and Products* (London and Rio Grande: The Hambledon Press, 1991).
Hall, A. R., and Kenward, H. K. (eds.), *Environmental Archaeology in the Urban Context* (London: Council for British Archaeology, Research Report 43, 1982).

Holt, Richard, and Rosser, Gervase (eds.), *The English Medieval Town: A Reader in English Urban History, 1200–1540* (London and New York: Longman, 1990).

Keene, Derek, *Winchester Studies*, ii. *Survey of Medieval Winchester* (Oxford: Clarendon Press, 1985).

Lobel, M. D., (ed.), *Historic Towns of the British Isles*, i. *Historic Towns: Maps and Plans of Towns and Cities in the British Isles, with Historical Commentaries from Earliest Times to 1800: Banbury, Carnarvon, Glasgow, Gloucester, Hereford, Nottingham, Reading, Salisbury* (London: Lovell Johns-Cook Hammond and Kell, 1969); *The Atlas of Historic Towns*, ii. *Bristol, Cambridge, Coventry, Norwich* (London, Scolar Press, 1975); *The British Atlas of Historic Towns*, iii. *The City of London from Earliest Times to c.1520* (Oxford: Oxford University Press, 1989; 2nd edn. 1991).

Maitland, F. W., *Township and Borough* (Cambridge: Cambridge University Press, 1898).

Platt, Colin, *The English Medieval Town* (London: Secker and Warburg, 1976).

Schofield, John, *Medieval London Houses* (New Haven and London: Yale University Press, 1994).

Urry, W., *Canterbury under the Angevin Kings* (London: Athlone Press, 1967).

Chapter 4

Ayres, J., *Building the Georgian City* (New Haven and London: Yale University Press, 1998).

Chalklin, C. W., *The Provincial Towns of Georgian England: A Study of the Building Process* (London: Arnold, 1974).

Clark, P., and Slack, P., *English Towns in Transition 1500–1700* (London: Oxford University Press, 1976).

Corfield, P., *The Impact of English Towns 1700–1800* (Oxford: Oxford University Press, 1982).

Cruickshank, D., and Burton, N., *Life in the Georgian City* (London: Viking, 1990).

Girouard, M., *The English Town* (New Haven and London: Yale University Press, 1990).

Hyde, R., *Gilded Scenes and Shining Prospects: Panoramic Views of British Towns 1575–1900* (New Haven: Yale Center for British Art, 1985).

Porter, S., *The Great Fire of London* (Stroud: Sutton, 1996).

Summerson, J., *Architecture in Britain 1530–1830* (5th edn., Harmondsworth: Penguin, 1969).

Tittler, R., *Architecture and Power: The Urban Town Hall and the English Urban Community c.1500–1640* (Oxford: Clarendon Press, 1991).

In addition to the above, specific references or quotations in the text have been taken from the following:

Clark, P., and Morgan, P., *Towns and Townspeople 1500–1780* (Milton Keynes: Open University Press, 1977).

Defoe, D., *The Complete English Tradesman* (repr. New York: Burt Franklin, 1970).

Drake, F., *Eboracum, or the History and Antiquities of the City of York* (repr. East Ardsley: EP Publishing, 1978).

Dyer, A. D., 'Probate Inventories of Worcester Tradesmen, 1545–1614', *Worcestershire Historical Society*, NS 5, *Miscellany II* (1967).

Farr, M. (ed.), *The Great Fire of Warwick 1694* (Publications of the Dugdale Society, 36, 1992).

The Journeys of Celia Fiennes, ed. C. Morris (London: Cressett Press, 1947).

Hewitson, A. (ed.), *Preston Court Leet Records* (Preston: George Toulmin & Sons, 1905).

Lloyd, D., *Broad Street: Its Houses and Residents through Three Centuries* (Birmingham: Studio Press, 1979).

Luce, R. H., *The History of the Abbey and Town of Malmesbury* (Malmesbury: Friends of Malmesbury Abbey, 1979).

Priestley, U., *The Great Market: A Survey of Nine Hundred Years of Norwich Provision Market* (Norwich: Centre of East Anglian Studies, 1987).

Sweet, R., 'The Production of Urban Histories in Eighteenth-Century England', *Urban History*, 23 (1996).

Chapter 5

Hall, P., *London, 2000* (London: Faber, 1963).

Hebbert, M., *London, More by Fortune than Design* (Chichester: John Wiley, 1998).

Jackson, A. A., *Semi-Detached London* (London: Allen & Unwin, 1973).

Jenkins, S., *Landlords to London, The Story of a Capital and its Growth* (London: Constable, 1975).

London Research Centre, *London '95* (London: London Research Centre, 1995).

Olsen, D. J., *The Growth of Victorian London* (London: Batsford, 1976).

Porter, R., *London: A Social History* (London: Hamish Hamilton, 1994).

Rasmussen, S. E., *London: The Unique City* (1st Eng. edn., London: Cape, 1934).

Sassen, S., *The Global City: New York, London, Tokyo* (Princeton: Princeton University Press, 1991).

Winter, James, *London's Teeming Streets* (London: Routledge, 1993).

Chapter 6

Adburgham, A., *Shops and Shopping, 1800–1914* (London: Allen & Unwin, 1964).

Alexander, D., *Retailing in England during the Industrial Revolution* (London: Athlone Press, 1970).

Birchall, J., *Coop: The People's Business* (Manchester: Manchester University Press, 1994).

Booker, J., *Temples of Mammon: The Architecture of Banking* (Edinburgh: Edinburgh University Press, 1990).

Jeffreys, J. B., *Retail Trading in Britain, 1850–1950* (Cambridge, Cambridge University Press, 1954).

Lancaster, B., *The Department Store: A Social History* (Leicester and London: Leicester University Press, 1983, and Cassell, 1995).
Mathias, P., *Retailing Revolution* (London: Longman, 1967).
MacKeith, M., *The History and Conservation of Shopping Arcades* (London and New York: Mansell, 1986).
Mui, H., and Mui, L. H., *Shops and Shopkeeping in Eighteenth Century England* (London: Routledge, 1989).
Winstanley, M. J., *The Shopkeeper's World, 1830–1914* (Manchester: Manchester University Press, 1983).

Chapter 7

Beresford, Maurice, *East End, West End: The Face of Leeds during Urbanization, 1684–1842* (Leeds: Thoresby Society, 1986).
Briggs, Asa, *Victorian Cities* (London: Odhams, 1963).
Daunton, M. J., *House and Home in the Victorian City: Working Class Housing, 1850–1914* (London: Edward Arnold, 1983).
Dupree, Marguerite W., *Family Structure in the Staffordshire Potteries, 1840–1880* (Oxford: Clarendon Press, 1995).
Garrard, John, *Leadership and Power in Victorian Industrial Towns, 1830–1880* (Manchester: Manchester University Press, 1983).
Lancaster, Bill, and Mason, Tony (eds.), *Life and Labour in a Twentieth-century City: The Experience of Coventry* (Warwick: Cryfield Press, 1985.)
Linstrum, Derek, *West Yorkshire: Architects and Architecture* (London: Lund Humphries, 1978).
Meller, Helen, *Leisure and the Changing City, 1870–1914* (London: Routledge, Kegan, Paul, 1976).
Pollard, A. J. (ed.), *Middlesbrough. Town and Community, 1830–1950* (Middlesbrough: Sutton Publishing, 1996).
Robinson, Fred (ed.), *Post Industrial Tyneside: An Economic and Social Survey of Tyneside in the 1980s* (Newcastle: Newcastle upon Tyne City Libraries and Arts, 1988).
Trainor, Richard H., *Black Country Elites: The Exercise of Authority in an Industrialized Area, 1830–1900* (Oxford: Oxford University Press, 1993).
Wright, Neil R., *Lincolnshire Towns and Industry, 1700–1914* (Lincoln: History of Lincolnshire Committee, 1982).

Bell, Lady, *At the Works: A Study of a Manufacturing Town (Middlesbrough)* (London: Edward Arnold, 1907).
Priestley, J. B., *English Journey during the autumn of the year 1933* (London: Heinemann, 1934).
Newbery, Maggie, *Picking up Threads: Reminiscences of a Bradford Mill Girl* (Bradford: Bradford Libraries, 1993).

Bennett, Arnold, *The Grim Smile of the Five Towns* (1907; Harmondsworth: Penguin, 1975).
Greenwood, Walter, *Love on the Dole* (London: Jonathan Cape, 1933).
Sillitoe, Alan, *Saturday Night and Sunday Morning* (London: W. H. Allen, 1958).

Chapter 8

Bagwell, Philip S., *The Transport Revolution, 1770–1985* (London: Routledge, 1988).
Barker, Theo, and Gerhold, Dorian, *The Rise and Rise of Road Transport, 1700–1990* (London: Macmillan, 1993).
Barker, T. C., and Robbins, Michael, *A History of London Transport* (London: Allen & Unwin), i. *The Nineteenth Century* (1963); ii. *The Twentieth Century to 1970* (1974).
Buckley, R. J., *History of Tramways from Horse to Rapid Transit* (Newton Abbot: David & Charles, 1975).
Daunton, M. J., *Coal Metropolis: Cardiff 1870–1914* (Leicester: Leicester University Press, 1977).
Freeman, Michael J., and Aldcroft, Derek H. (eds.), *Transport in Victorian Britain* (Manchester: Manchester University Press, 1988).
Hibbs, John, *The History of British Bus Services* (Newton Abbot: David & Charles, 1968).
Kellett, John R., *Railways and Victorian Cities* (London: Routledge, Kegan Paul, 1969).
Plowden, William, *The Motor Car and Politics in Britain* (London: Bodley Head, 1971).
Simmons, Jack, *The Railway in Town and Country, 1830–1914* (Newton Abbot: David & Charles, 1986).

Chapter 9

Daunton, M. J., *House and Home in the Victorian City: Working Class Housing 1850–1914* (London: Edward Arnold, 1983).
Dyos, H. J., and Reeder, D. A., 'Slums and Suburbs', in H. J. Dyos and M. Wolff (eds.), *The Victorian City: Images and Reality* (London: Routledge, 1973), 359–86.
Gaskell, S. M. (ed.), *Slums* (Leicester: Leicester University Press 1990).
Hardy, D., *From Garden Cities to New Towns*, 2 vols. (London: Spon, 1991).
Hasegawa, J., *Replanning the Blitzed City Centre* (Buckingham: Open University Press, 1992).
Horsey, M., 'Multi-Storey Council Housing in Britain', *Planning Perspectives*, 3 (1988), 167–96.
Meller, H., 'Urban Renewal and Citizenship: The Quality of Life in British Cities 1890–1990', *Urban History*, 22 (1995), 63–84.
Muthesius, S., *The English Terraced House* (New Haven: Yale University Press, 1982).
Ravetz, A., *The Place of Home: English Domestic Environments 1914–2000* (London: Spon, 1995).
Rodger, R., *Housing in Urban Britain 1780–1914* (Cambridge: Cambridge University Press, 1995).
Swenarton, M., *Homes Fit For Heroes: The Politics and Architecture of Early State Housing in Britain* (London: Heinemann, 1981).
Wohl, A. S., *The Eternal Slum: Housing and Social Policy in Victorian London* (London: Edward Arnold, 1977).

Chapter 10

Borsay, P., *The English Urban Renaissance* (Oxford: Clarendon Press, 1989).
Lancaster, Bill, *The Department Store: A Social History* (Leicester: Leicester University Press, 1983).
Neale, R. S., *Bath, A Social History 1680–1850* (London: Routledge, 1981).
Richards, Jeffrey, *The Age of the Dream Palace* (London: Routledge, 1981).
Russell, Dave, *Football and the English* (Preston: Carnegie, 1997).
Shields, Rob, *Places on the Margin: Alternative Geographies of Modernity* (London: Routledge, 1992).
Urry, J., *Consuming Places* (London: Routledge, 1995).
Walkowitz, Judith, *City of Dreadful Delight: Narratives of Sexual Danger in Late Victorian London* (London: Virago, 1992).
Walton, J. K., *Blackpool* (Edinburgh: Edinburgh University Press, 1998).
Williams, A., and Shaw, G. (eds.), *The Rise and Fall of British Coastal Resorts* (London: Cassell, 1997).

Chapter 11

Briggs, Asa, *Victorian Cities* (London, Odham's, 1963), chs. 4–5.
Brooks, Chris, *Mortal Remains* (Exeter and London: The Victorian Society, 1989).
—— and Saint, Andrew (eds.), *The Victorian Church* (Manchester and New York: Manchester University Press, 1995).
Cunningham, Colin, *Victorian and Edwardian Town Halls* (London and Boston: Routledge, 1981).
Esher, Lionel, *A Broken Wave: the Rebuilding of England 1940–1980* (Harmondsworth, Allen Lane/Pelican Books, 1981).
Evans, Robin, *The Fabrication of Virtue* (Cambridge: Cambridge University Press, 1982).
Girouard, Mark, *The English Town* (New Haven and London: Yale University Press, 1990), chs. 10–11.
Seaborne, Malcolm, *The English School: Its Architecture and Organization 1870–1970*, (London and Boston: Routledge, 1977).
Taylor, Jeremy, *Hospital and Asylum Architecture in Britain* (London: Mansell, 1991).

Chapter 12

Christ, Carol T., and Jordan, John O. (eds.), *Victorian Literature and the Victorian Visual Imagination* (Berkeley and Los Angeles: University of California Press, 1995).
Fawcett, Trevor, *The Rise of English Provincial Art: Artists, Patrons and Institutions outside London, 1800–1830* (Oxford: Clarendon Press, 1974).
Hyde, Ralph, *Panoramania: The Art and Entertainment of the All-Embracing View* (London: Trefoil in association with the Barbican Art Gallery, 1988).
James, Edward, *Science Fiction in the Twentieth Century* (Oxford: Oxford University Press, 1994).
Nadel, Ira Bruce, and Schwarzback, F. S. (eds.), *Victorian Artists and the City: A Collection of Critical Essays* (Oxford: Pergamon Press, 1980).
Sanders, Andrew, *The Short Oxford History of English Literature* (Oxford: Oxford University Press, 1996).
Solkin, David, *Painting for Money: The Visual Arts and the Public Sphere in Eighteenth-Century England* (New Haven: Yale University Press, 1993).
Timms, Edward, and Kelly, David (eds.), *Unreal City: Urban Experience in Modern European Literature and Art* (Manchester: Manchester University Press, 1985).
Walkowitz, Judith, *City of Dreadful Delight: Narratives of Sexual Danger in Late Victorian London* (London: Virago, 1992).
Wolff, Janet and Seed, John (eds.), *The Culture of Capital: Art, Power and the Nineteenth-Century Middle Class* (Manchester: Manchester University Press 1988).

Sources of Illustrations

15 Computer generated impression courtesy of Barratts Group
16 Figures supplied by Office for National Statistics
18 Barratts Group
19 London Properties plc
22 Commission for New Towns
28 CPRE and Countryside Commission
34 After plan reproduced in Brian Wacher:Towns of Roman Britain Batsford 1975
35 After plan reproduced in Brian Wacher:Towns of Roman Britain Batsford 1975
36 David Shotter
37 British Museum
38 Committee for Aerial Photography University of Cambridge
41 David Shotter
42 After plan reproduced in Brian Wacher:Towns of Roman Britain Batsford 1975
43 After plan reproduced in Brian Wacher:Towns of Roman Britain Batsford 1975
45 David Shotter
46 British Museum
47 Committee for Aerial Photography University of Cambridge
48 David Shotter
50 David Shotter
51 David Shotter
52 David Shotter
53 After plan reproduced in Brian Wacher:Towns of Roman Britain Batsford 1975
56 Suffolk County Council Archaeological Service
58 © Canterbury Hitage Museum
63 David Hinton
64 After C D M Metcalf: Thrymses and Sceattas
64 York Archeological Trust
66 Reproduced from A Vince:Saxon London 1996
67 © John Hodgeson. Print supplied by Southampton City Council
69 After C D M Metcalf: Thrymses d Sceattas
71 Dorset County Council Libraries and Arts Service
76–77 Museum of London
84 York City Archives
86 © Society of Antiquaries of London
88 National Monuments Record
89 © Winchester Excavations Committee
91 M638, f.41v The Pierpointgan Library/Art Resource, New York
97 British Library Royal MS 13A lll folio 41v
100 National Monuments Record
103 Peter Borsay
104 Hugh Meller/Tiggy Ruthven
106–107 West Air Photography
108 Reproduced by kind permission of Copeland Borough Council and The Beacon, Whitehaven
111 Guildhall Library, Corporation of London
112 Peter Borsay
115 J Allan Cash Photolibrary
122–123 Bristol Museums and Art Gallery
123 Illustrated London News Picture Library
126 Collection of John Davis
128–129 Guildhall Library, Corporation of London
133 Collection of John Davis
136–137 London Transport Museum
137 Hulton Getty Picture Collection
138 National Monuments Record
142–143 Hulton Getty Picture Collection
146 London Metropolitan Archives
158 The Francis Frith Collection, Salisbury, Wiltshire SP3 5QP
159 Rochdale Local Studies Collection
162 Hulton Getty Picture Collection
163 Hulton Getty Picture Collection
165 Rochdale Local Studies Collection
166 Jeffrey Richards
169 Sainsbury's Archives
171 Reproduced fromCo-operative Architecture 1945–1959 (print suppled by CWS Photographic Dept
173 Stuart Outterside, North News
176 British Library 2367bb18
178–179 Warrillow Collection Keele University
180 Potteries Museum and Art Gallery Stoke-on-Trent
188 R J Morris
191 Collection of R J Morris
192 Illustrated London News Picture Library
194–195 Bradford Industrial Museum
199 Leeds Library and Information Services
200 R J Morris
201 R J Morris
202 R J Morris
203 R J Morris
204 © Tim Smith
212 Gloucestershire County Library Service, Gloucestershire Collection
215 Mary Evans Picture Library
219 Reproduced by kind permission of Ealing Local History Centre
222–223 Pamlin Prints
224 Reproduced by kind permission of Ealing cal History Centre
225 Doncaster Libraries and Information Service
226 Mary Evans Picture Library
228 229 London Transport Museum
230 London Transport Museum
238 Centre for Urban History University of Leicester
239 Collection of Richard Roger
241 Centre for Urban History University of Leicester
245 E Howard:Garden Cities of Tomorrow Faber 1946/The Town and Country Planning Association
246 E Howard:Garden Cities of Tomorrow Faber 1946/The Town and Country Planning Association
247 E Howard:Garden Cities of Tomorrow Faber 1946 /The Town and Country Planning Association
248 London Metropolitan Archives
249 London Metropolitan Archives
252 Collection of Richard Roger
254 London Metropolitan Archives
255 London Metropolitan Archives
256 London Metropolitan Archives
258 Collection of Richard Roger
259 Reproduced from Leicester Today and Tomorrow 1968 (Photo credited to Leicester Mercury.)
260 The Record Office for Leicestershire, Leicester and Rutland (reproduced from the 1888 Ordnance Survey map)
261 © Crown copyright. All rights reserved. MC 030728
271 City of Salford Museums and Art Gallery
272 (Torquay illustration) Illustrated London News Picture Library
274 Reproduced by kind permission of Scarborough Bough Library
275 Reproduced by kind permission of Scarborough Borough Library
282 Chetham's Library
288 Sir Robert McAlpine Ltd
291 National Monuments Record
293 Reproduced from P Fleetwood-Hesketh: Murray's Lancashire Architectural Guide
296–297 Manchester Central Library, Local Studies Unit
300 Reproduced by permission of Birmingham Library Services
303 Laing Art Gallery, Newcastle upon Tyne (Tyne and Wear Museums)
305 Croydon Libraries
307 Geoffrey Tyack
311 Aerofilms
314 Geoffrey Tyack
318 British Museum
320–321 Luke Fildes:Applicants for admission to a casual ward, 1874. Royal Holloway and Bedford New College/ Bridgeman Art Library
323 Mary Evans Picture Library
325 Courtesy of Carlton TV
327 Mary Evans Picture Library
334 Mary Evans Picture Library
337 Eyre Crow: Dinner Hour, Wigan. Manchester City Art Gallery
338 Atkinson Grimshaw: Liverpool Quay. Tate Gallery London 1999
340 J A M Whistler: Old Battersea Bridge: Nocturne - Blue and Gold. Tate Gallery London 1999

In a few instances we have not been able to to trace the copyright owner prior to publication. If notified, the publishers will be pleased to amend the acknowledgements in any future edition.

Picture research by Anne Lyons

Index

Index of places begins on p.351

Index of places